ECONOMICS

SECOND EDITION

SEAN NAGLE

INSTITUTE of TECHNOLOGY TRALEE

First published 1996
Second Edition 1999

ISBN 0 9536762 0 X

PRINTED BY COLOUR BOOKS LTD.,
BALDOYLE INDUSTRIAL ESTATE,
BALDOYLE,
DUBLIN13.

Contents

Part 1 Microeconomics:-

Part 2 Macroeconomics:-

List of Tables

List of Diagrams

ix

Appendices

PREFACE

The first edition of this book was published in 1996. The second edition is fully revised. Facts have been brought up to date and the text revised to cover the recent changes, the development of economic theory and the evolution of government and EU policy since 1996.

As with the first edition the text is written for all students of economics. Its main aim is to meet the needs of third level students of economics whether full time or part time.

Chapters are arranged with microeconomics in the first part of the text followed by macroeconomics. There are questions at the end of each chapter designed to assist in assessing progress and understanding. A detailed glossary of terms has been included to provide an easy source of reference to the terminology of economics.

I am grateful to many people for their help, support and encouragement during the writing of this text. In particular I would like to thank Kevin Reidy of Waterford Institute of Technology for proof reading the text and for his very valuable comments and suggestions. My thanks to Eric O Brien of the Cork Institute of Technology for reading a draft of the text and for his many useful and constructive suggestions. I would also like to acknowledge Patrick Mc Elligott for drawing the diagrams and to Ciara O' Doherty of the of the Institute of Technology Tralee for her assistance.

Finally I wish to thank my wife Bernadette and daughter Emma for their help and support.

Sean Nagle August 1999

CHAPTER 1

AN INTRODUCTION TO ECONOMICS

Introduction:

This Chapter looks at the nature and scope of economics. There are many definitions of economics and all of them emphasise the allocation of scarce resources that have alternative uses. This is true of Robbin's definition, which states that "Economics is a science which studies human behaviour as the relationship between ends and scarce means that have alternative uses." Things people want are collectively known as economic goods. An economic good is anything for which people are willing to pay. It must be scarce in relation to demand for it, transferable and provide utility or satisfaction. An economy is a mechanism that allocates scarce resources among competing uses.

The Science of Economics:

Scientific method starts with the formulation of a theory concerning behaviour. Economists adopt a scientific approach by attempting to make an objective analysis of economic behaviour and this is known as positive economics. The idea is to establish why the economy performs as it does and to have a basis for predicting how the economy will perform when circumstances change. Predictions are made on the assumption of 'other things being equal' or ceteris paribus. For example, theory states that a rise in mortgage rates causes house building to fall, meaning that this relationship holds ceteris paribus - only if other things that affect house building do not change. Unfortunately other things do not stay the same and as a result tests of economic theories are rarely conclusive.

Positive and Normative Statements:

A positive statement states what is, was, or will be. A positive economic statement could be on the following lines " the rate of inflation will exceed 3% in 2000". This statement does not necessarily have to be true, but we can test the veracity of it at the end of 2000 by looking at the evidence. A normative statement is a statement of value: a statement about what ought or ought not to be, e.g. "old age pensions ought to be increased". Other examples could be - "should we have a more equal distribution of income"? "Or should we sacrifice more inflation for less unemployment"?

The Scope of Economics:

People's wants are unlimited whereas the resources needed to satisfy them are limited. Economics attempts through the economic system to meet people's wants or needs through the production of goods and services. Goods are tangible things like potatoes and washing machines; services such as education and transport are consumed at the same time as they are produced. Goods and services are produced to be consumed and it is through consuming goods and services that people satisfy their needs and wants. They can however only consume what their incomes will allow. The size of a household's income is an indication of its material standard of living.

Factors of Production:

All nations have resources available to them called factors of production. These can be classified as follows:

1. **Land** - This resource is provided by nature and in economics it means a productive resource given by nature and existing in its natural state. Natural resources such as oil are included. Land however must be distinguished from other resources for the following reasons:

    - land, is a gift of nature;
    - it is subject to the law of diminishing returns; and
    - it is limited in supply.

2. **Capital** - Man must create capital for himself. It is 'the produced means of production'. It includes machinery, buildings, offices, and social infrastructure such as roads, sanitation, communications systems and so on. Capital goods are not produced for their own sake to satisfy consumers but to assist in further production. It is increased by diverting part of the economy's resources away from the production of final consumer goods to the production of capital goods.

3. **Labour** - This is the physical and mental power of human beings. It is human effort of all kinds, mental, physical, unskilled, skilled, artistic or scientific.

4. **Enterprise** - This is sometimes included as a fourth factor of production and is the activity of combining the other factors. It is the acceptance of the risks of uncertainty in production. There is need for someone or a group to combine the factors of production, i.e. entrepreneurs. The efficiency with which the factors are used depends on the technology deployed. Technology is the application of science or knowledge to production and it can be embedded in capital goods.

Scarcity:

Even though advanced economies have grown very rapidly over the past fifty years and very high standards of living have been achieved the main economic problem is still scarcity of resources. No matter how well off a household is, it can become better off if its income increases since it can then consume more. In the Less Developed Countries (LDCS) the problem of scarcity manifests itself in malnutrition, starvation and disease. This is absolute scarcity in contrast to relative scarcity in developed countries. People have unlimited desires for goods and services but resources available are limited. Goods produced with our scarce resources are economic goods therefore they have a price. Goods that are not scarce do not have a price, e.g. air. All our wants cannot be satisfied so we are forced to choose. Scarcity forces people to compete with each other for scarce resources.

Choice:

As already stated people must make choices and the three fundamental choices are as follows:

- What goods and services to produce and in what quantities given that demand cannot be fully satisfied since the resources available to do so are inadequate? To make a choice we balance the benefits of having more of one good or service against the loss of some other good or service.

- How are goods and services going to be produced since usually there is more than one way of producing things? The method of production and the technology necessary to use this method must be chosen. In Ireland we must choose whether to use gas, coal, turf or oil to produce electricity. The method chosen will be the most efficient based on resources available to us.

- Who gets the goods that are produced? The question is- how is the nation's income to be distributed? There must be some mechanism for distributing among consumers the limited amount of goods and services produced.

Opportunity Cost:

Choice involves sacrifice. If a boy spends his pocket money on a computer game, he will have to postpone buying the latest compact disk. The compact disk is the opportunity cost of the computer game. Since resources are limited, having one thing means going without something else. The opportunity cost of any good is the most desirable alternative foregone. The majority of economic resources have more than one use and by using them for one purpose we have to go without the output that could have resulted from using them for another purpose. Choices are not always 'all or nothing' ones, but are usually about producing more of one good and less of another without relinquishing the latter absolutely. This is choice at the margin. If a farmer can produce either 100 tonnes of barley or 200 tonnes of wheat, then the opportunity cost of producing one tonne of barley is the 2 tonnes of wheat foregone. To a student the opportunity cost of buying a textbook is the night out he also wanted but has to go without. Since the consumer acts rationally, he will always choose the "best" alternative, so that oppurtunity cost is always the next "best". At a national level the opportunity cost of the country having another "tribunal" could be measured in terms of the number hip operations that could be done with the same amount of resources.

Production Possibility Curves:

It is possible to illustrate opportunity cost by means of a production possibility curve. The latter curve shows the various combinations of two goods that an economy can possibly produce when its resources are fully employed. Assume that the country using all its available resources produces just two goods food and clothing then Diagram 1.1 shows a typical production possibility curve.

PP_1 indicates all combinations of food and clothing that can be produced by this economy when its resources are fully used or employed. Points P, A, B and P_1 are all points of full employment. At point C there are unemployed resources. At point P the economy is producing only clothing, while at P₁ food only is produced. Production cannot take place beyond the curve, e.g. point D, as the nation does not have enough resources to do this. It is assumed that there are just two goods, food and clothing that can be produced and that there is only one type of clothing and one type of food.

A production possibility curve illustrates the issues of choice and opportunity cost. If a country produces more food it would have to give up the production of some clothing. The sacrifice of clothing is the opportunity cost of the additional food.

The production possibility curve is concave to the origin, because different factors of production has different properties. Land differs in different parts of Ireland, people have different skills and even though resources have alternative uses they are not equally efficient in all uses. As a country tries to produce more and more of a particular good, it has to use resources that are less and less suitable. In the example above the production of more and more food will mean an increasing marginal cost, so that ever increasing amounts of clothing have to be sacrificed for each extra unit of food produced.

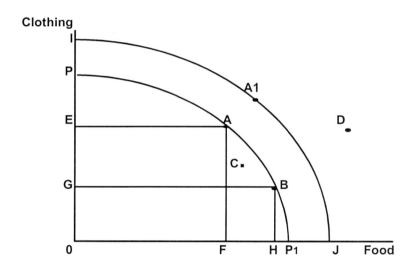

DIAGRAM 1.1 Production Possibility Curve

In Diagram 1.1 if the economy is initially at P producing only clothing, but then produces OF food, the opportunity cost of this is PE of clothing. This is the amount of clothing given up when food output goes up from zero to OF. However when the output of food increases from OF to OP₁ the opportunity cost is much greater at EO of clothing. When the output of food goes up from zero to OF, resources suited to production of food are used first but as production continues to increase resources more suited to clothing are used. These resources are comparatively inefficient in the production of food.

Over time the production possibilities of a country are likely to increase as a result of economic growth because, of technological advances, new sources of raw materials and an increase in labour productivity due to better education and training. We cannot however have economic growth without additional costs. There is opportunity cost since resources have to be diverted from consumption to investment in technology, education and training. Growth in potential output is shown by an outward shift in the production possibility curve. This enables actual output to increase from A to A_1, on IJ to where the production possibility curve has moved due to growth.

Economic Systems:

An "economic system" is the set of institutions within which a community decides what, how and for whom to produce goods and services. As already demonstrated all societies are faced with the problem of scarcity but their methods of dealing with it differ. At one extreme there is the centrally planned or command economy and at the other the free market economy. In between is the mixed economy that is some combination of the two extremes.

Centrally Planned or Command Economy:

A centrally planned or command economy is one where all decisions pertaining to economics are taken by a central authority. It is characterised by collective ownership of resources therefore the price mechanism does not operate. Examples in 1999 are Cuba and North Korea. Up to the late 1980's the USSR and other eastern European countries had command economies. In this type of economic organisation the government takes policy decisions and plans the allocation of resources at three levels:

- It plans the allocation of resources between current consumption and investment for the future.
- It plans the output of each industry and firm, the production techniques to be used and labour required.
- It plans the distribution of output between consumers.

Advantages of a Command Economy:

- National income can be distributed more equally based on needs.
- A low level of unemployment is possible, if the government allocates labour based on skills and production requirements.
- High growth rates are possible by directing resources into investment.
- Inefficiencies resulting from competition are eliminated.
- Monopoly power can achieve production benefits for the community.

Disadvantages of a Command Economy:

- If the state has complete control over resource allocation individuals lose much of their liberty.

- If there is no pricing system then planning can lead to inefficient use of available resources.

- If production is planned but individuals can spend their money as they wish, shortages and surpluses will arise.

- Much costly information must be collected and analysed before plans are made.

- State ownership diminishes the incentive of individuals and therefore effort.

- It is difficult to come up with incentives to produce a greater output without reducing quality. A large number of people are required to maintain quality.

Market Economy:

A market economy is a free enterprise, laissez-faire or capitalist economic system. Land and capital are privately owned. An economy that decides what, how and for whom goods and services are produced by channelling individual choice through a market is called a market economy. Markets consist of large numbers of buyers and sellers and price is determined by supply and demand. **Adam Smith** held that households and firms interacting in markets act as if they are guided by an " **invisible hand**", that leads them to desirable market outcomes. If the markets are fully competitive and flexible, equilibrium prices will be established at which demand and supply will be equal. Markets are unorganised and decentralised since there is no involvement by the government.

Advantages of a Market Economy:

- It works automatically therefore there is no need for expensive co-ordination.
- Competition is keen and no one individual has great power.
- Competition ensures that prices are kept down.
- Output is produced for profit so that the least cost method of production is used.
- Those able and willing to pay for output receive it and in this way the problem of for whom goods are produced is solved.

Disadvantages of a Market Economy:

- Luxury goods for some may be produced before others have the basic necessities of life.
- Competition between firms is often limited and a few big firms control the market for a particular good or service and can charge high prices thus making large profits.
- If competition is weak and prices are high firms will not necessarily be efficient.
- Community goods such as police and public amenities cannot be satisfactorily provided through the market, due to the fact that it is not possible to charge a price.
- Resources may remain unemployed as no one considers it profitable to employ them.
- Competition may lead to a waste of resources e.g. on advertising.

- There may be social costs, e.g. a chemical plant polluting the environment;
- Health services would be inadequate in a free market economy therefore the state must provide services so that they are adequate.

Mixed Economy:

In practice no country uses one system to the exclusion of the other. Ireland, together with most modern economies has a mixed economy in that it contains a mixture of private enterprise and state involvement in production and distribution.

Reasons for Government Intervention:

- to provide goods and services private industry will not or can not provide:
- to correct inequalities in the distribution of wealth between individuals:
- to curb monopoly power:
- to overcome frictions e.g. in the movement of labour:
- to relieve shortages e.g. housing.

The government controls a proportion of output by the provision of goods and services such as electricity, postal services, and infrastructure and by the operation of semi state bodies. It also controls part of output by transfer payments and through taxation.

Most countries including Ireland are mixed economies, though some are close to the free market economy, while others are nearer to the command economy. Overall it is the extent and shape of government intervention that distinguishes one type of economy from another.

Microeconomics:

The term "micro" comes from the Greek word for small. Microeconomics deals with small parts of the economic system and is a model that explains the behaviour of individuals and firms in the economy. Business firms and households make the microeconomic decisions of the economy. It also studies the way individual markets work.

Macroeconomics:

The term "macro" comes from the Greek word for large. Macroeconomics deals with the economy as a whole and studies the determinants of total output, inflation, employment and unemployment, national income and economic growth.

Questions.

1. Illustrate the practical importance of opportunity cost.

2. Explain the nature of a Production Possibility Curve and the assumptions made.

3. What are the three main forms of economic system? Do you consider a "mixed economy" to be the best type suited to Ireland ?

4. Distinguish between a positive and normative statement.

5. What are the advantages and disadvantages of the free market system in the allocation of scarce resources?

6. (a)Explain the mixed economy approach to the allocation of scarce resources.
   (b)What factors determine the extent to which an economy is mixed?

CHAPTER 2

DEMAND AND SUPPLY

Markets:

A market is any arrangement by which there is interaction between buyers and sellers of goods services, factors of production, or future commitment. It can be a street market, mail order system, shop, auction or whatever. These markets determine prices and ensure that the quantity people wish to buy equals the quantity people wish to sell. When we examine the workings of a market we must look at both the characteristics of demand for a good or service and the characteristics of supply of that good or service. The forces of demand and supply determine market prices.

The Functions of Price:

In a market economy, prices perform three main functions:

- **Incentive function**: For markets to operate efficiently buyers and sellers must respond to the incentives provided by the price mechanism. If the price of a particular good goes up consumers will buy less of that good. The supplier seeing that greater profit can be made shifts resources into producing the good whose relative price has gone up. This in turn may bid up wages and interest rates and other costs of production.

- **Signalling function:** Prices signal what goods and services are available and this enables suppliers to plan their economic activities. If incorrect information is transmitted it can lead to market failure.

- **Allocative function:** The price mechanism ensures that from the alternatives available the goods and services demanded are produced.

Demand:

In economics demand is how much of a good or service people in the market will buy at a given price over a given period of time. This is effective demand as it is backed up by the necessary purchasing power or money income. Demands are different from wants. Wants are unlimited desires and it is not possible to produce enough goods and services to satisfy all of them. Demand is a decision about which wants to satisfy, a decision that is influenced by the following factors:

- The price of the good or service.
- The prices of related or substitute goods or services.
- Expected future prices or shortages.
- Tastes of consumers for the good or service.
- Advertising.

- Population change.

Relationship between Price and the Quantity Demanded:

Price is dealt with separately because it is not only one of the important influences on demand but also on supply. The **law of demand** states that the quantity of a good demanded per period of time will fall as price rises and will rise as price falls ceteris paribus i.e. other things being equal. Quantity demanded of a good is therefore inversely related to price. Why does a higher price reduce the quantity demanded? If we assume that consumers have limited amounts of income that is divided as expenditure on a range of goods and services, then other things being equal, the higher the price of any particular good or service the smaller the amount that will be purchased. Why does a lower price, increase the quantity demanded? (1) Most goods have substitutes and as the price of a good rises relative to the prices of its substitutes then other things being equal consumers will buy less of the good and more of its substitute. (2) People can now afford to buy more with the same income and they will switch away from substitute goods and services the prices of which have not decreased.

The Demand Schedule and Demand Curves:

A demand schedule lists the quantities demanded at each different price, other things being equal. It shows the relationship between the price of a good and the quantity demanded. Table 2.1 sets out a demand schedule for milk. Average revenue (AR) is total revenue divided by the quantity sold. This demand schedule can be illustrated by drawing a demand or average revenue curve that graphs the relationship between the quantity demanded of a good or service and its price other things being equal. Diagram 2.1 shows the demand curve for Table 2.1. In addition, it slopes downward from left to right, indicating that as price rises quantity demanded falls and vice versa. Both the demand schedule and curve represent consumer plans because only a single price will prevail in the market at any one time. This means that all other price/quantity ratios are hypothetical.

Table 2.1 Demand Schedule for Milk

Price Of Milk (Pence / Litre)	Quantity Demanded Of Milk (Litres / Day)
70	50,000
60	100,000
50	150,000
40	200,000
30	250,000

Changes in Demand:

Assume that the demand schedule in Table 2.1 is based on an average consumer income of £150 per week. If this goes up to £200 per week, it will mean that now consumers will be willing and able to buy more milk at any price on the schedule. This means a new demand schedule arises, as shown in Table 2.2

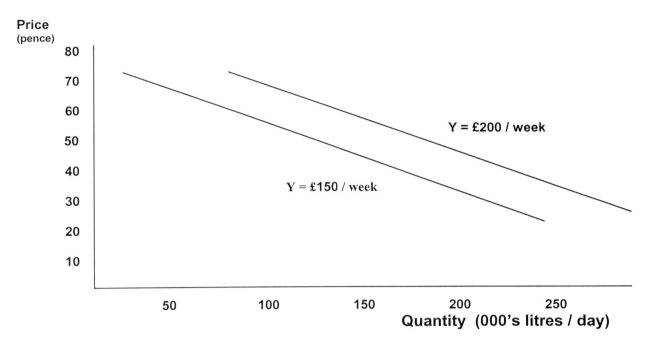

DIAGRAM 2.1 Demand Curve

Table 2.2 Demand Schedule for Milk given different Income Levels

Price Of Milk (Pence / Litre)	Quantity Demanded Milk with Income £150 / Week (Litres / Day)	Quantity Demanded Milk with Income £200 / Week (Litres / Day)
70	50,000	100,000
60	100,000	150,000
50	150,000	200,000
40	200,000	250,000
30	250,000	300,000

Diagram 2.2 shows the demand curves for different levels of income. The old demand curve has moved to the right from D to D₁. This shows an increase in demand at all prices, due to the favourable change in the conditions of demand. If there is an unfavourable change then the new demand curve moves to the left.

Underlying Conditions of Demand:

Anything other than price, which affects demand, is an underlying condition of demand. When we drew the demand curves in Diagram 2.2 we plotted a relationship between price and the quantity demanded, other things being equal. The "other things" are the underlying conditions of demand and when any of these change the demand curve shifts to a new position.

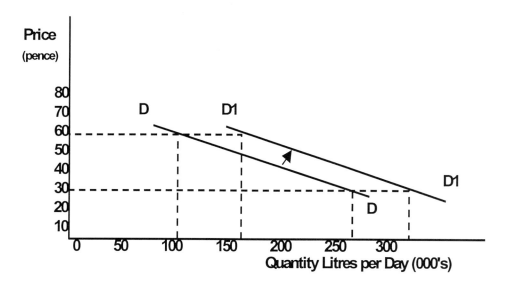

DIAGRAM 2.2 Demand Curve with New Quantities of Milk

The conditions of demand are as follows:

- **Income:** When income increases consumers buy more of most goods and vice versa. Increased income does not however lead to an increase in demand for all goods. Goods that do increase in demand as income rises are called **normal goods**. The effect of an increase in income on the purchases of milk is shown in Diagram 2.2. Goods that decrease in demand as income increases are known as **inferior goods,** which are not necessarily of inferior quality. Examples are margarine and black and white televisions. These goods have a negative Income Effect. **Giffen goods** are a special class of inferior good. When price increases demand increases. Giffen goods are goods such as bread and rice.

- **Complementary or joint demand:** When goods are complements, they are jointly consumed, cars and petrol. If the price of cars goes up fewer cars will be purchased and hence less petrol to run them. The opposite is also true and a fall in the price of one good, i.e. a car will cause an increase in demand for another, i.e. petrol.

- **Substitutes:** A substitute is a good that can be used in place of another good. For example if the price of pears goes up people will switch to apples. Demand for pears goes down and demand for apples goes up.

- **A change in tastes and fashions:** Taste is a very subjective matter and cannot be directly observed. It is sometimes possible to identify a trend or fashion that indicates changes in taste among large numbers of people. Consumers' tastes can be improved by a successful advertising campaign. When tastes change in favour of a product, demand goes up and when they change against the product, demand goes down. Clothing is subject to frequent change in fashion. Economists generally assume that changes in tastes or preferences occur only slowly and therefore are not that important an influence on changes in demand.

- **Changes in the size and composition of the population:** A general increase in population will bring about a rise in demand for most goods and services whereas a decrease will have the opposite effect. An increase in the population that consumes, for example, coke will result in increased demand for it, while a decrease will cause demand to fall. An increase in the number of people over 65 years of age will lead to demand for goods demanded by older people. The reverse will happen if the number of people over 65 years decreases.

- **Expectations:** If the price of a good is expected to rise, people will buy more of the good now and less in the future when its price is higher. If price is expected to fall, people buy less now and more later when the price falls.

Movements Along and Shifts of the Demand Curve:

A change in consumers' plans causes either a movement along the demand curve or a shift in it. A shift in demand is referred to as a change in demand while a movement along the demand curve is referred to as a change in the quantity demanded.

A demand curve is drawn on the assumption that other things remain equal. This means that a movement along the demand curve shows price alone changes and this: for example from 200,000 litres demanded to 50,000 when price rises from 40p per litre to 70p in Diagram 2.1.

If the price of a good remains constant but one or other of the underlying conditions change, a new curve must be constructed as the curve shifts. This shift is shown in Diagram 2.2 and it resulted from an increase in income that caused the demand curve to move to the right. If a change in any of the other underlying conditions occurs, causing demand to fall the demand curve will shift to the left.

Regressive (Perverse) Demand Curve:

Part of this curve slopes upward from left to right and shows that as the price for the good increases demand by the individual also increases. Goods, which have a regressive demand, are:

- Goods which are the standard food of the poor e.g. potatoes and bread. When the price of these goods rises, people will buy more of the goods rather than less. These goods are called Giffen Goods.

- Goods of ostentation, such as antiques or paintings that have a snob value. The higher the price an individual pays for this type of good the more exclusive it becomes. So when the price of this good is increased, the demand for it also increases.

- If the price of a good is constantly rising, then the demand for it may increase rather than decrease. Shares on the stock market are often affected in this way.

Diagram 2.3 shows the case of regression at the upper end of the curve. This may occur with goods of snob value such as jewellery. When price goes up from P to P1 the quantity demanded increases from Q to Q1. When their price falls, demand may also fall because a greater number of people can now afford to buy them and they start to lose their exclusiveness.

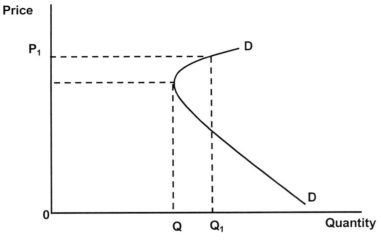

DIAGRAM 2.3 Demand Curve for Snob Goods

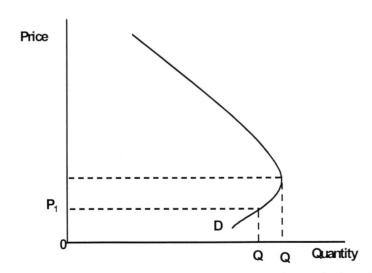

DIAGRAM 2.4 Demand Curve for Inferior Goods

Diagram 2.4 shows regression at the lower end of the curve. When price falls from P to P1 quantity demanded falls from Q to Q1.This, may occur with inferior goods. As their incomes rise, poor people buy more expensive goods such as meat instead of potatoes and bread.

Supply:

In economics supply refers to how much of a good will be offered for sale at a given price over a certain time period. The law of supply states that other things being equal when the price of a good rises the quantity supplied of the good also rises. Supply is not taken as the stock of something in existence, for example, the number of houses in Tralee at any one time. It is the number of houses for sale in Tralee at a particular time that constitutes supply. The higher the price of a good or service, the greater the quantity supplied, other things being equal. The quantity supplied depends on the price of the good and on the conditions of supply.

Supply Schedule:

The supply schedule is a table that shows the relationship between the price of a good and the quantity supplied. Table 2.3 is a supply schedule and shows the different quantities of milk that producers are willing and of course able to supply at different prices over a given time period. It can be for one producer, group of producers or for all producers, i.e. the market supply schedule.

Table 2.3 Supply Schedule for Milk

Price of Milk Pence Per Litre	Quantity Supplied Litres Per Day (000's)
70	300
60	250
50	175
40	100
30	50

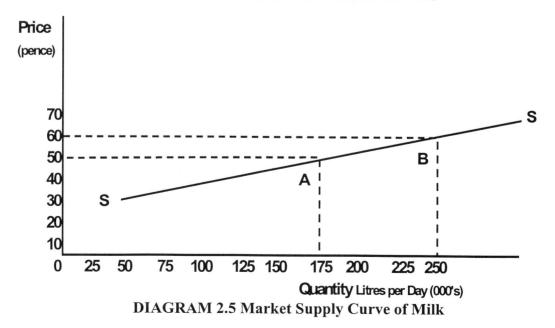

DIAGRAM 2.5 Market Supply Curve of Milk

Change in Supply:

Suppose there is a technical improvement in the dairy industry due to the introduction of a new improved milking machine that enables producers to supply more over the range of prices, then there is a change in the supply schedule. Table 2.4 shows the revised supply schedule.

Table 2.4 Revised Market Supply Schedule - Milk

Price of Milk Pence Per Litre	Quantity Supplied Litres Per Day (000's)
70	320
60	270
50	200
40	150
30	75

Diagram 2.6 shows the old and new supply curves. The supply curve has moved to the right from S to S₁ due to improved technical change. Any change in the underlying conditions of supply will cause a shift either to the left or right in the supply curve.

Conditions of Supply:

When a determinant other than price changes there is a change in supply, that is, a shift in the supply curve. An increase in supply shifts the supply curve to the right, a decrease to the left.

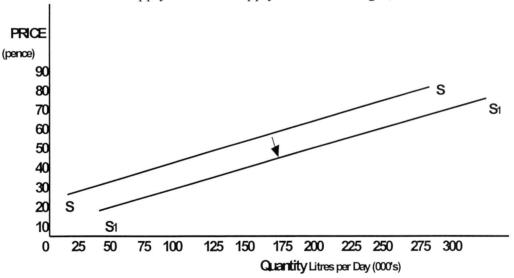

DIAGRAM 2.6 Revised Market Supply Curve Milk

The conditions of supply are as follows:

- **Prices of Factors of Production:** The prices of the factors of production are an important influence on price. An increase in the price of a factor such as labour will cause a

16

reduction in supply while a decrease will mean that a larger quantity can profitably be supplied at any price.

- **Prices of Related Goods:** The supply of a good can be influenced by the price of a related good. For example, if a farmer can produce, either mutton or beef, the quantity of beef produced will depend on the price of mutton. The two goods are substitutes in production. An increase in the price of a substitute lowers the supply of the good. Goods can be complements in production. This occurs when two things are, of necessity, produced together, for example, butter and cream from milk. An increase in the price of any of these increases the supply of the others.

- **Reduction in Tax on Expenditure on the Commodity:** A reduction in VAT on a commodity will mean that more can be supplied without reducing profitability. A subsidy on milk would enable producers to sell more at the given range of prices.

- **Favourable Climatic Conditions:** If weather conditions are favourable, grass yields and therefore milk yields will be high. Climatic changes can be unfavourable and can cause a decrease in supply.

- **Expected Future Prices**: If the price of a good or service is expected to rise then less will be sold to-day and more in the future. On the other hand if price is expected to fall it will pay to supply more now and less later.

- **Technology:** The introduction of new technology allows a larger quantity to be supplied over the range of prices.

- **Entry or Exit of Firms:** Entry of new firms will increase supply while firms leaving will decrease it.

Price and Output Determination:

The price mechanism brings demand and supply into equilibrium and the equilibrium price for a good or service where demand and supply are equal emerges. By combining our analysis of demand and supply we can show how the actual price of a good and the quantities bought and sold are determined in a free and competitive market. We use the data from Tables 2.1 and 2.3 to construct Diagram 2.7 and these figures are given again in Table 2.5.

Table 2.5 Market Demand and Supply of Milk

Price of Milk Pence per litre	Total Market Demand Litres (000's)	Total Market Supply Litres (000's)
70	50	300
60	100	250
50	150	150
40	200	100
30	250	50

Equilibrium is where the demand and supply curves intersect and have been brought into balance. At 60p per litre supply is 250,000 but demand is only 100,000 so that there is excess supply or surplus on the market each day of 150,000 litres. Since there are many suppliers and the commodity is perishable it is probable that some suppliers at least will lower price and that others will reduce output of milk. At 50p per litre demand and supply are equal and this is the equilibrium price and output. At 40p per litre 200,000 litres are demanded while 100,000 are supplied so that there is excess demand. In this case since there are many consumers, price will be pushed up, as suppliers will see that they can charge a higher price due to excess demand.

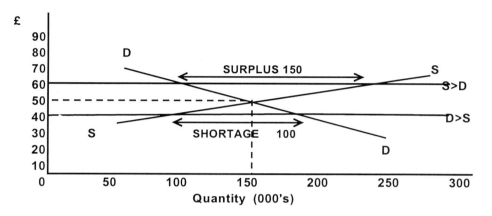

Diagram 2.7 Determination of Market Equilibrium (Milk Daily)

The equilibrium price can be referred to as the market-clearing price, since there is no surplus or shortage. The equilibrium price will remain unchanged as long as the demand and supply curves remain unchanged. If either of them shift, there is a new equilibrium price and quantity.

Changes in the Conditions of Demand and Supply:

If one of the underlying conditions of demand changes (other than price) the entire demand curve will shift. This results in a movement along the supply curve to the new point of intersection. This is illustrated in Diagram 2.8.

Suppose consumers taste changes and they now drink more milk, bringing about a change in the conditions of demand, the demand curve shifts to the right from DD to D_1D_1. At the original price of 50p per litre, we now have excess demand over supply of 50,000 litres. Competition between buyers will now push the price per litre up to 60p when 200,000 litres are demanded and supplied. The effect of the shift in demand, therefore, has been a movement along the supply curve from the old equilibrium to the new. The supply curve has not moved. A decrease in demand for milk due perhaps to a health scare will cause the demand curve to shift to the left.

If one of the underlying conditions of supply changes (other than price) the entire supply curve will shift Diagram 2.9. If for example the cost of producing milk increases, the supply curve moves to the left from SS to S_1S_1. Demand increases from A to B and there is now excess demand of 50,000 litres.

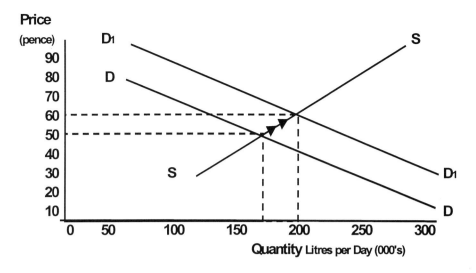

DIAGRAM 2.8 Effect of a Shift in the Demand Curve

If one of the underlying conditions of supply changes (other than price) the entire supply curve will shift as in Diagram 2.9. If for example the cost of producing milk increases, the supply curve moves to the left from SS to S_1S_1. There is now a shortage of 50,000 litres at the old price of 50p per litre. Price goes up to 60p per litre and supply falls from 150,000 to 100,000 litres. There is a movement along the demand curve from the old equilibrium to the new. The demand curve has not moved.

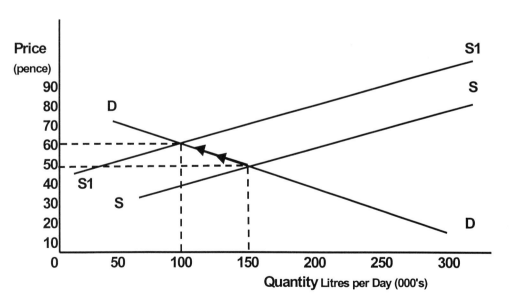

DIAGRAM 2.9 Effect of a Shift in the Supply Curve

Price Ceiling:

A price ceiling is a situation where a price is not allowed to rise to its equilibrium level. If the pricing authority considers that the equilibrium price of a good or service is too high, it can set a maximum or ceiling price. This is done for the benefit of the consumer. In Diagram 2.10 equilibrium is at price P_1 and quantity Q_1. Price P_1 is considered too high and a ceiling price of P_2 is fixed. Price P_2 reduces supply to Q_2 and demand increases to Q_3 where there is excess demand of $Q_3 - Q_2$. Suppliers cannot legally increase price to eliminate excess demand. To achieve the ceiling price the government must reduce effective demand by some form of rationing. This was done in many countries, including Ireland, during the Second World War. One problem with this type of rationing is that it involves administrative costs. If it is not fully supported by the public it could lead to the development of a black market.

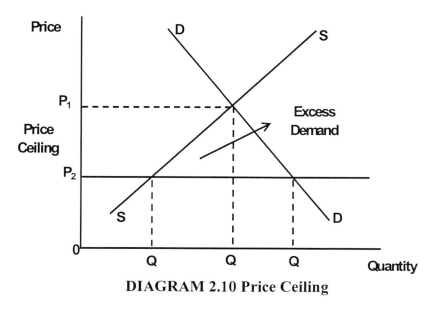

DIAGRAM 2.10 Price Ceiling

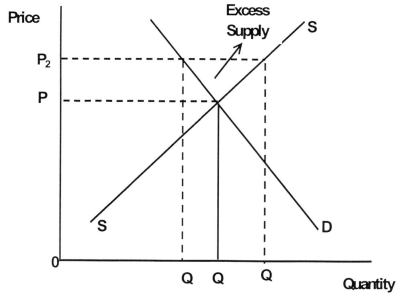

DIAGRAM 2.11 Price Floor

20

A price floor is the situation where the price is not allowed to decrease below a certain level. It only keeps the price from falling not from rising. If the pricing authority considers that the equilibrium price of a good or service is too low, it can set a minimum or floor price. This may be done to protect the incomes of producers. In Diagram 2.11 equilibrium is at price P_1 and quantity Q_1. Price P_1 is considered too low and a floor price of P_2 is fixed. Quantity demanded falls to Q_2 and supply increases to Q_3 resulting in excess supply of $Q_3 - Q_2$.

Questions

1. What is meant by 'effective demand'?

2. The following figures show the demand and supply schedules for beef.

Price of beef (£/ kg)	Quantity demanded of beef (kg/week)	Quantity supplied of beef (kg/week)
5	200	1,000
4	400	800
3	600	600
2	800	400
1	1,000	0

From these figures:

i.   Draw the demand and supply curves.

ii. State the equilibrium price.

iii. What is the excess demand or supply if the price is: £4 per kg? £1.50 per kg?

iv. Suppose that demand were now to decrease by 50% due to BSE disease at every price. Draw the new demand curve and state the new equilibrium price.

3. What is meant by demand? Explain the difference between a movement along and a shift in a demand curve.

4. What changes in the conditions of supply cause an increase in supply or a decrease in supply?

5. Using a typical demand curve diagram show the effect of a change in the price of a good and a change in the price of its substitutes.

6. Using diagrams show how the forces of supply and demand produce an equilibrium price and quantity.

7. Goods with snob value, such as antiques, may be demanded only because they are expensive. Does the demand curve slope downward?

8. From the following schedule suppose the government imposed a minimum price of £7 what would occur? From the same data show what the price would have to be to represent an effective price ceiling.

Price £	Quantity Demanded	Quantity Supplied
1	100	20
2	80	24
3	70	30
4	64	40
5	60	60
6	55	82
7	52	100
8	46	130
9	40	160
10	30	197

CHAPTER 3

ELASTICITY OF DEMAND AND SUPPLY

Introduction:

Elasticity measures the responsiveness of quantity demanded or supplied to changes in price or any other variable. When the quantity demanded is highly responsive to price changes demand is elastic, and when it is unresponsive, demand is inelastic. In Chapter 2 we saw that an increase in demand will result in a rise in both price and quantity while a fall in supply will result in a higher price and a lower quantity demanded. In this Chapter we show how price elasticity of demand, price elasticity of supply and income elasticity of demand are measured. We illustrate how a knowledge of the different elasticities are useful for firms and for the government.

Price Elasticity of Demand:

Price elasticity of demand refers to elasticity at a particular price and is a measure of the responsiveness of the quantity demanded to a change in price.

The general formula for measuring price elasticity is:

PED   =   <u>Proportionate (or percentage) change in quantity demanded</u>
                Proportionate (or percentage) change in price

We need to know the quantities demanded at different prices while all other determinants of demand are held constant. We can illustrate this by an example from the demand schedule in Table 2.1. When price falls from 60p to 50p per litre, demand for milk increases from 100,000 to 150,000 litres per day. The change in price is -10p, this must be related to the original price i.e. 60p or to the new price 50p.

One could therefore get two different answers for the same thing as follows:

Price elasticity of demand is therefore equal to:

$$\text{PED} = \frac{50,000}{100,00} \div \frac{-10}{60} = \frac{1}{2} \div \frac{-1}{6} = \frac{1}{2} \times \frac{-6}{1} = -3$$

A rise in the price of milk from 50p to 60p results in a drop in demand of 50,000

$$\text{PED} = \frac{-50,000}{150,000} \div \frac{10}{50} = \frac{-1}{3} \times \frac{5}{1} = \frac{-5}{3} = -1.67$$

We have two different answers describing the same situation so to avoid this situation we relate the actual change, to the mid point of the two prices.

Arc Elasticity:

To get over the difficulty of having two values for the elasticity depending on whether the price increases or decreases, we use the average price and quantity. Since elasticity falls from point to point moving down a negatively sloped demand curve, average elasticities should be measured only for small changes in price. The formula can be written as follows:

$$\frac{\Delta Q}{1/2 \, (Q_1 + Q_2)} \div \frac{\Delta P}{^1/_2(P_1 + P_2)} = \frac{\Delta Q}{\Delta P} \times \frac{(P_1 + P_2)}{(Q_1 + Q_2)}$$

ΔQ = Change in quantity demanded; ΔP = Change in price; Q_1 = Original quantity demanded; P_1 = Original price, Q_2 = Quantity demanded after the change in price; P_2 = New price.

From our example :

$$\frac{50}{^1/_2(100 + 150)} \div \frac{-10}{^1/_2(50 + 60)}$$

$$= \frac{50}{125} \div \frac{-10}{55} = \frac{2}{5} \times \frac{11}{-2} = -2.2$$

The price elasticity of demand is -2.2 regardless of whether the price increases or decreases. What is measured here is arc elasticity of demand and in Diagram 3.1 it is the elasticity between point X and point Y. Elasticity is measured over the arc of the demand curve rather than at one point.

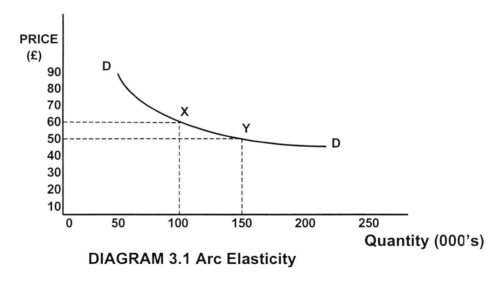

DIAGRAM 3.1 Arc Elasticity

Because demand curves slope downwards we are either dividing a positive proportionate/ percentage change in quantity by a negative proportionate or percentage change in price or vice verse. Therefore the result is negative. The sign is usually disregarded. This means that an increase in the price of a good will cause demand to fall and a fall in price will cause demand to rise. Examples are consumer durables and most clothing.

If it were positive it would mean that the demand curve is upward sloping so that an increase in the price of the good will lead to an increase in the quantity demanded. A fall in price will lead to a decrease. An example is maize used by people with very low incomes in less developed countries. When price goes up they may buy more maize and cut back on non-essentials.

Point Elasticity:

This is the measurement of elasticity at a point on a curve. The formula is $\Delta q/\Delta p \times p/q$ where $\Delta q/\Delta p$ is the inverse of the slope of the line xy tangent to the demand curve at the point in question A. In Diagram 3.2 Δq and Δp mean very small changes in quantity demanded and in price respectively.

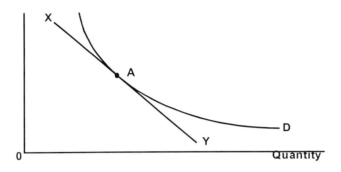

DIAGRAM 3.2 Measurement Of Point Elasticity

Panel (a) Diagram 3.3 illustrates infinitely inelastic demand by means of a vertical straight line. No matter what happens to price the quantity demanded remains the same. The more price is raised the greater the revenue. In absolute terms price elasticity of demand is equal to zero.

Panel (b) Diagram 3.3 illustrates an inelastic demand sloping downward from left to right. The relative change in the quantity demanded is less than the relative change in price. In absolute terms elasticity of demand will be greater than zero but less than one. The quantity demanded changes by a smaller percentage than does price.

Panel (c) Diagram 3.3 shows unit elasticity. This is represented by a convex slope due to the fact that if the elasticity of demand is to be kept constant the equal absolute price falls must be met with larger and larger absolute increase in quantity. The curve must therefore become flatter and flatter as prices become lower and lower. The relative change in quantity demanded is exactly equal to the relative change in price. In absolute terms price elasticity of demand is equal to one or unity.

Panel (d) Diagram 3.3 illustrates an elastic demand. The relative change in quantity demanded is greater than the relative change in price. In absolute terms elasticity of demand will be greater than one but less than infinity.

Panel (e) Diagram 3.3 illustrates an infinitely elastic demand: Purchasers are prepared to buy all they can get at a price and nothing at all if the price rises. A horizontal straight line shows this. In absolute terms elasticity of demand will be infinity. PED varies along the linear downward sloping demand curve from $-\infty$ to 0.

Determinants of Price Elasticity of Demand:

Price elasticity of demand varies widely between goods. The demand for some goods will be highly elastic whereas for others it will be highly inelastic. There are a number of reasons for this including the following:

- **The availability of substitutes at the prevailing market price:**
The number and closeness of substitute goods are the most important determinants. The greater the number and the closer they are the greater will be the price elasticity of demand. If a good has many substitutes consumers can switch to an alternative as its price rises. The situation is different when a good has few or no close substitutes. The demand for milk will be elastic as it has many close substitutes. However drinks as a whole have no close substitutes and therefore, their demand will be relatively inelastic.

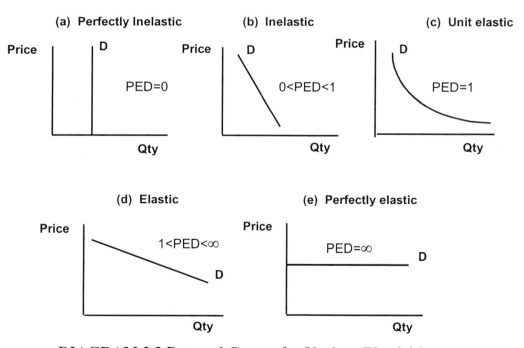

DIAGRAM 3.3 Demand Curves for Various Elasticities

- **Proportion of income spent on a good:**
The higher the proportion of income spent on a good the greater is elasticity. For example if mortgage interest rates rise, people may have to cut down on their demand for housing, buy smaller homes or rent them. Pepper, on the other, hand has a very low elasticity of demand since consumers would have little difficulty in paying a relatively large percentage increase in its price with little impact on their overall budgets.

- **The Time Period:**

Elasticity depends on the period of time that has elapsed since a price change. It takes time to find substitutes or to change spending habits so that, in general, the greater the period of time that has elapsed the higher the elasticity of demand. The response of buyers to a change in price depends on whether it is short-run or long-run demand. The short-run refers to the period just after a price change, and before the long-run starts. Long-run refers to the time required to complete all adjustments to a price change. The short-run response depends on whether the price change is seen as permanent or temporary. If it is assumed to be temporary then a price change results in a highly elastic response from the buyer. In the situation where price is high now buyers will wait for it to go down and if it is low now they will buy a great amount before it goes up again. When a price change is `considered to be permanent the quantity purchased does not alter much in the short-run, that is, demand is inelastic. The long-run demand curve comes about when every possible adjustment has been made, to a change in price. Long-run demand is more elastic than short-run.

- **Luxury or Necessity Good:**
If a good is a luxury it can be done without when its price rises, so that demand is elastic. Necessities cannot be done without therefore demand for them is inelastic.

- **The Durability of a Product:**
The longer a good lasts the more probable it is that its replacement will be postponed if its price rises. This type of good has a relatively elastic demand, for example, refrigerators.

- **The Possibility of New Purchasers:**
If price falls then new consumers may decide that it is worth buying the particular good. When these consumers are from an income group consisting of many people, a fall in price will result in a big elasticity of demand. If a fall in price affects an income group with few people, i.e. higher income group then the market demand schedule tends to be inelastic.

- **Addictive Goods:**
Goods such as alcohol and cigarettes are habit forming and this reduces users' responsiveness to changes in price.

Price Elasticity of Demand, Sales Revenue and Expenditure:

Total revenue is price multiplied by quantity, i.e. $TR = P \times Q$. This is gross revenue before the deduction of taxes or any other costs. This total revenue will be equal to total expenditure by consumers and revenue of firms. One of the important applications of price elasticity of demand concerns its relationship with firms sales revenue and this relationship is outlined as follows:

When elasticity of demand (E_d) is <1 a rise in price brings about a rise in total revenue (TR) and expenditure.
When $E_d > 1$ a rise in price causes TR and total expenditure to fall.
When $E_d = 1$ a rise in price does not change TR or total expenditure.
When $E_d < 1$ a fall in price leads to a fall in TR and total expenditure

When $E_d > 1$ a fall in price leads to an increase in TR and total expenditure.
When $E_d = 1$ a fall in price means no change in TR or total expenditure.

As can be seen when $E_d < 1$, price and TR move in the same direction. When $E_d > 1$, price and TR move in opposite directions.

When demand is inelastic as in panel (a) in Diagram 3.4 revenues can be increased by raising price while if it is elastic as in panel (b) revenue will be lost if price is raised. Revenue will increase if price is cut. In panel (a) the gain in revenue from increasing price is greater than the loss. In panel (b) the loss of revenue is greater than the gain from raising price.

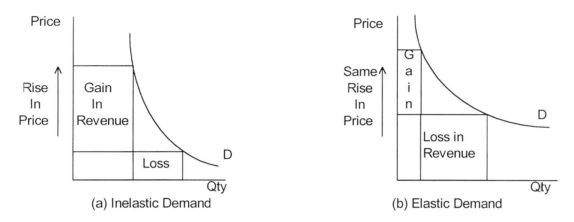

DIAGRAM 3.4 Effect of Elasticity on Revenue

The following examples illustrate the price changes a firm can make in order to increase revenue:

Example:

A firm that manufactures three different products finds Price Elasticity of Demand for the three products to be as follows:
Product X: - 3.0
Product Y: + 0.8
Product Z: - 0.2

Product X: Price elasticity is >1 which shows that the product is highly elastic. If the firm lowers the price the increase in demand will more than offset the price reduction and total revenue will increase.

Product Y: The plus sign means that price and demand move in the same direction so that if price is raised demand will increase as will total revenue which is price by quantity sold. If price is lowered demand total revenue will fall. This is a Giffen good.

28

Product Z: Price elasticity is < 1. This means the product is highly inelastic. A rise in total revenue due to an increase in quantity demanded will offset the fall in total revenue due to the fall in price.

Uses of Price Elasticity of Demand:

Price Elasticity of Demand and Taxes:

Knowledge of PED is important for government when it is imposing taxes on goods and services. The Minister for Finance is interested in knowing for example the effect of an increase in value added tax (VAT) on revenue. This VAT increase means a higher price for the consumer. The minister will find that if demand is elastic, revenue from this source will fall while if it is inelastic he/she will obtain more revenue. In most countries the heaviest taxes are on goods like alcohol and tobacco for which demand is inelastic. The minister does not always seek to maximise revenue. The less elastic demand is, the greater the tax burden on the consumer. As a politician the minister may not wish to increase this burden on the consumer and may tax goods with elastic demand when the tax has to be absorbed by producers having to cut their prices.

- **Price fixing by a Monopolist or Cartel:**

A monopolist or sole supplier of a good may find it difficult to decide whether to raise or lower his price. However he/she knows that if demand is inelastic at the going price and he raises his price his revenue will increase. It will pay him to go on raising price until the demand becomes elastic. In the early 1970s Organisation of Petroleum Exporting Countries(OPEC) producers increased their export revenues very substantially when they raised prices because demand for oil was inelastic. Since then demand for oil has become more elastic or less inelastic so that revenue has decreased.

- **Price Elasticity of Demand and Trade Unions:**

Trade unions will find it more difficult to obtain wage increases for their members without creating unemployment where the elasticity of demand for the product made is high.

Income Elasticity of Demand (IED):

Income elasticity of demand is the percentage change in the quantity demanded divided by the percentage change in income or

$$\text{IED} = \frac{\text{Percentage change in quantity demand}}{\text{Percentage change in income}}$$

We can express this in arc form as follows:

$$\frac{\Delta Q}{\Delta I} \quad X \quad \frac{(I_1 + I_2)}{(Q_1 + Q_2)}$$

ΔQ = Change in quantity demanded,
ΔI = Change in income,
Q_1 = Original quantity demanded,

Q_2 = Demand for good after the change.
I_1 = Income before the change,
I_2 = Income after the change.

An increase in real income, which is income expressed in units of goods usually, increases the demand for goods and services but to a varying degree. Income elasticities of demand can be either positive or negative. We look at three ranges, i.e. greater than 1 (income elastic) 0 to 1 (income inelastic) and less than 0 (negative income elasticity). The concept of IED is important for suppliers when forecasting the sale of their product when incomes are changing.

Example: You are given the following information:

Income Level (£)	Quantity Demanded
20,000	200
22,000	260

How sensitive is the quantity demanded to changes in income?

Income goes up from 20,000 to 22,000

$$IED = \frac{\Delta Q}{\Delta I} \times \frac{(I_1 + I_2)}{(Q_1 + Q_2)} = \frac{60}{2,000} \times \frac{20,000 + 2,000}{200 + 260} = \frac{6}{200} \times \frac{42,000}{460} = +2.7$$

The sign tells us the type of good it is. The plus sign means it is a **Normal** good whereas if it is minus it is an **Inferior** good. In our example we have a Normal good. The size of the figure refers to the sensitivity of quantity demanded to changes in income. The good in this case is income elastic because income elasticity of demand is greater than 1.

Determinants of Income Elasticity of Demand:

Degree of 'necessity' of the good: In advanced economies the demand for luxury goods increases rapidly as per capita income rises, whereas demand for basic goods such as potatoes increases just a little. If income elasticity of demand for a good is between 0 and 1 it is said to be **a necessity**, whereas if it is greater than 1 it is said to be **a luxury good**. If a rise in income brings about a fall in consumption, as consumers change over to other goods they can now afford, income elasticity of demand is negative. These good are called **inferior goods.**

Level of Consumer Income: Poor people will react differently than rich people to a rise in their incomes. For a given increase in income poor people may buy a great deal more meat, whereas rich people may buy just a little more.

Cross Price Elasticity of Demand (CED):

Cross elasticity is a measure of the responsiveness of demand for one product, A, to a change in the price of another B. If, the goods are complementary, a fall in the price of B, will bring about an increase in the demand for A. If the goods are substitutes a fall in the price of B will cause a fall in demand for A. The closer two goods are as substitutes or complements the larger the numerical value for cross elasticity. Magnitude can vary from - infinity to + infinity. It is positive for substitutes, negative for complements and zero means that the goods are independent so there is no relationship.

The formula for measuring cross elasticity is:

The proportionate change in demand for Good A
The proportionate change in the price of Good B

Example:
Cross elasticity of demand between Good 1 and 2 is = +2.1
Cross elasticity of demand between Good 1 and 3 is = +0.2
Cross elasticity of demand between Good 1 and 4 is = -0.5
Cross elasticity of demand between Good 1 and 5 is = -1.3

(a) Which of these goods are complements of Good 1?
(b) Which of these goods is the closest substitute for Good 1?

(a) Complementary goods are in joint demand e.g. cars and petrol. If the price of cars rises, demand for petrol falls so CED is negative and demand and price go in opposite directions. So Goods 4 and 5 are complements of Good 1.

(b) Cross elasticity of demand for a substitute good is positive + therefore demand and price go in the same direction. Goods 2 and 3 are substitutes for Good 1. The greater the numerical value of the substitute good, the closer the substitute.

Uses of CED:

Firms will wish to know the cross elasticity of demand for their product or a change in the price of a rival's product or of a complementary product. They can plan more effectively if they can gauge their customers' responses to a change in price or how their markets will react to a change in real income.

The government will wish to know how a change in domestic prices will affect the demand for imports. If cross elasticity of demand for imports is high because they are close substitutes for home produced goods and if prices go up at home due to inflation, then demand for imports will rise substantially. This increase will worsen the balance of payments.

Price Elasticity of Supply (PES):

Price elasticity of supply measures the responsiveness of supply of a good to a change in the price of that good.

$$PE_s = \frac{\text{Proportionate (or percentage) change in quantity supplied}}{\text{Proportionate (or percentage) change in price}}$$

Example: Suppose the price of milk increases from £1.50 to £1.65 a gallon and the amount dairy farmers produce increases from 5,000 to 5,750 gallons per day. Calculate price elasticity of supply.

$$\% \text{ change in price} = \frac{1.65 \times 100}{1.50} = 110 = 10\%$$

$$\% \text{ change in quantity supplied} = \frac{5750-5000}{5000} \times 100$$

$$= \frac{750}{50} = 15\%$$

$$PES = \frac{15}{10} = 1.5$$

Elasticity is greater than 1 showing that the quantity supplied moves proportionately more than price.

Since supply curves normally slope upwards from left to right elasticity of supply is usually positive.

Supply Curves for Various Elasticities :

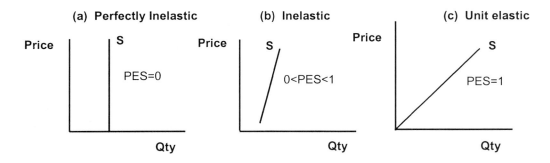

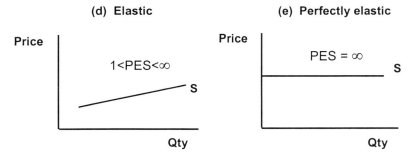

DIAGRAM 3.5 Supply Curves – Price Elasticity of Supply

Panel **(a)** Diagram 3.5 shows perfectly inelastic supply and Es = 0. A given amount of a commodity will be offered for sale whatever the market price. This applies to goods such as land and antiques.

In Panel **(b)** of Diagram 3.5 the quantity supplied changes less than proportionately to price i.e. by a smaller percentage, Zero < Es < 1. It shows relatively inelastic supply

Panel **(c)** Diagram 3.5 shows unit supply elasticity when Es = 1. Here the quantity supplied changes in proportion to the price i.e. by the same percentage.

Panel **(d)** of Diagram 3.5 shows relatively elastic supply when 1 < Es < infinity. The quantity supplied changes more than proportionately to price i.e. by a larger percentage.

Panel **(e)** Diagram 3.5 shows infinitely or perfectly elastic supply. Es = infinity and nothing will be supplied at prices below P, but when price P is reached an infinitely large amount will be supplied.

Determinants of Price Elasticity of Supply:

- **Time Period:** Supply periods can be divided into immediate, short-run and long-run.
In the **immediate time period** it is unlikely that firms can increase supply by much. This is due to the fact that supply is almost fixed and is therefore highly inelastic. In our example of milk supply, the factors of production such as land are fixed in the immediate period , so that elasticity is zero and the supply of milk is fixed. In the **short-run period** some inputs can be increased while others remain fixed. More fertiliser can be applied to the land but the supply of land cannot be increased over this period. The supply curve in the short run is more elastic than in the immediate period. In the **long-run period** all factors of production can be varied and supply will be highly elastic. Producers of milk can buy more land, build more milking parlours and buy more machinery. Supply is more elastic than it is in the short-run.

- **Resource Constraints:** If the firm has unused resources available it will be relatively easy for it to increase output. This ease will depend on how quickly additional resources can be bought or brought into production.

- **The Amount that Costs Rise as Output Rises:** The farmer's ability to purchase factors of production needed to increase his output of milk is subject to the cost of the factors. If costs rise rapidly as output is increased then any increase in profitability due to a price increase will be eroded by the increased costs. Supply in this situation will be inelastic. If however costs rise slowly as output goes up then supply may be relatively elastic, as will be the case if the firm has plenty of spare capacity.

- **Levels of Stock:** An increase in supply can be met from stock, if stock levels are high enough. The greater the level of stocks the greater the elasticity of supply. If stocks are not held due to high cost of storage then supply will be inelastic. If goods are perishable and cannot be held in stock then supply is inelastic.

1. Define elasticity and explain, using examples, its importance in its supply aspect. Why might supply elasticities be lower in the short- run than in the long- run?

2. A firm manufactures three different products and has price elasticities of demand as follows:
   Product A: - 4.00
   Product B: +1.00
   Product C: - 0.2
   What price changes, if any, should the firm make so as to increase its revenue?

3. Explain the terms:
   (a) price elasticity of demand
   (b) income elasticity of demand
   (c) Why might a manufacturing firm have an interest in the numerical size of these elasticities with regard to the products it sells?

4. By use of appropriate diagrams and examples explain how economists measure the price elasticity of demand.

5. Define cross price elasticity of demand and show how it is estimated. What does a high figure for cross elasticity mean?

6. Suppose that people going on business and on holidays have the following demand for airline tickets from Dublin to London :

Price (£)	Quantity demanded	Quantity demanded
	Business Holidays	
150	2,400	1,200
200	2,300	1,000
250	2,000	800
300	1,900	600
350	1,800	400

(A) As the price of tickets rises from £200 to £250 what is the price elasticity of demand for (1) business   (2) holidays ?
(b)Why might holiday makers have a different elasticity to that of business people ?

7. Define price and income elasticities of demand and outline the factors that determine them.

8. The following is the demand schedule of a product :

Price (£)	Demand (units per week)
8	40
,,	50
,,	60
,,	70
,,	80
,,	90
,,	100
,,	110

Calculate price elasticity of demand and comment on your results when (a) the price is reduced from £7 to £6 (b) the price is reduced from £3 to £2 .

9. A private tour operator found that price elasticity of demand for his tours was as follows :
Tour A: Price Elasticity of Demand = -1.6
Tour B: Price Elasticity of Demand = -1.0
Tour C: Price Elasticity of Demand = -0.5

He wishes to maximise profits and asks your advice as to what changes to make to price to achieve this goal. How would you advise him?

CHAPTER 4

DEMAND AND CONSUMER THEORY

Introduction:

We must consider how rational consumers behave so that we can carry out a more detailed examination of the slope of the demand curve. A rational consumer is assumed to be a person who will want to achieve the greatest possible satisfaction from his/her spending. Since our incomes are limited we must choose a combination of goods that will give us the greatest satisfaction. As far as consumption is concerned we must consider the relative costs and benefits to us of the alternatives on which we can spend our incomes. It is not suggested that all consumers act rationally all the time but the assumption that they do so is used to explain the behaviour of the representative consumer.

Utility Theory:

A number of theories have been put forward by economists to explain the behaviour of consumers and here we examine one of them, i.e. marginal utility theory. People buy goods and services because they get satisfaction from them and economists call this satisfaction "utility". Utility means the capacity of a good or service to satisfy consumers' wants. It is gained by the presence of pleasure and/or the absence of pain. Utility is a difficult concept because it is totally subjective and cannot be measured directly.

Total and Marginal Utility:

Total utility is the total satisfaction a consumer gets from the consumption of goods and services over time. It depends on the consumer's level of consumption as more consumption gives more total utility.

Marginal utility is the additional satisfaction derived from consuming one extra unit of a good in a given time period. Since utility is subjective, there is no way we can measure it. For our purpose here we will measure it in utils even though no one really knows what a util is. It is however useful to be able to state that utility has decreased or increased from say 8 to 6 or 6 to 8 utils respectively.

The total and marginal utility schedules and likewise, the total and marginal utility curves, show identical information but they show it in different ways.

Table 4.1 and Diagram 4.1 are based on the assumption that other things do not change. Things do change and they do so often. The utility the consumer gets from coke depends on what else he drinks. Each time other goods are consumed a new utility schedule must be drawn up and the curves shift. Utility is subjective and consumers change their minds for example when tastes change or their circumstances change.

Principle of Diminishing Marginal Utility:

This principle states that, as consumption of a good is increased, the consumer,s total satisfaction or utility will increase but at a diminishing rate. The decline in marginal utility outlined above is known as the "law" of diminishing marginal utility. This "law" or principle states that as more units of a good is consumed, additional units will provide less additional satisfaction than previous units. For this "law" to hold true consumption of all other goods must be held constant.

This principle is outlined in Table 4.1. If we take one good, say coke and estimate that a representative consumer gets 8 utils from one can per week and knows it. Consumption then goes up to 2 cans per week and total utility increases to 14 utils so that the consumer has gained an additional 6 utils. The increase in total utility due to an increase in consumption of one can of coke is the marginal utility of coke. The marginal utility of the second can is 6. If the consumer increases consumption to 3 cans per week then total utility will increase to say 18 utils. The marginal utility of the third can is lower than the second can, i.e. 4 utils. If the consumer continues to increase weekly consumption of coke, total utility will continue to rise but each successive increase will yield less and less utility. With 5 cans, total utility is at a maximum and no satisfaction can be got from the consumption of further units. Satiation is reached after five cans the fifth can giving zero marginal utility. A sixth can of coke gives no extra utility and marginal utility is negative, so that it may give the consumer displeasure.

Table 4.1 Diminishing Marginal Utility

Cans of Coke (number)	Total Utility (utils)	Change in Utility (marginal utility)
1	8	8
2	14	6
3	18	4
4	20	2
5	20	0
6	18	-2

Diagram 4.1 is drawn from the data in Table 4.1

Diminishing marginal utility is shown both by the diminishing rate of increase of the slope of the total utility curve drawn in Panel (A) and by the downward or negative slope of the marginal utility curve in Panel (B) Diagram 4.1. Satiation is reached after five cans of coke, the fifth drink yielding zero marginal utility. Total utility in Panel A starts at the origin since zero consumption yields zero utility. Satiation occurs where the marginal utility curve reaches zero becoming negative if further cans of coke are consumed, and at the highest point on the total utility curve.

Criticisms of the Law of Diminishing Marginal Utility:

A disadvantage of using this law is that it cannot be observed or measured. Much expenditure tends to become habitual because people do not carefully weigh the marginal utilities of all the things they buy particularly where small items are concerned. Another disadvantage is that it is not easy to show the exact effects of an income constraint on consumer spending.

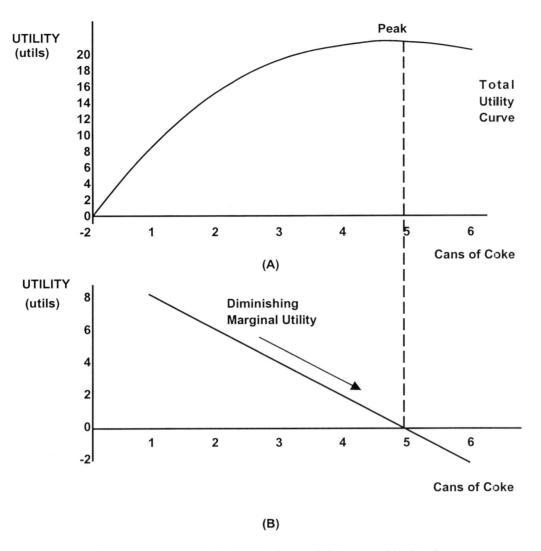

DIAGRAM 4.1 (A) Total Utility Curve (B) Marginal Utility Curve

Paradox of Value:

Adam Smith in the 1870's posed a paradox when he observed in the Wealth of Nations "Nothing is more useful than water: but it will purchase scarce anything: scarce anything can be had in exchange for it. A diamond, on the contrary, has scarce any value in use; but a very great quantity of other goods may frequently be had in exchange for it." A solution to this paradox was provided when W.S. Jevons made a distinction between total and marginal utility in 1871.

The total utility we get from water is very substantial. However we use so much water that the marginal utility diminishes to a tiny value. Diamonds, on the other hand, have a small total utility relative to water but because we purchase so few diamonds, they have a high marginal utility.

Relation between Price and Marginal Utility:

If we know that a consumer purchases 25 kg of potatoes per week at a price of 20p per kg but 20kg at 25p per kg, we know nothing of the total utility of potatoes to the consumer. We do not know how much the consumer is willing to pay rather than go without 10kg or 5kg or any potatoes at all. We know that when the consumer buys 20kg, the marginal utility of potatoes in his or her judgement is worth something that does not differ much from the price. Price is therefore an approximate measure of marginal utility to the consumer.

Equi-Marginal Utility:

Up to now we have concentrated on how a consumer decides how much to purchase of a particular good. We can use marginal utility analysis to show how a rational consumer decides what combination of goods to purchase. In Table 4.1 our consumer is a utility maximiser and will consume 4 cans of coke where total utility is greatest and there are no other constraints. There are however two other constraints in that the consumer's income is limited and expenditure must be spread over many different goods. The rule for rational consumer behaviour is known as the law of equi-marginal returns. It states that the consumer will get the highest utility from a given level of income when the utility from the last £1 spent on each good is the same. Algebraically this is when:

$$\frac{MUx}{Px} = \frac{MUy}{Py} = \frac{MUz}{Pz} \ldots \frac{MUn}{Pn}$$

Where X, Y and Z....... N are the different goods consumed. Table 4.2 gives marginal utility figures for a consumer wishing to spread an income of £22 among three commodities X, Y and Z.
To maximise utility income must be spread so that

$$\frac{MUx}{Px} = \frac{MUy}{Py} = \frac{MUz}{Pz}$$

The consumer purchases 2 litres of X, 4 litres of Y and 6 litres of Z. So that:

$$\frac{24}{4} = \frac{12}{2} = \frac{6}{1}$$

There is no other way of spending the full £22 that will give greater total utility.

Indifference Curve Theory:

Even though the multi - good version of marginal utility theory is useful it still does not allow us to measure utility in any absolute sense. Utility cannot be quantified. Indifference analysis does not seek to measure the amount of utility a person gains. Rather it ranks various combinations of goods in order of preference. It is assumed that the individuals are able to rank their preferences saying they prefer this bundle of goods to that bundle. The objective is to analyse without having to measure utility, how a rational consumer chooses between two goods. It can be used to show the effect on this choice of a change in consumers' income and a change in the price of one or both goods. It also enables us to examine the response of consumers to changes in price in greater depth, by analysing it in terms of the substitution and income effects of the price change.

Table 4.2 Equi-marginal Utility

Marginal Utility Derived From Each Litre

Litres Consumed	X £4/Litre	Y £2/Litre	Z £1/Litre
1	36	30	32
2	24	22	28
3	20	16	20
4	18	12	14
5	16	10	8
6	10	4	6
7	6	2	4

Indifference Curves:

The basic tools of indifference curve analysis are the indifference map and the consumers budget line. The indifference map consists of a large number of indifference curves. The main features of an indifference map can be summarised as follows:

-   **Indifference curves are convex to the origin:** They are convex because as the consumer gives up more of say good X he/she wants relatively more and more of Y to compensate him/her. This is due to the law of diminishing marginal utility or diminishing marginal rate of substitution.

-   **Indifference curves cannot intersect:** They cannot intersect because if they did it would mean that the combination of goods represented by the point of intersection would give equal satisfaction on two indifference curves, one with more goods than the other, e.g. 6 peaches plus 4 plums and 5 peaches plus 4 plums. This contradicts the principle that an indifference curve has the same level of utility along its length.

-   **Indifference curves slope downward from left to right:** Still assuming the consumer is rational he will want more of good Y when he gives up some of X. This means that the slope of the indifference curve is inverse or negative. (Diagram 4.2).

-   **An infinite number of curves:** It is possible to construct any number of indifference curves on the indifference map given the consumer's scale of preferences.

-   **Any movement of the indifference curve to the right is a movement to greater utility.** If we construct another indifference curve to the right of the original one, Diagram 4.3

this must show a situation where the consumer gets greater total utility because at each point on the curve the consumer is receiving more of both X and Y. In Diagram 4.3 point A_1 must yield more utility than point A and even more utility is yielded at A_2. This is an indifference map.

At every point on the indifference curve in Diagram 4.2 the consumer believes that he is receiving the same amount of utility.

Table 4.3
Indifference Schedule

Combination	Units of X	Units of Y
A	0	25
B	2	16
C	4	10
D	6	5
E	8	2
F	10	0

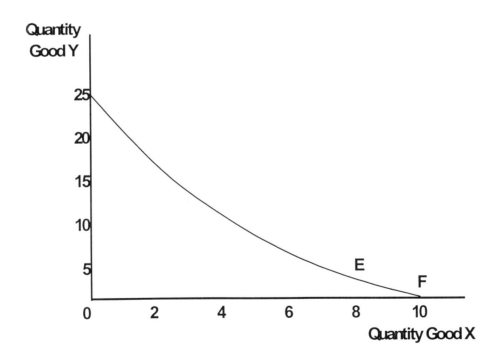

DIAGRAM 4.2 An Indifference Curve

41

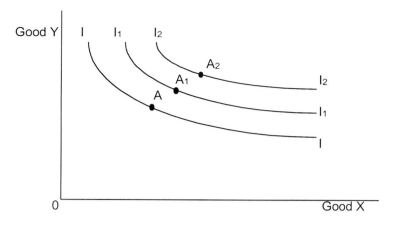

DIAGRAM 4.3 An Indifference Map

Budget Lines:

The limits to a household's consumption choices are described by its budget line. The budget line assumes that all income is spent. It is what is available to it not its preferences. Even though a consumer seeks to attain the highest indifference curve possible there are certain combinations of X and Y he cannot afford. The combinations he can afford are illustrated by an area bounded by his budget line in Diagram 4.4.

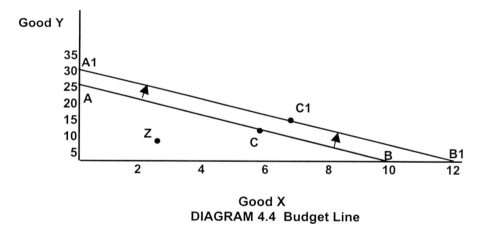

Good X
DIAGRAM 4.4 Budget Line

Suppose good X costs £5 and Y £2 and that the consumers' income is £50. In Diagram 4.4 the budget line goes from 25 units of Y point A, to 10 units of X point B, so that X exchanges for Y at a rate of 2.5 to 1.0, i.e. the price of X relative to the price of Y. If the consumer spends his entire income on good Y he will be at point A in Diagram 4.4 while if he spends it all on X he will be at point B. When these two points are joined we get the budget line. It is a straight line because the relative prices of X and Y are constant at £5 and £2 respectively. The consumer can attain any point on the line such as C or any point within the line, e.g. Z. Points such as Z within the line identify combinations of X and Y that the consumer can afford but which do not exhaust his income. He therefore spends less than his budget. Combinations of X and Y to the right of the budget line cannot be attained due to the income constraint of £50. If however the consumer's income increases by £10 the entire line moves to the right as shown in Diagram 4.4, i.e. AB to A_1B_1. Now more of both X and Y can be consumed

The Individual Consumers Equilibrium:

We combine the indifference curves of Diagram 4.3 with the budget line from Diagram 4.4 to show on Diagram 4.5 how individual consumer equilibrium is achieved. The consumer selects the highest indifference curve consistent with his budget constraint i.e. the one which is tangent to the budget line at point C. Indifference curve I_3 is unique as it is the only curve that touches the budget line AB at a tangent. Any indifference curve to the left of C, such as I_2 will not be chosen as the budget is not fully used and gives less satisfaction. This would be the case with point B. Indifference curves to the right of C such as I_4, cannot be obtained as they are outside the budget constraint. This would be the case with point D. The consumer therefore obtains maximum satisfaction by buying OD units of Y and OE units of X, given his income.

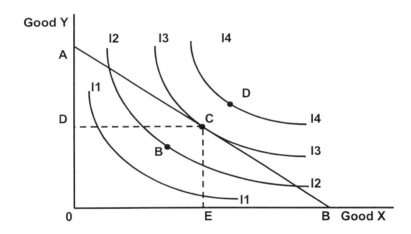

DIAGRAM 4.5 Consumer Equilibrium

A Change in Income:

As we saw in Diagram 4.4 changes in income lead to parallel shifts of the budget line. There: will be an equilibrium position for every level of income at which an indifference curve is tangent to the relevant budget line.

From Diagram 4.6 as income increases the budget line moves out from AB to CD to EF. The combination of good X and Y the consumer selects can be found by reading off the quantities of the two goods corresponding to points of tangency between the budget lines and indifference curves. By drawing a line through all the points of equilibrium we get the income consumption line. This line shows how consumption changes as income changes with relevant prices held constant. The slope of the income - consumption line depends on whether a good is normal i.e. a good whose consumption increases as income increases or inferior, i.e. a good whose consumption decreases as income increases.

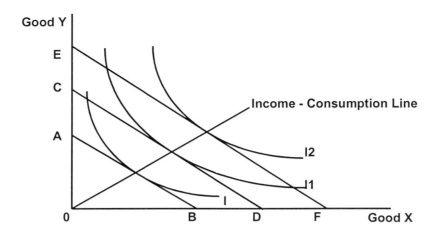

DIAGRAM 4.6 Income - Consumption Line

Price Effects:

If either the price of X or Y changes the budget line will pivot. If the price of X falls while that of Y remains constant, the budget line will swing outward. In Diagram 4.7 the initial budget line AB corresponds to the data in Table 4.3 where the budget was £50, the price of X was £5 and Y £2. Assume the price of X goes down to £2.50 while Y remains at £2. The new budget line AB_1 will cut the X axis at 20 or twice the quantity given by AB, but will still cut the Y axis at the same point. The curve has pivoted on point A. A series of budget lines can be drawn pivoting round point A. The price of X for each one is different but income and the price of Y is held constant. At each price there will be an optimum consumption point. The line that connects these points is called the price consumption line. The old optimum consumption point was at C and when the price of good X falls, a new optimum consumption point is established at C_1.

Derivation of the Demand Curve:

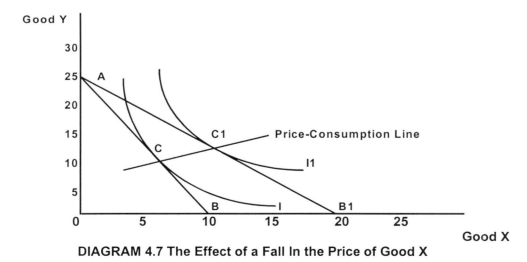

DIAGRAM 4.7 The Effect of a Fall In the Price of Good X

44

We can use indifference curves to show how an individual's demand curve is derived. The top part of Diagram 4.8 shows the effects of a price change similar to that in Diagram 4.7. In this case we can see that the price consumption line shows how demand for X increases as its price falls while the price of Y is unchanged. The lower portion of Diagram 4.8 shows the price of X against quantity demanded. If we correlate the various prices with quantities of X demanded along the price consumption line we derive a downward sloping demand curve.

In Diagram 4.8 price has fallen from OI to OJ to OK so demand has increased from OF to OG to OH. Since we can derive an individual demand curve we can also derive a market demand curve by aggregating all the individual demand curves.

The Income and Substitution Effect of a Price Change for one Commodity:

Income Effect: A change in the price of a good changes the consumer's real income and his demand for goods and services. It moves the consumer to a higher or lower indifference curve. The magnitude of the effect depends on the amount of total expenditure on the product and the size of the price change.

Substitution Effect: This is the effect on consumption of a price change when the consumer's real income stays at its original level. A fall in the price of a particular good will cause the consumer to buy more of it as it will now be cheaper than other goods. A rise in price will mean a reduction in demand, as the consumer switches to substitutes. Marginal rate of substitution is the rate at which a consumer will give up good X in order to get more of good Y and at the same time remain indifferent. The price change moves the consumer along a given indifference curve to a point with a new marginal rate of substitution.

We use the figures from Table 4.3 and assume again that the budget or income is £50. Two goods, X and Y are purchased and prices of £5 for X and £2 for Y are used. Suppose the consumer initially buys 6X and 10Y now 6X for £30 and 10Y for £20 making up the total income of £50. The price of good X falls to £2.50. We can now separate the two effects.

Income Effect: Our consumer can now buy the same amount of X and Y for £35 i.e. 6X now costing £15 and 10Y still costing £20. This means that he has £15 left over and his real income has gone up. As a result he can buy more of X and Y since X and Y are normal goods he will buy more of each, so that the income effect will be positive for both goods.

The Substitution Effect: If the consumer's income were reduced to just £35 he will have the same real income as previously in that he can buy 6X and 10Y as before and there is no income effect. Our consumer will not buy the same combination of X and Y since X is now relatively cheaper but will substitute X for Y. He might go for 10X and 5Y.

In Diagram 4.9 the price of a normal good X has risen and the budget line rotated from AB to AB_1. The consumption point has moved from C to D. This move can be broken down into a pure substitution effect from C to E due to relative price changes with the old real income plus a pure income effect for E to D as a result of a fall in real income at constant relative prices. The substitution effect reduces the amount of good X demanded from Q to Q_1 and the income effect reduces demand for good X from Q_1 to Q_2. In the case of a normal good both the income and substitution effects of an increase in price are negative. The substitution effect will reduce the quantity of good X demanded when its price goes up. The opposite happens as a result of the income effect for a good that is inferior.

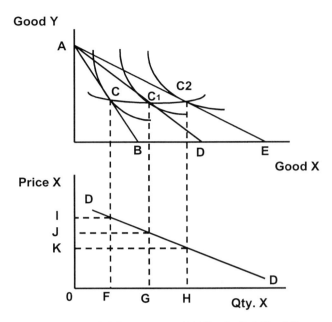

DIAGRAM 4.8 Derivation Of The Individiual Demand Curve

In Diagram 4.10 when price rises the budget line rotates from AB to AB_1. The substitution effect from C to E reduces the quantity of good X demanded from Q_2 to Q_1 but this is less than the increase in demand due to the income effect i.e. E to D a rise in demand from Q_1 to Q. In the case of a Giffen good the new equilibrium position E would lie to the right of C with more of good X consumed.

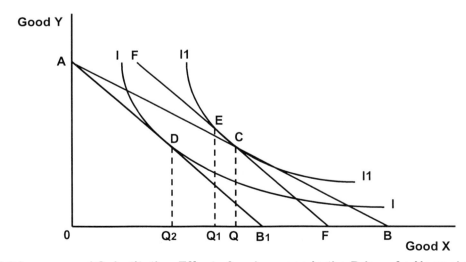

DIAGRAM 4.9 Income and Substitution Effect of an Increase in the Price of a Normal Good X

46

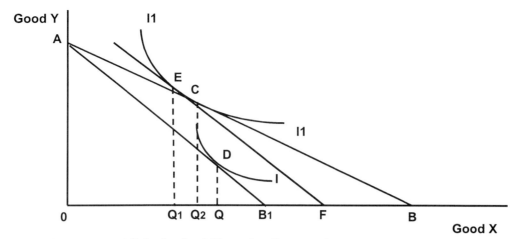

DIAGRAM 4.10 Income and Substitution Effect of an Increase in the Price of an Inferior Good X

Consumer Surplus:

Consumer surplus represents the difference between the maximum amount a consumer is willing to pay for each unit of a good and the price actually paid for the good. In Diagram 4.11 £200 is the market price of a television set and 200,000 are demanded and sold. However if the price is £275, 50,000 are sold and the purchasers must expect to get at least £275 of utility from the television. 100,000 will be bought when the price is £250. All purchasers pay the same price i.e. £200. Consumers willing to pay more than £200 receive extra utility for which they do not have to pay. Consumer 200,000th is the only one to equate utility with price. The area above the price line and below the demand curve i.e. hatched area is surplus utility derived by consumers but not paid for i.e. consumers' surplus.

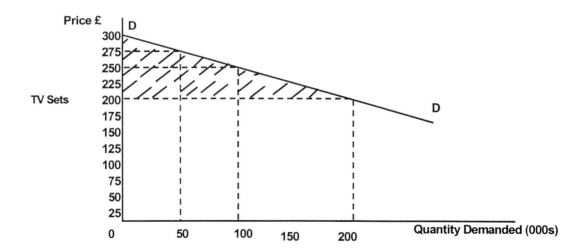

DIAGRAM 4.11 Consumer's Surplus

The notion of consumer surplus is useful for the following reasons:

47

First, changes in the surplus can be used to estimate the effect of price changes on consumers' utility. Secondly, if suppliers can control their prices, they can in principle extract all or part of the consumer surplus by practising price discrimination i.e. varying the price to different consumers.

Questions

1. Distinguish between total and marginal utility and use this distinction to explain the paradox of value.

2. Show that a change in the selling price of a good causes income and substitution effects.

3. " A problem with marginal utility analysis is that utility can not be measured. An alternative approach is to use indifference analysis." Discuss.

4. What are the main features of indifference curves?

5. Describe with the aid of a diagram the income and substitution effects of a change in the selling price of a good.

6. Suppose a child has £4 to spend on two goods, potato crisps and sweets. The marginal utilities he/she obtains from successive purchases are as follows:

Packets of either crisps or sweets purchased	Marginal utility of crisps in "utils"	Marginal utility of sweets in "utils"
1	70	80
2	46	64
3	34	42
4	24	34
5	16	28
6	12	24
7	8	20
8	4	16
9	2	14
10	0	8
11	0	6
12	0	4

If he/she spends the £4 and tries to maximise total utility:

a) How many packets of each good will he/she buy, if crisps cost 20p per packet and sweets 40p per packet?

b) If the price of sweets is reduced to 20p per packet how many of each will he/she buy?

CHAPTER 5

PRODUCTION, COSTS AND OBJECTIVES OF THE FIRM

Introduction:

The theory of production is an analysis of how inputs are transformed into output. A firm is an organisation that employs factors of production and organises them to produce goods and services. It may consist of a unit or a parent company with a number of subsidiary firms. An industry is defined according to the physical and technical characteristic of the output produced and includes all firms producing those goods. During the course of production the firm will incur certain costs and so we examine how these costs behave as output changes. To understand and predict the behaviour of the firm the objectives of the firm are described. The objectives are grouped under two headings: maximising and non-maximising.

Production Function:

The production function is the relationship between the quantity of inputs used to manufacture a good and the quantity of output of that good. There is a mathematical relationship between the output of a good and the inputs used to produce it. It can be written as Total Physical Product (TPP) = f (F1, F2, - - - --- Fn) where F1, F2 - - Fn are the quantity of each of the factors used. It summarises the technical opportunities open to the firm.

It is usually assumed that firms supply just one type of labour, one type of capital and one type of land. If just two factors are taken say capital and labour then the production function can be reduced to TPP = f(K,L) where K and L are amounts of capital and labour employed.

Production Time Frame:

The **short-run** is a period of time during which the quantity of at least one input, or factor of production is fixed and the others can vary. It is usual to assume labour to be variable while capital and land are assumed fixed. The length of the short-run period cannot be specified and it will vary enormously from firm to firm. Labour intensive firms can expand output quickly especially if it requires just a small amount of capital. A firm can hire additional workers and work their machines up to their maximum capacity. This however can only be done up to the point where output can no longer be expanded.

The **long-run** is a period of time in which the quantities of all inputs or factors of production can be varied but not so long that basic technology can change. The capacity or scale of operations can be increased to produce any output in the most efficient way.

The **very long run** is a period during which new technologies can be developed and put in place e.g. if the firm was to change from no computers to their widespread use in the production of output.

Production Measures:

When the firm varies one input while holding all others constant the changes in output can be measured in a number of ways depending on the purpose of the analysis.

Total Physical Product (TPP): This refers to the total quantity of output produced with a given amount of a particular input or factor such as labour with all other inputs held constant. TTP will increase as extra units of the variable factor are employed. It is physical output that is examined, not money value of output.

Table 5.1 shows the relationship between the firm's total product and the input necessary to produce it.

If 4 people are employed the firm's total physical product is 100,000 litres of milk. When an additional worker is added and other factors are held constant TPP goes up to 120,000 litres as shown in Table 5.1

Table 5.1 Milk Production Per Year For A Particular Producer

Number of Workers	Total Physical Product (000s Litres)	Average Physical Product (000s Litres)	Marginal Physical Product 000s Litres)
0	0	0	-
1	14	14	14
2	46	23	32
3	76	25.3	30
4	100	25.0	24
5	120	24	20
6	120	20	0
7	119	17	-1

Average Physical Product (APP): This is the firm's total product divided by the amount of the variable input, in this case labour used to produce it. When 4 people are employed 100,000 litres of milk are produced and the APP is 25,000 litres, as shown in Table 5.1.

Marginal Physical Product (MPP): MPP of any input is the increase in total product from an increase of one unit of that input. It is therefore the extra output produced with an extra unit of labour. From Table 5.1 when the number of workers is increased from 3 to 4 total product increases from 76,000 to 100,000 and MPP is 24,000. In other words the MPP of the fourth worker is 24,000 litres.

Relationship between APP and MMP:

I.   When MPP > APP, the average rises.
II.   When MPP <APP, the average falls.
III.   When the MPP= APP, the average is constant, neither rising nor falling.

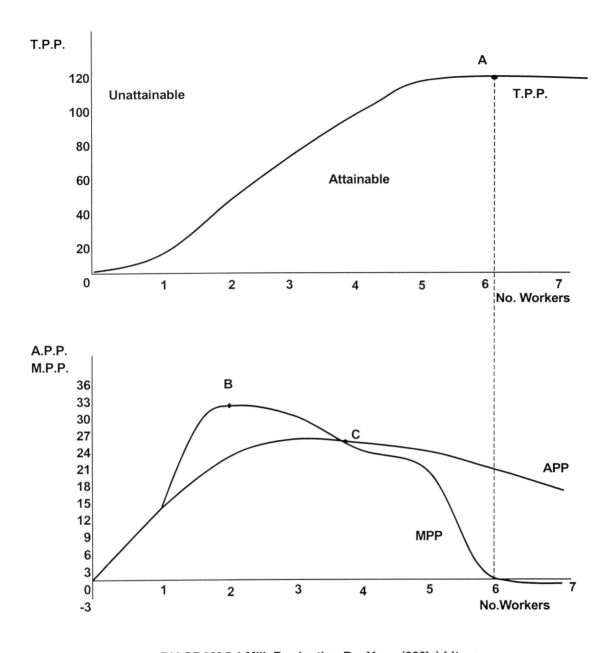

DIAGRAM 5.1 Milk Production Per Year (000's) Litres

Diagram 5.1 shows TPP on the top panel and APP and MPP on the bottom based on the data in Table 5.1.

TPP has a number of things in common with the production possibility curve (Diagram 1.1) since at points above the TPP curve output is unattainable while at points under the curve it is. Only points on the TPP curve are technologically efficient. The latter, however, are attainable but are technologically inefficient as a result MPP can be falling while average productivity is still rising. However at point A, TPP is at a maximum and an additional worker will add nothing to output. MPP = zero

APP rises at first and continues to do so as long as the addition to output from the last worker (MPP) is greater than APP, MPP pulls APP up and it continues to rise as long as MPP is above it. In Diagram 5.1, after point C MPP goes below APP and additional workers add less to output than the average. This brings down the average and APP falls. Even though MPP is falling APP can still rise as outlined below.

MPP peaks at point B, Diagram 5.1, and begins to diminish with the third worker who adds 30,000 litres to output and not 32,000 as the second worker did. APP rises until the fourth person is added. The fourth person produces less than the third person but is still more productive than the average of the first two workers. As a result MPP can be falling while average productivity is still rising.

Diminishing Returns:

The law of diminishing marginal returns states that if increasing quantities of a variable factor are added to given quantities of fixed factors, the MPP of the variable factor will decrease. It is sometimes called the law of variable proportions.

In our example of milk production we see that marginal output no longer rises when the third and subsequent workers are added. TPP continues to rise but the third worker adds less to output than the existing two workers. Now we have passed the point of maximum technical efficiency and there are fewer machines and other inputs per worker. As outlined above the contribution of the marginal worker is so small that APP per worker also falls with the addition of the fourth person. If workers are continuously added eventually the next worker will add nothing and the result could be a situation of negative returns.

The Components of Cost:

Costs can be divided into fixed and variable. Variable costs are those that vary with output while fixed costs do not so vary in the short run. It is also necessary to examine the concepts of total, average and marginal cost.

- **Fixed or Overhead Costs**

Total fixed costs (TFC) are costs that do not vary with the quantity of output produced. Certain inputs are required before production can start and they have nothing to do with the quantity produced. Fixed costs such as rent, interest on loans, depreciation of plant and equipment and rates are incurred even when there is no output. Our milk producer has a milking parlour and even if he now has no milk production he still has the maintenance cost of the building.

- **Average Fixed Costs (AFC)**

AFC is total fixed cost (TFC) divided by the number of units or output produced (Q) TF $\div$ Q.

- **Variable Costs**

A variable cost is a cost that varies with the output level. Total variable cost (TVC) includes all costs directly related to the level of output. TVC includes the cost of raw materials, wages and the cost of energy. When the level of output increases variable costs increase and when the level of output is reduced variable costs fall. Average variable cost (AVC) is equal to TVC÷Q. As output increases total variable cost (TVC) and Q increases therefore one cannot say whether AVC will rise or fall with output. However due to the law of diminishing returns we know that costs rise at a faster rate than output due to the fact that input use grows faster than output.

- **Total Cost (TC)**

TC is equal to total expenditure on inputs used for production and fixed costs always rises with output. TC = TFC + TVC is illustrated in Diagram 5.2 and the data used is contained in Table 5.2. Irrespective of the level of output FC is £4,000.

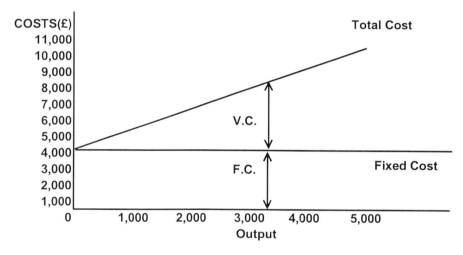

DIAGRAM 5.2 Total Costs

- **Average Total Cost (ATC)**

ATC = TC ÷ Q. This is the actual short-run cost of producing one more unit of output. It is U – shaped as shown in Diagram 5.3, indicating that ATC per unit of output first falls and then increases as output rises. ATC = AFC+ AVC declines as output increases because FC is spread over a larger output and ATC slopes downward. As output increases due to diminishing returns AVC rises and AVC slopes upward. The bottom of the U is the quantity at which ATC is lowest.

- **Marginal Cost (MC)**

MC is the addition to TC of producing one more unit of output. It is the change in total costs divided by the change in output i.e. MC = ΔTC ÷ΔQ. Δ is the Greek letter delta, and it represents the change in a variable. It is obtained by subtracting successive total costs (Table 5.2). MC is high when output is low at 400 (Table 5.2) as the firm is probably using simple production methods. As output increases more advanced technology can be used and MC falls. However as output rises still further the problems associated with managing a large firm appears. More staff, not directly involved in production is required to keep track of the business. Output as a result is now more expensive and MC increases and Diagram 5.3 shows this, as does Table5.2.

Table 5.2 Costs of the Firm

Workers	Output	Total Costs (£)			Average Costs (£)			
		FC	VC	TC	AFC	AVC	ATC	MC(£)
1	400	4,000	1,000	5,000	10.0	2.5	12.5	
								1.7
2	1,000	4,000	2,000	6,000	4.0	2.0	6.0	
								1.2
3	1,800	4,000	3,000	7,000	2.2	1.7	3.9	
								1.4
4	2,500	4,000	4,000	8,000	1.6	1.6	3.2	
								2.0
5	3,000	4,000	5,000	9,000	1.3	1.7	3.0	
								3.3
6	3,300	4,000	6,000	10,000	1.2	1.8	3.0	
								7.7
7	3,430	4,000	7,000	11,000	1.2	2.0	3.2	

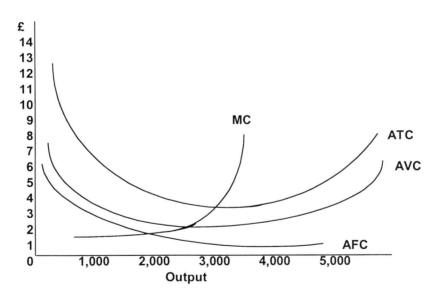

DIAGRAM 5.3 Average and Marginal Cost

In Diagram 5.3 the MC curve falls, flattens and then rises. It cuts both AVC and ATC when they are at a minimum due to the fact that MC bears a definite relationship to both AVC and ATC. In the case of ATC, MC lies below it when it is falling and above it when it is rising.

54

MC = ATC where ATC is at a minimum. In Table 5.2 this occurs between 3,000 and 3,300 units of output. At lower levels of output the MC values are less than ATC values, therefore ATC falls. At higher levels of output MC values in Table 5.2 are greater than ATC values so that ATC increases. The same analysis holds for the relationship between MC and AVC.

Relationship between ATC and MC:

- In the output range when MC is less than ATC then ATC is falling as output rises.
- In the output range when MC= ATC then ATC is at a minimum and will remain unchanged as output rises.
- In the output range when MC is greater than ATC then ATC is rising, as output rises.

A firm therefore produces at its lowest average cost when MC = ATC.

Costs in the Long-run:

In the long run all inputs are variable and as a result the law of diminishing returns does not apply and the firm can expand the scale of its operations.

- **Long Run Average Cost Curve (LRAC)**

As all costs are variable in the long run, the ATC in the short run differs from the ATC in the long run.

LRAC is derived, by visualising the ideal short-run AC curve associated with all levels of output. The shape of the LRAC curve is determined by the internal economies and diseconomies of scale and not by the law of diminishing returns that apply only in the short

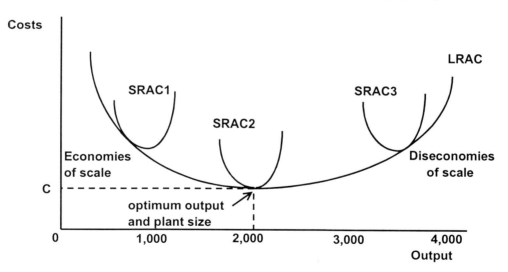

DIAGRAM 5.4 Long Run Average Cost Curve

run. In Diagram 5.4 these curves are SRAC at each level of output. It can be assumed that as the firm goes from one level of production to another SRACs do not change erratically, therefore LRAC is smoothly continuous. On it's downward course LRAC is a tangent to each SRAC before the point of minimum cost for each SRAC and this is known as the envelope curve. No point on the SRAC is ever below the LRAC, because the latter shows the lowest cost possible for each level of output. The theoretical LRAC falls as output rises, flattens and then rises. Optimum output is at 2,000 units and C cost as shown in Diagram 5.4. This output is referred to as the minimum efficient scale (MES).

Returns to Scale:

These are increases in output that results from increasing all the inputs by the same percentage. There are increasing returns to scale when LRAC decreases as output rises. There are constant returns to scale when LRAC is constant, as output rises. Decreasing returns to scale occur when LRAC increases as output rises. These three situations are illustrated in Diagram 5.5.

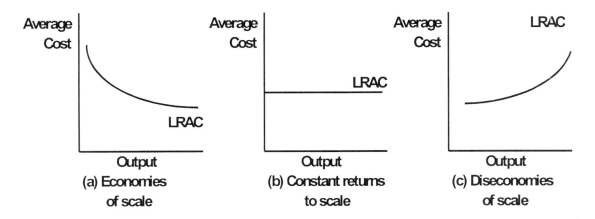

DIAGRAM 5.5 Returns to Scale and LRAC

Economies of Scale:

Economies of scale are present when an increase in output causes average costs to fall. When a firm is achieving economies of scale, it is getting increasing returns to scale from its inputs or factors of production. Thus as it increases output, it will be using smaller and smaller amounts of inputs per unit of output. Other things being equal it will be producing at lower average cost. Economies of scale can be grouped into the following categories:

– **Specialisation and Division of Labour:** There is great scope for specialisation in the long-run because there are no fixed factors of production. With specialisation, workers need less training and become very efficient at their particular jobs, special purpose machinery can be used and the result is an increase in the productivity of labour.

– **Indivisibilities:** A major underlying cause of economies of scale from specialisation is the indivisibility of factors. Indivisibilities occur when a production process is either technically impossible or not financially viable on a small scale. Examples of this are the production of cars, chemicals and steel.

– **Increased Dimensions:** Sometimes bigger is better. In the case of a container if the external dimensions are increased, the cubic capacity increases more than proportionately. A container measuring 3 metres by 3 metres by 3 metres has a cubic capacity of 27 cubic metres. If the dimensions are increased to 6 x 6 x 6 then capacity is 216 cubic metres. The new container requires a doubling of the original amount of material yet capacity has increased eightfold.

– **Financial:** Larger firms find it easier to obtain loans, because they can pledge more assets than smaller firms can. They can also negotiate lower interest rates than smaller firms.

– **By-products:** When large scale production takes place there may be sufficient waste products to make it possible for the firm to make some by-product.

– **Organisational:** As the firm gets bigger, individual plants can specialise in particular functions; managers can delegate day to day functions to administrative staff, so that they are free to concentrate on the more important tasks.

– **Multi-Stage Production:** Technical economies may be gained by linking processes together, e.g. a firm manufacturing cardboard boxes may be able to convert trees or waste paper into cardboard and then into boxes in a continuous process.

– **Commercial:** When a firm is large enough and can place a bulk order for materials the price quoted will be lower as the producer can take advantage of large scale production. If the firm has a large transport fleet it will usually be able to dispatch full loads whereas a small firm has to hire transport or dispatch part-loads. A large firm that manufactures a number of products can expect one to act as an advertisement for the others. A large firm can employ expert buyers and sellers, through division of labour.

– **Risk Bearing**: A large firm may have a number of products and is in a better position than small firms to withstand unfavourable trading conditions in one particular market. There is also the risk of running out of stock. In this case large firms need to hold proportionately less stock than smaller firms. This is due to the fact that a given change in demand represents a smaller proportion of total sales for the larger than for the smaller firm.

Diseconomies of Scale:

Increased scale can bring numerous advantages as outlined above but it can also bring disadvantages. When the firm gets beyond a certain size, cost per unit of output may increase as output increases and the reasons for this are as follows:

• **Managerial:** Diseconomies of scale arise due to the fact that management becomes more difficult as the firm becomes larger. Lines of communication get longer and there is a lack of direct involvement by management. The firm becomes bureaucratic and average costs may begin to rise as a result.

• **Industrial Relations:** Deterioration in industrial relations is another source of diseconomies. Workers may become alienated, resulting in frequent strikes and other forms of industrial unrest. Specialisation means greater interdependence among workers giving them greater bargaining power or the ability to maintain restrictive practices. A strike by a small group in a key area may halt production in the entire firm.

• **Production Process:** In a large firm, with mass production, if there are hold-ups in any part of the process they cause very serious overall disruption.

Revenue:

Revenues are receipts that a firm receives from selling its products.

Total, Average and Marginal Revenue:

Total Revenue (TR) is the total amount of revenue the firm receives and is equal to Price x Quantity or P x Q. Profit = Total revenue – Total cost.

Average Revenue (AR) is TR divided by the number of units sold, i.e. AR = TR/Q.

Marginal Revenue (MR) is the change in TR that results from selling one more unit of the firm's product. MR = ΔTR/ΔQ.

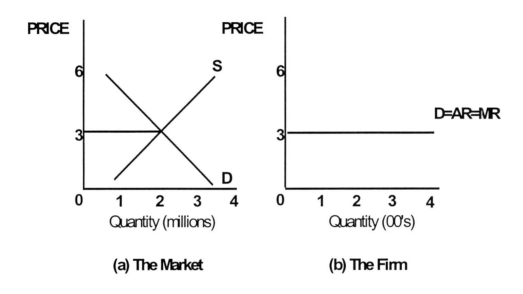

(a) The Market   **(b) The Firm**

DIAGRAM 5.6 AR,MR for a Price Taking Firm

Revenue Curves when Price is not affected by Output:

In this situation the firm must accept the market price determined by the intersection of supply and demand. It is therefore a price taker and is too small to be able to influence the market price. As a result it has a horizontal demand or average revenue curve at £3. AR is constant at £3 and must therefore lie exactly along its demand curve. The firm can sell any number of units and still have no effect on the price. If the AR curve is not changing then the MR curve must be the same as AR. If an extra unit is sold for £3 an extra £3 is earned. The TR curve will be a straight line through the origin as TR will rise at a constant rate since price is constant.

Revenue Curves when Price Varies with Output:

In this case the firm has a downward sloping demand curve and if it wants to sell more it must lower it's price. If it increases price it will have to accept a fall in sales.

Average Revenue:

The demand for the firm's product and AR lie along the same line because AR = P, therefore the curve relating price to quantity (D curve) must be the same as the curve relating AR to quantity (AR curve).

Marginal Revenue:

MR will be lower than AR and may be negative. If the firm wishes to sell more, other things being equal it will have to lower price. It must sell all units at the lower price. MR is the price at which it sells the last unit less the loss of revenue on the other units it could have sold at the higher price. From Table 5.3 if price is £14 then 2 units are sold. Suppose the firm now wishes to sell an additional unit and reduces price to £12. This results in a gain of £12 and a loss of £4 by having to reduce the price by £2 on the two units it could otherwise have sold for £14.The net gain is £12- £4 = £8. This is the MR of the third unit sold. AR, MR and TR curves are shown in Diagram 5.7 and are drawn on the basis of the data in Table 5.3

Table 5.3 Revenues for a Firm with Downward Sloping AR Curve:

Quantity (units)	Price = AR (£)	TR (£)	MR (£)
1	16	16	
			12
2	14	28	
			8
3	12	36	
			4
4	10	40	
			0
5	8	40	
			-4
6	6	36	

If demand is price elastic, a decrease in price will lead to a proportionately larger increase in quantity demanded and consequently an increase in total revenue. MR will therefore be positive. If demand is inelastic a decrease in price will mean a proportionately smaller increase in sales. The price reduction more than offsets the increase in sales and total revenue will fall. MR will be negative.

In Diagram 5.7 if sales are 4 or less the demand curve will be elastic at the relevant point because an increase in sales as a result of the price decrease leads to an increase in TR. Accordingly MR is positive. If MR is negative at sales of 5 or more, the demand curve is

59

inelastic at that point since an increase in sales leads to a fall in TR. In Diagram 5.7 (a) AR is elastic to the left of point X and inelastic to the right. The TR curve in Diagram 5.7 (b) rises at first and then falls. When MR is positive TR will rise and when MR is negative TR will fall. The peak of the TR curve will be where MR = 0 and price elasticity will be equal to -1.

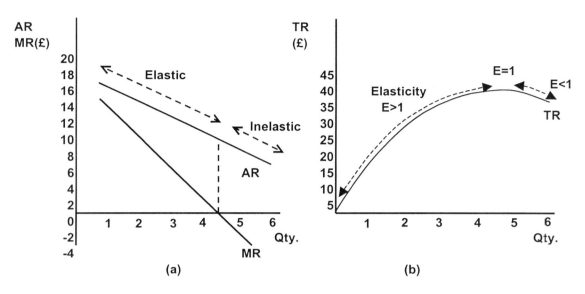

DIAGRAM 5.7(a) AR and MR, and
DIAGRAM 5.7(b) TR for a Firm With a Downward Sloping Demand Curve

Profit:

Profit is defined as a firm's total revenue (TR) less total costs (TC). **Normal profit** is the rate of return that is just enough to keep the factors of production in their current use. When AR = AC, normal profit is made. It is the opportunity cost of the entrepreneur and economists treat it as a cost of production whereas accountants do not. If AR falls below AC in the long run, the entrepreneurs will leave the industry. It is therefore an essential cost of production. When AR > AC or TR> TC, **supernormal profit** is made.

Objectives of the Firm:

The Firm:

A firm is a business or productive unit that buys or hires factors of production and organises them to produce and sell goods and services.

Profit Maximisation:

Profit maximisation is usually assumed to be the goal of the firm. We assume here that the firm operates in a market structure of imperfect competition. The traditional theory of the firm is that it seeks to maximise profits. In order to establish the profit maximising output for a firm we put costs and revenue together using total revenues and total costs. Average cost and average revenue curves can also be used. We look at both methods. If profits are to be maximised MR must equal MC. From Table 5.4 MR = MC when output is 3 units. In Diagram 5.8 MR = MC is at 3 units of output. If output rises from 1 to 2 units MC is £4, which is less than MR is, which is £12. If output rises from 3 to 4 units marginal cost is £8 which exceeds the marginal revenue of £4. At all levels of output below 3, MR is greater than MC and at all levels above 3, MR is less than MC. Profit is therefore maximised when MR = MC, as seen in Diagram 5.8 where $T\pi$ = £8.

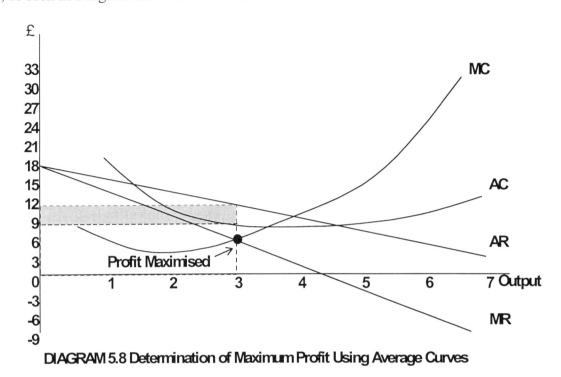

DIAGRAM 5.8 Determination of Maximum Profit Using Average Curves

Average profit $A\pi$ is AR - AC that is 12 – 9.33 = £2.67 at the profit maximising output of 3 units in Diagram 5.8. Total profit is equal to average profit by output i.e. $A\pi$ x Q. In this case it is 2.67 x 3 = £8 as seen in Table 5.4.

Total profit can be got from the total curves and is TR - TC = $T\pi$. Again from Table 5.4 total profit is greatest at output of 3 units i.e. £36 - £28 = £8

Model of Profit Maximisation:

This is a notion that the firm attempts to make as much profit as possible. It is based on two assumptions: first that the owners are in control of the day to day management of the firm and secondly the owner's objective is to maximise profit. However with the advent of the public limited company ownership and control are usually separated.

Profit is maximised where MR = MC i.e. when the revenue from selling an additional unit is equal to the cost of producing that additional unit. From Diagram 5.9 total profit (π) is maximised at output Q_1, where the vertical distance between total revenue (TR) and total cost (TC) is greatest.

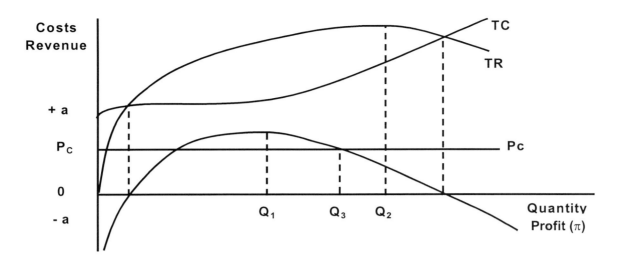

DIAGRAM 5.9 Variation of Output with Firm

Long-Run Profit Maximisation:

On the basis that AR and MR curves are the same in the long-run as in the short-run, profits will be maximised at output where MR = LRMC.

Table 5.4 Short-run Profit Maximisation: Using Average and Marginal Curves:

Output Units	P=AR £	TR £	MR	TC	AC	MC	Total Profit Tπ	Average Profit Aπ
0	18	0		12			-12	
			16			8		
1	16	16		20	20		-4	-4
			12			4		
2	14	28		24	12		4	2
			8			4		
3	12	36		28	9.33		8	2.67
			4			8		
4	10	40		36	9		4	1
			0			12		
5	8	40		48	9.60		-8	-1.60
			-4			18		
6	6	36		66	11		-30	-5
			-8			32		
7	4	28		98	14		-70	-10

The model of profit maximisation has been criticised on a number of grounds but the best known one is that it is unrealistic to assume that the firm will maximise profit when ownership is with the shareholders while control is in the hands of paid managers. Alternative models to profit maximisation have been proposed.

Alternatives to profit maximisation can be grouped under two headings: maximising and non-maximising goals. There are managerial and behavioural theories. Managerial theories rest on the primacy of managers within the firm where they behave so as to maximise managerial benefits. The behavioural theories view the firm as engaging in non- maximising behaviour.

Managerial Theories of the Firm:

Managerial theories of the firm are based on the primacy of managers in the firm. These theories stress some managerial objective but it is usually subject to a constraint. In any case the objective guiding the firm, will be set by the managers.

Sales Revenue Maximisation: Baumol (1959) proposed a model of the firm based on the principle that the primary objective of the managers of a firm is to maximise sales revenue not to maximise sales volume. His argument is that managers' salaries and other perquisites (perks) such as expense account, company car and luxurious office are more closely correlated with sales revenue than profits. The need to make profits is still recognised but they act as a constraint on managers rather than as an objective.

Williamson (1963) has a managerial theory similar to that of Baumol in that he stresses growth in sales. The model is based on the assumption that shareholders do not exert direct control over the management of the firm and that the firm is not operating in a highly competitive environment. In his model managers are more ambitious as they also seek utility or satisfaction through greater expenditure. In his opinion additional sales revenue is the easiest way of providing extra funds. Funds could also be provided from higher profits but part of this would have to be distributed to shareholders. It is a managerial utility model, which consists of three broad groups of expenditure made possible by greater sales revenue:
- Managerial salaries.
- Discretionary investment on items such as expensive motor cars and lavish offices.
- Expenditure on staff levels of the firm based on managerial discretion.

If management's sole aim is to maximise sales revenue then in Diagram 5.9 output would be Q2 where MR = zero as the last unit is neither lowering nor raising total revenue.
Constrained sales revenue maximisation or the difference it makes is shown in Diagram 5.9. If Pc is the minimum profit required to keep shareholders happy, then Q3 is the output which will maximise revenue under this constraint. Output between Q3 and Q2 would increase TR but would reduce profit below the minimum required Pc. The revenue-maximiser will charge a lower price than the profit maximiser to sell the larger output. Neither Baumol nor Williamson provide much analysis of where the profit constraint would be set and why it exists.

The 1964 Marris Model of Growth Maximisation: In this model managerial utility is a function solely of the growth rate subject to a job security constraint. It does however share the assumption of the Williamson Model, that managers aim to maximise their utility. Again there is a separation of ownership and management.

The Marris managers are motivated not so much by the achievement of absolute size, such as a given value of sales revenue, but rather by changes in size. Managers relate their salaries and status to the size of the firm.

Also essential to his analysis is the ratio of retained to distributed profit i.e. the so called "retention ratio". If most of the profit is distributed, shareholders will be happy and the share price will be high enough to prevent a take-over. If they distribute less of the profit they can reinvest the retained profit in the firm, thereby stimulating growth. However, shareholders will be less content and the share price lower, increasing the risk of a take-over. Management is faced with a 'trade off' between the dividend policy and retained profits and must seek the optimal balance between the two.

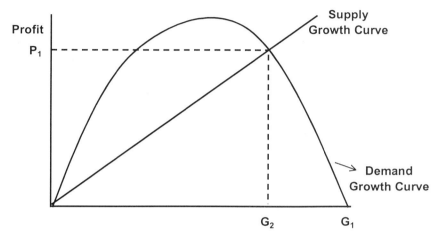

DIAGRAM 5.10 Marris's Growth Model of the Firm

In Diagram 5.10 the firm adopts the growth rate G_1 and profitability P_1 at point E. The supply growth curve can pivot clockwise from the vertical to the horizontal axis according to managerial discretion. Managers would like the supply growth curve to lie as close as possible to the horizontal axis. They do not behave in this way because of the security constraint i.e. the balance between dividend policy and retained earnings to ensure that the firm is not taken over.. A high proportion of profits going to retained earnings mean only a small amount is left for dividends. Low dividends mean a fall in the value of the shares that leaves the firm open to a take-over. Managers do not want this to happen, as it is a threat to their jobs.

Behavioural Theories of the Firm:

Behavioural theories seem to oppose the idea of maximising any objective and some of these are outlined below.

H.A. Simon (1959) describes the objective of firms as satisficing i.e. aiming to achieve a satisfactory level of attainment on a number of goals some of which are conflicting. The firm's management attempts to set itself minimal standards of achievement intended only to ensure the firm's survival and a level of profit acceptable to shareholders.

The satisfactory aspiration level of profits will be set according to past and future uncertainties. If the aspiration level is achieved without difficulty, it will be raised while if it proves difficult it will be lowered. In either case, the managers will instigate search behaviour using "rules of thumb" to discover why actual performance is not what was aspired to. The cost of the search will prevent the exploration of all alternatives, and so a satisfactory alternative will be chosen.

Cyert and March Model:

Cyert and March built on Simon's model and are more specific than he was in identifying various groups or coalitions within an organisation. They took a broad view of the groups that may influence the firm, including shareholders, managers, workers, customers, trade unions, suppliers and creditors. In order for decisions to be made, a 'coalition' of several of these groups must be formed to back one policy.

Workers may form one coalition wanting good wages and job security; shareholders want high profits; managers want status and power. Conflict will arise but this is resolved by continuous bargaining. When a group, say, the workers fail to have their goals satisfied, they are compensated by 'side-payments', for example, by higher wages, bigger office or promotion among other things.

Cyert and March state that their aim is to set goals, which resolve the conflict between opposing groups. This requires compromise and to encourage this a number of techniques can be used:

- By restricting bargaining time, groups must try harder to reach a compromise.
- Set some budgets at the start thus limiting the area of conflict.
- Payment in lieu of other demands can be used to reduce conflict.
- Standard operating procedures can be used to remove certain policies from the bargaining process, in that they are followed automatically, and so can not be argued over.

Evaluation of the Alternatives Theories:

- **Profit Maximising Model:** This model has been criticised because it does not take into account the separation of ownership and control in modern firms. It also assumes that the firm has complete and accurate information.
- **Managerial Theories:** These theories hold that managers control firms so as to seek to achieve their own objectives, subject to a minimum profit requirement or constraint. Their objectives are readily identifiable e.g. sales revenue maximisation, growth, status, share values and return on capital. They include a profit constraint but provide little advice on the level at which it is set. The profit constraint could be very much the same as that of a profit maximiser. In recent times institutional investors such as insurance companies are taking a more active role in firms. Their objective is to maximise profit or return for their investors. There is also the danger that managers who do not maximise profits will lose their jobs.

- **Behavioural Theories:** The emphasis here is on the framework of uncertainty and conflicting goals within which the firm operates. Behavioural theories have not developed a satisfactory alternative to profit maximisation. They have however given insights into how the system works.

Profit maximisation theories still form the basis of economic analysis. This may be an indication that ownership is not as divorced from the control as was previously thought. It would also suggest that businessmen have greater knowledge of their marginal costs than can be observed and are therefore in a better position to make the price and output decisions necessary for profit maximisation theories.

Questions

1. Explain the difference between increasing marginal costs associated with the law of diminishing returns and increasing LRAC associated with diseconomies of scale.

2. Explain the shape and relationship of the AC and MC curves.

3. Explain the law of diminishing marginal returns and show how it affects the costs of supply as output rises.

4. Complete the following table and establish the point at which:

   (a) Diminishing average returns occur; and

   (b) Diminishing marginal returns occur.

No. of workers	Total product	Average product	Marginal product
1	5		
2	15		
3	40		
4	100		
5	150		
6	180		
7	200		
8	210		

5. Using diagrams distinguish between the following:
   (a) Fixed and variable costs;
   (b) Marginal and average costs; and
   (c) Short-run and long-run.

6. Explain, with the aid of a diagram, the Baumol and Williamson model of sales maximisation subject to the earning of a target level of profit, as an alternative to profit maximisation.

7. Complete the following table and find the profit maximising output. Graph MC MR and show the profit maximising output on it. Graph AC and show the minimum unit cost of production for the firm.

Output	FC £'s	VC £'s	TC £'s	MC £'s	AC £'s	AR £'s	TR £'s	MR £'s	Profit £'s
0	300	0	0	0	0	0	0	0	
1		580				600			
2			1,220			600			
3						600			320
4		1,300				600			
5				160		600			
6					345	600			
7		2,220				600			
8					405	600			
9				1,160		600			1,000

8. Explain Baumol's view that sales maximisation is a more realistic representation of the goal of a firm than profit maximisation.

9. Economists often assume that firms seek to maximise profit. Explain this assumption and give your opinion of it.

CHAPTER 6

PERFECT COMPETITION AND MONOPOLY

Introduction:

Goods and services are supplied in a variety of market structures. Two of these structures, i.e. perfect competition and monopoly are examined in this Chapter. Perfect competition is a market structure where the decisions and actions of a single firm or consumer have no effect on market price. There are no restrictions on competition. In reality very few markets are perfectly competitive. At the other extreme in the competitive spectrum is monopoly where there is just one firm or where a number of firms act together to fix price i.e. a cartel so that there is no competition from within the industry. In either case the buyer is facing a single source of supply. We assume the firm is in business to maximise profits.

Model of Perfect Competition:

For a market to be perfect the following conditions have to be fulfilled:

- All units of the good are homogeneous (i.e. all units are similar) and it is of no consequence from which seller a buyer makes his purchase.

- There are large numbers of buyers and sellers in the market each buying or selling such a small amount of the product that anyone is unable to unduly influence market supply or demand.

- There must be freedom of entry into the market so that it is possible for any firm to enter the market and add to the supply, which will have the effect of lowering prices other things being equal.

- There must be perfect knowledge about market conditions among sellers and buyers. No one must have any privileged information.

- There must be freedom of entry and exit to the market so that everyone involved is a willing participant.

- It is necessary that the good in question should be capable of being easily transported from one area of the market to another.

- Buyers are always able to buy from the seller offering the lowest price.

These conditions are never fully satisfied in the real world but some markets have many of the characteristic features of perfect competition. The model of perfect competition is highly theoretical. The conditions are very extreme and there is little possibility of finding an example of perfect competition. The stock exchange is close to representing this type of competition. In spite of these shortcomings economists are able to use the model of a perfect market to gauge the level of competition in real world markets.

Short-Run Output of the Firm under Perfect Competition:

A perfectly competitive firm has a horizontal demand curve. Therefore it can sell as much output as it wishes at the going market price. If it raises its price even a little, demand for its output disappears.

The going market price is established by the intersection of market supply and demand curves. We have already established that the firm's demand or AR curve is horizontal. This is illustrated in Diagram 6.1. Given a fixed price, AR will always be equal to MR, since both are equal to the price of one unit.

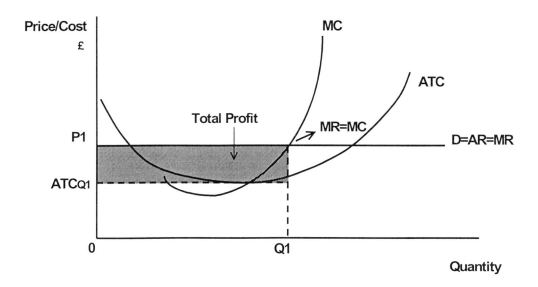

DIAGRAM 6.1 Short-Run Equilibrium Under Perfect Competition

The MC, AVC and ATC curves of the firm are U shaped. The firm will maximise profit where MR = MC i.e. at Q_1 output given that price is P_1. If the firm stops short of producing Q_1 units then revenue from selling on additional unit will exceed the cost of selling another unit. The firm can increase profits by raising its output up to Q_1. If the firm's output exceeds Q_1 the MC of all the units in excess of Q_1 will be greater than the additional revenue, which the firm can get from selling them. All units sold after Q_1 will lose money therefore total profit will be reduced and will be smaller than what can be obtained at lower outputs. In Diagram 6.1 since the ATC curve is below the AR curve at Q_1 the firm is earning supernormal profits shown by the shaded area. As long as MR exceeds MC, additions to profit are positive. Profit = $(P_1 - ATC_{Q1})Q_1$ that is numerically equivalent to the size of the shaded area.

Diagram 6.2 shows that the firm is making an economic loss. The ATC curve is at all points above AR. The firm's decision now turns on how to minimise its losses. In Diagram 6.2 between outputs Q_1 and Q_3, price (AR) exceeds AVC. Output at Q_2 corresponds to the output where MR = MC and this is where the firm is minimising its losses. It is making losses equivalent to the shaded area. In the short run the firm will stay in business, since AVC is below AR and the excess is a contribution towards FC. The firm will try to reduce costs and will hope for an increase in price.

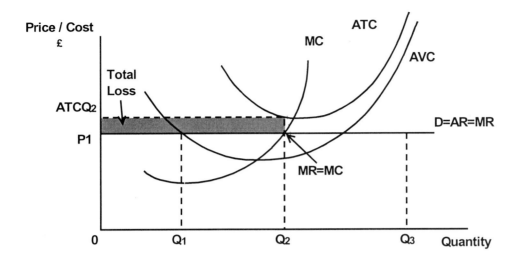

DIAGRAM 6.2 Short-Run Loss Minimising under Perfect Competition

In Diagram 6.3, price does not cover AVC at any output. Producing where MR = MC the firm will have an output of Q_1. If the firm continues to produce it will increase it's losses therefore the firm should temporarily cease business.

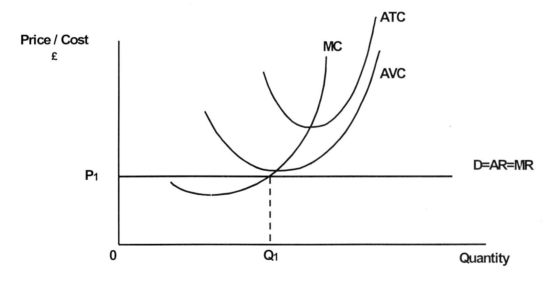

DIAGRAM 6.3 Close down Position for a Perfectly Competitive Firm

Perfectly Competitive Firms Short-run Supply Curve:

The firms supply curve represents the relationship between the price of a product and the quantity of output the firm is willing to supply at that price. In perfect competition P = MR and MR = MC therefore P = MC, so that the supply curve and MC follow the same line as shown in Diagram 6.4.

If price rises the demand curve of the firm shifts upwards and if price falls it shifts downward as shown in Diagram 6.4. If price is £3 per unit output is 3,000 units i.e. MR = MC and MC = Price = £3. If price rises to £5, MR has shifted upwards to £5 so that MC = $MR_1 = P_1 = £5$ and 6,000 units of output. Price then rises to P_2 and MR to $MR_2 = P_2 = £7$ per unit. Now MC = $MR_2 = £7$ and 9,000 produced. In each case profit is maximised where MR = MC.

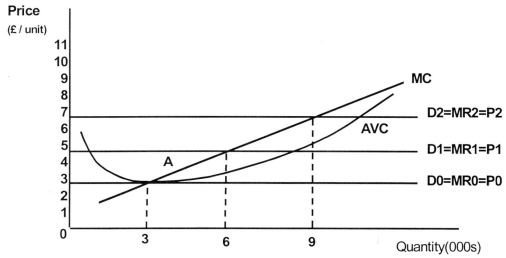

Diagram 6.4 Short-Run Supply Curve for a Perfectly Competitive Firm

The firms supply curve is dependent on costs of production and this is why it slopes upwards because MC rises as output rises due to the law of diminishing marginal returns. A higher price is needed to induce a firm to increase its output. The firm will not produce below its AVC curve. In Diagram 6.4 the supply curve is that portion of the MC curve above point A.

Long-Run Industry Supply Curve:

The long-run industry supply curve represents the minimum price at which firms will supply goods over the long run. The long run applies when firms have sufficient time to enter or leave the industry it is also a period long enough for firms to adjust capacity to the lowest cost level. Diagram 6.5 shows a number of long-run industry supply curves under perfect competition.

In Diagram 6.5 in all three panels there is an increase in demand from D to D1. Equilibrium in the short-run goes from X to Y where D1 and S or $\sum MC$ (the sum of the MC curves of the firms in the industry intersects). When price goes up new firms enter due to the supernormal profit available. Short-run supply curve shifts to S_1 and equilibrium shifts to point Z. The long run effect of the increase in demand is to move the equilibrium point from X to Z. As shown the long-run supply curve (LRSC) goes through points X and Z.

71

Panel (A) in Diagram 6.5 shows the long run supply curve (LRSC) as horizontal. This will be the position if price goes back to its original level going through points X and Z that are at the same price. Costs in the industry are constant.

In panel (B) when new firms enter the industry they bid up the price of the factors of production that are now in short supply. The firm's LRAC will shift up vertically. Therefore long run equilibrium will be at Z and the LRSC will slope upwards as shown. This situation is due to increasing industry costs.

Panel (C) shows what happens when costs fall due to external economies of scale. The LRSC will slope downwards.

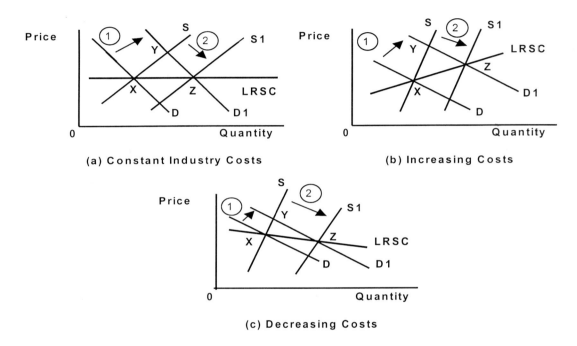

(a) Constant Industry Costs

(b) Increasing Costs

(c) Decreasing Costs

DIAGRAM 6.5 Various Long-Run Industry Supply Curves under Perfect Competition

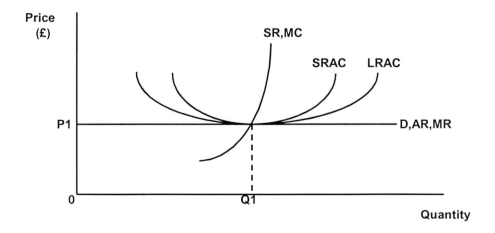

Diagram 6.6 Long-run Equilibrium of a Perfectly Competitive Firm

Long-Run Equilibrium of the Perfectly Competitive Firm:

If firms are making supernormal profits in the long run, new firms will enter and/or existing firms will expand. This results in increased supply as the market supply curve shifts to the right and as a result price falls assuming the market demand curve remains unchanged. Price continues to fall until only normal profits are made. This occurs as shown in Diagram 6.6 when the demand curve touches the bottom of the long-run average cost curve (LRAC) assuming that all firms have the same cost structure or set of cost curves. Long-run equilibrium is where $MR = MC = AR = AC = LRAC$ and quantity Q_1.

Advantages of Perfect Competition:

There are a number of advantages that can arise from a situation of perfect competition

- Price is just sufficient to give the firm a normal profit therefore the consumer is not exploited and gets the product at the lowest possible price.

- Each firm must produce at the most efficient output and inefficient firms are forced out of the industry.

- The public obtains the greatest output from the resources used in producing the good.

- Firms will wish to make supernormal profits so they will develop new technology.

- There is no point in advertising and this means that the AC curve will be low, so those prices will be lower than they would be with advertising.

- There is an automatic reallocation of resources in response to changes in demand. When demand changes so does supply. This happens automatically because of the profit motive that causes firms to enter and leave the industry.

Disadvantages of Perfect Competition:

- There is no guarantee that goods will be equitably distributed to the members of society.

- Firms are small and there may be large- scale duplication among them resulting in waste.

- Firms may not be able to afford the necessary research and development needed to develop new technology due to their small size. They may be afraid that others will copy them due to the fact of their having perfect knowledge and operating in a very competitive environment.

- Since perfectly competitive firms produce undifferentiated products, this may not suit all consumers as their preferences can vary greatly.

- In some industries large firms achieve economies of scale and can produce at lower cost than small firms. In the long run many firms cannot exist in such industries, so that the market structure is no longer purely competitive.

Monopoly Model:

Assumptions underlying monopoly:

- There is only one firm, with complete control of the firm in the hands of the industry.
- A single product is produced and there is no close substitute for it.
- Information is not freely available to firms interested in entering the industry.
- There are barriers to the entry of new firms.

Monopolist's Demand Curve:

The firm's demand curve is also the industry's demand since there is only one firm in the industry. We assume a normal demand curve so that it is necessary for the monopolist to reduce price to increase sales. To do this the price of all goods must be reduced therefore MR will always be less than AR because when AR is falling MR must be less than AR. The monopolist faces a downward sloping AR curve with the MR curve below it. The firm in this case is a price maker. When price elasticity of demand is inelastic MR can be negative. This happens when price is reduced and quantity demanded goes up but this increase is small so that total revenue falls.

Barriers to Entry:

Barriers to entry must exist if a firm is to maintain its monopoly position. Barriers can be divided into legal and natural barriers.

Legal Barriers:

These barriers arise when law protects the monopoly.

- Some semi state bodies are statutory monopolies. In Ireland at present it is illegal to compete with An Post in the delivery of letters and the ESB has the sole right to supply electricity.
- A patent is a legal restriction on entry. Patents protect inventors for a limited period of time and in this way encourage invention by preventing others from copying them. Patents however do run out after sixteen years.

Natural Barriers:

- Natural barriers can arise due to geographical conditions of supply. De Beers in South Africa own 80% of the worlds diamond mines.
- Natural monopoly can also arise because of economies of scale. Chemical companies for example has relatively high set up costs. Once they are established they may have succeeded in reducing fixed costs per unit so that a new firm cannot compete since its output would be at a relatively low level of production. The minimum point on the firm's AC curve occurs at a level of output almost equal to the market size, which means that there is room for only one firm.

Other Barriers to Entry:

- A firm may have a monopoly because it was first in the field and no other firm has the ability or customer goodwill to enter the field.

- A firm may have control over wholesale or retail outlets through which the product must be sold and as a result can bar the access of its rivals to consumers.

- The monopolist can enter into trade agreements with other firms.

- An established monopolist can temporarily lower price to show potential entrants that they will lose if they enter and is involved in a price war.

- The monopolist can build up brand loyalty that forces new entrants to compete against products that are well known and established in the market.

Limits of Monopoly power:

The monopolist cannot control demand and because of this has two options:
- Fix the price and allow demand to decide the quantity supplied;
- Control supply and let demand determine price.
- Has control over price or quantity but not both.

Price and Output Decisions of the Monopolist:

We assume that there is no control by the government over the monopolist's price and output decisions. The objective of the firm is to maximise its profits. As already stated the firm's AR curve is the same as that of the industry. Diagram 6.7 illustrates the revenue and cost functions of a firm operating under conditions of pure monopoly.

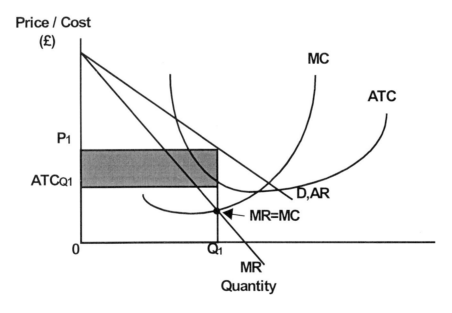

DIAGRAM 6.7 Profit Maximising Price and Output of a Pure Monopolist

As already explained a firm maximises profit where MR = MC. In Diagram 6.7 this is where output is Q_1 and average revenue or price is P_1. Since the firm faces a downward sloping demand curve, marginal revenue is less than average revenue and in equilibrium supernormal profit is obtained as shown by the shaded area (P_1- ATC_{Q1}). .Average cost is assumed to include normal profit. Since no new firms can enter, the only difference between the short-run and long-run equilibrium is that in the long run the firm will produce where MR = long-run MC. In this case supernormal profit remains the same. ATC may not be at a minimum so that the firm does not operate at maximum efficiency.

Why does the monopolist not charge any price he wants?

As already stated he maximises profit where MC=MR and if he charges a higher price he will not do so. He competes for the available purchasing power and if his price is too high some consumers may do without the product even though there is no substitute for it. He will also fear that the Competition Authority established by the state may set a maximum price for his product so that he earns only normal profit.

Monopoly and Welfare:

Conventional wisdom is that monopoly is 'bad' and against the public interest. It is seen as imposing a cost on society by raising price and reducing output relative to levels under perfect competition. The monopolist charges a price aboveMC.

Diagram 6.8 shows welfare loss due to monopoly. It shows the hypothetical case of converting a competitive industry into a monopoly. Long-run industry equilibrium is at point E. Price is equal to the long run MC of production. At Pc and Qc consumer surplus is CEPc. When the firm is converted from a competitive market structure to a monopoly, price is increased to Pm and output reduced to Qm resulting in consumer surplus of CAPm. Monopoly profits are PmABPc. The welfare loss is AEB. Who gets the real income represented by AEB? The answer is no one as it just disappears when the monopoly is set up.

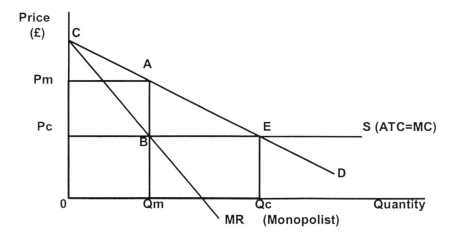

DIAGRAM 6.8 Loss of Welfare due to Monopoly

76

Advantages of Monopoly:

- **Economies of Scale:**

A monopoly may be able to achieve substantial economies of scale and if its MC curve is substantially below that of the same industry under perfect competition the monopoly will produce a higher output at a lower price. In Diagram 6.9 the monopoly produces Q_1 when price is P_1 but the perfectly competitive industry produces at Q_2 at the higher price of P_2. The monopoly MC curve must be below point B on the diagram. If the monopolist was to follow the P = MC rule observed by perfectly competitive firm's price would be lower at P_3 and output higher at Q_3.

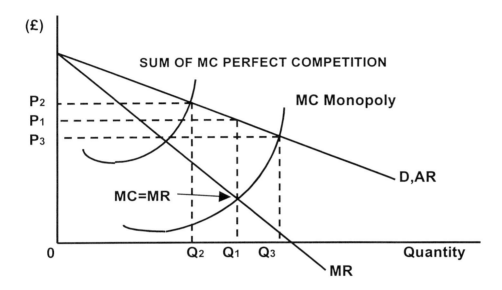

DIAGRAM 6.9 Equilibrium of Industry Under Perfect Competition and Monopoly with Different MC Curves

- **Long Term Planning:**

The monopolist does not have to worry if he will be still in business in the future to reap the reward of any innovation he may be making now.

- **Research:**

Only very large firms can afford to carry out the amount of research needed to establish a monopoly in a particular industry. Only monopoly gives the stability in the market that will encourage innovation.

- **Patents:**

These help preserve technological superiority and to legally keep rivals out.

- **Sole Ownership of Raw Materials:**

If a firm has sole ownership to raw materials it is the only firm that can produce that particular product.

Disadvantages of Monopoly:

- The monopolist sets price or output at a level to earn supernormal profit. Price is higher and output lower than they would be if there were a competitive market instead of a monopoly. The consumer is exploited as the monopolist sets price above MC.

- The monopolist earning supernormal profit does not produce where average costs (AC) are minimised therefore they are not efficient producers. The lack of competition makes the monopolist even less efficient. He has no incentive to improve when he is already making excess profits due to his monopolistic position.

- Monopolists can engage in price discrimination to increase their supernormal profits.

- If a monopoly controls a vital resource it may make decisions detrimental to the public interest

- A monopoly may prevent competition by taking over smaller rivals. Diseconomies of scale may arise in a large monopoly.

Control of Monopoly:

The growth of monopolies is controlled in Ireland by:

The Competition Authority:

This Authority was established under the 1991 Competition Act. The Act introduced the following in relation to price -fixing arrangements:

- a general prohibition of anti-competitive behaviour ;

- price fixing agreements into competition legislation; and

- offers legal redress to anyone adversely affected by anti-competitive behaviour.

Price Discrimination:

Price discrimination is the practice of charging some customers a higher price than others for an identical good or of charging an individual customer a higher price on a small purchase than on a large one.

Conditions Necessary for Price Discrimination to Work:

- For a firm to employ price discrimination the following conditions must be satisfied: The seller must have some degree of monopoly power so as to be able to control supply.
- The firm must face a downward sloping demand curve so as to have some discretion in the price it charges, to buyers of its product. The seller must have the ability to make rather than take price.
- The firm must have easily identifiable groups of customers with different types of demand for the product. Demand elasticities must differ in at least two markets.
- The firm must be in a position to segregate its sales to each group of customers so that customers paying the lower price cannot resell the item to customers paying a higher price.

There are three major types:

First Degree Price Discrimination:

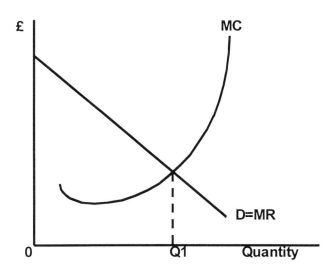

DIAGRAM 6.10 Profit Maximising Output under First Degree Price Discrimination

This type of discrimination occurs when each unit is sold for the maximum obtainable price. Examples of this are a lecturer giving private grinds. In this case the individual selling the service is dealing with the customer on a one to one basis and has a good idea of the person's ability to pay. It is possible for first degree discrimination to take place when different customers are charged a different price for the same product according to their willingness to pay or when the same customer is charged different prices for the same product. This is shown in Diagram 6.10. Price is lowered only for the extra unit sold therefore the additional revenue gained from the last unit MR will be its price to that consumer. Profit is maximised at Q_1 where MC =MR equal to the price of the last unit. Consumer surplus is eliminated.

Second Degree Price Discrimination:

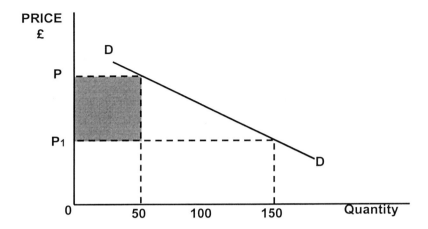

DIAGRAM 6.11 Second Degree Price Discrimination

This type of discrimination occurs when the consumer pays a certain price for some units and a different price for additional units of the good. It therefore involves discounts. Quantity discounts are often a successful of price discrimination as a customer's willingness to pay for an extra unit decreases as the customer buys more units. Diagram 6.11 shows that the first 50 units are sold at price P and the next 100 units at price P_1. Profits rise because the discriminating firm is able to increase revenue from selling a given quantity. The amount of consumer surplus gained has been reduced. The shaded area shows the revenue gain compared with selling 150 units at the single price of P_1.

Third Degree Price Discrimination:

This occurs when the same product is sold to different customers at different prices, in two or more independent markets. It is the most common type of price discrimination and it is illustrated in Diagram 6.12.

Panel (3) in Diagram 6.12 shows MR and MC curves for the entire firm. To get this MR curve the MR curves in markets A and B are summed horizontally, to get MR_{A+B} in Panel (3). With output at 200 units in market A and 400 in market B adding to 600 units, revenue rises by £8 if one additional unit is sold either in market A or market B. Total profit is maximised as usual where MR = MC, i.e. 600 units. Output must be divided between the two markets so that MC = MR is the same in each market i.e. at £8. If this is not the case then switching output to the market with the greater MR could increase revenue. Profit maximising output in market A is 200 units sold at a price of £12 each and in market B, 400 units at £10 each. The demand curve is less elastic for market A than it is for B therefore the higher price is charged in market A.

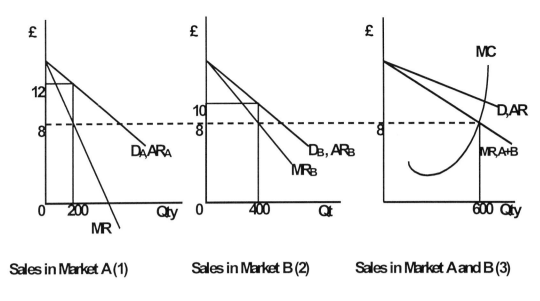

Diagram 6.12 Price Discrimination

Examples:

Peak Rates – Off Peak Rates:

The following are examples of products that cannot be stored or resold therefore time is important.

- Commuter travel –different fares at different times.
- Electricity-different charges at different times e.g. night saver
- Telephone calls-different charges at different times.

These are examples of services that cannot be transferred from the cheaper to the more expensive market.

Status of the Consumer:

Students and senior citizens are charged a lower price as follows:

- Cinema
- Travel
- Services such as hair cuts and public lectures.

Is Price Discrimination Good or Bad?

Since profits are higher with discrimination than without, there is a redistribution of income from consumers to the seller. Firms can also use price discrimination to drive competitors out of business. If, for example a firm has a monopoly at home it can charge a high price, while if it is in oligopoly (See Chapter 7) in the export market it can charge a low price there by subsidising its products from its high profits at home.

Customers with more elastic demand curves who are charged the lower prices are likely to have lower incomes than those in the less elastic market so that the economically weak benefit. Discrimination can improve competition by encouraging more price experimentation. This is due to the fact that, a firm unwilling to engage in across-the-board price changes, may be willing to test the effect of a price change in one market or on one class of customer.

Questions

1. Under conditions of perfect competition, a firm's price is probably be less and its output greater than under monopoly conditions. Comment on this statement.

2. "A monopolist will always charge a higher price and produce a lower output than a competitive firm." Critically evaluate this statement.

3. Outline using diagrams the short-run and long run profit maximising price and output for a perfectly competitive firm.

4. By means of a diagram show the profit maximising price and output for a firm operating under conditions of monopoly. Why are monopolies considered to be harmful?

5. Explain why a monopolist is normally expected to charge a higher price and produce a smaller output than under competition? In what circumstances might this not apply?

6. Distinguish clearly, with the aid of a diagram, the market conditions in which a firm is a 'price taker' and those in which it is a 'price maker'.

7. Explain illustrating your answer with a diagram the long-run equilibrium of a firm in perfect competition.

8. Does a monopolist or a competitive firm face a more elastic demand curve? What characteristics of the good being sold lead to a larger elasticity?

9. What is price discrimination? Explain with the assistance of diagrams how third degree price discrimination occurs.

CHAPTER 7

IMPERFECT COMPETITION

Introduction:

Imperfect competition occurs between the two extremes of perfect competition and monopoly. There are two types of imperfect competition i.e. monopolistic competition and oligopoly and these are discussed here. Under monopolistic competition there are a large number of suppliers of products that are slightly differentiated. Oligopoly refers to markets that are dominated by a few sellers.

Monopolistic Competition:

Under monopolistic competition there will normally be a large number of relatively small firms. There are therefore many firms competing but each firm does have some degree of market power as well as some discretion as to what price to charge. The firm will have a downward sloping demand curve made possible by product differentiation.

Assumptions of Monopolistic Competition:

♦ There are many buyers and sellers with each firm having an insignificantly small share of the market and acting independently of rivals.

♦ There is freedom of entry and exit into the industry.

♦ Each firm produces a product that is slightly differentiated from that of its rivals.

♦ Each firm is aware of the level of profits being earned by all firms in the industry.

♦ The aim of the firm is to maximise profit.

Price and Output Decisions of Monopolistically Competitive Firms:

Short-Run:

Since the firm's product is differentiated it does not have a perfectly elastic demand curve but in general it will be a fairly elastic. The short-run equilibrium of the firm will be exactly the same as for that of the monopolist, as shown in Diagram 7.1. Profits shown by the shaded area are maximised where MR = MC i.e. at price P_2 and output Q_2. ATC at Q_2 units of output is $ATCQ_2$. The firm is not producing where MC= ATC and where ATC is at a minimum. The firm could produce a greater quantity more efficiently than it actually does do in equilibrium and as a result there is over capacity since the firm is producing below the level its resources would allow. This means the cost of production is not as low as it could be and resources are being wasted.

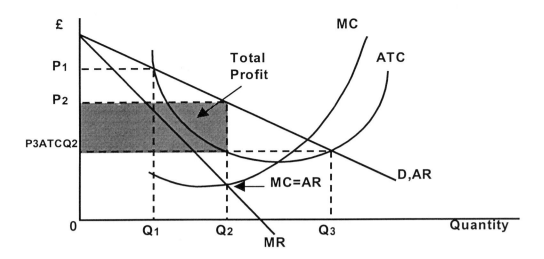

DIAGRAM 7.1 Short Run Equilibrium for a Monopolistically Competitive Firm

Long-Run:

If supernormal profits are made in the short run new firms will have an incentive to enter the industry. When this happens each firm can expect to sell less as its market share declines and this will continue until excess profits are no longer being earned. The only curve that has shifted between the short-run and the long-run is the demand curve, as seen in Diagram 7.2

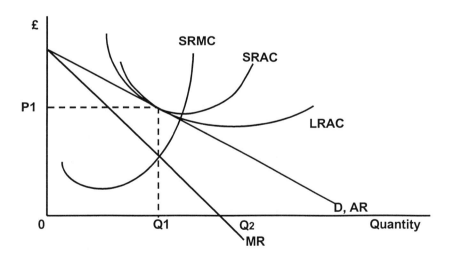

DIAGRAM 7.2 Long-Run Equilibrium for a Monopolistically Competitive Firm

In Diagram 7.2, the long-run equilibrium position of a monopolistically competitive firm is shown. AR is shown tangent to the SRAC and LRAC curves at the profit maximising output Q_1 and price P_1. Since price equals SRAC at Q_1 the firm is just covering all its costs (including implicit and opportunity costs) and the firm will be making a normal profit. When this is the case, no more firms will enter the industry. Output Q_1 is below the optimum output that is Q_2 in Diagram 7.2 and the firm is producing to the left of the minimum point of the

LRAC resulting in excess capacity. The firm produces a lower output than that which minimises ATC therefore the consumer pays more than the minimum ATC. Only if the demand curve of the firm is elastic, is the long-run equilibrium at the point of minimum average total cost. The demand curve slopes down because of product differentiation and it is the latter that produces excess capacity.

Limitations of the Model:

♦ Information may be imperfect so those potential entrants to the market are unaware of super normal profits being profits being made. Therefore they will not enter the market.

♦ Since firms in the industry produce different products it is practically impossible to derive the demand curve for the industry as a whole. The analysis must therefore be done on the firm.

♦ It is possible that existing firms are making supernormal profits but it may happen that when new firms enter the industry that profits will go below normal. Therefore there will be no further incentive for new firms to enter.

♦ The model concentrates on price and output decisions but it must also be borne in mind that monopolistically competitive firms engage in non price-competition.

Non Price Competition:

There are two broad types of non-price competition, i.e. product differentiation and advertising.

Product Differentiation:

The main aim of product development is to differentiate the product by brand names, packaging, sales promotion and advertising. This gives the firm the ability to maintain excess profits even in the long run. It will also ensure stability of sales if consumers remain loyal to the product. Consumers benefit in that they get a consistent product so that they know what they are buying. Different products cater for different consumer tastes and income levels. There are a number of disadvantages associated with product differentiation as follows:

♦ It reduces competition among existing firms because consumers tend to remain loyal and this loyalty also makes it more difficult for new firms to break into the industry.

♦ Too much is spent on packaging, design change and advertising.

♦ Too many brands make it difficult for the firm to avail of full economies of scale.

Advertising:

The main objective of advertising is to sell the good or service. If successful it will move the firm's AR curve to the right and make it a little less elastic (slope becomes steeper) as well.

As long as the firm's revenue increases by more than enough to cover the advertising expenses and additional costs associated with extra output then with the additional profit it can put off adjustment towards long-run equilibrium. It is however difficult for the firm to forecast the change in demand likely to occur after advertising. The consumer usually through higher prices pays for additional costs.

Monopolistic Competition versus Perfect Competition:

In the long-run in perfect competition P = LMC = minimum long-run ATC as shown in Diagram 7.3 (a). Both SRATC and LRATC are tangent to the perfectly elastic demand curve. Price is Pc and quantity produced is Qc that equals LRMC. In panel (b) of Diagram 7.3 the demand curve Dm is sloping downward. $SRATC_2$ = LRATC at Qm.

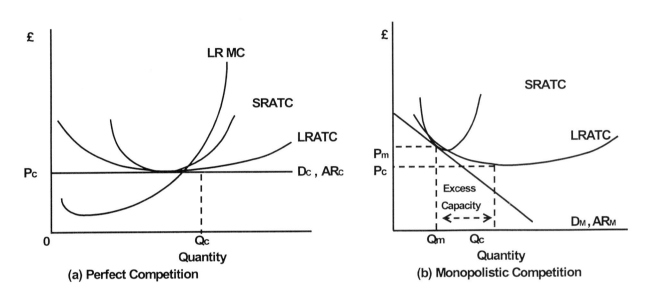

DIAGRAM 7.3 Comparison Perfect Competition and Monopolistic Competition

Given that cost conditions are the same under both market structures how do they compare? For monopolistic competition, Pm > LRMC, Pm > minimum LRATC so that firms are not producing at the least cost point. In perfect competition, P= LRMC. Because P > minimum LRATC, consumers under monopolistic competition pay a higher price than they do under perfect competition when P = minimum LRAC. (Diagram 7.3 Panel (a)) With price Pm greater than Pc and Qm smaller than Qc, the consumer pays a higher price and output is lower under monopolistic competition. In both cases P=AC so that neither makes an economic profit. This is so in the case of monopolistic competition because the firm's ATC = AR. Under monopolistic competition there is excess capacity as shown in Diagram 7.3 (b).

Oligopoly:

Oligopoly represents a market structure in which a few firms dominate in the production of a good or service. When there are only two firms, in the industry is called a duopoly. It is now the most prevalent market form in the industrialised world. This is due to the availability of economies of scale that has encouraged the growth of large-scale firms. As firms grew in size the number of them supplying the market fell. This process continues and oligopoly is now the most common market form. Industries can produce homogeneous products or differentiated products so that these do not determine whether a firm is an oligopoly or not. What is important is the degree of market power possessed by the industry's leading firms. The principal effect of fewness of firms is to give each firm such a high profile position in the market that its decisions and actions have far reaching repercussions on the other firms. Even though there is great interdependence among firms, each firm will do the best it can in the market depending on what it thinks its rivals might do. Interdependence means that it is impossible to predict the effect on the firm's sales of say a change in price without first making assumptions about the reactions of other firms. Different assumptions will give different predictions so that there is no single acceptable theory of oligopoly.

Perfect and Imperfect Oligopoly:

Perfect oligopoly exists when the oligopolists produce a uniform product. Major petrol suppliers form a perfect oligopoly. When the products produced are differentiated an imperfect oligopoly exists e.g. detergents.

Competitive and Collusive Oligopoly:

Competitive oligopoly exists when rival firms are interdependent to the extent that they take account of the reactions of one another when deciding strategy without reference to them. A firm can never be certain of how rivals will react but uncertainty can be reduced or eliminated by firms colluding together to fix prices or through a cartel agreement.

Cartels:

 A **cartel** is the establishment of a central body to fix price and output. As a rule it is responsible for sharing the output between the members. The best-known cartel is the Organisation of Petroleum Exporting Countries (OPEC) which was set up in 1973. It was successful from 1973 to the early 1980's when a world wide economic slump occurred. As demand for oil has fallen exporters have had to cut production to maintain prices. Nigeria and other countries with major economic problems refused to cut supply, preferring to cut prices. Prices were higher in the early 1990's as Iraq put pressure on OPEC members to cut production. Since 1993 prices were cut as demand for oil continues to fall. OPEC failed because disagreements between the members could not be resolved.

The Central Selling Organisation (CSO) set up in 1930 to reduce fluctuations in the price of diamonds is a very effective cartel. De Beers runs it and if they collude in this way they act as a monopoly. Collusive oligopoly exists when all the firms in the oligopoly charge the same price as a monopolist would, and split the output between them. It has all the disadvantages of monopoly; i.e. restricts output, and increases price, productive and allocative inefficiency and loss of consumer choice. Collusive oligopolies are normally illegal since they are against the public interest.

Traditional Models of Oligopoly:

We examine two theories under this heading, the first being the kinked demand curve model and the second being the dominant firm model.

Kinked Demand Curve Model:

In this model, developed by Paul Sweezy in 1939, the firm is held to believe that if it cuts price, rivals will follow quickly with their own price cuts. This results in limiting the gain in sales of any one firm to its share of the overall gain in industry sales. Rivals may see a price reduction as an attack on their position and will make a counter attack. The result of this is that all firms lose. If one firm increases price the others will not follow but will expect to gain customers from the price increasing firm.

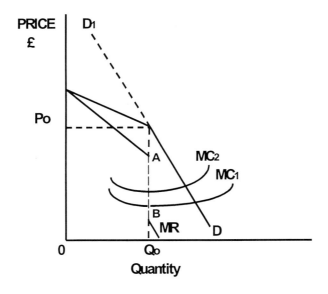

DIAGRAM 7.4 Kinked Demand Curve

In Diagram 7.4 the firm faces a downward sloping demand curve that has a kink at price P_0. At prices above P_0 the demand curve is relatively elastic. This reflects the fact that if one firm raises price, none of the others will follow and the firm increasing its price will suffer a large fall in the quantity demanded. At prices below P the demand curve is less elastic. This reflects the fact that if one firm cuts price all others will follow and the firm will only gain a small increase in demand.

The kink in the demand curve D creates a break in the MR curve at Q_0. The firm produces where MR = MC so as to maximise profits. However output Q_0 is where the MC curve passes through the discontinuity in the MR curve, or the gap $|AB|$. If MC fluctuates between A and B as shown in Diagram 7.4 with MC, and MC$_2$, the firm will change neither price nor output. If MC goes outside AB it will change both.

The kinked demand curve model yields five predictions about the market behaviour of oligopolistic firms:

◆ A firm will not independently raise price for fear that it will cause a drop in its profit, sales and market share.

◆ A firm will not independently cut price in the knowledge that rivals will follow so that the cut brings no gain.

◆ Oligopolists will charge the same or nearly the same price for their goods because their goods are substitutable and consumers will go to the lower price seller.

◆ Price and output of an oligopolistic firm have a tendency to be rigid in the face of small cost changes.

◆ Price will tend to be sticky but output will tend to be responsive to small changes in demand conditions.

All of these predictions are consistent with observed behaviour in oligopolies.

Faults with the Kinked Demand Curve Model:

Frequent price changes disrupt customer relations by introducing an element of uncertainty as to future prices. Firms will not wish to have frequent price changes as this means altering price lists and upsets customers when firms are supposed to sell their products at 'nationally advertised prices'. The model does not explain how oligopolists initially arrive at the prevailing price. It explains how the model shows price stability but not how price is determined. Sweezy could not predict where the kink would occur, therefore he could not predict the price. The assumption that when one firm increases price, others will not follow does not always hold. When all firms experience the same rise in costs or change in demand conditions, there is an incentive to change price. If one firm leads the way it can be confident that others will follow.

Game Theory:

The essence of game theory is that the firm assesses the payoff from a given strategy in the light of strategies adopted by competitors. It goes beyond the general reaction patterns of earlier theory, to more explicit assessments of strategy and counter strategy. Oligopolistic markets are suited to this analytical technique since the major producers are few in number and highly interdependent. A strategy is a game plan describing how each player will act in every possible situation. The players in the game endeavour to maximise their profits. Equilibrium occurs when each player chooses the best strategy, given the strategies being followed by the other players. This is known as the Nash equilibrium after John Nash who first proposed it.

	Advertise	Not advertise
Advertise	Firm X 140 Firm Y 160	Firm X 80 Firm Y 200
Not Advertise	Firm X 200 Firm Y 100	Firm X 160 Firm Y 180

Consider the health care industry as an example and assume that the matrix in Figure 1 shows the possible actions that two firms might undertake and the result of these actions. The top left rectangle represents the results or payoff if both X and Y advertise; the bottom left is where X advertises but Y does not; the top right represents when Y advertises but X does not; and the bottom right shows the payoffs if neither firm advertises. If firm X can earn higher profits by advertising than by not advertising, whether or not firm Y advertises, then firm X will advertise. Firm X compares the left- hand side to the right- hand side and sees that it earns more by advertising no matter what firm Y does. If Y advertises and X advertises then X earns 140; but if X does not advertise it earns 80. If Y does not advertise then X earns 200 by advertising and 160 by not advertising. Firm Y will earn 160 by advertising and 100 by not advertising, if firm X advertises. By advertising firm Y will earn 200 but only 180 not advertising, if firm X does not advertise. Both firms would be better off if neither advertised; X would earn 160 instead of 140 and Y would earn 180 instead of 160. However both must advertise, as they would lose more if the other firm advertised and they did not. This is the prisoners' dilemma i.e. a situation in which the best outcome is not chosen because actions depend on other firms. None of the health care firms wish to spend money but they must and this demonstrates their interdependence.

Price Leadership:

Price leadership is a pricing behaviour in oligopoly markets whereby firms set the same price as an established leader from within the industry. Firms choose to follow the leader but are free to follow a different policy. This leader may be the biggest or most respected firm in the industry and as a result this is known as dominant firm price leadership. Over time a leader may emerge and be seen as the best barometer of market conditions and this is known as barometric firm price leadership.

Dominant Firm Price Leadership:

This means that there is an unwritten or tacit agreement that the biggest firm sets the price for the industry as a whole. Diagram 7.5 outlines the dominant firm model. D is the industry demand curve. $\sum MCf$ is the horizontal sum of the MC curves of the competitive fringe firms. The latter set MC = P and thus act as price takers. Dd is the demand curve of the dominant firm and MRd is its marginal revenue curve. MCd is lower than MCf because of economies of scale or greater efficiency.

At any given price the dominant firm derives its demand curve by looking at what fringe firms will do. In Diagram 7.5 at price P_1 fringe firms will supply the whole market demand as $\sum MCf = D$. At prices below P_1 the fringe firms cannot supply the whole market and that part of the market available to the dominant firms is obtained by getting the difference between $\sum MCf$ and D at points below where $\sum MCf = D$. The dominant firm sets the price for this part of the market. Going on its own MCd and MRd it sets price at Pd, where fringe suppliers, supply Qf. Since $Qd + Qf = Q_t$ market supply and demand are equal at Pd.

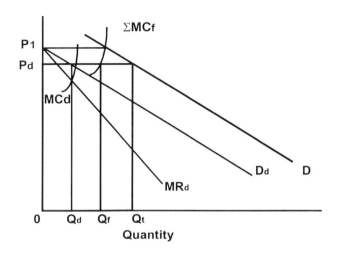

DIAGRAM 7.5 Dominant Firm Price Leadership

Contestable Markets:

The theory of contestable markets refers to oligopolistic markets where there are no barriers to entry and no exit barriers from the market. In equilibrium MR= MC =AC =AR as in perfect competition. Only normal profit will be earned and output will be where AC is at a minimum. If firms produce where AC is not minimised or if they raise prices to earn super normal profit, other firms will enter the market. An important influence on the ease of exit and entry is the degree to which costs are sunk or unavoidable, i.e. are irretrievably committed to the market. The greater the level of sunk costs, the more risky entry becomes. The level of profit is not associated with the number of firms in the market, as suggested by traditional theory of the firm.

91

Questions

1. Compare and contrast the long-run equilibrium of the monopolistically competitive firm with that of the perfectly competitive firm.

2. It is claimed that monopolistic competition does not achieve optimum allocation of resources. If this is the case does it mean that the consumer gains more from perfect competition than from monopolistic competition?

3. "One obvious way of arriving at a common price policy in an oligopolistic industry is for one firm to serve as a price leader." Discuss using the dominant firm model.

4. Critically evaluate the Kinked Demand Curve Model as a theory explaining the oligopolistic behaviour of firms.

5. "In an industry consisting of only a few firms each one must consider the reactions of its rivals so that prices are relatively stable." Explain and critically evaluate this statement.

6. Discuss the theory of contestable markets in the context of barriers to entry.

7. "Game theory describes interdependent decision-making in which each player chooses a strategy." Critically evaluate this statement.

CHAPTER 8

INCOMES AND PRICING OF PRODUCTION

Introduction:

Income is a reward for the use of assets: wages for the use of workers skills and time, rent for renting land and buildings, interest for the use of temporary capital and profit for the provision permanent capital. Income is received by households as a flow over time, so much a day, week, month or year. A household's income derives from its wealth that is the household's stock of assets. Distribution theory is based on **Alfred Marshall's (1842-1924)** convention of dividing inputs for the production of output into four factors of production. In this Chapter we examine how the value of output is distributed as factor incomes to the owners of the inputs that are sold or hired to firms so that output can be produced.

Factors of Production:

Factors of production are the inputs or resources used in production and they are labour, capital, land and enterprise. The owners of the factors receive an income from the firms that uses them. Income in the case of labour takes the form of wages and salaries. For land it is rent, for capital it is the profit or interest earned by the owners of it, while it is profit for enterprise. In the case of labour or human capital we speak of wages as the selling price whereas with land and capital we speak of income earned from their use.

Given the quantity of the different factors a household possesses, its income depends on the price it can get for them. Factor markets can be examined by looking at supply and demand, but some special characteristics must be looked at separately.

Demand for Factors as a Derived Demand:

Firms require labour, raw materials, machines, land and other inputs to produce the goods and services that they sell. This is a derived demand as it depends on the demand for the commodity that is being produced. Total demand for a factor is the sum of its derived demands in all of its productive uses.

In Chapter 5 we saw what happens to output when a firm increases it's inputs of a variable factor when other factors are fixed. Average physical product (APP) and marginal physical product (MPP) of the variable factor increases initially but eventually decreases because of the law of diminishing returns. MPP is a purely physical phenomenon. If we take labour as the variable factor, the value of its MPP is determined by the price of the final product. Suppose the firm is producing footballs and can sell them for £10 each and the MPP is 100 the value of MPP is £1,000. This addition to the firm's revenue from employing one more unit of labour is called marginal revenue product (MRP) of labour.

Average physical product (APP) is the output per worker and the average revenue product (ARP), is the revenue produced per worker. APP x price = ARP.

Table 8.1 shows the ARP and MRP as a result of employing different numbers of workers derived from Table 5.1. It is assumed for Table 8.1 that it is a perfectly competitive market where the milk sells for 50p a litre.

Diagram 8.1 shows the ARP and MRP from Table 8.1. The portion of the MRP curve below the ARP curve is the firms demand curve, for labour indicated by the dotted line. The fourth worker brings in an extra £12 so that the firm will pay him £12. The fifth worker brings in £10 in revenue so he will be paid £10.

Table 8.1
Average Revenue Product and Marginal Revenue Product

No. of Workers	APP (from table 5.1)	MPP (from table 5.1)	ARP (APP x 50p)	MRP (MPP x 50p)
	000's litres	000's litres	£	£
1	14	14	7	7
2	23	32	11.5	16
3	25.3	30	12.7	15
4	25.0	24	12.5	12
5	24	20	12.0	10
6	20	0	10.0	0
7	17	-1	8.5	-0.5

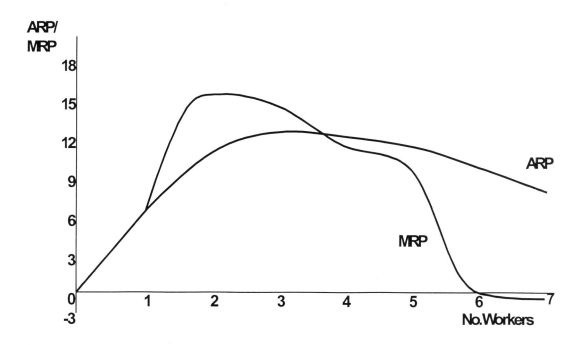

DIAGRAM 8.1 Demand Curve for a Factor

If there is perfect competition in the labour market as well as the product market then the wage rate will be already determined for the firm. The MC of labour will be a horizontal straight line at the given wage. At a wage of £12 an hour, 4 workers will be employed, but wages would have to fall to £10 an hour if 5 workers are to be employed A profit maximising firm will hire no workers if the wage rose above £12.70 an hour.

Elasticity of Demand for Factors:

The demand for any factor will be more elastic:

- The more elastic the demand for the product;
- The easier it is to substitute other factors of production for the one in question;
- The more elastic the supply of substitute factors; and
- The more important the factors contribution to the firms total costs.

The Supply of Factors:

To understand factor prices we need to examine the supply of factors and must distinguish between the different factors of production. The most important supply curve in the factor market is that of labour.

Labour Supply:

We have already seen in Chapter 1 what constitutes labour and we now examine it in more detail. Labour supply in competitive markets is highly elastic. Overall supply of labour depends on the following:
- size of the population;
- number of people available for work;
- number in paid employment;
- average number of hours worked by each employee per week;
- the participation rate i.e. the ratio of the number of economically active people of working age (employed or seeking employment) to the total population

Specialisation or Division of labour:

The division of labour means breaking down the production process into specialised tasks. It is well established that division of labour greatly increases the quantity of goods and services that can be produced. The advantages are as follows:

- Increased level of skill in the work force resulting in increased production.
- Time is saved through having a trained staff working at speed and not moving from job to job.
- The talents of individuals are catered for.

- It makes possible the use of more specialised capital equipment.

There are also **disadvantages** as follows:

- Repetitive work can become monotonous and can lead to lack of interest, strikes and absenteeism.
- Highly specialised workers may become scarce and may prevent the firm from expanding.
- There is an increased risk of unemployment due to the specialised nature of the work. It also becomes easier to replace workers with capital.
- Dependency on other people will increase .

We must determine how aggregate supply of labour is obtained and the way in which wage rates and labour supply are interrelated.

Individuals Labour Supply:

An individual must choose between time spent earning a wage and time spent doing things while not earning a wage from working which we will refer to as leisure. The decision then is how many hours a day or a week to supply. A supply curve relates the quantity of work offered to different wage rates. Diagram 8.2 shows the labour supply curve of an individual in Panel (A) and the aggregate supply curve for labour in Panel (B).

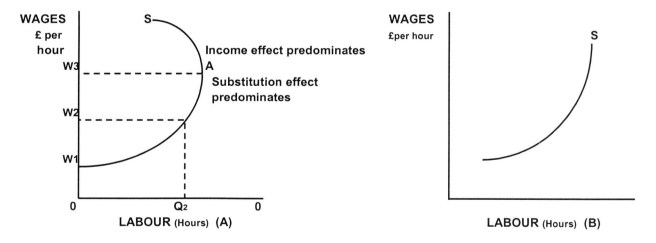

DIAGRAM 8.2 Individual and Aggregate Supply Curves for Labour

In Panel (A) at a wage rate at or below W_1 the worker will prefer not to work at all as more utility is obtained from leisure. Above W_1 hours of labour supplied by the individual increase as wages increase. When wages rise from W_1 to W_2 the number of hours of labour supplied rises to OQ_2. As wages rise the worker is encouraged to substitute hours of work for hours of leisure. This substitution effect is offset by an income effect. As wage rates rise so does income and since leisure time can be considered to be a normal good then demand for it will rise as income rises. The income and substitution effects pull the worker in opposite directions. If the substitution effect is greater than the income effect higher wages encourage more hours of labour. In Diagram 8.2 (A) the substitution effect is greater than the income effect between W_1 and W_3 when the slope is positive. Above W_3 the income effect is greater than the substitution effect and the supply curve is negatively sloped. At point A income and substitution effects are equal and the supply curve begins to slope backwards.

Aggregate Supply of Labour:

The aggregate supply curve of labour shows the total amount of labour supplied at all the different wage levels. This curve is typically upward sloping as shown in Diagram 8.2 (B). Even though an individual may have a backward sloping curve the aggregate curve will be positive because many workers will work more hours and more workers will enter the labour force. Indeed some people may be willing to work for less than W_1

Land:

Land consists of all types of natural resources used in the production of wealth. The total supply in any area, e.g. Ireland, is fixed in that it cannot be moved to another geographic location. In this case the supply curve is vertical. There is no cost of production to society as a whole but there is a cost to the individual or firm since a purchase price or rental must be paid for its use. However, when we talk about a certain quality of land in a certain area supply is not totally inelastic since land can be improved by irrigation or reclaimed. In the short-run the supply of land is perfectly inelastic while in the long-run it is less than perfectly inelastic as shown in Diagram 8.3 panels (a) and (b) respectively.

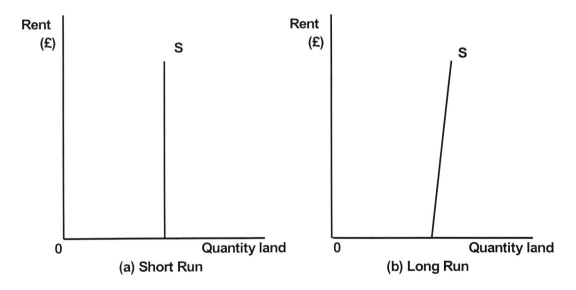

DIAGRAM 8.3 Supply of Land

Although the supply of land is fixed and supply is inelastic, each individual firm operating in a competitive land market faces an elastic supply curve, because it can acquire the land it demands at the going rent arrived at in the market. If land markets are very competitive firms are price takers. Demand for land as a factor of production is a derived demand.

Capital:

Capital is a stock of wealth existing at any one moment of time and can be defined as a sum of finances that can be invested in different ways. Alternatively, it may be defined as the physical means of production used to augment the productivity of labour. The financial markets link the two by channelling people's savings into productive investment. Capital takes many forms but what all those things have in common is that they are produced means of production.

It can be sub-divided into two types, fixed capital and working capital. Fixed capital is not used up in the production process but is kept within the firm. It includes plant, equipment, premises, machinery and vehicles. Working capital is used up in the course of production and consists of stocks of raw materials, work in progress and finished goods.

Demand for Capital:

The marginal efficiency of capital (MEC) represents the firm's demand for capital curve and is the rate of return on the last unit of capital, or internal rate of return. It slopes downwards indicating that the greater the level of investment per period, the lower the rate of return. There are two reasons for this as follows:

1. The greater the level of investment in a given period, the greater the demand for new capital goods. This results in an increase in the price of these capital goods which means a reduction in the return on the investment. If for example a piece of equipment was purchased for £1,000 and the return on investment was £100 or 10%. Suppose the price of the equipment increased to £1,200 and the return remains the same i.e. £100. Then the rate of return on the investment has dropped to 8.34%.

2. In Diagram 8.4 as the firm invests more and its stock of capital grows, MEC will fall due to diminishing returns. Investment should continue so long as MEC is greater than i when stock of capital is Q and investment is just enough to replace worn out equipment. As the rate of interest increases the stock of capital contracts and as it decreases it expands.

Supply of Capital:

The amount of capital supplied depends on the amount of savings that households undertake. Supply of capital therefore depends on how much of its income the household saves. The main factors determining a household's savings are (A) its current and future income and (B) the rate of interest. A household with a low income now compared to its expected future income saves little and could in fact have negative saving as previous savings are now being spent. A household with a high income now compared to expected future income will save more now in order to spend later. The stage in the household's life cycle is the main determinant as to whether current income is low or high, relative to expected future income. If households are young they have low current income relative to expected future income. This means that young households have negative savings and older people positive savings. The life cycle hypothesis is explained in Chapter 10.

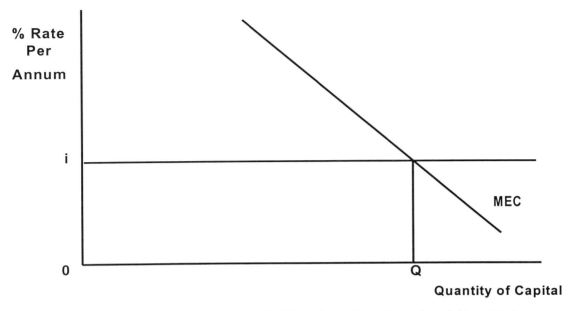

Diagram 8.4 Profit Maximising Stock of Capital

Market Supply of Capital:

Market supply curve of capital services is the sum of the quantities of capital supplied by all the individual firms. The short-run and long-run supply of capital are shown in Diagram 8.5 and as shown the supply of capital SS is inelastic as capital is heterogeneous and the long-run supply LS is elastic since additional capital equipment can be produced. If the interest rate is higher than r, savings increase while if it is below r savings decrease.

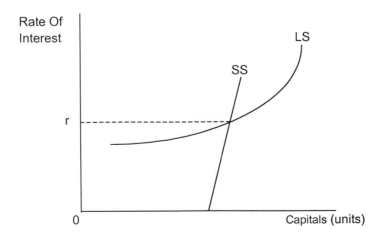

DIAGRAM 8.5 Short and Long-Run Supply of Capital

SAVINGS:

Saving is non-consumption or that part of disposable income that is not spent in the current period.

Supply Curve of Savings:

Do individuals and firms supply more savings out of a given income if interest rates increase? The answer seems to be no. Savings are relatively price inelastic as interest rates change as shown in Diagram 8.6 (a). Income is much more important than price in determining the supply of savings, as shown in Diagram 8.6 (b). This means that as income goes up, a decreasing fraction of it goes to consumption, so an increasing fraction of it will be saved.

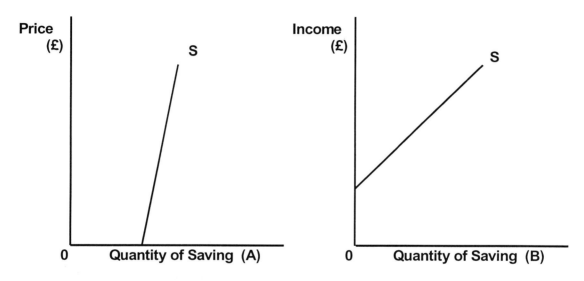

DIAGRAM 8.6 Supply Curve of Savings

Enterprise:

The activity of combining land, labour and capital is called enterprise and can be included as a fourth factor of production. Profit is the price of enterprise and it is the factor of production provided by the entrepreneur. The traditional view of the entrepreneur was as the owner - manager of a business. The modern view is that a group of shareholders who have put money into a business but are not involved in the day to day running of it are also entrepreneurs.

The entrepreneur must have the initiative and skill to organise the factors of production, i.e. land, labour and capital so that business opportunities can be exploited. He or she must be able to identify needs and opportunities and to respond to these in a creative way. There is no guaranteed reward yet responsibility for the risks involved falls on the entrepreneur. If the enterprise is successful the reward is profit, but if it fails the firm makes a loss. It is the only factor that can earn a negative return i.e. a loss.

Economic Rent:

This idea came from **David Ricardo (1772-1823)** and applied to land but can now be applied to any factor of production. Ricardo made two assumptions, first that the supply of land was fixed and secondly that land had only one use, i.e. to grow food. At the time demand for land was very high because Napoleon had cut off European grain from the UK market. As a result landlords were able to charge very high rent for land, on which to grow grain. Since supply was fixed landlords did not create more land but were receiving more money. If demand for land fell, rents also fell, but the supply of land did not change. Ricardo said rent was a producer's surplus.

The fact that land had only one use and that supply was perfectly inelastic is shown in Diagram 8.7.

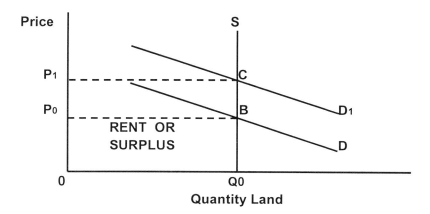

DIAGRAM 8.7 A Factor Earning only Economic Rent

Q_0 amount of land is available regardless of the price of land. D is the demand curve for land and price is P_0. Earnings of landlords of OP_0BQ_0, would consist of economic rent since nothing needs to be paid to attract land into use. Suppose the price of corn goes up and the derived demand for land rises to D_1 the new price of land P_1 merely increases economic rent by $P_0 P_1 CB$.

Ricardo's views have been modified in two important ways:

- It is now accepted that the supply of land is only fixed in the global sense. There are a number of markets for land for example agriculture, housing and property. A change in the price of land for one use causes land to shift from use to use so that there is some elasticity of supply built up.

- The modern view of economic rent is that it is a form of surplus payment to any factor of production over and above the minimum necessary to keep it in its current use. It is a payment to a factor over and above its supply price. A soccer player may earn £2,000 a week because his skills are in great demand. If he was not such a good player he may play for £500 a week. His transfer earnings are £500. The remaining £1,500 is his economic rent which equals total earnings minus transfer earnings.

Economic Rent and Labour:

To obtain the use of labour, you must pay it's supply price or transfer earnings that are the minimum amount a factor must earn in a specific use in order to stop it transferring to an alternate use. In the case of labour it is what people must be paid to persuade them to stay in their present job. If the earnings of a factor fall it will transfer to some other use. If a plumber's weekly wage rate is £500 then to obtain his services you must pay him £500 per week. Suppose he becomes a professional rugby player and earns £2,000 per week, then his economic rent is £1,500.

Economic Rent and Land:

Land is supplied by nature and man to increase the overall supply can do little. Supply price is zero. All payments for the factor of production land is considered to be economic rent.

Economic Rent and Enterprise:

Normal profit is the supply price of enterprise and in the long run production will not take place if it is not earned. If supernormal profit is earned the entrepreneur is earning more than is necessary to keep him in production. Supernormal profit is also economic rent as it is more than he would get in his next best alternative employment that must be at least equal to a normal profit.

Transfer Earnings:

Transfer earnings are the minimum amount a factor must earn in a specific use in order to stop it transferring to an alternate use. In the case of labour it is what a person must be paid to persuade him or her to stay in his or her present employment. If the earnings of a factor fall it will transfer to some other use. They can be seen as the opportunity cost of keeping a factor in its current use.

Separating Economic Rent and Transfer Earnings:

In general the earnings of the factor will be made up of both economic rent and transfer earnings. If we take the market supply curve for nurses in Diagram 8.8 we see that starting at point X and moving to point Y in Diagram 8.8 as the wage rate rises more nurses are attracted to the profession. At each higher wage new nurses are getting just enough to entice them to transfer into the profession, so that their wage is entirely transfer earnings. Nurses already in, get economic rent because they are now getting more than the minimum necessary to keep them in the profession. Workers' economic rent is the difference between the actual wage rate and the point on the supply curve at which they entered the market. In Diagram 8.7 at the market wage of Wm the total economic rent of all those employed is shown by area 1 which is the area above the supply curve and below the going wage. Area 2 shows transfer earnings.

Diagram 8.9 shows the extreme position of a totally inelastic supply curve. Some very specialised types of labour are in inelastic supply. This is particularly true of singers who have a very special talent, which can not be duplicated. Janet Jackson has a unique talent and the quantity of Janet Jacksons is fixed. Due to this fact her income is determined entirely by demand and is all economic rent. The supply curve is inelastic fixed at 1 in Diagram 8.9.

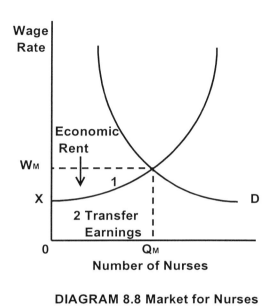

DIAGRAM 8.8 Market for Nurses

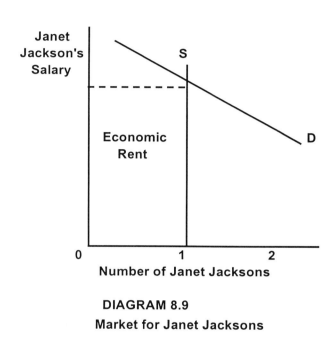

DIAGRAM 8.9
Market for Janet Jacksons

Questions

1. Using diagrams separate economic rent from transfer earnings.

2. What determines the demand for labour? Explain why an individual supply curve for labour may slope backwards at some sufficiently high wage level.

3. With the aid of a diagram explain economic rent and show how it arises. Examine the ways in which the concept can be applied to factors other than land.

4. "The size of economic rent earned by a particular type of factor depends upon the elasticity of supply of that factor and how the particular type of factor is defined." Critically evaluate this statement.

5. Explain why a world famous entertainer's earnings are mainly economic rent.

CHAPTER 9

MARKET FAILURE AND GOVERNMENT INTERVENTION

Introduction:

In Chapter 1 we looked at economic systems i.e. centrally planned, free market system and the mixed economy which is a mixture of the two. We then examined the operation of the market system. Even in the market system there are failures when market forces alone bring about an inefficient outcome. Government then intervenes in an effort to produce a more efficient outcome. The main examples of market failure examined in this Chapter are in:

- Production of public goods;

- Externalities in the production or consumption of goods and services;

- Merit and demerit goods;

- The absence of sufficient competition; and

- Problems with the distribution of income and wealth.

Public Private and Mixed Goods:

A pure **public good** is a good or service every one consumes and from which no one can be excluded. Public goods are an example of market failure, when the price system fails to produce a socially optimal quantity of a good or service, e.g. national defence. It is a category of goods that the free market, whether perfect or imperfect, will under produce or may not produce at all. A **private good** is a good or service each unit of which is consumed by only one person. Most goods are private goods and have two characteristics, i.e. excludability and diminishability. Excludability means that the owner of a good can exercise private property rights, preventing others from using it or enjoying its benefit's. Diminishability is when one person consumes a good, less of the benefits are available to others. Public goods have the opposite characteristic, i.e. non-excludability and non-diminishability. Many goods are called **mixed goods** and lie between a pure public and a private good. Castle Street in Tralee is a pure public good until it becomes congested when it becomes a private good.

Non Excludability:

This means that once the good is provided you cannot prevent anybody from getting the benefits from it. Security provided by the gardaí is a good example. It is virtually impossible to exclude any person in Ireland from enjoying the benefits of the security provided. Economists however argue that in the case of pure public goods there arises the free rider problem. A free rider is anyone who enjoys the benefits of a good or service without paying for it. It would be impossible for a private company to provide footpaths all along the streets of Tralee and then charge people to walk on them. The market fails because it fails to provide a service for which there is a need; therefore, the government provides the service.

Non-diminishing Consumption:

One person's consumption of a pure public good does not reduce the amount available for someone else. For example, your consumption of the security provided by the Gardaí does not decrease the security of anyone else. One family's enjoyment of network television does not take from the enjoyment of other families. It does not, however, mean that everyone benefits to the same extent. A criminal for example may not like the efforts of the Gardaí to provide security.

Market Failure Public Goods:

Goods supplied by private markets tend to be rival in consumption and have low exclusion costs. With rival consumption and exclusion, private firms can recover costs by charging prices that consumers must pay. The cost of excluding non-payers is sufficiently low so that it is possible to exclude them. In the absence of externalities competitive markets produce private goods efficiently.

Public goods are subject to market failure that occurs when the price system fails to produce a socially optimal quantity of a good or service e.g. national defence. A partial market failure occurs when private markets produce too little of a good. A total market failure occurs when private markets are unable to produce any of the good. With this type of good free riders will have little incentive to pay since they can obtain the good or service without paying, as it is too expensive to exclude them. Together with this the consumption of the free riders does not take from the consumption of others so that a public good will be underproduced or not produced at all by private markets.

Externalities:

Externalities are the positive or negative effects that the activities of production and consumption can have on third parties. An externality is therefore a special type of public good or public 'bad' which is 'dumped' on those who receive or consume it. This is likely to result in social inefficiency because individuals normally only consider the private costs of their decisions. Whenever other people are affected beneficially there are said to be external benefits and when they are affected adversely there are said to be external costs.

External Costs of Production:

Marginal social cost (MSC) is the cost incurred by the producer of a good plus MC imposed as an externality on others. An electricity generating station using coal has external negative costs of production such as acid rain, pollution, the 'eyesore' provided by the station itself and pylons which distribute the electricity around the country. The MSC of electricity production exceeds the marginal private cost (MC). A negative externality would result if the discharge of industrial waste into rivers decreased the catch of commercial fishers. Another example is intensive farming, which removes hedges and ditches thus destroying wildlife. Diagram 9.1 shows that the MSC curve is above the MC curve. The socially optimum output for the firm is Q_2 when P = MSC. Production is at Q_1, which is greater than the social optimum (Q_2) so that external costs result in overproduction from society's point of view.

External Benefits of Production:

A pure production externality is generated in production and it is passed on to other firms, either as an increase in their costs in the case of a negative externality or a reduction when positive externalities are received. The air corps spends money training pilots and each year some of these pilots leave to work for private companies. These companies' costs are reduced since they do not have to train such pilots. Society has benefited from their training even though the Air Corps has not. The marginal cost of air transport is less than the marginal private cost. Another example of external benefits in production is that of research and development undertaken by a particular firm if other firms have access to the results.

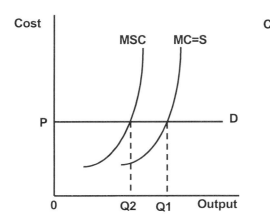

DIAGRAM 9.1 External Costs in Production

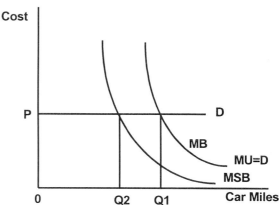

DIAGRAM 9.2 External Costs in Consumption

External Costs of Consumption:

External costs of consumption are outlined in Diagram 9.2. Marginal social benefit (MSB) is the £ value of benefit from one additional unit of consumption, including any external benefit. Cars cause traffic congestion, pollution and noise, so that the MSB of using them is less than the marginal private benefit or marginal utility. The optimal distance travelled for the motorist is Q1 miles: i.e. MU = P as shown in Diagram 9.2. Price is the running costs of the car. The social optimum would be less i.e. Q2 miles where MSB = P. Another example of an external cost of consumption is litter on the streets and beaches.

External Benefits of Consumption:

There are many commodities, which are partly public and are likely to be the type of good or service where social benefits exceed private benefits. An example of this is Iarnrod Eireann that makes commercial losses and is subsidised by the government. This is not a pure public good since people who do not pay the fares are excluded from the trains. The social benefits of travel by public rail transport are greater than the private benefits. People who travel by train contribute to a reduction of traffic congestion, as there is less exhaust and fewer road accidents. The marginal social benefit of rail travel is greater than the marginal private benefit. There are external benefits of consumption from rail transport. Another example is the benefit accruing to a commercial beekeeper from the gardens of private households.

Externalities - Government Intervention:

The main methods of government intervention are:

- **Changes in Property Rights:** One cause of market failure is the limited nature of property rights. There are many assets owned by the community such as water and land and private individuals and firms often pollute these. When private land is polluted the owner can sue the culprit. If a neighbour has a large heap of top soil over grown with weeds and it is in full view through your sittingroom window there is nothing you can do since you have no property rights over the neighbour's lawn or lack of it. The atmosphere is not owned. People living near Dublin Airport object to the extension of the runway because of the noise factor. It is, of course, impractical to suggest that aircraft be diverted because an individual on night shift cannot sleep during the day. As regards a neighbour playing loud music and having noisy parties it should be possible to prevent this under the noise abatement Act. In general the government must take action to prevent pollution of land, water and so on.

- **Persuasion**: Government can run public campaigns to persuade people to do things or not to do things. For example, the public can be encouraged to protect property from theft and be discouraged from smoking.

- **Taxation and Subsidies:** Taxation and subsidies can be used to make up the missing market in the externality. If the cost of negative externalities, e.g. pollution is established then a tax can be imposed on the person or firm responsible for the pollution. This provides on incentive lacking in the market for less of the negative externality. The firm must now include this cost in its price. If this tax is set so that the adjusted price to the consumer equals MSC an allocatively efficient level of production and consumption may be achieved. In the case of pollution, it may be that this tax will give the polluter an incentive to evade it by dumping waste at night to avoid detection.

- **Regulation and Controls**: Government can ban production of certain goods such as drugs.
When a negative externality exists firms can be prohibited by law from producing more than the socially efficient output. There will however be no incentive for firms to reduce pollution, so that a better method is to place a legal maximum on the amount of pollution the firm can produce. Dangers from machinery may be impossible to exclude from certain

methods of production but acceptable levels can be established which is less than the market system would choose.

Merit Goods:

Merit goods are those which the government believes are socially desirable and they are distributed on the basis of merit or need rather than by price. Merit good such as education is a good or service from which the social benefits of consumption to the whole community exceed the private benefits to the consumer. For this reason the government intervenes to ensure that consumption of these goods and services is higher than it would be under the free interplay of market forces. Higher consumption is achieved by way of subsides or in some cases by compulsion. Whereas markets may fail to supply any quantity at all of a pure public good such as defence, they can certainly provide services such as health and education. Reflected in the existence of private hospitals and schools where fees are paid. However if hospitals and schools are available only through the market at prices unadjusted by subsidy, people, particularly the poor, will consume too little of these services. The government therefore encourages consumption by means of subsidies or by providing them free of charge.

Demerit Goods:

These are goods whose consumption the government discourages as they impose negative externalities on society rather than just on the individual consumer. The social costs to the whole community which result from the consumption of a demerit good such as tobacco or alcohol exceeds the private costs incurred by the consumer. Cigarette packets carry a government health warning, so the dangers of smoking are well known. The price of cigarettes is not related to the cost of providing the health care smoking needs so that cost falls partly on the taxpayer. Provision through the market is inefficient because the market price leads to over consumption in relation to the socially optimal level. Drugs and pornography are other examples of demerit goods.

Market Failure and Perfect Competition:

Perfect competition is used as a standard against which to judge market failure in monopoly and imperfectly competitive markets. Even if the conditions of perfect competition listed in Chapter 6 were found in the real world market failure is still very likely to occur for the following reasons:

- Perfect competition can only achieve economic efficiency in the absence of economies of scale (Chapter 6). Even if economies of scale are possible it may not achieve productive efficiency because there may not be room for large numbers of firms all benefiting from economies of scale.

- Markets must exist for every single good or service not only now but also in the future. Markets that could exist but do not are known as missing markets and the latter is an important type of market failure.

- All markets within the perfectly competitive market economy worldwide must be in simultaneous long run equilibrium to have economic efficiency throughout the economy.

Market Failure Monopoly and Imperfect Competition:

Marginal cost must equal the marginal benefit of output in all markets if the allocation of resources is to be socially optimal. Under monopoly and imperfect competition the marginal condition will not be met. The profit maximising monopolist produces at an output where price is greater than marginal cost. Government can intervene here to increase output and lower price so as to reach social optimum. It can also tax away super normal profits.

Policies to Reduce Monopoly Power:

The following are some of the measures available for dealing with this type of market failure:

- When artificial barriers protect the monopoly the government can reduce or remove them.

- The government can nationalise the industry.

- Rules regarding price, the government can lay down output and rates of return. It can also set down minimum standards for such things as quality, standards and productivity.

- Taxation can be used to take away excessive profits.

Monopsony:

Monopsony firms are in a position to use their market power to force the prices of goods and services they purchase below those which the competitive market would determine. Price and output are not at their optimum and as a result resources are misallocated. An example of this arises in a town where one or two firms are sole employers of labour. The government can deal with these in the same way as outlined for monopoly.

Cobweb Model:

This is a model of a market which assumes that producers' output decisions respond with a lag to price changes. This type of market failure is associated with expectations and is particularly associated with agricultural products. Take potatoes as an example. With the supply and demand curves shown in Diagram 9.2. quantity demanded initially is Q_1 and price is P_1. Estimating that this will be next year's price, growers now plant Q_2 that they are willing and able to sell at P_1. However when they come to sell it is found that they can only sell Q_2 at price P_2. This leads them to estimate that next year's price will be P_2 so that they will grow Q_1 next harvest time and the price will go back to P_1. If price changes get bigger over time we have a divergent cobweb when the demand curve is steeper than the supply curve. If price changes get smaller over time we have a convergent cobweb when the supply curve is steeper than the demand curve.

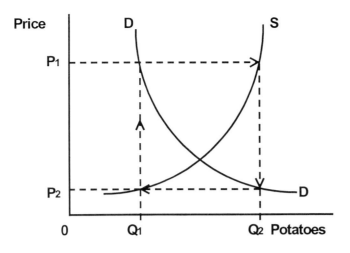

DIAGRAM 9.3 Cobweb

Lumpy Investment:

This is where expansion takes place through large units of investment. If for example demand is rising for the goods of a particular oligopoly with four firms in the industry, they probably all make sizeable investments in plant and machinery to take advantage of the additional demand. It is very likely that this will result in excess capacity and losses for all, resulting in market failure. On the other hand, if none of the four firms expand demand will not be met, and economic rent will be earned. This problem of lumpy investment can only be cured if one firm from the industry is allowed to expand.

Imperfections Affecting Factor Behaviour:

When factors are relatively immobile, supply will tend to be inelastic in the short-run so that even though price is increased substantially it will not bring about any sizeable factor movement. Workers may be unaware of job vacancies because the market does not properly communicate them. Unions may interfere with the free movement of labour by limiting membership while at the same time having closed shops.

Imperfections Affecting Consumer Behaviour:

In general goods are supplied to satisfy the tastes of consumers and if this is done the market system will work. However consumers must have correct information about the goods they buy and if this is not supplied, the market will fail.

Income and Wealth Distribution:

So far we have looked at markets with regard to economic efficiency and have taken market failure to mean that markets have not been economically efficient in the use of resources. We must now look at equity, which means justice or fairness. The free operation of markets leads to vast inequalities in the distribution of income and wealth. The government can intervene in a number of ways to reallocate income:

- It can use a progressive tax system so that the proportion of income paid in tax increases with the level of income. Making the better off contribute more than the poor are a form of redistribution. This may have disincentives for work and may also lead to a poverty trap where poor people are discouraged from working because any extra income they earn is largely taken from them in loss of benefits and taxes..

- Transfers in kind can also be given and may include supplementary benefits for the unemployed, free fuel and many other benefits.

- The government can intervene in the market, e.g. control of rents or prices.

- To redistribute wealth the government can put taxes on inheritances and other forms of wealth.

Questions

1. What is an externality? What effects do externalities have on the allocation of resources?

2. What are public goods? What government policies can be introduced to 'correct' the deficiencies of the free market?

3. Distinguish between social and private costs.

4. Outline the manner in which the price mechanism co-ordinates a market economy. Detail the circumstances in which a failure of the market mechanism may occur.

5. "Externalities are the positive or negative effects which the activities of production and consumption can have on third parties". Discuss the external costs and benefits of production and consumption.

6. What is meant by market failure and how is it caused? How can the government correct market failure?

CHAPTER 10

NATIONAL INCOME

Introduction:

National income is the sum of incomes received by the residents of a country as a result of economic activity. It is a money measure of production during a period of time, generally one year and it is the flow of goods and services produced in the year in question. This flow differentiates it from the stock of goods at a point of time and it is this difference that distinguishes national income from national wealth. It is the total income received by citizens in Ireland from all sources at home and abroad for a given year.

The government needs to know-:

- the value of the nations output and how it is changing over time;
- incomes generated in the course of producing that output; and
- How output is allocated between different uses.

This information is contained in the National Income and Expenditure Accounts compiled by the Central Statistics Office.

The main problem in compiling national accounts is the provision of a summary of the large numbers of individual transactions that take place in the economy. The problem of aggregation is solved by grouping together similar transactions into broad categories which are, consumption (C) investment, (I) government expenditure on goods and services, (G) exports (X) and imports (M)

National Income =C +I+ G+ X – M.

An attempt is made to measure a country's total production of goods and services for the following reasons:

- So that economists can test theories of how the macro-economy operates against real world data.

- By use of these theories, government officials and economists endeavour to come up with policies that will increase the country's production level and national welfare.

- Data for the past enables business people plan for the future by providing them with a basis for estimating future trends and needs.

Gross Domestic Product (GDP):

Total output in money terms or total income from production of the economy is known as Gross Domestic Product (GDP) and it is made up of the value of all final goods and services produced over a year. It is calculated, at factor cost, i.e. excluding subsidies and taxes imposed on goods and services. Essentially it is the total cost of production. Most international comparisons are based on GDP, particularly within the EU.

Gross National Product (GNP):

Gross National Product (GNP) means the value of all final goods and services produced in an economy in a given period of time usually a year, plus any net factor income it obtains from abroad. It measures a flow of goods and services over the year, is calculated gross and is the most commonly used index of economic welfare. However, in the course of production machinery wears out and stocks are used up resulting in, depreciation of capital. If we do not allow for this and just add new investment goods produced then we have GNP. Total output should only include net investment. This represents the value of new investment goods and stocks less depreciation on existing capital stocks used up. The result is Net National Product (NNP) - Table 10.1 for 1997. Firms claim the amount of depreciation allowed for tax purposes. This may not be an accurate measure of depreciation so GNP is used in preference to NNP.

GNP includes net factor income from abroad, that is negative due to debt service payments to non residents, and multinational companies in Ireland repatriating their profits to their parent companies abroad. GNP is GDP plus net factor income from abroad. In Ireland's case GDP is greater than GNP since net factor income from abroad is negative. For this reason, GNP is used, for international comparison.

GNP at Market Prices:

- Add depreciation to NNP to obtain GNP at factor cost

- Add taxes and subtract subsidies to obtain GNP at market prices.

- To obtain GNP from GDP add net factor outflow (which is negative for Ireland).

Gross National Disposable Income (GNDI):

Figures for GNP do not take into account international transfers that are not in exchange for goods and services. Transfers coming in to Ireland include grants from the EU, which are very substantial. Outgoing transfers include Overseas Development Aid (ODA) and contributions to EU. When net transfers from the rest of the world are added to GNP, GNDI for 1997 is obtained (Table 10.2).

National Income per Capita or per Person:

GNP divided by total population is the basic measure of living standards and this is known as per capita income. When national income per capita is used to make comparisons it can be misleading. Two countries may have the same income per capita even though in one country most people have nearly the same income while in the other some few are very rich and the majority very poor. The rich pull up the average. A better measure would be the median income where 50% of the population have less than this figure and 50% have more. GNP can also be measured as per head of employed population and this allows us to compare how much the average worker produces. GNP at constant 1990 market prices per head of population shown in Table 10.3 shows a steady increase over the period 1992/97 as does the same measure for per person at work, over the same period.

Table 10.1
National Income 1997
Relationship between GDP at Market Prices and National Income

	£ MN
Gross Domestic Product at Market Prices	48,241
Plus Net Factor Income from abroad	-6,322

Gross National Product at Market Prices	41,919
Less Indirect Taxes	-7458

	34,461
Plus Subsidies	2,010

GNP at Factor Cost	36,471
Less Depreciation	5,113

Net National Product at Factor Cost **(National Income)**	31,358
	======

Source: National Income and Expenditure Accounts 1997 (Table10.3) CSO

GDP Growth:

Prior to 1990 Ireland's growth rate was unexceptional. There has been controversy over the Irish GDP figures and opinion is that they are artificially inflated. This opinion is based on the fact that multinational companies' profits are part of Irish GDP and that they artificially increase these by transfer pricing. Transfer pricing in this case is used to minimise the company's tax liability, internal prices being set so that the greatest profit is earned in those countries with the lowest rates of company taxation. Repatriated profits cause a gap between GDP and GNP and this has widened over the past number of years.

Table 10.2
Gross National Disposable Income 1997

	£Million
GDP at Market Prices	48,241
+ Net Factor Income from Abroad	-6,322
GNP at current Market Prices	41,919
+ Net Transfers from Abroad	1,290
Gross National Disposable Income (GNDI)	43,209

Sources: National Income and Expenditure 1997, CSO

Table 10.3
Irish National Product Main Aggregates 1992 - 1997
Per Head of Population and Per Person at Work

Year	1992	1993	1994	1995	1996	1997
Per Head of Population £'s						
GDP Current Market Prices	8,400	9,077.2	9,824.5	10,917.8	11,843.0	13,177
GNP Current Market Prices	7,521	7,903	8,827.5	9,665.9	10,422	11,450
GDP Constant (1990) Price	8,062.6	8,241.2	8,764.1	9,636.9	10,247.0	11,113.0
GNP Constant (1990) Market Prices	7,138.1	7,293.0	7,809.8	8,460.8	8,909.0	9,504
Per Person at Work £.						
GDP Current Market Prices	26,310.	128,161.3	29,655.4	31,502.5	33,108.0	36,055.0
GNP Current Market Prices	23,507.0	25,105.1	26,646.0	27,890.2	29.137.0	31,329.0
GDP Current (1990)Prices	25,032.7	25,567.6	26,454.5	27,086.5	28,648.0	30,407.0
GNP At Constant (1990) Market Prices	22,162.4	22625.9	23,574.1	24,413.0	24,905.0	26,004.0

* Preliminary

Source: National Income and Expenditure 1997 Table A. ESRI February 1999

Between 1992 and 1997 real GNP per person in Ireland increased from £7,138.1 to £ 9504.0 a rise of £2,365.9 or 33%. GNP is used since it includes net factor flows whereas GDP does not. This is shown in Table 10.3.

Irish GDP grew by an estimated 10.6% in 1997 making it the fastest growing economy in the EU (Table 10.4).The estimate for 1998 is 11.4% while it is 3.0% for the Euroland and 2.9 for EU(15). Table 10.5 shows percentage growth for E.U. and selected countries for the period 1986 to 1990, 1991 to 1994 and estimated growth for 1995. Economic growth for the EU in 1996 is forecast at 2.5%.

Table 10.4

GDP Annual Average Change 1986/1990 and 1991/1995 and Percentage Change Constant

Price on Preceding Year 1996 to 2000

	1986/1990	1991/95	1995	1996	1997	1998*	1999*	2000*
Germany	3.4	2.1	2.2	1.4	2.2	2.8	2.2	2.6
United Kingdom	3.3	1.3	2.3	2.3	3.5	2.5	1.3	2.1
France	3.2	1.1	2.5	1.6	2.3	3.1	2.6	2.8
US	2.8	2.1	3.0	3.6	4.0	3.3	2.1	2.2
EU	3.3	1.5	2.5	1.8	2.7	2.9	2.4	2.8
Spain	2.3	0.5	2.4	1.3	1.8	3.0	2.8	3.0
Portugal	5.5	1.8	3.6	3.2	3.7	4.2	3.4	3.6
Ireland	4.6	6.2	9.5	8.3	10.6	11.4	8.2	9.0
Japan	4.6	1.4	0.9	3.9	0.9	-2.5	0.6	1.7

*Forecast

Source: European Economy EU Supplement A Economic Trends No 10 October 1998.

Reconciling Different Measures of GNP:

A. Measures of National Product:

Net Domestic Product at Factor Cost

+ Net Factor Income from Abroad
= Net National Product at Factor Cost

= National Income
+ Depreciation

= Gross National Product at Factor Cost

 - Subsidies

+ Indirect Taxes

= Gross National Product at Market Prices

B. Gross National Disposable Income:

GDP Market Prices

+ Net Factor Income from Abroad

= GNP at Market Prices

+ Net Transfers from Abroad

= Gross National Disposable Income.

GNP Adjusted for Terms of Trade:

Terms of trade can be measured by the ratio:

$$\frac{\text{Index of Export Prices}}{\text{Index of Import Prices}} \times \frac{100}{1}$$

An increase in the ratio means a given quantity of exports will purchase more imports, giving an improvement in the terms of trade. A decrease means more exports have to be sold to purchase a given quantity of imports, resulting in a deterioration in the terms of trade.

Consider the example of countries X and Y, each has 5 per cent growth in real GNP. Country X has a favourable movement in its terms of trade; import prices increase by 5% while export prices go up by 10%.

Country X's command over resources can be obtained as follows:

$$1.05 \times \frac{1.10}{1.05} = 1.1 = 10\% \text{ increase in command over resources.}$$

Country Y has unfavourable terms of trade and import prices increase by 10% while export prices increase by 3%. Command over resources is given by:

$$1.05 \times \frac{1.03}{1.10} = 0.98 = 2\% \text{ decrease in command over resources.}$$

Terms of Trade Adjustment:

This is the difference between the value of exports deflated by the price of imports and exports deflated by the price of imports i.e. $\frac{X}{PM} - \frac{X}{P}$

Country X's purchasing power has increased by 10% while that of country Y has fallen by 2%. This adjustment is in Table 8 of the National Income and Expenditure Accounts, CSO.

When the terms of trade for goods and services are better than in the base year the adjustment is positive. In years when there is an improvement in the terms of trade, the adjustment is larger than that in the preceding year so that the increase in the availability of goods and services to the community is larger than the change in GNP at constant prices.

Table 10.5 shows adjustments for terms of trade 1991 to 1997, 1990 is the base year and Px = Pm = 100 so that the effect is zero in 1990. Where the terms of trade for goods and services are better than in the base year the adjustment is positive. When there is an improvement in the terms of trade the adjustment is larger than that of the previous year. The adjustment is cumulative from the base year. The effect in 1997 was £-1825-(£-1657). In 1997 the terms of trade adjustment reduced GNP by 5.2%. The volume of GNP increased by 8.2% and GNDI grew by 8% after the adjustment effect.

Real National Income - GDP Deflator:

Inflation is a particular problem when national income is used as a measure of national wealth. The nominal national income for any year is national income at current or prevailing prices in that year. Real national income is national income after allowing for inflation and is said to be measured at constant prices. The constant price series is the current price series deflated by the relevant deflator.

The procedure for converting nominal GDP to real GDP is as follows:

- Measure each year's GDP at the price that ruled in a selected base year, say 1990;

- Establish the difference between price in the base year and the year for which the statistic is being calculated;

- Express average prices each year as an index with the index for the base year being 100; and

- The formula is:

$$\frac{\text{Real GDP}}{\text{Year A}} = \frac{\text{Nominal GDP}}{\text{Year A}} \times \frac{\text{Price Index Base Year}}{\text{Price Index Year A}}$$

Table 10.5
Gross National Disposable Income at Constant (1990)
Market Prices Adjusted for Terms of Trade 1991- 1997

Description	1991	1992	1993	1994	1995	1996	1997*
			£millons				
GNP at constant (1990)market prices (average estimate)	24,809.7	25,376.0	26,065.0	28,006.1	30,467.4	32,302.0	34,793.0
Terms of trade Adjustment	-432.5	-639.4	-315.8	-848.9	-1,590.7	−1657.0	-1825.0
Net current transfers from abroad at constant(1990) prices	1,570.7	1,231.2	1,239.8	1,064.9	981.6	1,205.0	1,139.0
Gross national disposable income at constant (1990) market prices	25,947.9	25,967.8	26,989.0	28,222.1	29,858.3	31,851	34,106.0
Index of gross national disposable income at constant (1990) prices	101.0	101.1	105.1	109.9	116.3	124.0	132.8

* Preliminary

Source: National Income and Expenditure 1997 Table 8

Measurement of National Income:

There are three different methods of measuring it:

- The income method;
- The output method; and
- The expenditure method.

Theoretically measurement by any one of these methods will produce identical results. This allows the accuracy of all three to be checked against each other.

National Income ≡National Output≡ National Expenditure

Income Method:

Using this method the value of national product is obtained by adding together all incomes earned by the basic factors of production. Total value of national product using this method is known as 'national product at factor cost' and counts all incomes from productive activity such as wages, salaries, profits and rent.

Table 10.6
National Income
Income Method 1997 and 1998

	£Millions 1997	£Millions 1998*
Income from Agriculture Forestry and Fishing	2,371	2,252
Non Agricultural Income	37,239	42,284
	39,610	44,536
Adjustment for Financial Services	-1,930	-2,282
	37,680	42,254
Net Factor Income from the rest of the World	-6,322	-7,682
Net National Product at Factor		
Cost National Income	31,358	34,572

Estimate*

Source: Income and Expenditure Accounts 1997. Table 1. ESRI February 1999

Only incomes that are the reward for productive activity should be counted and incomes in kind must also be included. These are received in non-monetary form and an example of this is the consumption of part of his output by a farmer. All transfer payments must be excluded (pensions, sickness benefits, interest on national debt, etc.). These payments do not add up to current marketable output, they merely transfer the power to purchase output from those who have produced it in the first place (usually tax payers) to those who receive the transfer payments. If we included it again we would be double counting. Another problem is that profit is overstated when the value of stock increases because of inflation. This is known as stock appreciation and must be deducted when all incomes are added. Details using this method are shown in Table 10.6.

Output Method:

All expenditure on the goods and services that have been produced in the country are added. It is sometimes referred to as the 'value added' method. Double counting must be avoided.

Double Counting:

The following example illustrates the method of counting assuming the cost of wheat to the farmer is £0:

Sale of wheat to millers£100, value added £100
Sale of wheat flour to bakers, £140, value added £40
Sales of bread to customers, £180, value added £40

Here, wheat and flour are intermediate goods that contribute to making bread that is a final good. When sales of all three goods are added, the total is £420, clearly an overestimate since all that is available to the consumer is £180 worth of bread. If, however, the value of each stage is measured, it will add up to £180 or the value of the "final" good.

Table 10.7
National Income
Output Method 1997*

	£ millions
1.Agricultural Production (farming, forestry and fishing)	2,372
2.Industrial Production	15,156
3.Distribution, Transport and Communications	6,731
4.Government services (Civil Service and Defence)	2,011
5.Other domestic (rent and remuneration of employees)	13,427
6.Adjustment for stock appreciation	-87
7.Adjustment for financial services	-1930
8.Net factor income from the rest of the world	-6,322
Net National Product at factor cost = National Income	31,358
Add Depreciation	5,113
Gross National Product at Factor Cost	36,471
Plus Taxes on Expenditure	7,458
Less Subsidies	-2,010
Gross National Product at Market Prices	41,919

Preliminary*
Source: National Income and Expenditure 1997

This method has the advantage that it shows:

- The separate contribution of all sectors to total output; and

- As all firms keep accounts of goods purchased and total sales, it is easy to calculate their value added.

Output of services must be included. It is difficult to value non- marketed services such as government services, this problem is solved by counting the cost of supplying the service as the

value of its output.

As the total of all value added is divided between the factors of production that contribute to it, the output measure also gives national product at factor cost. As it gives a breakdown of total output by sector, it is usually known as 'national product at factor cost by sector of origin'. This is shown in Table 10.7.

Black Economy:

Certain transactions not recorded or when their full value is not given so as to avoid tax, are referred to as the "black economy". The EU, in a report from the Commissioner for Social Affairs estimated that it amounts to 10% of Irish GDP. Output figures are understated and this reduces the reliability of the statistics.

Multinational Companies (MNCs):

MNCs sell raw materials and components to subsidiaries at artificially low prices to maximise profits in low tax countries. This practice artificially increases Irish output.

The Expenditure Method:

The aim here is to add up all expenditure on goods and services produced in the country during a particular year. There are a number of pitfalls that need to be avoided:

- Only expenditure on 'final' goods must be counted; expenditure on intermediate goods must be excluded otherwise it leads to double counting. An example of intermediate expenditure would be spending by the dairy co-operatives on milk (used to make butter). If we recorded the spending on butter and milk, the milk would have been counted twice since its cost goes to make up the final price of butter. This was explained under the output method.

- Transfer payments must be excluded.

- Total expenditure includes imports and this figure must be deducted so as to arrive at the amount spent on home production.

- Expenditure on second hand goods must be excluded. All sales of second hand houses, cars, and other goods must be omitted when compiling national accounts using this method as they add nothing to this year's product.

By adding all expenditure a figure for national product at market prices is obtained. To equate this figure with national product at factor cost, indirect taxes must be subtracted and subsidies added. Indirect taxes are deducted because they do not enter into factor incomes while subsidies are added because they do. Indirect taxes raise the market prices of goods and services while subsidies lower them. Details of expenditure data for Ireland in 1997 are shown in Table 10.8.

The main problem in compiling national accounts is the provision of a summary of the large numbers of individual transactions that take place in the economy. The problem of aggregation is solved by grouping together similar transactions into broad categories which are, consumption (C) investment (I) government expenditure,(G) exports (X) and imports (M)

National Income = C +I+ G+ X – M.

Uses of National Income Calculations:

A. To Indicate Standard of Living:

GNP is used to indicate the overall standard of living or income per head of the people of a country. To find how living standards change from year to year, constant market prices should be used. The national income cannot be accepted on its face value and the following qualifications must be made:

- Allowance must be made for the rise in the general level of prices from one year to another. We can correct for price changes very easily if all prices have moved to the same degree. When prices change in different degrees or directions, as they often do, the price problem becomes more difficult. Comparison of real GNP from one year to the next is arbitrary to some extent.

- If the population of a country is also increasing, the best figure for measuring economic growth is GNP per head of population.

- An increase in national income may be the result of longer working hours, inferior working conditions or increased urbanisation and therefore national welfare may not increase at all..

- If national income increases are due to military expenditure, it is misleading to look at this increase in income as an increase in the standard of living.

- Any labour or service that does not pass through a market is not counted as part of national income. Examples of this are roadside selling and do-it-yourself activity. Generally, the non-market sector is larger in rural than in urban areas and is less developed in developing economies than in developed.

- When people pay for services they previously performed themselves national income is inflated. If a married woman returns to work and employs someone to take her place in the home, she adds to the national income twice – yet her own work is the only net addition to services.

- National income or real GNP per head may be up even after allowing for inflation and an increase in the population but the standard of living may not have risen. There are three main reasons for this:

1. Ireland may have to pay more for imports due to a worsening in its terms of trade;

2. The increase in income may go to a small number if distribution of income is unequal; and

3. The increased income may be used for investment and in this case it will benefit the people later rather than now.

Table 10.8
National Income
Expenditure Method 1997 (1)

	£ millions	As % GDP
(C) Personal expenditure on consumer goods + and services.	25,191	52.2
(I) Gross domestic physical capital formation	9,448	19.6
+ Value of physical change in stocks +	539	0.01
(G) Net Expenditure by public authorities on current goods and services +	6,669	13.8
(X) Exports of goods and services	40,614	84.2
(M) Imports of goods and services	-34,220	-70.8
= Gross Domestic Product at current market prices (GDP)	48,241	100.0
+ Net factor income from the rest of the world (F)	-6,322	
= Gross National Product at current market prices (GNP)	41,919	

1 Preliminary
Source: National Income and Expenditure Accounts 1997, CSO Table 5.

B. For Standard of Living Comparisons:

Comparisons must be made in order to make certain decisions. How much help should developed countries give to less developed ones? Which countries are very rich and which countries are very poor?

National income figures must be subjected to qualifications on top of those mentioned in A. above:

1. Per capita figures should be used so as to allow for different population sizes. We need an estimate of per capita income, i.e.

    $$\text{NNP at factor cost} = \frac{\text{Per capita income}}{\text{Population}}$$

    Therefore growth in NNP must exceed population growth for living standards to rise.

2. Figures are expressed in different currencies and have to be converted into a common denominator, such as the US dollar. The use of exchange rates to convert National Income statistics into a common currency unit may produce unreliable results for comparative purposes. If an IR£1 is converted into US dollars it may not buy the same amount of goods in Ireland as in the US.

3. It is very difficult to measure GNP in a country with a large subsistence sector in agriculture. Output of unsold food must be estimated and this is further aggravated if it accounts for a large part of food production, as it does in many Third World countries. In the latter, food may be produced for household consumption and not for the market so that, it is not included in GNP in these circumstances and will understate real living standards.

4. Difference arises from climate or geography. Inhabitants of cold countries must spend a relatively large proportion of their income on keeping warm, while people in warm countries spend relatively little on this. Sparsely populated countries spend relatively more on transport and communications than densely populated countries. It does not necessarily follow that living standards are lower where expenditures are lower.

5. There are differences in income distribution in one country as against another and little is known about this. An oil producing state may have a high measured GNP but 80% of this may accrue to a very small group of people, leaving the mass of people worse off than those in a country where GNP is much lower but where income in distributed more evenly.

6. We have very little knowledge concerning the amount of GNP available for consumption. Government may take a large share in taxation and spend it on projects that may not benefit the average person directly.

C. To Calculate the Rate at which Income is Growing :

National Income figures, by showing a relationship between the level of investment and growth or between profits and the level of investment, is useful to the planning process.

D. Relationship between Different Parts of the Economy:

Having figures for the various components of the national income such as consumption spending and foreign trade assists central government planning.

E. To Assist the Government in Managing the Economy:

Equity in the distribution of the national income is important to the government for political and taxation purposes. Figures for national income assist in the achievement of this objective.

Factors Determining a Country's Material Standard of Living:

The major factors determining a country's material standard of living are examined below. For a country involved in economic relationships with the rest of the world, these factors can be classified into internal and external.

Internal:

- **Nature of People**

The standard of living will be higher the greater the proportion of workers to the total population and the longer their working hours. The quality of the labour force, i.e. health, skills, ability to organise and co-operate, energy, adaptability, enterprise, education and training, determines the standard of living.

- **Original Natural Resources**

This covers minerals, sources of energy, climate, fisheries and the quality of agricultural land. Exhaustion of mineral resources reduces output. Countries dependent on agriculture are subject to variations in the weather that may cause output to fluctuate from year to year. Endowment of natural resources is a major factor differentiating the rich from the poor countries. Saudi Arabia and Kuwait for example are rich because of their oil resources. Others like the US and Australia based their industrial development on natural resources.

- **Capital Equipment**

This is essential for the development of natural resources and labour. Machinery is necessary to extract copper and a turbine generator to harness a waterfall. Hotels are necessary to exploit game parks and other tourist attractions.

- **Organisation of the Factors of Production**

To achieve maximum output the factors must be organised efficiently. Far Eastern countries like Japan and Singapore are rich because of their ability to organise industrial production, effectively.

- **Political Situation**

An able and stable government is an incentive to investment particularly in long term capital projects and output is consequently greater.

External:

a) Terms of Trade

The rate at which one nation's goods exchange against those of other countries is referred to as the Terms of Trade. If the terms of trade move in the nation's favour, it means that it gets a larger quantity of imports for the same given quantity of exports.

b) Gifts and Grants from Abroad

When gifts and grants are used to further the economic development of the country receiving them the standard of living improves.

Questions

1. Describe the various methods of measuring the National Income. What difficulties occur in measuring it?

2. Explain the term 'standard of living'. Outline the factors that determine the standard of living in an industrialised country.

3. "For comparison of levels of economic and/or human welfare over time or between countries, GNP statistics suffer from certain deficiencies." Critically evaluate this statement.

4. Explain the differences between GNP, GDP and NNP.

5. National Income accounts are an important source of information and an indicator of economic trends, but care must be exercised when using them. Outline the apparent limitations in using them for analysis and comparison.

6. Distinguish between Gross National Product and Gross Domestic Product. State giving reasons, which of these you consider being the better indicator of the Irish standard of living.

7. You are given the following data for a hypothetical economy:

IR £m

Interest	240
Profit	360
Wages	1,320
Exports	720
Imports	840
Consumption expenditure	960
Government expenditure on goods	600
Government transfer payments	60
Investment expenditure	720
Subsidies	240
Income tax	240

a) What is the value of GDP at market prices?
b) What is the value of GDP at factor cost?
c) What is the value of the trade surplus?
d) What is the value of savings?

8. Explain the output method of measuring GNP and indicate how it differs from the income and expenditure methods.

CHAPTER 11

DETERMINATION OF NATIONAL INCOME

Introduction:

John Maynard Keynes (1883 1946) an Englishman put forward a model of income determination that is still considered the core of modern macroeconomics. Up to the 1930s economic thought was dominated by those who subscribed to the classical school whose philosophy was based on the operation of market forces. Keynes challenged this in his most famous work, The General Theory of Employment, Interest and Money, published in 1936. He was opposed to the laissez faire approach and gave a much greater role to government. From the 1950's to the 1980's many governments adopted his model of income determination. In this Chapter we study the accelerator theory that relates net investment to the rate of change of output. The circular flow of receipts and expenditure between firms and households is discussed. Simple models of income determination based on the idea of the circular flow of income are examined. The multiplier, which shows by how much national income increases following an increase in expenditure, is outlined.

The Keynesian Approach to the Determination of the National Income:

He used a simple model of aggregate demand and aggregate supply to explain how national income is determined. Equilibrium is where aggregate demand (AD) equals aggregate supply (AS). Aggregate supply is the total supply of all the goods and services available from domestic production to meet aggregate demand. The level of output is demand driven or determined by aggregate demand. He believed that the government taking measures to increase or decrease AD could manage the national economy. He suggested that there could be equilibrium at less than full employment. Unemployment could be high and may show no tendency to fall. He held that the most effective weapon of government economic strategy is its fiscal policy. To stimulate the economy to bring about full employment, it can increase aggregate demand through fiscal policy.

Aggregate Demand:

Aggregate demand is planned expenditure on national output. The quantity of output is demand determined, while the level of demand in the economy as a whole is known as aggregate demand. Keynes put forward a model of income determination in the 1930s, suggesting that the main factor behind short-term fluctuations is change in spending by households and firms.

The four components of demand or expenditure are consumption, investment, government expenditure and net exports. Aggregate (monetary) demand is equal to $C + I + G + X - M$. Since Y stands for national income, then national income is in equilibrium when $Y = C + I + G + X - M$ or $C + I + G + NX$ where NX equals net exports.

The factors influencing consumption, saving, investment, government sector and foreign trade are now examined.

Consumption - Consumer Spending:

It includes expenditure on imports but not investment. The level of the household's measured income, variability of its income, the rate of interest, availability of credit and expectations of inflation, unemployment and income, mainly determines a household's demand for consumption goods. We look at aggregate consumption that is the sum of all households' consumption. It is also dependent on wealth and savings as purchases can be made out of assets and savings of consumers and those with savings are more likely to spend.
Consumption is the spending by all the households in the economy upon goods and services. Keynes suggested that the amount spent on consumption goods depends mainly on the level of real income so that as income increases, the level of consumption increases. He maintained that each successive increment to real income would be matched by a smaller increment to consumption spending, the remainder being saved.

Personal consumption expenditure makes up approximately 58 per cent of total expenditure or aggregate demand in Ireland. The largest part is spending on non-durable goods such as food, clothing, energy - all items with relatively short economic lives. Next comes spending on services such as health, education, banking, insurance and entertainment. The third category is spending on durable consumer goods such as refrigerators, motor cars and radios.

Consumption Function:

The Consumption Function is the relationship between planned consumption and income and may be stated mathematically as follows:
Equation (1) $C = F (Yd)$ where Yd is disposable income and C is consumption. This equation states that the level of planned consumption, C, is dependent upon (or is a function of) the level of disposable income Yd. Disposable income is income less direct taxes or income tax. Here, we assume there is no government sector, therefore there is no tax, so that $Y = Yd$. Equation (1) does not tell us anything about the exact nature of the relationship between planned consumption and disposable income but equation (2) expresses this.

Equation 2: $C = a + bYd$: When income is zero, consumption equals a. What is the economic meaning of this value "a"? If income is zero, we have to run down our savings in order to survive and "a" represents this minimum requirement. As income rises, consumption also rises by a fixed proportion. The ratio of the increase in consumption to the increase in disposable income is known as the marginal propensity to consume (MPC) which in equation (2), is given by "b". An increase in consumption cannot be greater than an increase in income, therefore, MPC lies between zero and 1 and is expressed in decimal form.

In Diagram 11.1, consumption is measured on the vertical axis and income on the horizontal axis. Assume that a minimum of £500 is needed to survive, and that as disposable income increases, consumption increases by 0.8 (for every extra £ of income, £0.8 is consumed). Equation (2) is now $C = 500 + 0.8Yd$. The 45° line represents points where all income is spent, i.e. consumption is equal to disposable income. Consumption positions fall below this line except for where, due to extreme poverty, society is unable to save anything and all income goes on consumption (point s £2,500). If national income is £2,000, C=£2,100 S £100. If national income is £3,000 C=£2,900 and S=£100

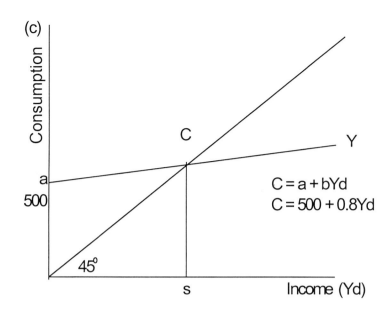

Diagram 11.1 Consumption Function

Factors other than Income Affecting Consumption:

Besides the level of income, spending decisions are affected by:

- **Changes in disposable income**: We have assumed that there is no government activity but in practice, government activity affects spending and increased direct taxation for example reduces disposable income. The C curve in Diagram 11.1 is lowered.

- **Distribution of wealth in the community:** As the proportion of income saved usually increases with income, greater equality of incomes is likely to reduce savings and therefore increase consumption. If income is redistributed from rich to poor then consumption rises as poor people spend a higher proportion of their incomes than rich people.

- **Anticipated change in the value of money:** If people expect prices to rise, then they spend now rather than save for the future. Spending planned for the future will be brought forward and again C rises.

- **Hire purchase and other credit facilities:** If the initial deposit is reduced, it will encourage consumption. The same applies if bank credit is made easier.

- **Time lag in adjusting spending habits:** It takes time for people to alter spending habits as income increases in the short term, therefore, savings increase. In this case C falls.

- **Invention of new consumer goods:** Over the past number of years, spending on televisions, cars and other consumer durable goods has increased, assisted by advertising and the necessity to keep up with the neighbours. These cause C to increase.

These changes bring about a change in the propensity to consume and the whole C line moves or changes its position. If income changes, movement is along the C line.

Propensity to Consume:

- Average propensity to consume (APC) concerns the proportion of total income spent or consumed. If income is £10,000 and the person spends £8,000, then:

$$APC = \frac{Total\ Consumption}{Total\ Income} = \frac{C}{Y} = \frac{£8,000}{£10,000} = 0.8$$

- Marginal propensity to consume MPC is a measure of the rate at which consumption changes as income changes. It is the proportion of a rise in national income that goes on consumption or that fraction of a person's additional income that is spent on consumer goods.

If, when income Y increases by £500, C increases by £400 then,

$$MPC = \frac{\Delta C}{\Delta Y} = \frac{£400}{=£500} = 0.8 \text{ where } \Delta = \text{change in}$$

The marginal propensity to save (MPS) is the proportion of an increase in national income saved. Since income is either consumed or saved MPC + MPS =1. MPC is the more important of the two concepts as the size of the multiplier is determined by it as we will see later in the chapter.

Table 11.1 shows the value of APC and MPC for different points on a consumption function.

Table 11.1
APC, MPC and the Consumption Function

	National Income £ bn	Planned Consumption C £ bn	Average Propensity To Consume (APC)	Marginal Propensity To Consume (MPC)
A	0	3	–	–
B	3	5	1.67	0.66
C	6	7	1.16	0.66
D	9	9	1.00	0.66
E	12	11	0.92	0.66
F	15	13	0.87	0.66
G	18	15	0.84	0.66
H	21	17	0.81	0.66
I	24	19	0.79	0.66
J	27	21	0.78	0.66
K	30	23	0.77	0.66

Diagram 11.2 is drawn from Table 11.1. MPC stays constant as Y rises, whilst APC declines. This occurs whenever a consumption function is a straight line as it is in Diagram 11.2.

APC can be calculated from any point on the C line e.g. H:

APC $= C/Y = 17/21 = 0.81$.

MPC is the slope of the line between two points, e.g. H and I: MPC $= 2/3 = 0.66$ = slope of the consumption function. The conclusion therefore is that the co-ordinates at any point on a consumption function will give the value of APC.

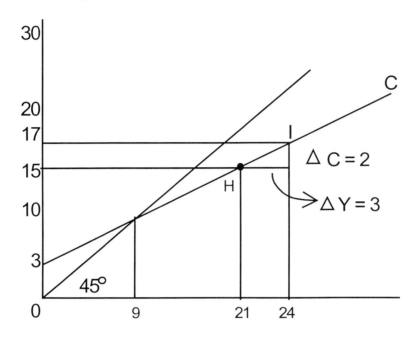

Diagram 11.2 National Income (£ Billion)

Modern Theories of the Consumption Function:

Permanent Income Hypothesis:

Milton Friedman developed this theory in 1957 and it is based on two hypotheses; first, people's incomes fluctuate and secondly, people do not like fluctuating consumption.

He holds that planned consumption is proportional to expected or permanent income. Friedman distinguished between permanent and transitory or windfall income received on a once off basis. Consumption depends on permanent income that is people's average (discounted) income in the long run. When income is seen to be temporarily high, people will not increase consumption but will increase savings to see them through when income is unusually low. If people consider that the rise in permanent income is more likely to continue they will increase current consumption, adjust their standard of living upwards and their APC will not fall.

The Life Cycle Hypothesis:

Franco Modigliani developed this theory, and it is very similar to the Permanent Income Hypothesis. It is useful to distinguish between contractual and non-contractual savings. Contractual saving is when people save early in life to buy a house and all through their working lives to finance retirement. These savings are contractual in the sense that they are contributions to pension funds, life assurance premiums and payments to building societies. Regular saving is done over the working years and then dissaving when the house mortgage is paid off or on retirement.

Non contractual savings can be for a once off decision to take a holiday or to buy Christmas presents. Dissaving in another part of the year follows saving for part of the year and they cancel one another out over a period of months or a year. Diagram 11.3 outlines the lifecycle theory of consumption.

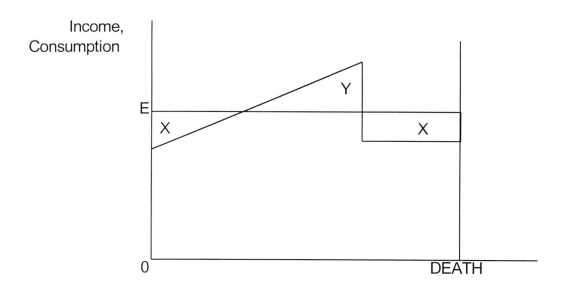

Diagram 11.3 Life Cycle Theory of Consumption

Actual income rises over a householder's lifetime and on retirement it falls to pension level. In Diagram 11.3, permanent income is the constant income level OE. Let consumption equal permanent income then the areas marked X show total dissaving and that marked Y total saving, so that X + X = Y. The household can therefore dissave early and late in life.

Propensity to Save:

If we take the amounts saved and express it as a proportion of income we arrive at the propensity to save.

(a) Average Propensity to Save (APS):

That proportion of total income that is saved is described as the average propensity to save. APS is S/Y so that if Y = £100m and S = £20m, then APS = 0.2. Since income is either spent or saved, APC +APS =1. Poorer households will spend a large part of their incomes so their APC will be close to 1, and APS will be very small.

(b) Marginal Propensity to Save (MPS):

MPS is that part of any small increment of income that is saved. If Y increases by £1 and S increases by 20 pence, then the marginal propensity to save is 0.2.

$$MPS = \frac{\Delta S}{\Delta Y} = \frac{20}{100} = \frac{1}{5} = 0.2.$$

Since any increment in income must be either spent or saved, MPC + MPS = 1.

The Savings Function:

As with consumption the major determinant of savings is income. The consumption function tells us not only how much households plan to consume, but also how much they plan to save. Diagram 11.4i and 11.4ii demonstrate this.

Diagram 11.4i shows the consumption function and 11.4ii shows the savings function, derived from the consumption function. The vertical distance between the C line and 45 degree line shows the planned saving at that income level. When income is OD, consumption is BD and saving as shown is AB. The 45 degree line makes OD = AD. In Diagram 11.4ii, saving is FG. We obtain the savings function by plotting the difference between the C line and the 45° line as positive and negative amounts of saving. Savings are zero at OE income level as all income is spent. Below OE, dissaving takes place, while above OE, saving is positive. Households spend more than their current income by dissaving, i.e. borrowing and running down their assets.

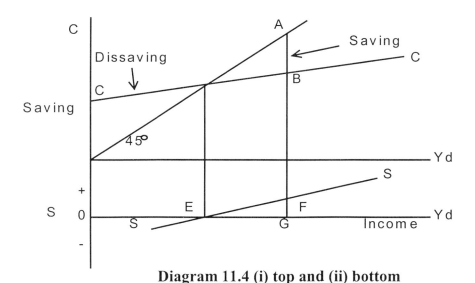

Diagram 11.4 (i) top and (ii) bottom

Diagram 11.4 Consumption and Savings Function

136

Factors other than income affecting savings are as follows:
Personal Saving:

- **Government Policy:**
There are a number of ways the government can influence savings and peoples attitudes towards savings. The Post Office attempts to stimulate savings by income tax concessions. The Post Office does not charge for handling Savings Bank Deposit Accounts, and tax is not deducted from interest earned on Savings Certificates and National Instalment Savings. Special deposit accounts with financial institutions at 15 per cent deposit interest retention tax DIRT is now allowed under certain conditions.

- **Contractual Savings:**
Building societies and insurance companies encourage regular savings which can be classified as contractual savings.

- **Psychological Attitudes:**
This type of saving is a provision against such things as sickness, unemployment and old age.

- **Speculation:**
Saving is undertaken to enable the saver to speculate should the opportunity present itself.

- **Business Saving:**
Saving by business is undertaken when the shareholders have received their share of the profit for the year. The portion kept back as retained earnings can be "ploughed back" into the business.

Factors affecting Business Savings:

- Profits are the main determinant here.

- Much depends on how forward-looking the business is and its determination to provide for future commitments.

- Taxation policy with regard to dividends would also have a bearing since if tax on them is increased it may be better to retain more of the profit.

Government Saving:

- The main source of government saving is through a budget surplus when revenue exceeds expenditure.

- Saving by semi state bodies would come under this heading since they are basically under government control.

- Local authorities could have a 'budget surplus'.

Investment Function:

Investment means expenditure on new capital goods by government or firms. For a given firm, an investment project would be worth undertaking if in very general terms, it were expected to be profitable. It is expenditure on aids to production such as machinery and infrastructure such as roads.

Investment is a flow concept, which measures spending on these items over a period, for example, one-year. Estimates of future returns depend to a large extent on expected future demand and on current supply capacity. High future net cash flows will stimulate investment unless there is adequate spare capacity to meet the expected demand without further capital investment.

A businessperson will invest in new capital equipment only if he expects to obtain revenue from it equal to its cost. Its cost is likely to be made up of the purchase price and the price of funds locked up in it. The purchase price is not likely to vary in the short term but the price of funds or interest rates can change. If investment is to be financed by bank borrowing or fixed-interest-stock issues, the rate of interest will be very important. While equity financing will be cheaper the higher the general level of stock market prices.

Over the long term, investment is affected by the relative costs of labour and capital. Different techniques of production are characterised by different ratios of labour to capital equipment, and choice of technique is influenced by the relative costs of the two factors.

Keynes recorded the level of aggregate investment to be mainly determined by (a) expectations of businesspersons about future profitability and (b) the rate of interest. Not all economists are convinced of the absolute importance of the rate of interest apart from its effect on profitability and they argue that expectations alone determine the level of investment. There is agreement that the level of investment is not directly linked to national income in the same way as consumption is. Here we assume that investment expenditure is independent of the level of the current national income, therefore, the investment function can be represented by a line parallel to the income axis for all income levels as in Diagram 11.5. When consumption and investment expenditure are taken into account, aggregate demand is represented by C + I.

Savings and Investment:

The Classical economists assumed that savings always equal investment and that savings re-entered the economy as expenditure on goods and services. Keynes held that since the same people are not necessarily both savers and investors, actual investment might not equal actual planned savings. However, actual investment must equal savings when planned investment is greater than savings and hence greater than actual investment. This means that stocks are being run down and could cause firms to increase production hence increasing income. When planned investment is less than savings and actual investment, this suggests that stocks be built up. This may cause firms to cut back production and so reduce national income and output.

	Unplanned Stocks	Income
Planned Investment > savings	falling	rises
Planned Investment < savings	rising	falls
Planned Investment = savings	zero	constant(equilibrium)

Determinants of Investment:

- **The Rate of Interest:**

The rate of interest measures the cost of capital to the firm. The higher the rate of interest the more expensive it is for firms to invest so that firms will invest more the lower the rate of interest. There is little agreement on how responsive total investment in the economy is to changes in interest rates. Keynesians look on the relationship between interest rates and investment as a highly stable one. In times of depression interest rates will have little bearing on investment, as opportunities to invest are very limited at such times.

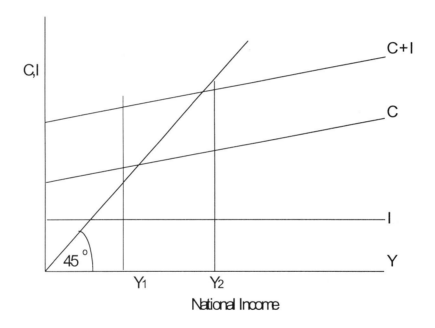

Diagram 11.5 Investment Function

- **Increased Consumer Demand:**

Increased productive capacity is provided only when consumer demand increases. The greater the increase in consumer demand the more capacity or investment required. This does not mean that investment depends on the level of consumer demand but it does mean that it depends on how much it has risen. The relationship between increased consumer demand and investment is looked at when the 'accelerator' principle is examined.

- **Cost and Productivity of Capital Goods:**

A new process that reduces the cost of capital goods will make investment more profitable. For example, if the rate of interest is 15 per cent and a machine costs £10,000 down from £15,000, the interest cost is down from £2,250 to £1,500.

A new invention that makes capital equipment more productive will make investment more attractive. Technological progress is an important determinant here.

- **Expectations:**

Expectations of future demand conditions and cost conditions have a strong influence on the level of investment since it is made in order to produce output for the future. If business people are pessimistic about the future, low rates of interest will not encourage them to borrow whereas if they are optimistic, high rates of interest will not necessarily put them off.

Sometimes expectations about the future can change dramatically and quickly, and was described by Keynes as the animal spirits of business persons. A sudden swing from pessimism to optimism about future projects can result in a large increase in desired investment while the reverse ends in drastic cutbacks in investment plans.

Investment and Income:

Investment is not totally independent of national income, as part of firms' investment is to replace worn out or outdated equipment. This type of investment will depend on the level of national income since the greater the current level of national income the greater the stock of capital and consequently more will have to be replaced each year. If the level of national income is high firms' profits are high, therefore, they can invest more.

Investment that arises when a firm wishes to satisfy an increase in demand for its product is called induced investment. This type of investment is related to the rate of change in income and is the basis for a theory of investment known as the acceleration principle.

Instability of Investment: Acceleration Principle:

The acceleration principle is based on the argument that when income is increasing, it will be necessary to invest so as to increase capacity to produce consumption goods; investment may also be high because business expectations based on the rising trend of sales may be favourable. If, however, income is falling, it may be necessary to replace capital equipment as it wears out; also expectations may be unfavourable due to falling trends in sales. Investment is, therefore, a function of changes in income. The accelerator theory rests on the assumption that there is a fixed relationship between output and the amount of capital needed to produce it, i.e. the capital-output ratio.

If £4m of capital is needed to produce £1m of annual output, the capital-output ratio is 4:1. Table 11.2 gives the effect of a constant rise of income. If output is to grow by £1000m, then an extra £4000m of net investment will be required and since, income rises by the same rate, there is no change in net investment.

Table 11.2
Effect of a Constant Rise in Income

Period	Income (£m)	Extra Income (£m)	Extra Capital Needed (Net Investment) £m
1	1,000	1,000	4,000
2	2,000	1,000	4,000
3	3,000	1,000	4,000

Table 11.3 shows the effect of a slow down in the increase in income.

Table 11.3
Effect of a Slow down in Increase in Income

Period	Income (£m)	Extra Income (£m)	Extra Capital Needed (Net Investment) £m
4	3,750	750	3,000
5	4,250	500	2,000
6	4,500	250	1,000
7	4,600	100	400
8	4,650	50	200
9	4,650	0	0
10	4,650	0	0

In period 4, income grew by £750m requiring net investment of £3,000m. There is a fall of £1000m from period 3 shown in Table 11.2. Investment falls when growth in the economy slows down. If the rate of growth of income decelerates, net investment declines. Table 11.4 shows that if the growth of income accelerates, net investment increases and again the capital output ratio is 4:1.

Weaknesses of the Accelerator Theory:

- The upward leverage effect of the accelerator only takes effect if the industry is operating at or near full capacity. If firms have excess capacity and/or carry stocks left over from a previous upsurge in demand, they can, by using this capacity, increase output without the need to invest in additional fixed capital.

- It is too mechanical in that it assumes all firms react to increased demand in the same way. Some firms will wait to see if increased demand is permanent while others will order more machinery than they need.

- Demand for capital goods may increase when industries producing them are at full capacity. Prices will go up and may cause firms to economise in the use of capital. In other words, the capital output ratio will change.

Firms may make investment plans a long time in advance and may be unable to change them quickly.

Table 11.4
Effect of a Rise in Increase in Income

Period	Income £mn	Extra Income £mn	Extra Capital needed (Net Investment) £mn
1	6,000	-	-
2	6,500	500	2,000
3	7,000	500	2,000
4	7,750	750	3,000
5	8,750	1,000	4,000
6	10,000	1,250	5,000

When income rose by £500m per period, net investment was constant at £2000m per period. In period 4, income rose by £750 m and investment by £3,000m or an increase of £1,000m.

The Government Sector:

The public sector includes both central and local government and semi-state bodies. The government raises revenue by means of direct taxes (i.e. taxes on income and profits) and indirect taxes (taxes on expenditure). Expenditure by public authorities is broadly of three kinds: capital expenditure (hospitals, roads, railways, airports, etc.), current expenditure on goods and services and payments of grants and transfers. This demand for goods and services in the domestic economy provides income for the suppliers of factors of production used in their production i.e. Aggregate demand (AD) or Effective Demand = C + I + G. Total demand (AD) in the economy is increased by public expenditure (G), directly through current and capital spending. Taxation reduces total demand and represents a leakage from the system. Diagram 11.6 shows the separate C, I and G schedules.

Government has the power to raise the level of aggregate demand through increases in government spending not matched by taxation increases. This is fiscal policy. It can lower AD by increases in taxation not matched by increases in expenditure. Decisions to increase or decrease G are made by the government usually once a year and these are expressed in the current and capital budgets.

Exports and Imports (X and M):

Demand for domestic goods and services by foreign countries (i.e. exports) provide income in the domestic economy for the suppliers of the factors of production that are used in producing the exports. Demand for imports does not provide income in the domestic economy. An increase in exports will raise domestic income while an increase in imports will lower it.

The demand for exports and imports is dependent on purchasers' preferences, income, exchange rate and relative prices. Taking preferences as given, it follows that the demand for Irish exports depends on the general level of world demand and on the prices of Irish goods relative to those of competitors. Demand for imports will depend on the level of home demand and on the prices of imported goods relative to those competing with goods produced at home.

The influence of demand is clear but the question of relative price is complicated due to the frequent alteration of exchange rates. If exchange rates were fixed, then changes in relative prices in world markets would depend on differences in rates of inflation. Prices can vary when exchange rates can vary.

Exports are determined by external factors while imports are a function of the level of national income and can be related to income, i.e. $M = f(Y)$. If the relationship were $M = 0.4Y$, then 40 per cent of Irish GNP is spent on imports and for any increase in income 40% would leak out of the economy on foreign goods in each expenditure round.

The Marginal Propensity to Import (MPM) is computed utterance follows:
$$\frac{\Delta M}{\Delta Y} = \frac{\text{Change in Imports}}{\text{Change in Income}}$$

We now have an aggregate demand function comprising of consumption, investment, government and foreign trade (exports minus imports).

$AD \equiv Y = C + I + G + (X - M)$ and this is shown in Diagram 11.6.
An increase in exports will increase the aggregate demand function, while autonomous imports will produce an identical effect. A fall in exports or increase in imports will reduce aggregate demand.

Aggregate Supply:

National product when measured by the output method shows the volume of goods and services produced in the economy over the year. In a closed economy, supply of goods will equal demand (national product as measured by the expenditure method). In an open economy, the amount of goods available in any one- time period may not be equal to the amount of money which people wish to spend on them at ruling prices. Three things can happen:

- If there are unemployed resources, they can be used to increase aggregate supply until it equals aggregate demand.
- If resources are fully employed, prices will rise due to excess demand so that aggregate supply value equals the amount which people wish to spend.
- Imports may rise if the economy is open with no restrictions on imports so that goods from abroad augment domestic supply to equate it with demand.

In the national accounts, GNP (output method) always equals GNP.(expenditure method) Whether this equality is achieved by increases in employment, prices or imports, depends on the circumstances of each particular economy.

Equilibrium Full Employment National Income:

The full employment level of national income is the level at which there is no deficiency of demand. When aggregate demand equals aggregate supply, national income is said to be in equilibrium. This is shown in Diagram 11.6. Equilibrium is where the aggregate demand function $C + I + G + (X - M)$ cuts the 45 degree line. At this point, expenditure and output are equal and equilibrium level of national income is at E when income is YE and expenditure is E_1. In the 1950's, 1960's and 1970's governments sought to achieve this full employment income, by influencing the level of aggregate demand.

Deflationary Gap:

If equilibrium national income Y_1 on Diagram 11.7 is less than the level required to generate full employment in the economy, then there is a deficiency of demand or a deflationary gap, as seen in Diagram 11.7. The deficiency of AD at full employment is the vertical distance AC and this can be removed by government policies that raise aggregate demand.

A Deflationary gap is the excess of national income over expenditure at the full employment level of national income and withdrawals exceed planned injections. Equilibrium level of National Income is at C when $C + I + G + (X - M)$, the total level of demand cuts the 45° line. This is at National Income of £200m at B while the full employment level of National Income is FE £300m. The deflationary gap or the difference between full employment level of national income and the equilibrium level of national income is the vertical distance AC shown in Diagram 11.7.

Inflationary Gap:

An inflationary gap is the excess of national expenditure over national income at the full employment level of national income and injections exceed planned withdrawals. When equilibrium national income exceeds the full employment level, an inflationary gap exists and policies to reduce demand will have to be pursued to remove it, otherwise prices will rise to ration the available supply between competing demands. Injections must be reduced or withdrawals increased or a combination of both.

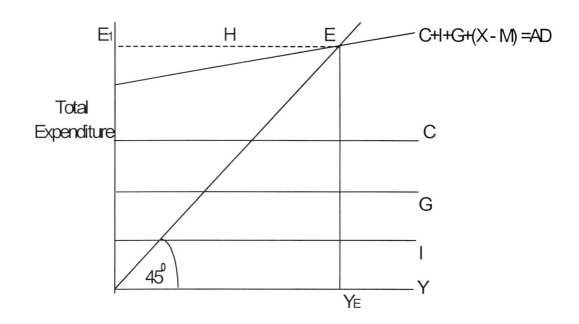

Diagram 11.6 Equilibrium National Income

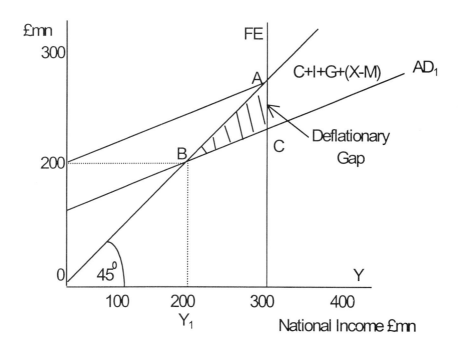

Diagram 11.7 Deflationary Gap

In Diagram 11.8, the vertical distance XZ shows the Inflationary Gap. In an open economy where goods can be imported to satisfy demand, there would be a lessening of inflationary pressures that over full employment in the domestic economy would cause. The AD line would move downwards as (X - M) becomes smaller or negative as imports exceed exports.

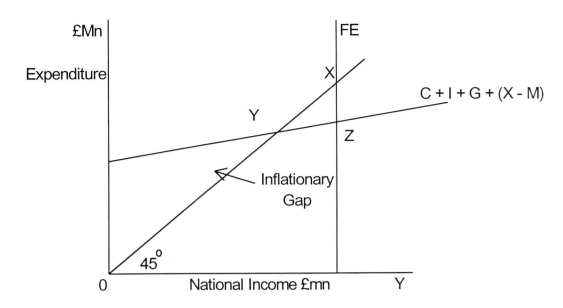

Diagram 11.8 Inflationary Gap

Circular Flow of Income:

Prior to 1936, when J.M. Keynes wrote 'The General Theory of Employment, Interest and Money,' many economists held the belief that the interaction of demand and supply in a market economy ensured that resources were fully employed.

In the late 1920's and 1930's, there was depression and very high unemployment. This was blamed on 'market imperfections', trade unions and on too much or too little government spending. The cure was to cut public spending and wages so that more workers could be employed. Governments tried this but it only made the situation worse. Cuts in Government spending increased the number unemployed and wage cuts reduced consumer demand and therefore the incentive to produce more. Keynes put forward the theory that it was possible for an economy to be in equilibrium at a point where all those who wished to work were unable to find employment. The remedy he proposed was to increase injections into the economy, thus increasing aggregate demand and through this, the level of employment. Where exports and investment showed no tendency to increase, Keynes proposed that an increase in Government expenditure should be the force to get the economy moving to a higher level of income. This increase in expenditure could be met by borrowing in the short term with an increase in taxation to repay this borrowing being delayed until private investment responded to the new higher level of aggregate demand sufficiently, to allow a retrenchment in net government expenditure.

Government has control over one injection, i.e. government expenditure and one leakage, i.e. taxation. These are, according to Keynes, the main weapon a government has at its disposal. Another attraction is the multiplier which means that National Income would rise by some multiple of the initial injection of government expenditure. Keynes suggested the circular

146

flow of income as a conceptual framework. It is not a means of measuring national income but gives a picture of the way money flows around the economy and shows the sources of injections and leakages. Households provide productive services to firms and in return receive the factor rewards of rent, wages, interest and profit.

Closed Economy:

This is an economy that is self -sufficient and does not involve itself in international trade. Diagram 11.9 shows the Circular Flow of Income operating in a closed economy with two sectors, households and firms and ignoring the government sector for the time being. National Income (Y) is made up of Consumption (C)+ Investment (I) i.e. Y= C+I i.e. Yd=Y. The incomes of households depends on the output of firms. Production of firms depends on the expenditure of households. If we assume that there are no savings then, Income = Output =Expenditure. We return to the simplest form of Circular Flow of Income in which there is no international trade. (Figure1.1) And again, we assume that people spend 0.8 of each additional pound they receive. MPC is therefore 0.8.

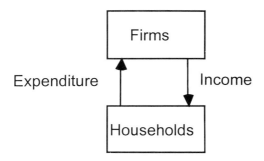

Diagram 11.9 Circular Flow of Income (Simplest Model)

The following points must be noted:

i. Income equals expenditure – if expenditure is £1000 then income will be £1000.

ii. Expenditure brings about production and income. £1000 spent has created income of £1000.

iii. Expenditure comes from income and if householders consume all the income they receive, the circular flow of income is complete.

Saving and Investment:

We now make the C+I model more realistic by considering savings and investment S+I. Income is either spent (consumption) or saved. Spending means that income stays in the circular flow but saving is a leakage of money from it, Diagram 11.10. Leakage means withdrawal of demand from the circular flow and withdrawals consist of saving, increased taxes, imports, interest rates and repatriation of profits. Not all household income is automatically passed back to firms nor does all expenditure come from income.

Along with consumption, there is investment spending by businesses, which does not come out of current income. It is usually from borrowing or from a firm's reserves and it is spending on capital goods such as factories, machinery and infrastructure generally.

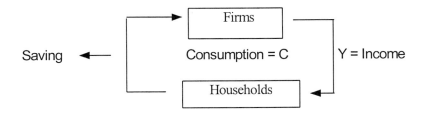

Diagram 11.10 Circular Flow – Savings

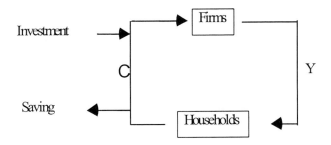

Diagram 11.11 Circular Flow – In a Two Sector Economy

Investment is an expenditure that does not come from the flow of income as it is an injection of demand into the circular flow. Injections are spending on domestic output that comes from outside the household sector. There are the following types; investment, government spending, exports, increased expenditure, reduced taxes and reduced interest rates. Diagram 11.11 introduces saving and investment.

It is unlikely that the level of planned savings will equal planned investment as households and firms make saving and investment decisions for different reasons. If planned saving exceeds planned investment there is a net leakage of demand from the circular flow. Savings vary with the level of income and due to this leakage income falls and continues to fall until at a lower level income, planned saving equals planned investment. If planned investment exceeds planned saving there is a net injection of demand into the circular flow and income rises until planned savings equal planned investment. The equilibrium in the two sector model is when S = I.

An Open Economy:

This is an economy that engages in international trade.

The Four Sector Model:

We must extend our model further to include the government and foreign trade sectors. The demand for the country's exports (X) and government expenditure (G) is injections. Demand for imports (M) and taxes (T) net of transfer payments are leakages. There are three injections and three leakages and these are shown in Diagram 11.12.

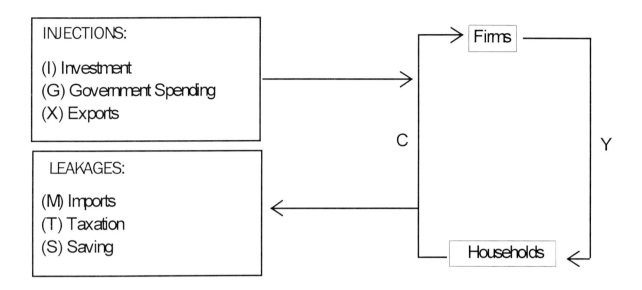

Diagram 11.12 Circular Flow Four Sector Model of the Economy

The sizes of the injections are influenced by factors outside of national income as follows:
- Investment is influenced by profitability, level of interest rates, and by overall confidence in the economy.
- Government expenditure is influenced by political decisions.
- The general level of world economic activity, political stability and the exchange rate influences exports.

The size of leakages depends on the size of the national income.

Expansions in the Circular Flow:

If planned investment exceeds planned saving, ceteris paribus there is a net injection of demand into the circular flow. This means that income and expenditure increase, caused not by consumption but by injections. Assume that income is £1000 and that 10 per cent is saved. (£100). To spend £1000, investment of £100 is required. This is shown in Diagram11.13

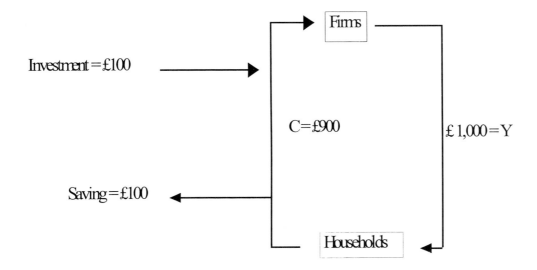

Diagram 11.13 Initial Position

If injections exceed leakages, i.e. if I > S, (planned investment > planned saving), production and income increase, as shown in Diagram 11.14

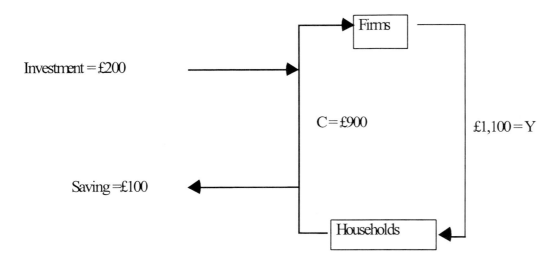

Diagram 11.14 Planned Investment greater than Planned Saving.

In Diagram 11.14, saving is £100 while investment is greater at £200 and expenditure(C+I) is £1100. Production increases to £1100 with a similar increase in income. When investment is greater than saving, income expands, until saving increases to £200 and there is an upswing in the economy.

As income rises, so does saving, so that when income reaches £2000, savings at 10 per cent of Y will be £200 and will then equal investment so expansion stops. The equilibrium position is shown in Diagram 11.15.

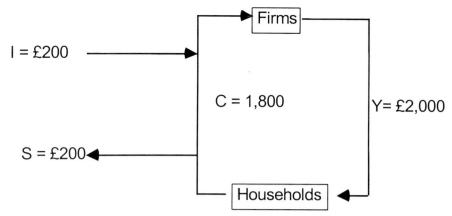

Diagram 11.15 Equilibrium at Income £2000

Contractions in the Circular Flow:

If investment falls so also does income and as before, we assume that 10 per cent of income is saved. Diagram 11.16 shows the effect of a fall in investment from £200 to £150. The

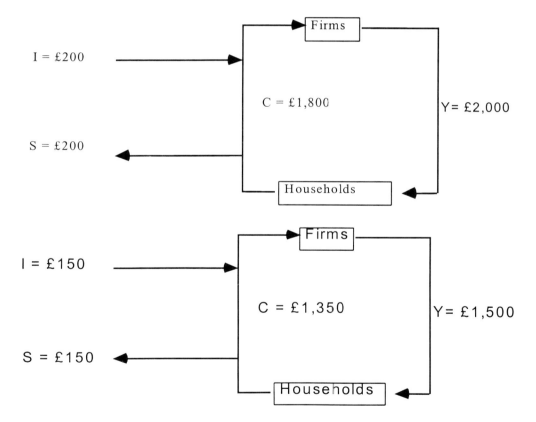

Equilibrium at Income £1,500

Diagram 11.16 Effects of a fall in Investment

result is equilibrium at a lower level of income. If planned saving is greater than planned investment there is a net leakage of demand from the circular flow. Savings vary with the level of income and due to this leakage income falls and continues to fall until at the lower level of income planned saving equals planned investment (Diagram 11.16).

To reach the full employment level of national income, a high level of aggregate demand is required and to attain this, a high level of injections (investment) is needed. The injection must match the leakages that occur at the full employment level of income.

The Multiplier:

The multiplier is a very important concept in modern economics, and is used by governments when making decisions. As regard's income formation, it is important for if the fraction of income that the public uses to increase its consumption is known, the final affects on any change in expenditure can be estimated. It plays a vital role in Keynesian analysis of the workings of the economy as a whole. It tells us how much output changes when there is a shift in aggregate demand. It describes the fact that additions to spending (or decrease in spending) have an impact on income that is greater than the original increase or decrease in spending itself. Keynes used k as the symbol for the multiplier.

If injections are only £150, then the full employment level of £2000 will not be achieved. Income is £1500 when injections of £150 equal leakages of £150 (10 per cent of £1500) as seen in Diagram 11.17. This £50 of spending missing in Diagram 11.17 is called 'deficiency of demand' and in this situation, there is a recession in the economy. If injections were higher, then required aggregate demand at full employment level would be excessive. Production cannot increase, therefore, prices rise and cause 'demand pull inflation'.

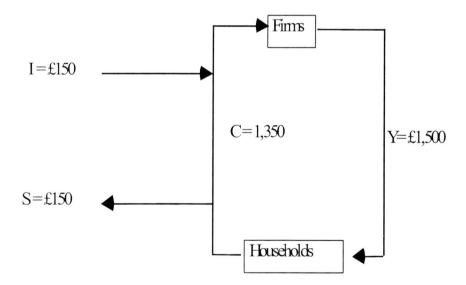

Diagram 11.17 Equilibrium at a lower National Income

We return to the simplest form of Circular Flow of Income in which there is no international trade. (Diagram 11.17) and again, we assume that people spend 0.8 of each additional pound they receive. MPC is therefore 0.8 and since all income is either spent or saved, MPS is 0.2 or 1 - MPC = 0.2.

Table 11.5
Calculating the Multiplier

Step	Change in Y	Change in C	Change in I
		(0.8 x change in Y)	
1	0	0	1
2	1	0.8	0
3	0.8	0.8 x 0.8	0
4	$(0.8)^2$ or 0.64	$0.8 \times (0.8)^2$	0
5	$(0.8)^3$ or 0.512	$0.8 \times (0.8)^3$	0

Here we have a one-unit increase in investment demand as firms see their stocks falling. At Step 2, output is raised by 1 unit in reaction to the increase in demand in Step 1. Consumption changes by a further 0.8 or MPC times the change in income and output. At Step 3, firms increase output by 0.8 to meet the increased consumption demand in Step 2. This increases consumption demand by 0.64 (0.8 times increase in income.). The process continues and to obtain the multiplier we add increases in output from each step in Table 11.5 and keep going.

Multiplier = $1 + 0.8 + (0.8)^2 + (0.8)^3 + \ldots\ldots$The value of the sum of the numbers is known to be

$$k = \frac{1}{1-0.8} = \text{Multiplier or } \frac{1}{1 - MPC} = \frac{1}{1 - 0.8} = \frac{1}{0.2} = 5$$

When MPC in Table 11.5 is 0.8, the multiplier is 5. Any part of an entire unit of income not spent on extra consumption must be spent on extra savings, therefore

$$1 - MPC = MPS \text{ Therefore, } k = \frac{1}{MPS} = \frac{1}{0.2} = 5$$

Investment of £1,000,000 brings about extra spending in the economy amounting to £5,000,000. Savings increased by £1mn, which is equal to the increased injection (investment). The size of the multiplier depends on the size of MPC - the higher the MPC, the greater the multiplier. If MPC were 0.5 for the above example, then the multiplier would be 2 and extra spending £2,000,000 and the increase in S would still be £1m (£2mx 0.5).

This is the multiplier for a closed economy that is self-sufficient and does not engage in international trade.

Example:	Income (£)	Saving (£)
Stage 1. £1m spent on investment in the domestic market provides an income to domestic suppliers of goods	1,000,000	Nil
Stage 2 Recipients of £1m have MPC = 0.8 providing income for others of £800,000 and £200,000 is saved.	800,000	200,000
Stage 3 People receiving the £800,000 have MPC = 0.8 so that others receive income of £640,000 and savings are £800,000 less £640,000.	640,000	160,000
tage 4 People receiving £640,000 have MPC = 0.8 and save 0.2 of £640,000 or £128,000.	512,000	128,000
Stage 5 Next Stage 409,600 102,400		' ' '
etc.		' ' '
etc.		' ' '
etc.		

Increase in Income	£5,000,000	
Equilibrium Increase in Savings		£1,000,000

The marginal propensity to import,(MPM), is that fraction of each extra unit of income that is spent on imports and it is a leakage out of the circular flow of income. Marginal propensity to pay tax (MPT) is the proportion of each extra unit of income that leaks out of the circular flow of income through taxation Taxes are a leakage and reduce the amount available for consumption at each stage of the process. The value of the multiplier will be reduced and it can be written as:

$$k = \frac{1}{MPS+MPM+MPT}$$

If MPS = 0.2, MPM= 0.4 and MPT= 0.3: then

$$k = \frac{1}{0.2+0.4+0.3} = 1.11$$

Graphical Presentation of the Multiplier:
Diagram 11.18 shows the effect of a rise in investment which causes the expenditure function to move upwards, resulting in a new higher equilibrium level of GNP. Equilibrium points are located on the 45^0 line.

Point E_1, gives the original intersection between the 45° and the expenditure function $C + I_1 + G$. When investment increases from I_1 to I_1 a new expenditure function results. This is shown by the line C + I$_2$ + G, and equilibrium is at E$_2$. Movement from equilibrium point E$_1$ to E$_2$ along the 45^0 line brings about a change in GNP equal to the change in expenditure. E$_1$ to X must equal X to E$_2$, i.e. the change in GNP. The change in investment (I) is part of the distance X to E$_2$. The change in GNP is greater than the change in investment. As consumption is a function of GNP it will also rise. This is induced consumption because it is brought about by the increase in GNP. Government spending is autonomous and fixed, therefore the change in consumption ΔC is the rest of the expenditure change shown in moving from X to E$_2$ in Diagram 11.18

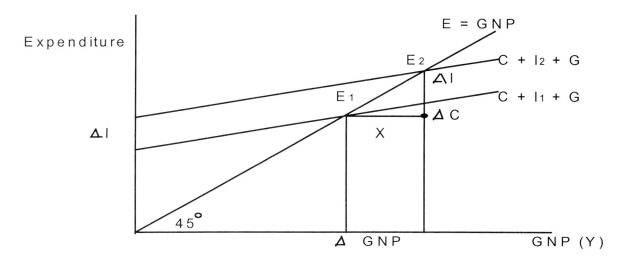

Diagram 11.18 Effect of the Multiplier

Limitations of the Multiplier:

The multiplier suggests to policy makers that if there is unemployment an increase in government spending will set off a multiplied increase in national income. There are limitations as follows:

- It is only relevant when there is demand deficient unemployment. If unemployment is mainly voluntary increased spending will generate more unemployment rather than employment as people will be better off unemployed rather than employed.

- Due to time lags circumstances may have changed before injections work their way through the economy possibly making extra spending inappropriate.

- Marginal propensity to consume may be unstable making the multiplier effect unreliable. Keynes thought that the MPC was stable in the short run, but factors such as interest rates may have more effect than he thought, therefore making the multiplier unstable.

- High marginal tax rates and marginal propensities to import may reduce the value of the multiplier and by increasing government spending the balance of payments may be worsened via higher imports rather than domestic output being increased. Ireland has a high marginal propensity to import and a relatively high marginal tax rate.

Empirical Evidence of the Multiplier for the Irish Economy:

Ireland is a small open economy where MPM is high by international standards and is generally taken to be 0.4. Income tax and indirect taxes are also high and as a result the marginal rate of tax or MPT is taken as 0.24. Estimates of MPC vary between 0.74 and 0.8 and if MPC is taken as 0.75 then MPS is 0.25. If extra spending by the Government means additional borrowing, then interest rates may rise. As a result investment falls and consumers spend less therefore the multiplier effect of government spending is reduced. When increased spending is on an industry operating at full capacity, there is no multiplier effect.

Inserting the above values into the formula we get

$$k = \frac{1}{MPS + MPT + MPM}$$

$$k = \frac{1}{0.25 + 0.24 + 0.40} = \frac{1}{0.89} = 1.12$$

An increase of £1 million in C, I, G or X or a reduction of £1 million in M will increase GNP by £1.12 million. This is only a marginal increase instead of the multiple increase as outlined under the simple Keynesian model. This is due to the fact that the leakages are so large together with the other two factors mentioned above. However, an increase in aggregate demand (AD) does bring about an increase in the equilibrium level of GNP. Efforts by the government to boost the Irish economy by fiscal measures are severely restricted by the level of leakages.

This simple Keynesian multiplier has lost much of its appeal due to the fact that everybody concerned with the working of the economy realises that it is more complicated than this model suggests.

Paradox of Thrift:

The fact that income must always move to the level where the flows of savings and investment are equal, leads to one of the most important paradoxes in economics, the Paradox of Thrift. It draws attention to the fact that an increase in the Marginal Propensity to Save (MPS) can result in a reduction in the level of income while bringing about no increase in the actual level of savings.

An attempt to save, when it is not matched with an equal willingness to invest, will cause a gap in demand. This means that firms will not get back enough money to cover costs of production or costs will be cut resulting in lower incomes. As incomes fall, savings will also fall because ability to save is reduced. The result of the effort to increase savings may be an actual reduction in savings. Classical economists claimed that saving was a virtue and that it would lead through lower interest rates to a higher rate of growth. In the Keynesian model saving is an evil in that it causes a reduction in national income and as a result a rise in unemployment. If individuals save more they will increase their consumption possibilities in the future, but if society as a whole saves more it may reduce factor income and consumption.

Illustration of Paradox of Thrift:

Case 1:- Injection £1000 MPS = 0.2 Multiplier = $\dfrac{1}{MPS} = \dfrac{1}{0.2} = 5$.

$\Rightarrow$ Increase in income £5000; Increase in savings 5000 x 0.2 = £1000

Case 2:- Injection £1000 MPS = 0.4 Multiplier = $\dfrac{1}{MPS} = \dfrac{1}{0.4} = 2.5$.

$\Rightarrow$ Increase in income £2500; Increase in savings = 2500 x 0.4 = £1000

The increase in income is smaller in the second case, while the level of savings has not increased despite the increase in MPS, assuming that everything else remains unchanged.

Questions

1. If there is an injection of £100 m in the economy, state, giving reasons, in which of the following circumstances would you think the multiplier effect would be greater?

(a) a small open economy at full employment?
(b) a small open economy with unemployed factors of production?

2. Explain the accelerator theory of investment and give reasons for the difficulty involved in trying to forecast the accelerator effect with any degree of accuracy.

3. Evaluate using diagrams where appropriate, the contributions of the life cycle theory of consumption and the permanent income hypothesis to our understanding of consumer behaviour.

4. Distinguish between an inflationary gap and a deflationary gap and explain the importance of this for policy makers.

5. Define the terms "marginal propensity to consume" and the "multiplier". Explain their importance in influencing the aggregate level of consumption.

6. Explain the term "the multiplier". What factors determine the magnitude of the multiplier?

7. Complete the following table for a hypothetical economy. Assume that the consumption function is a straight line and that investment is constant at all levels of income.(all figures £b)

Y	C	S	I	APC	MPC
0	50		50		
200	200				
400					
600					
800					
1,000					

(a) From this data graph the consumption function and aggregate demand. Below this graph draw another to show investment and savings.

(b) State and show the equilibrium level of national income.

(c) Suppose Investment increases to £50bn. what will the new level of national income be and what is the value of the multiplier?

CHAPTER 12

MONEY AND BANKING

Introduction:

We begin this Chapter by examining the nature and functions of money and the banking system. The traditional role of the Irish Central Bank and its new role in the European Monetary Union (EMU) is described. The meaning of monetary policy is explained and policy objectives are outlined. Theories to explain the rate of interest are explored. The structure and operations of the European System of Central Banks (ESCB) are outlined. The monetary instruments of the European Central Bank are detailed.

What is money?

If there is no money, goods and services must be exchanged under a system of barter-the buying or selling of products in exchange for other products. A mutual coincidence of wants must exist, between buyer and seller. Suppose a person wishes to trade a T.V. set for a refrigerator, he must find someone with a refrigerator willing to exchange it for a T.V. set. The parties must agree that the two items are of equal value, something unlikely to occur when there are many trades and many commodities in the market. Barter is inefficient because of the energy and time wasted trying to establish coincidence of wants. Money is anything that is generally accepted as a means of exchange for goods and services. It takes a variety of forms: shells, salt, cattle, gold, cigarettes, paper and many other commodities have been used as money. Whatever is used must be convenient, unquestionably accepted in exchange for goods and services, reliable in use and people must feel that it will retain its value by remaining relatively scarce.

Functions of Money:

- ## Medium of Exchange:

In a money economy such as Ireland, money serves as a medium of exchange and one side of almost every transaction takes the form of a money payment. Without money a barter system operates.

Any commodity generally acceptable as a means of payment for goods and services can be used as a medium of exchange. When the medium ceases to be acceptable, it loses its monetary function. To remain acceptable, it must be limited in supply. Other desirable qualities are:

1. Homogeneous - all units must be identical in quality;
2. Portable - easily carried around to make payments;

3. Divisible - capable of sub-division into small units to facilitate the purchase of inexpensive items;
4. Durable - it must retain its value over time; and
5. Recognisable - its authenticity must be easily recognisable.

The development of money greatly facilitates trade and helps individuals to specialise their production and move away from a subsistence economy.

Measure of Value and Unit of Account:

Money is a measure of value and a unit of account, making possible the operation of a price system and automatically providing the basis for keeping accounts. Prices can be quoted and people can compare them.

Standard of Deferred Payment:

It is a standard of deferred payments - the unit in which loans and future contracts are fixed provided its value is stable. People can make a contract or an agreement now to exchange goods or settle a debt in the future, agreeing now in monetary units the payment to be settled in the future.

Store of Wealth or Value:

It is a store of wealth - the most convenient way of keeping any income, surplus to present needs. It can be used to make purchases in the future. Fruit would not be good 'money' in this respect, as it is perishable. There are other stores of value such as land, antiques and works of art. Many of these may be better as a store of value because inflation erodes money's purchasing power over time while the prices of these assets tend to rise in inflationary times.

Development of Money:

There were three steps in the development of money:

• Commodity Money:

As already mentioned, a wide variety of things have served as money but almost everywhere man has adopted metallic money using precious metals, gold and silver. Gold and silver are acceptable in all parts of the world no matter what the level of development. The reasons are that these are wanted for their own sake, are portable, divisible and not subject to deterioration and so are a store of value. They are readily recognisable and limited in supply.

Gresham's Law is named after Sir Thomas Gresham (1519-79) and states that bad money drives good money out of circulation. Currency had been debased in the sense that sweating of coins took place. There was, as a result, a fall in the value of the coinage and sellers would not accept it at face value and weighed coins to determine their value. As a result prices increased and when new coins went into circulation people kept them and the worn coins continued in circulation.

When Ireland joined the European Monetary System (EMS) in 1979, we broke the link with Sterling because the UK did not join and as a result the Irish £ was worth less than the £ Sterling. For a time after the break, Irish people exchanged sterling coins at a premium in Irish money. Sterling coins could be compared to the coinage in Gresham's time in that they quickly disappeared from circulation, as they were the good money.

- **Paper Money:**

Goldsmiths are credited with this stage in the development of money. Holders of gold deposited it with the goldsmiths for safekeeping and received a receipt. These receipts began to pass from hand to hand in exchange for goods in place of the original gold and so paper money with 100 per cent gold backing evolved. Goldsmiths discovered that much of the gold, which backed these receipts, lay idle in their safes. They saw that so long as they kept sufficient gold to meet day to day withdrawals, they could issue receipts in excess of their stock of gold, thereby making loans on which they could charge interest. Goldsmiths, at this stage, had become bankers. Goldsmiths had to maintain reserves in gold, which had to be immediately available to meet depositors' demands.

The reserve ratio is the ratio of reserves to deposits. Profit depended on the amount lent and there was a temptation to lend to excess. In the early days of banking depositors sometimes got scared and tried to redeem their money causing a run on the banks. In Britain and the U.S. in the eighteenth and nineteenth centuries, there were many bank failures. The Bank of England in 1844 became the note issuing authority in the UK and bank notes were convertible into gold or silver but this is no longer so.

Fiduciary Issue refers to bank notes issued, not backed by gold or silver (bullion). These notes are issued in good faith and since the government gives it legal tender status, people have confidence in it. Monetary authorities can alter the note issue as they wish. Denied the power to issue notes, bankers substituted bank deposits, readily transferable by means of a cheque. Banks credited the account of the borrower and the latter could withdraw notes or transfer sums in settlement of transactions by cheque. Banks had to hold reserves and the third stage in the evolution of the modern monetary system had begun.

- **Legal Tender or Fiat Money:**

Legal tender is that which must be accepted in legal settlement of a money debt and taxes. In Ireland, Central Bank notes are legal tender up to an unlimited amount. Coins issued by the Central Bank are legal tender as follows:

50p and 20p up to £10, 10p and 5p up to £5, and 2p and 1p up to 20p. Notes and coins are called cash and they have face values, which differ greatly from their intrinsic value. Even though it has little intrinsic value it has the force of law behind it and is sometimes called Fiat Money.

Financial Institutions - Power to Create Money:

If people have money on deposit, they can write cheques to the value of the deposit. When a bank makes a loan, it gives the recipient the power to draw cheques to the value of the loan. Every loan creates a deposit. A deposit is a liability to the bank in that the bank must honour the cheques drawn for this amount. Since the bank is owed this amount, it has an asset. This means that bank deposits are money and that banks have the power to create money.

If Mr. X deposits €5000 in the bank, he can draw cheques to the value of €5000; if Mr. Y is given a loan of €5000, he can also draw cheques for €5000. Most of today's business is transacted by cheque. The amount of credit banks can create depends on the reserve ratio. This ratio is defined by the Central Bank for each category of eligible balance sheet items included in the reserve base. The ratios are used to calculate reserve requirements. The more banks can get people to use cheques, credit cards, etc., the lower the percentage of their assets they need to hold in cash form.

Example of Credit or Money Creation:

Assume that there is only one bank and that it has obtained an addition to its cash of say, €1000. We assume the public does not wish to hold any notes or coins, so that none of the additional cash leaves the bank and the addition to money supply is entirely in the form of bank deposits. Assume that the primary ratio is 10 %, and that the bank does not keep any excess reserves. The change in the balance sheet is as follows:

Assets	Liabilities
Cash €1000	Mr. A. €1000

The bank has acquired an asset as additional cash and a liability as a deposit. The situation after the bank has extended its lending activities is as follows:

Assets		Liabilities
Cash	€1,000	Deposits €10,000
Loans	€9,000	
	€10,000	€10,000

A cash ratio of 10 per cent has allowed the above bank to carry out an expansion of deposits equal to €1,000 x10 = €10,000.

Money Multiplier = $\dfrac{1}{\text{Reserve Ratio}}$ x Increase in Deposits

$$\frac{1 \times 1000}{1/10} = 10 \times 1000 = €10,000$$

162

When there are several banks in the system, the process of deposit creation is more complex. Suppose instead of one bank we now take three: Bank A has 60% of total banking business, Bank B has 30% and Bank C 10 %. Again, €1000 is lodged in Bank A.

Bank A Balance Sheet

Assets		Liabilities
Cash	€1000	Deposits €1000

Bank A has 60 per cent of business so that there will be a leakage of €400 cash from it as shown below.

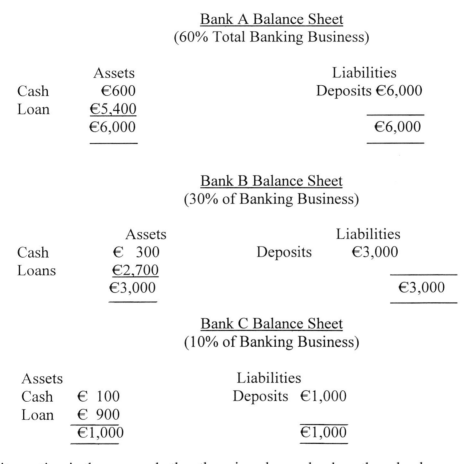

Bank A Balance Sheet
(60% Total Banking Business)

	Assets	Liabilities
Cash	€600	Deposits €6,000
Loan	€5,400	
	€6,000	€6,000

Bank B Balance Sheet
(30% of Banking Business)

	Assets	Liabilities	
Cash	€ 300	Deposits	€3,000
Loans	€2,700		
	€3,000		€3,000

Bank C Balance Sheet
(10% of Banking Business)

	Assets	Liabilities	
Cash	€ 100	Deposits	€1,000
Loan	€ 900		
	€1,000		€1,000

Credit creation is the same whether there is only one bank or three banks.

Constraints on the Credit Creation Process of Banks:

- The size of the cash ratio; if banks must hold 10 per cent of deposits in cash, then the extra €1,000 of cash deposited in the absence of an internal cash drain leads to the creation of €10,000 extra deposits. If the ratio were 20%, then there would be an increase of €5,000 in deposits.

- Internal cash drain; Banks are limited not only by their own cash ratio, but also by cash holdings of the non-bank public.
- The credit creation process depends on the original deposit and the credit created all staying within the one banking system. If the loans are spent on imported goods, the foreign banking system will benefit instead of domestic banks.
- The banks' ability to attract creditworthy customers is important since if no one wishes to borrow there is no multiple expansion of deposits.
- The banks' ability to grant loans is dependent upon their ability to acquire cash lodgements.
- Public confidence in the banking system; and
- People may be hoarding the money and if the bank loses reserves there is a multiple reduction in credit.

Money Supply In Ireland:

Prior to the 1970's there was no importance attached to having an accurate definition of the money supply since it was the Keynesian view that 'money did not matter,' in the macro-economic management of the economy. Monetarism in the 1970s made control of the money supply an important part of economic management.

Components of the Money Supply in Ireland:

The money supply refers not only to current assets but also includes other assets of a highly liquid nature. The main components are as follows:

- Notes and coins, i.e. currency outstanding;
- Money deposits in the Post Office and Trustees Savings Banks;
- Money deposits in State Sponsored Financial Institutions;
- Money deposits in Building Societies; and
- Deposits in government savings' schemes.

Measuring the Money Supply:

There are three measures of the money supply in Ireland, as shown below, M1 the total of notes and coins in circulation plus current accounts in associated banks. M2 consists of M1, plus deposit accounts with agreed maturity up to two years with both retail clearing and non-clearing credit institutions in associated banks less inter bank balances. M1 refers to narrow money supply while M3 is broad or wide money supply. M3E comprises the publics' holdings of notes and coins, plus current and deposit accounts denominated in both Irish pounds and foreign currencies. It includes accrued interest of residents of private sector entities within the State offices of licensed banks, building societies, TSB Banks, State sponsored financial institutions and Post Office deposit accounts. The Irish contribution to the Euro area money supply is shown in Table 12.1.

Table 12.1
Irish Contribution to Euro Area Money Supply January 1999

Currency	€ millions
Current Accounts M1	=12,090
Deposit Accounts M3	=67,197
M3E	=68,669

Source: Central Bank of Ireland. Table A3 January 29th1999.

Irish Financial Institutions:

Development:

The first banks appeared in the latter part of the eighteenth century and these were private partnerships limited to six partners, all of which had unlimited liability. Irish stock banks began in the early nineteenth century with shareholders from the landed gentry, who had unlimited liability. Merchants were involved in the mid- nineteenth century but some of their banks collapsed and in 1756 they were not allowed to have banking interests if they were involved in foreign trade.

Between 1824 and 1836 seven joint stock banks were set up while at this stage Bank of Ireland was already in operation. Daniel O' Connell formed the National Bank of Ireland in 1834 to provide banking facilities for the catholic rural population in Ireland.

In 1879 shareholders in banks were given limited liability protection, but throughout the nineteenth century there was no Central Bank to help them. Bank of Ireland from time to time helped banks in difficulty, but in 1845 due to the Bankers Ireland Act, it was required to compete with the other banks that interfered with its role of assisting them. After Independence the Bank of Ireland continued as Government Banker until the Central Bank Act of 1971.

Associated Banks:

These are four in number and they are privately owned public quoted companies. They are Allied Irish Bank, Bank of Ireland, Ulster Bank and National Irish Bank. They are called "Associated Banks" because the Central Bank Act of 1942 gave them a special place in the banking system. They are also known as commercial banks and they can create credit as already outlined. These are essentially banks that accept deposits and make loans. They offer an increasing range of services to their clients. Some relate to handling of money i.e. deposit accounts and loans while others relate to services such as advice. Money transfers can be made by cheque and this is the most important retail banking service. A customer can also draw money by using the Automatic Teller Machine (ATM) System. There are about 300,000 ATMs world wide with about 600 in Ireland. Other services offered include foreign exchange, mortgages, loans and credit cards.

Non - Associated Banks:

There are essentially two types i.e. Merchant Commercial and Industrial banks. Since they do not have an extensive branch network like the Associated Banks, they rely on large personal and corporate accounts, industrial funds and funds raised abroad particularly on the London money market.

Merchant Commercial Banks:

These are also called Non-Clearing banks and they operate mainly in the wholesale area of banking. They include North American banks established in late 1960's and early 1970's when EU banks also arrived. The former came due to the setting up of American and Canadian businesses in Ireland while the latter set up due to Ireland's entry into the EU. These banks had access to international expertise and could do business without Central Bank permission while the Associated banks required permission. In spite of their competitive advantage a number of these banks were unable to make a profit and they closed. They are however more specialised in their lending than the Associated banks.

There is a certain amount of overlapping between merchant and commercial banking e.g. both is involved in the provision of foreign exchange. There are, however, activities which clearly belong to merchant banks, and these are outlined below.

Industrial Banks:

Industrial banks provide instalment credit, hire purchase and term loans. Loans to purchase consumer durables can be obtained. Associated banks are unwilling to lend for this type of purchase but they have established their own lending outlets by way of subsidiaries. A flat rate of interest is quoted but it is not the true rate of interest. This is because it is the rate of interest charged on the full amount of the loan until the final instalment is repaid. A rule of thumb to establish the effective rate of interest is to double the flat rate and deduct one. If the flat rate is 10% then the effective rate is approximately 19%.

State Sponsored Financial Institutions:

The Agricultural Credit Bank and the Industrial Credit Corporation are state owned banks. They were set up as development banks for agriculture and industry respectively.

Hire Purchase Finance Companies:

These are not licensed banks and their main business is the extension of instalment credit. They cannot accept deposits from the public and much of their business is in the area of financing the purchase of motor vehicles. Interest rates can be calculated as outlined above.

There are three parties involved; seller, purchaser and finance house. It is the most expensive form of capital as interest is charged on the initial capital cost whereas for other sources, interest is on the average amount outstanding over the life of the agreement.

Building Societies:

Building Societies were set up to provide people with mortgages to purchase houses. Initially they were all mutual institutions i.e. they are owned by the members. Since 1989 they can change their status to public limited companies in which case they can provide traditional banking services. They are controlled by the Central Bank rather than by the Registrar of Friendly Societies.

Credit Unions:

These are savings co-operatives controlled by the Credit Union Act 1966 and the Industrial and Provident Act 1978. The Department of the Environment, in conjunction with the Registrar of Friendly Societies, controls credit unions. They provide low cost loans to members on a non profit basis and encourage savings.

Currency in Ireland:

Gold and silver were used as a medium of exchange in Ireland but took the form of ornaments such as rings rather than coins, which appeared first around the year 990. The first Irish currency was established in 1460 by the Irish Parliament. Fifteen Irish pence were worth twelve English pence (shilling) and this was the first devaluation. The British allowed harp coinage in the sixteenth century, in acknowledgment of a separate Irish currency. Copper coinage first appeared in 1601.

Towards the end of the seventeenth century when the banking activities described earlier began in Ireland, coins were in short supply and part of the economy still operated on a barter basis. There was a mixture of coins from other countries in circulation. These varied in quality and design and this hampered their use as a medium of exchange.

A Mr. Wood was allowed to issue coinage in the 1720's but this was withdrawn after two years on the basis that the increase in supply would increase prices. Shortages continued and merchants issued their own coins to facilitate trade.

In the early nineteenth century the value of Irish currency dropped and the Irish Currency Report 1804 blamed it on credit expansion. Gold convertibility was suspended in 1797, with no effect on exchange rates. It was reintroduced in 1821. In 1826 due to the monetary union of Ireland and Britain the Irish currency was abolished.

After 1922 and Independence the 1926 Coinage Act allowed the Minister for Finance to issue new Irish coins. The Parker - Willis Banking Commission was set up in 1926 and in 1927 recommended the introduction of the Saorstat pound. Backing for this new currency unit consisted of 100 per cent sterling reserves and it was freely convertible into sterling. It also recommended the setting up of the Currency Commission that was set up in 1927 to issue and administer the new currency. It lasted until 1942, when its function of overseeing the issue of legal tender notes was taken over by the Central Bank set up in that year. Legal tender notes were introduced in 1928 and the clearing banks were no longer allowed to issue their own. Currency notes and notes in circulation at the time had to be withdrawn. In 1979 when Ireland joined the European Monetary System (EMS) and the Exchange Rate Mechanism (ERM) the link with sterling was broken. Regarding note issue, backing changed from mainly sterling to more dollar investments as sterling weakened. When Ireland joined EMS roughly 5% of notes were backed by dollar and dollar securities. After joining some dollars were switched to currencies and securities of other EU member states and European Currency Units (ECU).

The Central Bank of Ireland:

The Parker - Willis Commission recommended that a Central Bank should not be established while a second Banking Commission 1934 - 1938 recommended that it should. When war broke out in 1939 the Irish monetary authorities realised that something more than just the Currency Commission was needed. The latter was abolished in 1942 as already stated and replaced by the Central Bank of Ireland in 1943. It not only assumed the powers of the Currency Commission but had additional duties and powers conferred on it by the Central Bank Act of 1942.

The Central Bank is the national monetary authority with responsibility for formulation and implementation of monetary policy, provision of notes and coins, management of the exchange rate and official external reserves. It supervises the banks, building societies and other financial institutions. The Exchequer account is held by it.

Functions of the Central Bank: 1942 Act:

The main function of the Central Bank is to safeguard the integrity of the currency, i.e. to safeguard the purchasing power of the currency. The State owns the capital of the bank and any profits made are paid into the Exchequer.

The 1942 Act authorised the Bank to hold balances on behalf of the associated banks for the purpose of clearing cheques. It was however 1958 before clearing balances began to be maintained with the Central Bank for inter-bank settlements.

It was allowed purchase Irish Government securities plus certain other approved securities in order to enable it to act as a lender of last resort, if the banks were short of legal tender notes. Since 1955 the Bank has done this by discounting Exchequer Bills and Bills of Exchange. Rediscounting commercial bills ceased in 1959. It was not allowed to keep the Government account, which remained with the Bank of Ireland. It was it allowed to set reserve requirements for the banks and commercial banks held their reserves in the London money market.

The Central Bank 1971 Act:

This Act increased the power of the Central Bank. As already stated new banks (subsidiaries of foreign banks) had set up in Ireland and existing banks had merged so that the banking industry had grown substantially. The Central Bank had very little control over the new banks and the 1971 Act increased its power. During the 1960's sterling was devalued on a number of occasions and this led to a movement from it as a reserve currency. To counteract this move England in an agreement in Basle in 1968 promised to make good losses suffered by countries holding sterling if its value dropped below one pound = $2.40. This however only covered balances held by central banks. Most of Ireland's external assets were held in sterling balances in London by the commercial banks but they were then transferred to the Central Bank. It is mainly due to this move that external reserves are now with the Bank and their movement enables the Central Bank provide support for an Irish Money Market.

Due to the growth of licensed banks it was realised that changes were needed to provide the Bank with more formal control over the banking system. The main features of the 1971 Act were:

- It gave the Central Bank authority to issue banking licences, a function of the Revenue Commissioners until then. Certain conditions must be met and the Bank can refuse or withdraw a license with the consent of the Minister for Finance.
- The Bank received formal power to require holders of banking licences to maintain a specified ratio between certain assets and liabilities. There are two ratios and they were established in 1972.

1. **Primary Liquidity Ratio:** This is the ratio of primary liquid assets in the form of notes and coins and deposits with the Central Bank to current and deposit account liabilities of the bank. This rate was 3% in 1998 and for every £100 banks have in deposit and current accounts the banks must keep £3 in notes, coins or Central Bank deposits.

2. **Secondary Liquidity Ratio:** This is the ratio of the holding of a bank of government bonds or stock to its deposit liabilities. This ratio was abolished in December 1993.

- The Exchequer Account was transferred to the Central Bank from the Bank of Ireland thus becoming the Government bank. In this capacity it handles all revenue and expenditure business and also managed the national debt until the National Treasury Management Agency (NTMA) an independent body was set up in 1990.
- A provision of the Currency Act in 1927 was that the Irish pound be kept at parity with the pound sterling. In 1971 this became discretionary and even though no change was made up to 1979 when Ireland joined EMS it facilitated the break with sterling at that time.

The 1989 Central Bank Act:

Building societies trustee saving banks and hire purchase companies were brought under the control of the Central Bank so that the licensing and supervisory capacity of the Bank was increased. A deposit interaction account was set up to protect bank depositors' money in the event of a bank failure as in the 1980's there had been a number of bank failures. This Act provided for the regulation of money brokers. It also got a supervisory role over certain financial institutions in the Irish Financial Services Centre (IFSC). The Minister of Finance obtained the power to change the exchange rate or exchange rate arrangements of the Irish pound after consultation with the Bank.

The goal of maintaining a stable exchange rate means that the Central Bank must maintain sufficient resources to deal with fluctuations in the demand for Irish currency as well as any unforeseen exceptional demands. The role of the Bank in this regard was tested during the currency crisis 1992/1993 when external reserves were run down.

Official external reserves are the country's holdings of foreign currency, gold, SRDs plus Irelands Reserve position in the IMF. Table 12.1 shows the external reserve position as at the end of January 1999.

The Building Societies Act 1989 gave the Bank supervisory and regulatory power over building societies, while allowing the latter to operate almost as banks. The Trustees Savings Bank Act 1989 gave it similar powers over the Trustees Savings Banks. The Unit Trust Act 1990 and the Industrial Credit Company and Agricultural Credit Corporation Acts in 1992 gave the Bank similar powers. From 1992 therefore all financial institutions are under the supervision of the Central Bank so that they can all be treated similarly.

Table 12.2
Official External Reserves € Millions January 1999.

Gold	SDRs	Reserve position IMF	Foreign Exchange	Total
48	166	468	5,057	5,739

Source: Central Bank Ireland Spring 1999

The Irish Money Market:

Up to 1979 the exchange rate for the Irish pound was identical to that of sterling and Irish interest rates moved in line with those of the UK. There was no necessity for an Irish money market. In the 1960's there was a relatively small inter- bank market mainly between the non - associated banks.

A committee was appointed in 1967 to examine the possibility of setting up a Money Market. It reported in 1969 and suggested the setting up of a dealership - based money market. In order to do this it recommended that the encashability of Exchequer Bills be improved and medium and short term bond markets should be set up. The Central Bank started two- way dealing in short- dated government securities and in 1974 included five years maturing securities.

Transfer of external reserves to the Central Bank started in 1968 and continued helped by the fact that the Bank began to offer a wide range of short -term deposit facilities at competitive interest rates.

Inter Bank Market:

The Inter Bank Market facilitates institutions wishing to lend or borrow funds. It started in the 1960s and developed during the 1970's with only the non-associated banks participating. The associated banks supplied funds to the market rather than use it as a source of liquidity themselves. They had customers' deposits as a source of funds. This source was also available to the non -associated banks but not to near the same extent. A number of money brokering firms set up in Dublin in the 1970's and this helped in the development of the Market.

When Ireland broke the link with Sterling in 1979, exchange controls between the UK and Ireland were put in place. This led to an increase in activity on the Dublin Inter Bank Market. There was also an exchange risk between Sterling and the Punt and the Central Bank could determine Irish interest rates for the first time. Borrowers now preferred to borrow at home because of the exchange risk. This put pressure on liquidity, which now became important in determining short-term interest rates. The Central Bank could affect market liquidity and help to smooth out interest rate fluctuations.

The Inter Bank Market is the means by which banks with surplus funds can lend to banks with inadequate funds. Lending can be for as short a period as a day. This market which has no exact location is a source of day to day liquidity for the banking system.

Liquid assets are assets that can be quickly converted into money with little or no loss. Non liquid assets are those whose values cannot be readily realised in the short - term and do involve losses. If a bank needs additional liquidity it can increase its borrowing from these banks. The debits and credits that come through the bank clearing system determine a particular bank's liquidity on a particular day. The number and nature of transactions maturing on that particular day also affect it. These cause money to move into and out of a bank, thus affecting liquidity. Settlements as a result of the previous day's business can also be a factor. Interbank Market liquidity is made up of individual bank liquidity, with some of them in deficit and others with surpluses.

Demand and supply fix the inter bank interest rate. This interest rate is now influenced by the ECB through the rate at which it is willing to lend to the banks.

Interest Rate Determination:

Interest is the payment made by a borrower for the use of money. The rate of interest is expressed as a percentage of the sum borrowed or outstanding. When demand is high, interest rates will rise and when supply is high interest rates will fall. The Classical Theory on interest rates is known as the Loanable Funds Theory, while the Keynesian explanation of this concept is put forward in the Liquidity Preference Theory. Both theories are examined and a comparison is made.

Loanable Fund Theory of Interest:

The Classical economists put forward the Loanable Funds Theory. They saw society divided into two groups, i.e. those who had surplus funds they wished to supply at the highest possible rate of interest and those who wished to borrow at the lowest possible rate. The theory was based on supply and demand. The interest rate, used to equate the flow of savings to the flow of investment, is seen as the price paid for the use of loanable funds and is determined by supply and demand. The supply of loanable funds comes from:

- Current savings out of income;
- Money saved in the past but not lent out; and
- Additional money through credit creation by banks or additional currency issued by the state.

These funds are made available if the rate of interest is right. The rate will be at a level to equate what lenders are prepared to lend with what borrowers are prepared to borrow.

The Classicals believed that Savings (S) = Investment (I), a situation brought about by flexible rates of interest (r) for loanable funds. The investment schedule as shown in Diagram 12.1 is downward sloping because as r increases demand for investment decreases. Savings represent a supply of loanable funds and the curve is upward sloping as the higher the interest rate the more people save and deposit with financial institutions. In Diagram 12.1 if the interest rate is above r (at r_1), financial institutions will have surplus funds and will have to lower r to attract borrowers. If the rate is below r (at r_2), financial institutions will be short of funds and will have to raise the rate of interest.

Demand and supply determine the rate of interest and supply is fixed by the Central Bank, and is independent of the rate of interest. As a result the supply curve for money is vertical. Demand is determined by the rate of interest and the amount people wish to hold in cash is called liquidity preference.

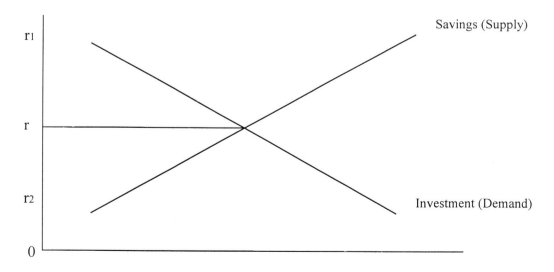

Diagram 12.1 Quantity of Loanable Funds

Liquidity Preference Theory or Keynesian Theory of the Rate of Interest:

Demand for Money - Keynesian Theory:

Keynes suggested three reasons why people might choose to hold money, and they were:
1. Transactions motive;
2. Precautionary motive; and
3. Speculative motive.

1. The Transactions Motive:

Money is a medium of exchange and hence the amount of money held is related to the number of transactions people expect to undertake. It is not possible to get perfect synchronisation between the receipt of income and the spending of that income. A person receives income weekly or monthly but spends that income every day. If, for example, the person is paid £140 a week and spends it evenly over time, the average holding of money is £70. Suppose the person is paid £20 daily, average money holding is £10 and real income is unchanged. Money acts as a temporary store of purchasing power. An economy's system of payments and receipts changes only slowly over time and hence we may assume that the principal determinant of the transactions motive is the level of national income. As national income rises, other things being equal, the demand for

money increases. This motive is not affected by the rate of interest and the demand curve for money is vertical.

2. The Precautionary Demand:

This demand is explained by the necessity to hold money to finance unplanned expenditures. People hold extra money to cover unforeseen emergencies like a visit to a doctor or unexpected car repairs. Money is held because no other assets have the same degree of liquidity. This demand depends to some extent on expectations. Perhaps the best approximation to use is the level of national income. As income rises, so do unforeseen expenditures. The lower the opportunity cost of holding money, the higher the level of funds held for the precautionary motive is likely to be. The size of the rate of interest will determine how much money will be held for this reason.

3. The Speculative Motive:

This is the element of demand for money that is most likely to be subject to considerable fluctuations. Money balances held in excess of those required for transactions and precautionary purposes are speculative balances. Why should people prefer to hold a sterile asset rather than an income-earning one? Government securities are risk free from the point of view of default but there is a risk of capital loss.

Example:

Suppose a person purchases ten undated government securities, face value €1000 each bearing interest at 15 per cent, at €600 each in the open market. Cost is €6000 and annual income is €1500, a yield of 25 per cent. Suppose further that a prospective purchaser thinks that security prices will fall and holds on to his money. If he is correct and if price drops to say €300, €6000 will now purchase 20 securities giving an annual return of €3000 (50%). By waiting a year, the investor has sacrificed €1500 in income foregone but he will have a net gain of €1500 per annum so long as he holds these securities. Falling security prices increase liquidity preference while expectation of rising prices will reduce liquidity preference. When the rate of interest is low the speculative demand for money will be high and large amounts of money will be held in liquid form. When the rate of interest is high the speculative demand for money will be low and small amounts of money will be held in liquid form.

Prices of Securities and Rate of Interest:

When the prices of fixed interest securities change, the rate of interest changes. The rate of interest is the current yield on undated government securities. This is the 'basic' rate of interest since the government can borrow at a lower rate than any other borrower.

The following example sets out the relationship between security prices and the rate of interest:

An undated 10 per cent security, nominal value €100 (holder gets €10 per annum) stands at €80. Yield $= \dfrac{10}{80} \times \dfrac{100}{1} = 12.5$ per cent = current rate of interest.

Price of Security falls to €60. Yield $= \dfrac{10}{60} \times \dfrac{100}{1} = 16\ 2/3$ per cent = current rate of interest.

Price of Security rises to €120. Yield $= \dfrac{10}{120} \times \dfrac{100}{1} = 8 1/3$ per cent = current rate of interest.

Thus the rate of interest varies inversely to the market prices of fixed interest securities. As the security price rises the interest rate falls in exact proportion. Speculative demand exists when people believe that interest rates are going to rise, and they sell securities in the belief that their value will fall as the rate of interest rises. The opposite takes place if they believe interest rates will fall.

Liquidity Preference Theory:

Liquidity refers to the speed and the certainty with which an asset can be converted back into money. If financial holders of cash hold larger or smaller amounts at different times, it stands to reason that the greatest inducement to them is to vary the rate of interest. When the interest rate is low, the opportunity cost of holding cash is small and when the rate is high, the opposite holds. There is an inverse relationship between the rate of interest and the willingness to be liquid and it is known as liquidity preference. More cash is held when rates are low and less when rates are high. This is shown in Diagram 12.2.

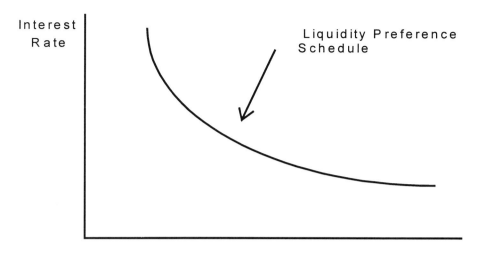

Diagram 12.2 Amount of Money People Wish to Hold in Cash

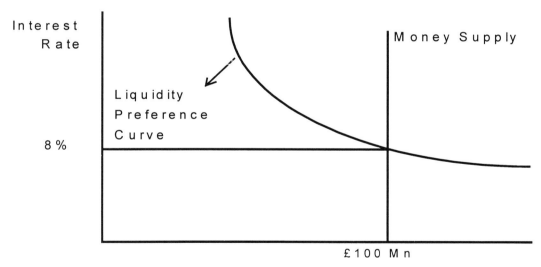

Diagram 12.3 Determination of National Interest Rate

Interest rates, therefore, determine whether people wish to hold more or less cash. What determines the interest rate? The different desires to hold cash and the amount of money that exists determine the rate. We can look on the interest rate as being determined by supply of and demand for money. The supply of money is determined by the Central Bank and is independent of the rate of interest. As a result the supply curve is vertical so that the monetary policy of the Central Bank determines the rate of interest (Diagram12.3). At 8% people wish to hold €100 million but there is only €90 million available. The money supply has fallen from S to S1(Diagram12.4).

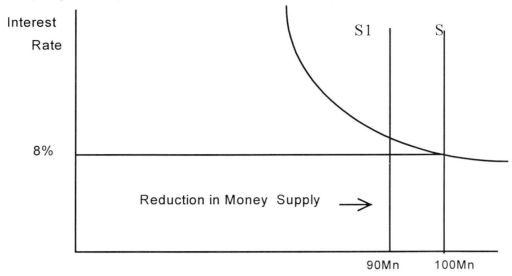

Diagram 12.4 Change in Quantity of Money

They do not realise this but feel they are not liquid enough. They will wish to make their holdings bigger by selling securities. However, selling does not create a single pound of money but there is a transfer from one holder to another and the interest rate changes. As already stated, as the price of securities falls, the yield on them rises from 8% to 9%. There is a new equilibrium that is shown in Diagram 12.5. As the interest rate rises say to 9 per cent, people are willing to hold less money i.e. €90 million. The supply of money falls from S to S1. There is no further attempt to get liquid and there is a new equilibrium rate of interest at A.

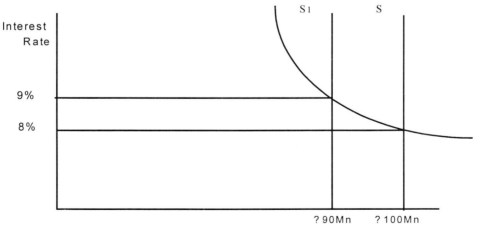

Diagram 12.5 New Equilibrium

The Liquidity Trap:

Keynes claimed that the demand for money is elastic with respect to the rate of interest. He held that in some circumstances, the interest elasticity of demand for money may become infinite, i.e. at a sufficiently low rate of interest everybody may prefer to hold cash rather than bonds. Liquidity preference would become absolute. It would be impossible to sell new bonds to finance investment and thus increases in saving would not be matched by increases in investment. Unemployment would persist for long periods. This is the liquidity trap and it is shown in Diagram 12.6.

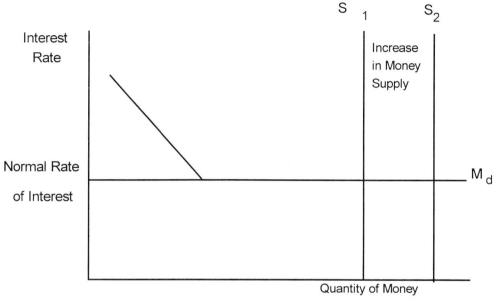

Diagram 12.6 Liquidity Trap

Most monetary economists agree that it is unlikely that a perfectly elastic section of the demand curve for money exists, or is likely to be observed. This perfectly elastic demand for money is at the 'normal rate of interest' and is known as a 'Liquidity Trap'. If a liquidity trap exists, then further increases in the money supply will not lower the rate of interest but will go to consumption, resulting in inflation and Balance of Payments difficulties.

Comparison of Loanable Fund Theory with Liquidity Preference Theory:

Liquidity Preference shows that investment and the level of savings is not chiefly determined by the rate of interest. Loanable Funds makes the rate of interest the mechanism that brings about equilibrium between supply and demand for savings. Loanable Funds Theory states that all income is either spent or saved and savings are immediately invested. This assumes that there are no leakages from the circular flow of income and that therefore slumps in the economic system do not occur. Liquidity Preference would differ from this as it takes account of leakages and also of cyclical slumps. This showed up deficiencies in the Loanable Fund Theory, which overall is regarded as an oversimplification.

Marginal Efficiency of Capital (MEC):

MEC is the rate of return on the last unit of capital employed or internal rate of return. It is the discount rate that makes the net present value of an investment equal to zero. In Diagram 12.7 as the firm invests more and its stock of capital grows, MEC will fall due to diminishing returns. Investment should continue so long as MEC is greater than r when stock of capital is Q and investment is just enough to replace worn out machinery. As the rate of interest increases, the stock of capital contracts and vice versa. MEC is the demand curve for capital.

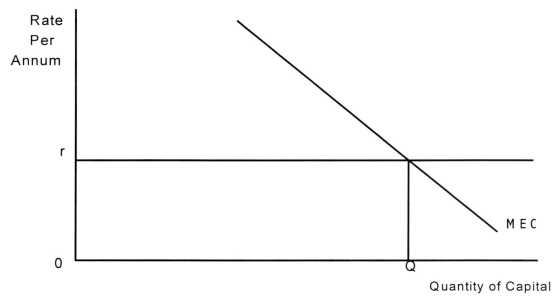

Diagram 12.7 Profit Maximising Stock of Capital

Real Versus Nominal Interest Rates:

Interest is measured in pound terms not in terms of goods in general. The nominal rate measures the yield in pounds per year, per pound invested. However, the pound as a measure can become distorted. Prices change due to inflation so that the interest rate in pounds does not measure what a lender earns in terms of goods and services.

The nominal interest rate is the rate on money in terms of money. Interest rates quoted for banks and other financial institutions in newspapers or on their premises are nominal rates.

The real interest rate is defined as nominal interest rate minus inflation. Suppose the nominal rate is 12% per annum and that the inflation rate is 2% per annum, the real rate is 12 - 2 that is 10%. If inflation goes up to 5% the real rate falls to 7%, whereas if inflation falls to say 1% the real rate rises to 11%. This means that real rates have risen although nominal rates have not changed.

Wholesale and Retail Rates:

Wholesale rates are those pertaining to the Inter-Bank Market and applying to lending and deposits by one bank to another. It also applies to rates quoted by banks specialising in large deposits or the making of large loans. Best known was the Dublin Inter-bank offer rate (DIBOR), now under EMU the euro-wide Euribor. The three- month Euribor rate was 3.1% at the end of February.

Retail rates are those paid to depositors (non-bank) and charged to borrowers (non-bank). These are fixed by the rates applying in the Inter-Bank Market and are usually higher than the wholesale rates. Retail rates are referred to as 'matrix' rates because they form a matrix as follows:

Prime rate: The prime rate formerly known as AAA, which is the lowest retail rate is applied to large commercial borrowers for short-term borrowing, to schools, hospitals and of course government and local authorities.

AA: A degree higher than the prime rate and applies to small and medium sized businesses, farmers and reflects a greater degree of risk for the lender; and

A: the rate that is highest in the matrix and charged to personal borrowers.

Effects of Change in Interest Rate Levels:

A Rise in Interest Rates:

- Borrowing will become more expensive and the increased rate of return will bring about an increase in savings but will, due to higher cost, reduce borrowing. This will have a deflationary effect on the economy. Business costs rise while spending by customers is reduced.

- Consumer spending will be reduced and this in turn will cause aggregate demand to fall resulting in the economy being depressed. People with existing mortgages or other loans will have to pay more so that they will cut back on other areas of spending. This happened during the currency crisis of 1992/1993.

- Costs will rise and margins will be cut. In the case of exports this will make firms less competitive and employment will be adversely affected. Inflation will increase in the short run adding to the cost of production and will adversely affect competitiveness.

- Short-term speculative investment, particularly foreign, will be attracted and this will tend to move the exchange rate upwards. It also disrupts the balance of trade and renders monetary policy less effective.

- Savers with deposits in financial institutions will gain provided they do not have borrowings to offset the gains on savings.

- Government borrowing will be more expensive and this could be very substantial depending on the increase in the interest rate. There is the added strain on the Exchequer in that when interest rates go up, tax take will go down.

- A rise in interest rates in Ireland will attract an inflow of funds into the country thus increasing the already stated demand for the Punt. As a result, the price of the Punt rises, i.e. its rate of exchange.

A Fall in Interest Rates:

- Investment will increase as the cost of capital is reduced.

- Consumer spending will increase and this will give a boost to the economy.

- Cost of production will decrease and this will make exports more competitive resulting in greater demand and employment.

- In the short run the level of inflation may fall and this will reduce pressure on costs especially the wage element of them. This will also make exporting firms more competitive.

- On a personal level the borrower will now have less to pay on mortgages and will have more to spend on goods and services. This in turn will increase aggregate demand resulting in increased economic growth.

- Interest received by banks will be reduced as will the interest paid by them on deposits.

- Government debt service will be less, therefore government finance will be available for purposes other than debt service. Taxes will contribute more to the Exchequer, therefore it is possible that the budget deficit will be less.

- A reduction in the interest rate will adversely affect people on fixed incomes (such as pensioners) since they receive less interest and as a result their income will decrease. There will be less incentive to save in the short run.

Irish Interest Rates:

Up to 1979 the Irish pound was fixed to sterling on a one-to-one basis. There was no way of making either a profit or a loss by switching money between UK and Ireland. Irish and UK interest rates did not differ and the UK dictated Irish rates because of the much greater size and sophistication of the money market there.

The Irish Central Bank could not use interest rates to control the growth of the money supply. If Irish rates were reduced to increase credit, mobile funds left Ireland to earn higher interest in the UK leaving a smaller amount available for lending in Ireland. An increase in the Irish rate to reduce credit would attract funds from the U.K. thus negating the effect of the increase.

However, with the break from sterling in 1979, the Central Bank, began to pursue an independent interest rate policy. In December 1978 Exchange Control Regulations came into effect on capital movements between Ireland and the United Kingdom as part of preparations for joining the European Monetary System (EMS). For the first time it was possible for Irish and UK interest rates to differ without the certainty of undesirable inflows or outflows of capital. It was expected at the time that Irish interest rates would fall and approach the German rate that was lower than the UK rate. Opinion was that if the Irish rate remained above the German rate, capital would flow into Ireland. This did not occur initially as there was a lack of confidence in the ability of the Irish authorities to keep the exchange rate at the agreed level.

With the change of government in 1987 and the start of financial rectitude, interest rates fell automatically. For a number of years prior to the currency crisis of 1992/1993, Irish interest rates were within 1% of German short-term rates due to the Irish economic performance in terms of external payments surplus, inflation and Exchequer borrowing. This position changed in September 1992 when pressure came on to the Irish pound and sterling left the ERM. Approximately £4 billion of Irish National Debt consisted of domestic gilts, held mainly by a small number of German financial institutions that helped to keep interest rates down. There was great fear that the Punt would be devalued vis- a- vis the Deutschmark and the Germans sold back the gilts to Irish banks. Liquidity of the banks' was strained and as a result interest rates were forced up, to 13.75% for the STF rate-4.25 percentage points greater than the Bundesbank's Lombard rate of 9.5%. The Irish monetary authorities could do nothing to counteract this, therefore policy of any description was inapplicable. Eurocurrency refers to commercial bank deposits outside the country of issue. In January 1993 the Dublin Inter-bank rate was 22.5% while Euro-Sterling was 6.31% (three months rate), Euro-DM 8.44% and Euro-Dollar 3.25%. The Central Bank Short Term Facility (STF) was down to 7.5% in June after thirteen reductions. The Dublin Inter-Bank rate in June 1993 was 6.75%.

The Irish government decided not to leave the narrow band of the ERM and not to devalue. To maintain this policy it had to maintain the high interest rates necessary to prevent capital outflows and to maintain confidence in the Irish Punt. As it turned out the currency was devalued in January 1993, so that a large question mark hangs over the policy followed at that time. So long as the exchange rate was mis-aligned it was necessary to keep interest rates high.

Another factor that contributed to the weakening of the currency was the sale of Punts by Irish exporters for sterling. There was a widely held view that Irish interest rates would attract a high risk premium over ERM countries and that this would slow down the rate of decrease in Irish interest rates. This of course did not happen but would have if the conditions that caused the currency crisis were still present. However, weak sterling and high German interest rates had caused the crisis but subsequently Sterling got stronger and German rates came down.

Again policy makers in Ireland had no influence over what occurred. The expectation was that if Ireland devalued, interest rates would stay high, but this was not what occurred.

The currency crisis showed that the capital market i.e. the market for medium and long-term loans is under utilised thereby over burdening the money market leading to interest rate volatility and crowding out of industry in competition for funds. What is needed is an integrated European capital market. The Central Bank can only influence interest rates within the constraints imposed on it by the markets.

As long as there was exchange rate parity there was no chance of making a capital loss or gain by shifting money between Britain and Ireland. If Ireland had her own interest rate policy working, capital flows would have occurred and this would have interfered with the exchange rate.

In July1997 whilst Irish rates were 6.3 per cent compared to 3.1% for the Euro DM. By January 1st 1999 Irish and Euro zone states were the same i.e.3 per cent. The rate was reduced to 2.5% on April 8th 1999.

Control of Interest Rates:

Since January 1st 1999 the European Central Bank controls the level of interest rates and is not required to disclose the basis for its interest rate decisions.

Irish Monetary Policy:

As already mentioned, in 1826 monetary union took place between Ireland and Britain. Currencies remained the same up to 1979 when Ireland joined the European Monetary System (E.M.S.). Even though Ireland had political independence in 1922, she didn't have control over the banking and financial system, in the sense that she followed Britain's lead regarding money, exchange and interest rates, long after this.

The Irish financial system had not developed up to the start of the 1970's, due to the fact that the Irish Government did not give the Central Bank sufficient powers before 1971. Powers conferred on the Central Bank in 1942 had not been used much so that even if additional powers were given prior to 1971 they may not have been used earlier. All that concerned Ireland regarding monetary policy over all this period was to maintain the Irish Pound on a one-to-one basis with sterling. Exchange rate policy dominated monetary policy over the period.

The Irish Central Bank has a number of powers as already outlined. Its ability to use these powers is conditioned by the economic environment within which it operates. Up to 1979 when Ireland broke the link or parity with sterling the Irish Central Bank could not operate what would be considered an independent monetary policy. Even when the link was broken the EMS also brought constraints.

The Operation of Traditional Instruments of Monetary Policy in Ireland:

Open Market Operations:

Open market operations were not possible due to the small size of the Dublin Stock Market during the 1960s. At that time if the Central Bank had dealings of any sufficient size to influence the money supply it could cause fluctuations in the prices of government securities thereby undermining confidence in them. This of course would make it very difficult for the government to raise money. At this time also it is probable that even if open market operations were possible that it would have very little external effect on the money supply. Commercial banks had a large proportion of their external assets in sterling and as a result could replace cash lost to the Central Bank as a result of Open Market Operations from that source thus achieving their desired level of credit expansion within Ireland. If the Bank called for Special Deposits these were ineffective for the same reason as cash lost to the Central Bank was easily replaced from the commercial banks external market reserves. When Ireland became a member of the EMS, the scope for open market operations was still limited by the size of the Irish market for government securities and interest rates.

Credit Guidelines:

Credit guidelines were introduced by the Central Bank in 1965 in an effort to regulate bank credit. By controlling credit it was intended to keep growth in the money supply in check. Around this time clearing or associated banks were experiencing liquidity problems and they approached the Central Bank to fix the size of future growth in their credit. By 1970 all banks, including foreign banks, were included and credit guidelines were aimed at a total annual increase in lending by all banks.

In 1973 partially reflecting the failure of credit guidelines and their adverse effect on inter-bank competition, the Central Bank used its power under the 1971 Central Bank Act and introduced liquidity ratios. As already stated there are primary and secondary liquidity ratios and they can have a significant impact on total bank activity. They can also introduce severe rigidities into the monetary system. Credit guidelines came back again in 1977 but were then aimed at private sector credit creation. These guidelines were exceeded and from 1979 the Central Bank required supplementary deposits with itself. The interest rates were penal. In 1981 foreign currency based lending was included as part of allowed private sector credit expansion thus enforcing a greater restriction. Credit guidelines were abandoned in 1985 when demand for credit fell considerably.

The public sector in the late 1970's and 1980's was responsible for credit expansion and the Central Bank had no control over it, all it could do was complain about it. Demand for credit by the private sector fell during the 1980's and credit guidelines were no longer effective.

External Reserves:

Since the link with Sterling was broken, the Central Bank's role is one of managing the official external reserves and the external value of the Punt. This duty impedes the Central bank in the exercise of its power within Ireland. If, for example, interest rates are relatively low, spending will increase and part of it will be on imports and may mean an excess of imports over exports. If this happens, demand for Irish Punts is less than supply on foreign exchange markets and this may mean a depreciation of the Irish currency.

The Central Bank can use some of its external reserves to buy the Punt when an excess supply exists to keep the exchange rate stable. There is a limit to this buying as was the case during the currency crisis of 1992/93.

European System of Central Banks (ESCB):

The ESCB comprises the ECB and the national central banks of each of the participating or eurozone countries. Its activities are carried out under the Statute of the European System of Central Banks. The Governing Council of the ECB is responsible for the formulation of monetary policy while the Executive Board implements it. The ECB has recourse to member central banks to carry out the operations that form part of the tasks of the ESCB. It has adopted the term 'Eurosystem' to denote the composition in which the ESCB performs its basic tasks. If and when all 15 EU member states participate in the eurozone, the term Eurosystem will become a synonym for the ESCB.

European Central Bank (ECB):

The ECB officially came into operation on June 1st 1998 and an Executive Board and Governing Council manages it.

- **Executive Board:**

This is made up of the President, Vice President and four others appointed by 'common accord' by the heads of the eurozone states for eight years (non-renewable terms). It is responsible for day to day implementation of monetary policy.

- **Governing Council:**

The Governing Council has a seventeen -member board comprised of the full-time six person Executive Board and eleven national central bank governors. They meet once a month and each has one equal vote except for some technical matters where votes are weighted according to the country's shareholding in the ECB, which is based on GDP and population. The only senior Irish representative at the ECB will be the Governor of the Central Bank of Ireland, in his role as a non- executive director. It is the most important decision making body in the ECB and will decide monetary policy in the eurozone.

EMU Monetary Policy:

Monetary policy in the eurozone resides with the ECB and the national central banks of the participating countries. The Treaty on European Union assigns to monetary policy in EMU the primary objective of maintaining price stability. The Governing Council has defined price stability, which is defined as a year-on year increase in the Monetary Union Harmonised Index of Consumer Prices (MUHICP) of below 2% for the eurozone. All EU States introduced MUHICP in January 1997. It covers a range of consumer goods and services for which the measurement of change is harmonised. The coverage is gradually being increased. MUHICP is designed for international comparisons of consumer price inflation and they are not intended to replace national Consumer Price Indices. The ECB therefore focuses on eurozone inflation. It will base its monetary policy on developments in the eurozone as a whole. This means that it will not react to specific national developments. MUHICP of 2% or less which is to be maintained over the medium term. This is achieved through a "stability-oriented monetary policy strategy for the Eurosystem'(ESCB plus governors of national central banks of eurozone states).

This strategy involves three elements as follows:

- he first element of the strategy is the setting of interest rates for the Eurosystem's monetary policy instruments. On January 1st 1999 the initial level of ECBs main refinancing rate was 3%. This was reduced to 2.5% in April 1999.

- The second element is the assignment of a quantitative reference value for the growth of a broad monetary aggregate, M3 .The reference value for monetary growth must be consistent with price stability and must also consider the medium term trend in real GDP and changes in the velocity of circulation. The first reference value for M3 was set at 4.5 percent annual increase and this will be monitored by a three month moving average of the monthly 12-month growth rates of M3. The money supply is appropriate as a policy target only if there is a stable link between inflation and money. This has proved to be extremely difficult in national economies. It will be much more difficult for the ECB to establish reliable euro wide measures of money and inflation.

- The third element is a continuing assessment of the outlook for price developments and the risks to price stability in the eurozone.

The ESCB must also support the general economic policies in the EU.

The Governing Council of the ECB at its twice- monthly meetings takes monetary policy decisions when each member has an equal say. The Maastricht Treaty guarantees the independence of EMU monetary policy. The treaty states that the ECB must not take or seek instructions from national governments. Initially the ESCB had difficulty in deciding whether to go for inflation targeting or money aggregate targeting. Eventually it was decided to opt for a compromise between the two.

Framework for the Implementation of EU Monetary Policy:

The framework consists of monetary instruments and procedures. The ESCB ensures participation of a broad range of counterparts or financial institutions. By means of its instruments the Eurosystem can influence liquidity and interest rates in the eurozone. These in turn impact on money and credit growth, economic activity and ultimately inflation. The implementation of monetary policy is conducted in a decentralised manner. As a result all monetary operations with counterparts in Ireland are carried out by the Central Bank of Ireland.

EMU Monetary Policy Instruments:

These include the following and they are detailed in Appendix 12.1:

- open market operations;

- reverse transactions;

- refinancing operations;

- fine- tuning operations;

- structural operations;

- foreign exchange swaps;

- outright transactions;

- collection of fixed-term deposits;

- Eurosystem standing facilities;

- marginal lending facility;

- deposit facility; and

- minimum reserve ratio.

The Central Bank of Ireland in EMU:

With the advent of the Euro, the Irish Punt has been substituted by the new currency. Monetary policy for Ireland is now decided by the ECB and is determined by influences that affect the overall Euro zone.

The Central Bank of Ireland can carry out the following functions:

- execute reverse transactions;

- main financing operations;

- longer-term refinancing operations;

- fine tuning reverse operations;

- structural reverse operations;

- outright transactions;

- foreign exchange swaps; and

- collection of fixed-term deposits.

The Central of Ireland provides the ECB with daily liquidity forecasts and carries out its money market operations with Irish financial institutions. It monitors and reports on local market conditions and relays this information to the ECB.

Eurosystem liquidity providing operations are based on underlying assets. There are two categories of assets i.e. tier one and tier two. Tier one consists of marketable debt instruments fulfilling uniform euro area eligibility criteria specified by ECB e.g. ECB debt certificates. Tier two consists of additional assets, marketable and non-marketable, that are of particular importance for national financial markets e.g. equities traded on a regulated market.

The Central Bank of Ireland operates The Trans-European Automated Real-time settlement Express Transfer system (TARGET). This consists of eleven national real-time gross settlement (RTGS) systems and the ECB payment mechanism, that are inter-linked to provide a uniform platform for the processing of cross border payments. The content of the Bank's statistical returns denominated in Euros has been expanded significantly. It is producing Euro coins in 1999 and will print Euro notes in 2000. Euro notes, and coins will be introduced in 2002.

Questions

1. Discuss the options open to the European Central Bank if it considers that there is a shortage of liquidity at the prevailing interest rate.

2. What is money and what are the main functions of money? To what extent are these functions affected by high inflation rates?

3. "The European Central Bank can carry out structural intervention to smooth out the fluctuations in liquidity and it can influence the level of interest rates by forcing the banks to borrow through a number of channels." Describe the instruments used in intervention and the channels provided.

4. Explain using a numerical example how commercial banks create money. Is there any limit to the amount of purchasing power that they can create?

5. Explain the liquidity preference theory of interest rate determination using diagrams where appropriate.

6. Outline the role of the Irish Central Bank in the EMU.

7. What are the possible economic effects of the present low interest rates on the Irish economy?   In order to achieve it's objectives, the European System of Central Banks has at its disposal a set of monetary policy instruments."

8. Keynes distinguished three reasons for holding assets in monetary form. Explain these reasons and the factors that influence them.

Appendix 12.1

- ## Open Market Operations:

Open market operations play an important role in the monetary policy of the ESCBs for the purpose of managing the liquidity situation in the market, steering interest rates and signalling the stance of monetary policy. National central banks are the intermediaries between the counterparts and the ECB. Standard tenders will normally be used for supplying liquidity through open market operations, but provision is also made for quick tenders or bilateral procedures.

Open market operations are initiated by ECB and it decides on the terms and conditions for their use. Reverse transactions are the main open market operations. They can be divided into four categories: main-refinancing operations, longer-term refinancing operations, fine- tuning operations and structural operations. In addition ESCB has three other instruments for conducting fine tuning operations: foreign exchange swaps, outright transactions and collection of fixed-term deposits.

- ## Reverse Transactions:

These refer to operations where the ESCB buys or sells eligible assets under repurchase agreements. They are used for the main refinancing operations and the longer term refinancing operations.

Main Refinancing Operations:

The main refinancing operations are regular liquidity providing reverse transactions with a weekly frequency and maturity of two weeks. The ECB fixed its main refinancing rate at 3% on December 22nd 1998. This rate was deemed to be a level consistent with the maintenance of price stability in the eurozone in the medium term.

Longer-term Refinancing Operations:

The longer-term refinancing operations are liquidity providing reverse transactions with a monthly frequency and a maturity of three months. They are executed in a decentralised manner by the national central banks. The Eurosystem does not intend to send signals to the market and therefore normally acts as an interest rate taker.

Fine- tuning Operations:

Fine- tuning operations are executed on an ad hoc basis with the aim of managing the liquidity situation in the market and of directing the interest rate. Fine-tuning operations are primarily executed as reverse transactions but can also take the form of outright transactions, foreign exchange swaps and the collection of fixed -term deposits. These operations are normally executed by the national central banks.

Structural Operations:

The ESCB can carry out structural operations by issuing debt certificates, reverse transactions and outright transactions. These operations are carried out by national central banks.

Foreign Exchange Swaps

These are operations where the ESCB buys or sells euro spot against a foreign currency and, at the same time sells or buys it back forward at a specified repurchase date.

Outright Transactions:

This is when ESCB buys or sells eligible assets outright on the market. It is a full transfer of ownership from seller to buyer.

Collection of Fixed-term Deposits:

The ESCB may invite counterparts to place remunerated fixed-term deposits with the national central bank. Deposits are for a fixed term and with a fixed rate of interest.

Eurosystem Standing Facilities:

Eurosystem uses two standing facilities for its monetary policy operations. The aim is to provide and absorb overnight liquidity, signal the general stance of monetary policy and provide a ceiling and floor for overnight market interest rates. These facilities are available to national central banks on their own initiative subject to operational criteria.

These facilities are outlined as follows:

- **Marginal Lending Facility: Deposit Facility**

This is one of the standing facilities outlined above and it can be used by counterparts to obtain over night liquidity against eligible assets. It is intended to satisfy counterparts' temporary liquidity needs. The national central banks can provide liquidity under this facility either in the form of overnight repurchase agreements or as overnight-collateralised loans. The interest rate of 4.5% on this provides a ceiling for the overnight market interest rate.

- **Deposit Facility:**

Counterparts can use this facility to make overnight deposits. The interest rate at 2.0% provides a floor for the overnight interest rate. No collateral is given to the counterpart in exchange for the deposits.

- **Minimum Reserve Ratio:**

The ECB requires credit institutions established in Member States to hold minimum reserves on accounts with the national central banks within the framework of the ESCBs minimum reserve system. The amount to be held by each institution is determined in relation to its reserve base.

The main aim is to stabilise money market interest rates creating or enlarging a structural liquidity shortage. These elements relate to overnight deposits, deposits with agreed maturity up to 2 years; deposits redeemable at notice up to 2 years, debt securities with agreed maturity up to 2 years and money market paper. Liabilities vis-à-vis other credit institutions and liabilities vis-à-vis the ECB and national central banks are excluded. The reserve requirement of each credit institution is calculated by applying to the amount of eligible liabilities the current reserve coefficient of 2%. Compliance with reserve requirements is determined on the basis of an institution's average daily reserve holdings with the Central Bank over a maintenance period. This period lasts for a month starting on the 24th day of each month and ending on the 23rd day of the next. The ECB pays a rate of interest on these deposits at the average level of the main refinancing rate over the maintenance period.

If an institution fails to comply with all or part of the minimum reserve requirement, the ECB may impose any one of the following:
- A payment of 5% above the marginal lending rate;
- A payment of up to two times the marginal lending rate; and
- The requirement for the institution to establish non-interest bearing deposits with the ECB.

Many of the elements of this framework for implementing monetary policy in the euro area were present in the Irish system before EMU.

CHAPTER 13

THE I S - LM AGGREGATE DEMAND AND SUPPLY

Introduction:

In this Chapter the ISLM model showing simultaneous equilibrium in the goods market (I=S) and the money market (L=M) is discussed. This model allows us to examine the effects of fiscal and monetary policy on both national income and interest rates. The Keynesian and Monetarist positions with regard to the effectiveness of fiscal and monetary policy are compared. The aggregate demand and supply model which is a technique used as a method of macro economic analysis is outlined.

The methods used so far to analyse national income, especially the 45° line and the aggregate demand curve are limited because they ignore the monetary and asset sector of the economy. The IS -LM model tries to overcome this, by including both the real and monetary sectors.

IS - Curve:

The IS curve is defined as all possible combinations of the interest rate and level of GNP that keep the economy's commodity market (the real economy) in equilibrium. The IS schedule shows the different combinations of income and interest rates at which the goods market is in equilibrium. It represents all those combinations of income and interest rates at which the supply of goods and services equals the demand for goods and services. The IS curve slopes downward and it is shown in Diagram 13.1. For goods market equilibrium, a higher interest rate must be accompanied by a lower income level since the aggregate demand schedule must be lower.

Elasticity of IS Curve:

The elasticity of the IS curve is the responsiveness of national income to changes in interest rates. The more sensitive is investment to the rate of interest the flatter is the IS curve. Keynesians argue that the IS curve is fairly inelastic because investment is unresponsive to changes in interest rates. They also hold that savings are unresponsive resulting in a small shift in the I and S curves in response to a change in interest rates therefore national income change is small. Monetarists argue that investment and savings are relatively responsive to changes in interest rates and the IS curve is relatively elastic.

Shifts in the IS Curve:

A change in interest rates will cause a movement along the IS curve but a change in any of the other determinants of saving or investment will shift the whole curve. This is because it will change the equilibrium level of national income at any given rate of interest. Changes in government expenditure will shift the IS curve to the right if it is increased and to the left if reduced. An increase in government expenditure will shift the IS curve to the right, and a reduction to the left. Changes in the rate of income tax also cause a shift to the right if reduced and to the left if increased.

LM CURVE:

The LM curve is concerned with equilibrium in the money market and represents the monetary sector of the economy. It shows all the various combinations of interest rates and national income at which the demand for money equals supply (L = M). (Diagram 13.1). The LM curve slopes upwards since with a higher income level it needs a higher interest rate to cut off money demand and maintain money market equilibrium with an unchanged money supply.

Elasticity of the LM curve:

The elasticity of the LM curve is the responsiveness of interest rate changes to a change in national income. The greater the marginal propensity to consume (MPC), the more will the transaction demand for money rise as national income rises, and thus the more will the L curve shift to the right. As a result of this shift the interest rate rises and the LM Curve gets steeper. The greater the interest elasticity of the speculative demand for money the flatter the curve. The more sensitive the transactions demand for money the steeper the LM curve. Keynesians suggest that the L curve is likely to be relatively flat given the responsiveness of the speculative demand for money to changes in interest rates. Monetarists think it is relatively steep because they regard demand for money as insensitive to changes in interest rates.

Shifts in the LM Curve:

A change in national income will cause a movement along the LM curve to a new equilibrium. An increase in the money supply shifts the LM curve to the right and reductions shift it to the left. An increase in demand for money other than as a result of income will shift the LM curve to the right, while a decrease in demand for money will shift the LM curve to the left.

LM is at first horizontal because of the liquidity trap, then it slopes upward and is vertical when money is completely held in active balances. The IS curve slopes downwards left to right. For the goods market to be in equilibrium we must be on the IS curve. For the money market to be in equilibrium we must be on the LM curve. They cross at point E where interest rate and income are the same. Here the monetary and real sectors of the economy are in equilibrium and therefore the economy as a whole is in equilibrium. This occurs where interest rate is r_0 and national income y_0 at point E in Diagram 13.1.

Fiscal and Monetary Policy and IS-LM Model:

The model can be used to examine and illustrate the effects of fiscal and monetary policy.

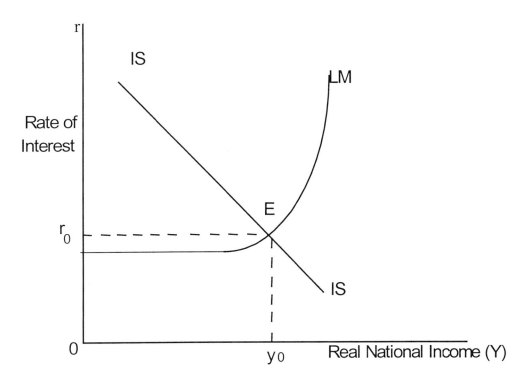

Diagram 13.1 IS/LM Curve and Macroeconomic Equilibrium

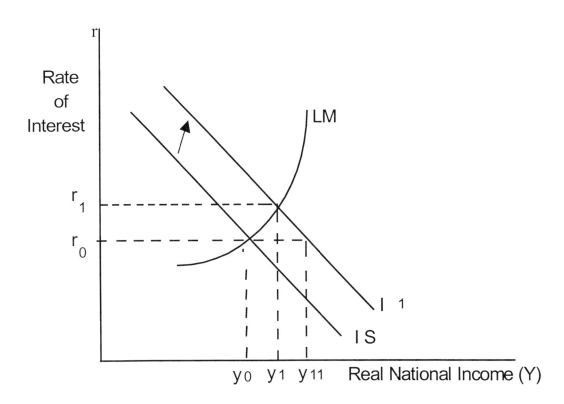

Diagram 13.2 Expansionary Fiscal Policy

Diagram 13.2 shows the effect of an increase in government expenditure (G) or cut in taxes (T) with no increase in the money supply. The IS Curve shifts from IS to IS^1. If the interest rate remains constant, income rises to Y_{11}. This is the full multiplier effect. Income rises from Y_0 to Y_1 as interest rate rises to r_1 because the increase in income brings about an increase in interest rates. There is less room left for private expenditure and some private investment is crowded out by government expenditure. This reduces the size of the multiplier. Higher interest rates result from the need to offer higher rates on government bonds to encourage the public to buy them as well as the increased demand for money as income rises. It is difficult to measure the magnitude of crowding out.

Diagram 13.3 shows the effect of 100% crowding out of fiscal policy. Here the IS curve intersects the LM curve when the latter is vertical. Movement in IS from IS to IS^1 doesn't alter income which stays at Y^c. Interest rate rises from r^0 to r^1 so that it crowds out completely the increase in government expenditure (G). The result is that if the economy is on the vertical part of the LM curve fiscal policy affects the interest rate but not income.

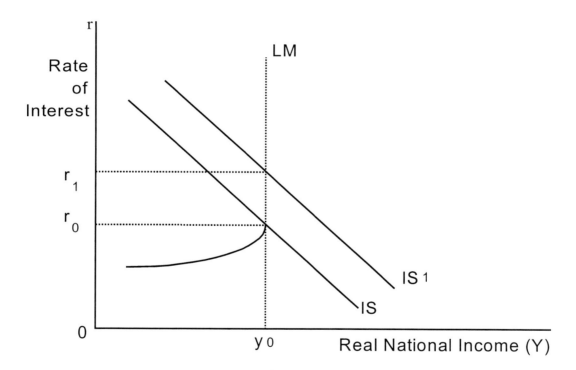

Diagram 13.3 100% Crowding Out from a Fiscal Expansion

Diagram 13.4 shows the case of no crowding out from fiscal policy. Here the IS curve intersects the LM curve when the latter is horizontal so that interest rate does not change so neither does investment but income rises Y_0 to Y_1. The multiplier has its full effect. This is the only way the simple multiplier will work.

Expansionary Monetary Policy:

In Diagram 13.5 it is seen that an increase in the money supply moves the whole LM curve to the right. Income increases and interest rate falls from r_0 to r_1 whereas in expansionary fiscal policy interest rate rises. Income rises to Y_1.

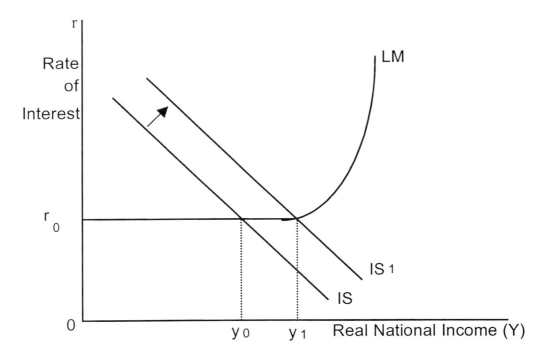

Diagram 13.4 No Crowding Out from a Fiscal Expansion

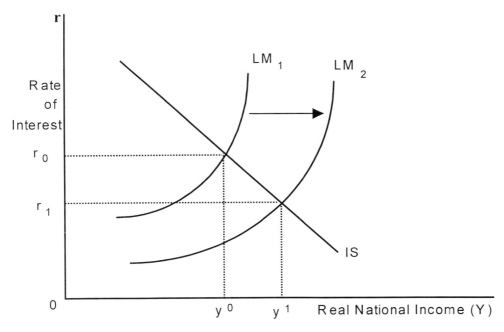

Diagram 13.5 Expansionary Monetary Policy

Monetary Policy Ineffective:

Diagram 13.6 shows the IS curve intersecting the LM curve on its horizontal section, the liquidity trap. At this point an increase in the money supply has no effect on income or the interest rate. This is due to the desire to hold idle money balances (liquidity trap) and the consequent absorption of the increased money supply into idle balances. Monetary policy is therefore ineffective in the liquidity trap while fiscal policy would be effective.

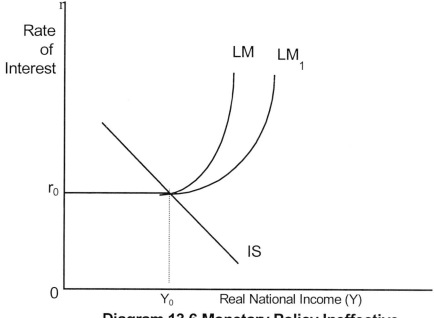

Diagram 13.6 Monetary Policy Ineffective

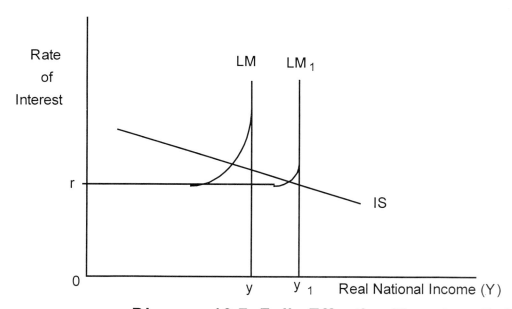

Diagram 13.7 Fully Effective Monetary Policy

Fully Effective Monetary Policy:

In Diagram 13.7 the IS curve cuts the LM curve at its vertical section. Income increases by exactly the amount of the horizontal movement in LM.

Expansion of Fully Effective Monetary Policy:

Diagram 13.8 outlines the result of higher government expenditure or lower taxes when financed by an increase in the money supply. There is no rise in interest rates and as a result no crowding out of private expenditure takes place. Income increases by a greater amount than when fiscal and monetary policies are used separately.

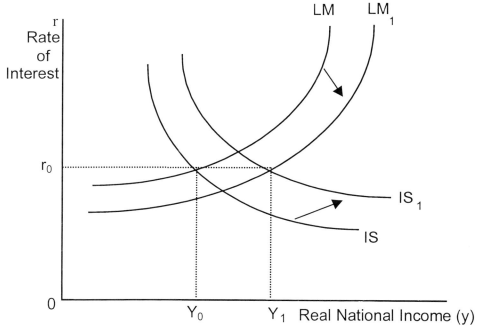

Diagram 13.8 Expansionary Fiscal and Monetary Policy

Effectiveness of Fiscal and Monetary Policy:

The effectiveness of fiscal and monetary policy depends on the slopes of the IS and LM curves. Fiscal policy is most effective when IS is steep and LM shallow. When LM is shallow IS moves to the right, interest rate increases by a small amount whereas when IS is steep, an increase in interest rates will cause only a small reduction in investment. Crowding out is minimised and national income increases substantially.

Monetary Policy is most effective when LM is steep and IS shallow. When LM is steep a move to the right will result in a large fall in interest rates, whereas when IS is shallow. This drop in interest rates will bring about a relatively large increase in investment and therefore in national income.

Keynesian Vs Monetarists

Keynesian Position:

Keynesians make the following assumptions, about the shapes of the LM and IS curves:

- The LM curve is relatively flat or shallow, because the liquidity preference curve (L) is relatively flat because of the importance of speculative demand in the overall demand for money.

- The IS curve is relatively steep because the investment demand curve is relatively inelastic due to the unresponsiveness of investment to changes in interest rates. Savings also follow the same pattern.

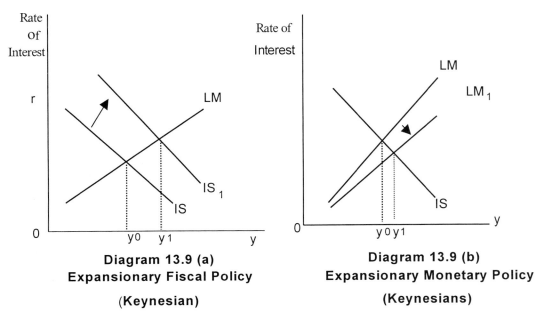

Diagram 13.9 (a)
Expansionary Fiscal Policy
(Keynesian)

Diagram 13.9 (b)
Expansionary Monetary Policy
(Keynesians)

Diagram 13.9 Keynesian Analysis of Fiscal and Monetary Policy.

Expansionary fiscal policy brings about a bigger increase in national income in (a) than an expansionary monetary policy does in (b). Keynesians argue that this is due to the fact that an increase in the money supply leads to greater holding of idle balances and therefore a reduction in the velocity of circulation. Keynesians argued that during a depression output is low and so the economy is in a liquidity trap, so that monetary policy is totally ineffective. The only way out of the depression is to use fiscal policy.

Monetarists Position:

Monetarists make the following assumptions:

- LM curve is relatively steep or vertical because the demand for money is inelastic or has zero interest elasticity and the speculative balances of money play a minor role.

- Investment is interest elastic therefore IS has a shallow or flat slope.

Diagram 13.10 shows Monetarist analysis of fiscal and monetary policy. Panel (b) shows a greater increase in income with expansionary monetary policy than with expansionary fiscal policy, in Panel (a). Monetary policy is according to them more effective than fiscal policy. They hold that fiscal policy is weak due to crowding out as shown in panel (a) due to the steepness of the LM curve. Increase in income results in increased transactions demand leading to much higher interest rate. This is the result of few speculative holdings of money so that a substantial interest rate increase is necessary to bring forth enough money balances to meet the now higher transactions demand.

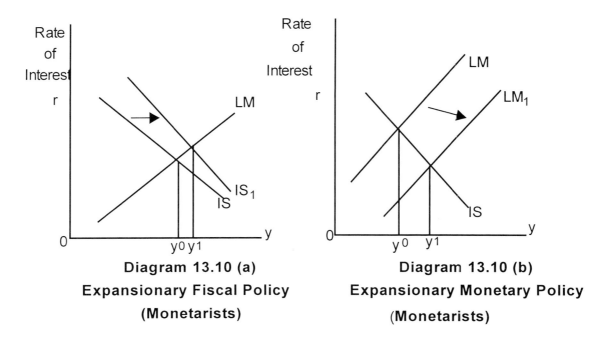

Diagram 13.10 (a)
Expansionary Fiscal Policy
(Monetarists)

Diagram 13.10 (b)
Expansionary Monetary Policy
(Monetarists)

Aggregate Demand Aggregate Supply Model:

Aggregate demand is the amount that firms and households plan to spend on goods and services at each level of income. Aggregate supply is the total supply of goods and services in a given period. It is the relationship that exists between the price level and the amount produced in the economy. The aggregate demand aggregate supply model of macro economic analysis is now in wide scale use.

Aggregate Demand Curve:

The aggregate demand curve (AD) is a curve that shows the different levels of expenditure on domestic output at different price levels. It can be derived graphically from the IS - LM model with the price level as an endogenous variable. It shows the relationship between AD and the price level. For a given price level one can read off the level of real national income Y from the AD curve.

The AD curve is shown in Diagram 13.11 as downward sloping just like the demand curve for a single good or service. There are differences in that the price level is the average price level and movements along the curve are not explained in the same way as for a single product.

When prices rise, interest rates usually rise causing a fall in demand for goods such as cars and investment goods because many of them are purchased with loans. AD will fall.

When prices, rise this causes a fall in the real value of assets denominated in money terms such as cash or bonds for example. Their purchasing power drops so AD falls. This is referred to as the wealth effect.

If prices rise faster than those in foreign countries, domestic goods become relatively dearer and fewer are purchased by our citizens and on the export markets. Again AD falls.

Shifts in Aggregate Demand:

There are a number of factors that increase AD and shift it out to the right. These can be divided into policy variables and external variables and are shown in Diagram 13.12.

Policy Variables:

- In the case of monetary policy an increase in the money supply brings down interest rates thereby improving credit conditions. This leads to increased investment and consumption of durable consumer goods, at any given price level.

- By way of fiscal policy increases in expenditure, tax reductions, increased social welfare payments, all raise income and result in greater consumption, at any given price level.

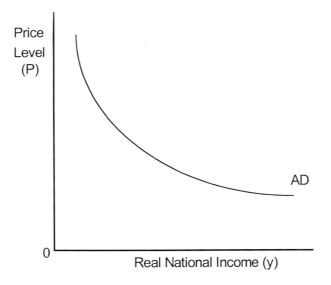

Diagram 13.11 Aggregrate Demand

External Variables:

- An increase in output growth abroad leads to increased demand for our exports.

- Changes upwards in asset values will increase the wealth of households and thus consumption.

A rise in the amount of desired consumption, government investment or net expenditure at each price level shifts the AD curve to the right AD_1, while a decrease will shift it to the left AD_{11} in Diagram 13.12.

Aggregate Supply Curve (AS):

AS curve is the relationship that exists between the price level and the amount produced in the economy. For a given price level we can read off the level of real national income (Y) from the aggregate supply curve. The AS curve is assumed to slope upwards to the right as firms' marginal costs rise as output is increased.

There is need to distinguish between a short and long run aggregate supply curve.

Short Run Aggregate Supply (SRAS):

SRAS curve shows what will be produced and offered for sale at each price level assuming unit input prices are fixed. It slopes upwards from left to right, i.e. as prices increase as does output and as price decreases output falls.

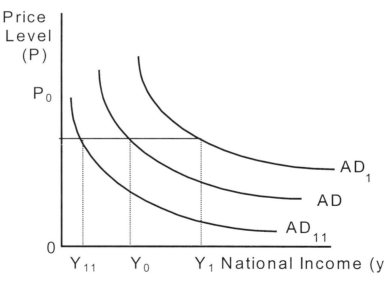

Diagram 13.12
Shifts in Aggregate Demand Curve

Although the unit cost of inputs is constant in the short run, the firm's unit costs can still increase. This may be due to marginal workers who are less efficient being employed or workers paid overtime. Firms will only increase output if they get higher prices to cover the higher costs so that as the economy moves to the right along the SRAS curve prices are rising. If firms reduce output the reverse happens (Diagram 13.13).

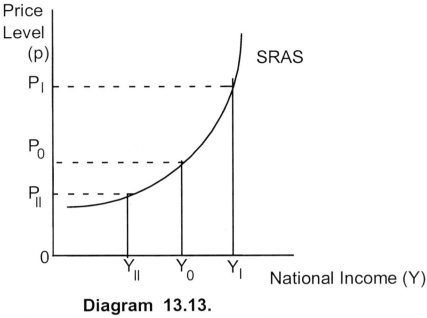

Diagram 13.13.
Short Run Aggregate Supply Curve

Shifts in SRAS Curve:

These shifts are sometimes described as supply side shocks. If we no longer assumed that input prices are constant, shifts can occur:

- A rise in unit input prices brings about a fall in profit and producers seek to raise prices to cover the difference in costs. This causes SRAS to shift upwards and to the left, as in Diagram 13.14 equivalent to moving from point A on $SRAS_0$ to point C on $SRAS_1$.

- Firms could maintain prices after an increase in input prices reducing output to Y_1 and moving from A to B in Diagram 13.14. This is also the equivalent to a shift in the SRAS curve to the left.

Equilibrium AD and AS:

Diagram 13.15 shows that equilibrium is where aggregate supply and aggregate demand intersect and determines the economy's price level and total output. When price is higher than the equilibrium price AS is greater than AD and at lower prices AS is less than AD.

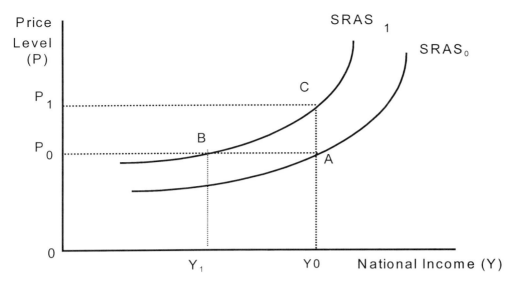

Diagram 13.14
Shift in Short Run Aggregate Supply Curve

Equilibrium is at point E where SRAS = AD. The economy's total output is Y_0 and price level P_0. If price is higher than P_0 at P_1 national income is not at equilibrium but output of Y_1 only is demanded and producers would wish to produce at Y_2 i.e. there is excess supply in the economy. The surplus would force price down to P_0. If price is lower than P_0 then there is excess AD and price will have to increase to restore equilibrium.

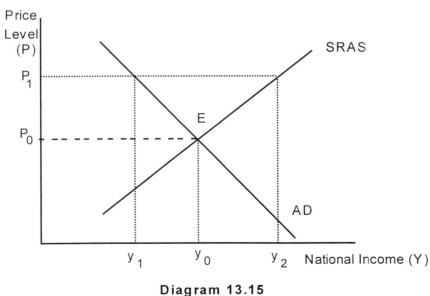

Diagram 13.15
Equilibrium SRAS and AD

Long Run Aggregate Supply Curve (LRAS):

LRAS is a vertical line at the potential level of national income. It is now viewed by most economists to be a vertical line Diagram 13.16 relates the price level to equilibrium real national income after all input costs have been fully adjusted to eliminate any excess supply or demand. LRAS is a vertical line at Y_P and since the adjustments take time, it is described as long run.

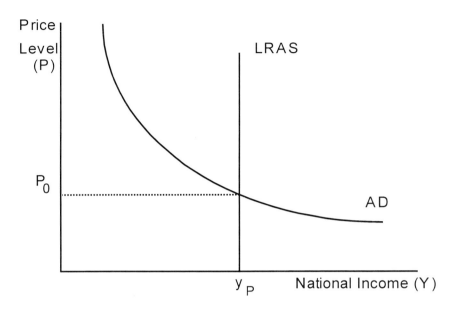

Diagram 13.16
Long Run Aggregrate Supply Curve

The Classical Approach - Aggregate Supply:

This approach is based on the assumption that changes in AD affect the price level but have no impact on output and employment. Wage and price flexibility mean that the real level of spending is enough to maintain full employment.

In Diagram 13.17 suppose AD falls to AD_1 so that at P, spending falls to B. Wage and price adjustments follow and price falls to P_1 (wages also fall). Full employment is re-established at C and total output is back to potential output. If AD moves to the right there is excess demand and price would move up so that the LRAS curve is again reached.

There is no scope for changes in AD to raise output even in the short run and the only effect of such policies will be to raise the price level and cause inflation.

Output can only be increased by moving LRAS to the right and this can only come through better methods of production and skills.

204

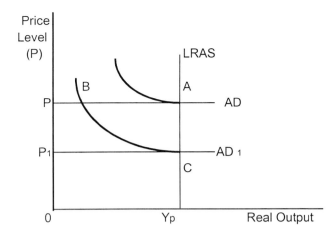

Diagram 13.17 Classical Approach

The Keynesian Model:

Diagram 13.18 illustrates the Keynesian version of the AS curve and it is in the form of a "reversed L".

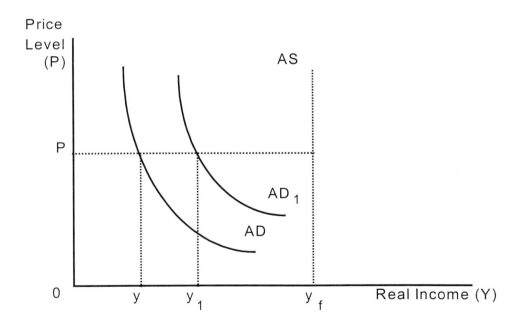

Diagram 13.18 Keynesian Aggregrate Supply Curve

AD can be increased along the horizontal portion of AS thereby expanding output and employment with no conflict with the price level. When the full employment level is reached any further increase in AD raises prices but not output.

An In-Between AS Function:

Many take the view that there is a position between the two extremes. Diagram 13.19 shows this AS curve as sloping upward and as a function of price level, becoming steeper at higher levels of real output or income. An increase in AD from AD_1 to AD_2 in the Diagram results in increased output and inflation. At low levels of output, i.e. where the curve is almost horizontal the main effect is on real output but as it nears full employment, the AS curve is practically vertical the main effect is on prices.

All these models indicate the limitations on government ability to influence the economy through their policy measures.

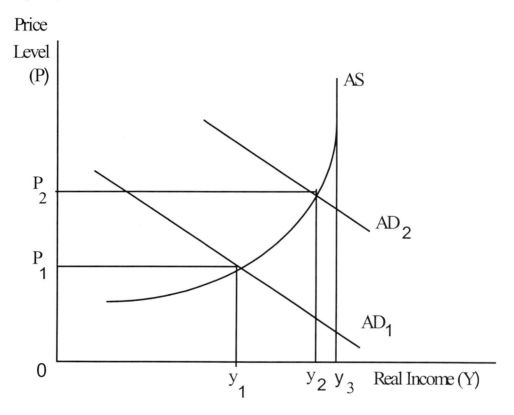

Diagram 13.19 Upward Sloping AS Curve

Questions

1. What does the IS curve represent and why does it slope downwards? What does the LM curve represent and why does it slope upwards?

2. " The extreme Keynesian position is that fiscal policy is effective and that monetary policy is ineffective in influencing GNP." Using IS/LM analysis, critically evaluate this position.

3. "Monetarists argue that fiscal policy is ineffective and that monetary policy has a strong effect on nominal GNP." Using IS/LM analysis critically evaluate this argument.

4. "The effectiveness of discretionary fiscal policy is reduced by crowding out." What is 'crowding out' and what determines its size?

5. Distinguish between the Keynesian and Neo- Classical versions of the AS curve.

6. "The IS/LM framework can be used to illustrate issues concerning the relative effectiveness of fiscal and monetary policy." Using diagrams critically evaluate the Keynesian and Monetarists positions.

Chapter 14

FISCAL POLICY

Introduction:

Fiscal policy is the part of a government's overall economic policy that aims to achieve the government's economic objectives through the use of the fiscal instruments of taxation, public expenditure and budget surplus or deficit. Since January 1st 1999 it is the only means of macroeconomic intervention in the economy. The government tries to manage aggregate demand, output and income by use of these instruments. The government's basic aim is to have a stable level of output and growth and this is known as stabilisation policy. Fiscal policy is enunciated and introduced in an annual budget. The government first decides what it wishes to spend and then determines the ways in which it will raise the required revenue usually through taxes. There is, however, one constraint in that potential revenue is not infinite. Trends in the current and capital budgets and Public Sector Borrowing Requirement (PSBR) are reviewed. The Pact for Stability and Growth for Eurozone member states together with the Irish Stability and Growth Pact Programme 1999-2001 are set out. The history of and current status of the Irish national debt is detailed.

Keynesian Fiscal Policy:

In the Keynesian era 1945 to the mid 1970's -when inflation became the greatest concern - fiscal policy was looked on as the prime means of controlling aggregate demand. However this required the use of the overall levels of public spending, taxation and budget deficit to manage the level of aggregate money demand in the economy, with the objectives of achieving full employment and stabilising the business cycle. This policy contained the following elements:

- If a market economy was left unregulated, it would lead to unemployment, low economic growth and an unstable business cycle;

- Due to lack of aggregate money demand, caused by too much saving in the private sector and too little investment, the economy settles in an 'under-full employment equilibrium' characterised by demand-deficient unemployment. This is a deflationary gap as outlined previously;

- By deficit financing, the government, through using fiscal policy as an instrument for demand management, can put spending power into the economy. As a result, deficient demand can be eliminated and full employment is achieved;

- When full employment is reached, the government can then use fiscal policy in a discretionary way so as to meet any new circumstances that arise; and

- Fiscal policy was directed at the 'demand side' of the economy, with the 'supply side' considered to be of secondary importance.

The Limits of Keynes:

- Keynes was largely concerned with finding a cure for mass unemployment which was , the outstanding problem of his day. Nowadays, governments aim at a complex of economic objectives. They seek stabilisation, not only of employment, but also of, the balance of payments and prices.

- Many of the Keynesian methods have been rendered less than adequate due to changes in the institutional framework of the economies of countries. Unemployment now is due mainly to structural changes. Inflation has been caused by cost push rather than demand –pull factors.

- There is a lack of precision in implementing demand management techniques due to lack of reliability of the data and forecasts on which decisions are based. The exact value of the multiplier is not known and as a result, the amount of change which will result from a particular fiscal action, is not precisely predictable. Lags in implementation may blunt the effect of a particular measure and could, in fact, be harmful instead of helpful.

Monetarists' Fiscal Policy:

Monetarists are those who attribute inflation solely to rises in money supply. In the mid 1970's inflation became the overriding concern and policy changed to the control of the money supply. Monetarists' fiscal policy has been pursued by some countries since. It is basically an attempt to increase the role of markets and of private sector economic activity and to reduce the economic role of the state. They argue that it can only be effective if accompanied by monetary policy and that even then, it is the latter that is affecting aggregate demand.

The main elements in this policy are:

- A rejection of the use of public spending and taxation as discretionary instruments of demand management.

- Medium term policy in place of short-term policy to reduce public spending, taxation and government borrowing. They hold that under Keynesian policy, government spending crowded out the private sector. This means that the government by increasing its expenditure will bring about a corresponding decrease in private sector expenditure.

- The macroeconomic elements of Keynesian fiscal policy have been subordinated to a more microeconomic fiscal policy. This includes reductions in public spending and taxation and offers of incentives with the objective of improving the economic performance on the supply side of the economy.

- Fiscal policy is subordinated to the needs of monetary policy.

Methods of Increasing Aggregate Demand:

- Increase consumption, for example, by reducing taxation and increasing benefits such as children's allowances, thus increasing disposable income for expenditure on consumption. There are only short time lags between tax or benefit changes being announced in the Budget and the measures actually being implemented.

- Private investment can be increased by subsidising it;

- Increase government expenditure G by increasing expenditure on consumption goods and services without, at the same time, increasing taxes. This will create a full multiplied rise in national income as all the money is spent; and

- Government can increase its own expenditure on investment, for example, on roads, schools hospitals, etc. without increasing taxes.

In deciding which fiscal method or methods to use, several criteria must be considered:

- The speed of application is reduced because of deficiencies in statistics and the time taken to collect them. Government expenditure takes time to be activated unless some projects are actually ready to start. The quickest way to increase effective demand is by reducing taxes such as VAT. In general, a reduction in taxes paid by the poor will be more effective than a similar reduction in taxes mainly paid by the rich. This is due to the fact that the rich are likely to save a greater proportion of their increase in incomes. It is however difficult to measure exactly how much of the tax cuts will be spent.

- If unemployment starts in one industry or area, then specific measures are necessary. There are regional variations within a country with, for example, above average unemployment in some areas. Tax reductions do not help but subsidies do in such situations. Investment aid can be given to particular areas. It is also possible that government investment can be directed to particular areas.

- It is important that what is produced is useful. It is, perhaps, better to employ people on projects of low value rather than have them unemployed. Investment expenditure whether public or private is preferable to tax reductions that increase consumption particularly in an open economy where a great deal of consumption expenditure is on imports. Tax cuts, however, are quicker to implement.

- The effect of a measure must be examined to find its effect on the other goals of fiscal policy. For example, if growth is a priority, then the idea is to increase demand by investment rather than by consumption.

Limitations of Policy in a Small Open Economy:

In classifying economies, the words 'small' and 'open' are used in a precise technical sense. Here 'smallness' means that relative to total world supply of traded goods or assets, a small economy is one that supplies such a small proportion that it cannot influence their prices. At a macroeconomic level, it means that any change whether expansion or contraction, will have little effect on economic activity in the rest of the world. For example, an expansionary fiscal policy in Japan or Germany can cause an expansion of world trade while a similar policy in Ireland will have a negligible effect.

What are the implications for economic policy of being a small open economy, like Ireland? It is extremely susceptible to external shocks such as the oil price rise in 1974. The effect of domestic fiscal and monetary measures, tend to have more effect on the balance of payments than on the level of domestic prices and employment. A further constraint of macroeconomic policy is that consistency with a tenable balance of payment's position is essential, otherwise the country will suffer from a loss of external reserves, and if this continues for any length of time, a devaluation of the currency may be unavoidable.

Automatic Stabilisers:

The fiscal system has automatic stabilisers built into it. These are for example, changes in fiscal policy that stimulate aggregate demand when the economy goes into recession without the government taking any deliberate action. These can be defined as anything that tends to cause injections to decrease or leakages to increase as national income rises, with no government assistance and vice versa when national income falls. They therefore reduce both upward movements and downward movements in national income. They act to reduce business cycle fluctuations, in part, but cannot wipe them out completely.

When the economy is close to full employment, a high degree of built-in stability will be useful because it will dampen down inflationary pressure. However an economy in depression may be prevented from making a fast recovery because of the same degree of built-in stability.

These stabilisers are primarily of two types.

1. Automatic Changes In Tax Receipts

The most important automatic stabiliser is the tax system. In a recession government revenue falls automatically since it is related to economic activity. This automatic cut in tax increases aggregate demand, therefore it reduces the size of the economic fluctuations.

2. Transfer Payments

Government expenditure acts as an automatic stabiliser. At a time of recession there is greater unemployment and more people are on social welfare. Benefits pump funds into or out of the economy and this occurs even though there is no increase in the amount of benefit or eligibility. This automatic increase in spending increases aggregate demand when it is not enough to maintain full employment.

In Ireland we have a progressive tax system and when incomes begin to fall tax receipts fall without any change in the tax system or rates. When income rises tax receipts increase. If there is an unexpected change in the economy, a change in tax may be just what is needed. If output falls, tax receipts will automatically fall so that personal incomes and spending will be cushioned. But the individual taxpayer who retains his job still pays the same amount of tax. Output will not fall by as much as it would without stabilisers. In inflationary times an increase in tax will lower incomes and reduce consumption spending and aggregate demand. This will slow down the upward trend in wages and prices.

Limitation of Automatic Stabilisers:

In the multiplier model a shock to spending on investment, net exports or government spending will have a multiplied impact on output. Taxes automatically take away a fraction of each extra £ of income thus reducing the size of the multiplier. For example if MPC is 0.8 without taxes, the multiplier would be five $\frac{1}{1-0.8}$. If taxes took one quarter of all income then the multiplier will be reduced to two and one half i.e. $\frac{1}{1-.8(1-.25)} = \frac{1}{1-.6} = \frac{1}{0.4}$

= 2.5 having their effects on GNP multiplied 5 times because of the automatic stabilising effect of taxes the impact will be smaller.

Effectiveness of Automatic Stabilisers:

Automatic stabilisers will not maintain full stability as outlined and can have adverse effects on aggregate supply, unemployment, may create poverty traps and cause the problem of fiscal drag.

- **Adverse Supply Side Effects**

High taxes discourage initiative and effort. The higher the marginal propensity to tax the higher the stability provided by the tax system. However taxes act as a disincentive to investment and work.

- **Unemployment Trap**

Higher benefits may discourage people from work and this increases unemployment and offsets the effect on employment of the automatic stabiliser. It will also increase the level of unemployment for any given level of inflation i.e. moves the Philips curve (given in Chapter 18) to the right.

- **Poverty Trap**

A poverty trap arises when poor people are discouraged from working or getting a better job because any extra income they earn will be largely taken away in taxes and lost benefits. The more people are discouraged the lower will be the level of aggregate supply. There is a link between the poverty trap and unemployment trap, i.e. the "Black Economy". People give up work so as to claim unemployment benefit while working in the informal "Black Economy" in order to escape the poverty party.

- **Fiscal Drag**

This is the tendency of automatic fiscal stabilisers to reduce the recovery of an economy from recession by reducing the size of the multiplier. It occurs in a progressive tax system when the government fails to raise tax thresholds to keep pace with inflation.

Taxation:

A tax is a compulsory contribution made by the taxpayer to the State towards its expenditure. It is levied on a "base" determined by the taxing authority. It is, however, not a price because the tax payable bears no relation to the services received. Even though the main purpose is to raise revenue, it also helps to:

- **Lessen the inequality of incomes;** this is done by progressive taxation, which means the higher the income, the higher the tax.
- **As an instrument of control of the level of economic activity;** Deficit budgeting to combat unemployment when taxation raised is not enough to cover expenditure; Surplus budgeting or raising more revenue than required and for other reasons to combat inflation.
- To influence consumption and production by sales taxes, value added tax and customs duties.

Attributes Of A Good Tax System:

In his work "An Inquiry into the Nature and Cause of the Wealth of Nations, **Adam Smith** gave four principals or Canons of taxation. In general terms these are as follows:

- **The tax on each person should be related to the person's ability to pay.** People in the same economic circumstances should pay the same. For example, all smokers pay tax on tobacco while non-smokers do not.

- **The amount of tax a person must pay should be certain and clear.** He/she should also find it difficult to evade payment.

- **The manner and timing of payment of taxes should have regard to the convenience of the taxpayer.** Bad debts and evasion are reduced if the above is done.

- **The cost of collection should be small relative to the yield.** Yield should at least cover the cost of collection with something to spare to offset the vexation caused. In practice, a single tax with a high yield is better than a number of taxes having a small yield. The Minister for Finance should be able to estimate the yield from a tax if the budget is to be used for adjusting overall demand.

Nowadays, the ideal tax should also include the following attributes:

- **It should be adjustable up and down as policy changes.** Here, due to trade agreements and competition from imports, customs and excise duties may not lend themselves to a wide degree of flexibility.

- **It should not discourage effort and initiative.** This is especially true in relation to high marginal rates of income tax demonstrated by the backward bending supply curve of labour. High rates will induce the taxpayer to take his income in the form of leisure or reduce his willingness to undergo training or seek promotion. On the other hand, a person with a mortgage, or hire-purchase payments, may have to work harder to meet repayments, when his income is reduced. Some people may enjoy work and prefer it to leisure. Most workers have to work a normal week and can only vary their hours as regards overtime. High marginal rates of tax will affect investment. Capital is mobile and foreigners may make investment decisions, affecting the Irish economy. The level of taxation will influence them, and this may act as a disincentive to investment.

- **It should be consistent with government policy.** The tax structure should be reviewed regularly to see how individual taxes can be used to further government policy.

- **Taxes should be equitable in their distribution.** This can be classified according to the proportion of a person's income, which is deducted in tax.

Types of Taxation:

- **Progressive Taxation:**

In a progressive system the proportion of a person's income paid in tax increases as income rises. The Irish system is progressive whereby after the exemption of low incomes under a certain level the rate of tax increases in stages so that the proportion of income taken increases with rising income. The main advantage with this system is that it reduces inequalities of wealth. For tax to be progressive the marginal rate must be higher than the average rate. A disadvantage of the system is that, at high income levels, the choice between more income and more leisure is distorted in favour of the latter resulting often in reduced output by the most productive or skilled people in the labour force. Taxes on luxury goods bought mainly by the higher income groups are also progressive.

- **Regressive System:**

In a regressive tax system, as a person's income rises the proportion paid in tax falls. The higher the income the lower the proportion paid in tax because the amount paid by each person is fixed. The marginal rate of tax is less than the average rate. Beer and tobacco taxes are high revenue earners for the Government. The poor spend a much higher proportion of their income on them than the rich therefore they are regressive. Indirect taxes such as a television license is regressive in that the sum payable is fixed irrespective of income.

- **Proportional Taxation:**

In this system a fixed proportion of income is taken in taxation. The marginal and average rates are equal. This is sometimes called a "flat rate" tax. Taxes on goods where expenditure does not change as income rises are proportional.

Diagram 14.1 shows that a tax is progressive, regressive, or proportional depending on whether the proportion of income paid in tax rises, is constant or falls as income increases.

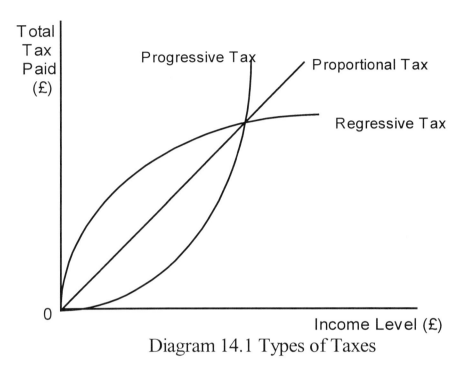

Diagram 14.1 Types of Taxes

The tax system should have a stabilising effect on the economy and this means that there is change but there are not wide fluctuations in the economy. Tax revenue tends to be high when economic activity is high and vice versa when it is low. Taxes can be looked on as automatic stabilisers in that when economic activity is high they take an increasing proportion of purchasing power from the private sector and a decreasing proportion when activity is low. They lessen the extent of fluctuations but do not eliminate them since their stabilising effect occurs only in response to the initial fluctuations.

The Structure of Taxation:

No single tax is perfect, therefore, there must be a structure of taxation, consisting of a number of taxes that the government can vary from time to time as policy changes.

Direct Taxation:

This involves a direct levy on an individual or corporate body by reference to a specific tax base. It is a tax on income and wealth.

Advantages:

- Here the person makes direct payment to the revenue authority and it is related to ability to pay. Personal and other allowances are used to ensure that the payment of taxes does not prevent people providing themselves with the necessities of life.

- The person is aware of the amount he is liable for. Allowances and rates of tax are set out in legislation and are available to everybody.

- Cost of collection is low as seen in the method of PAYE (Pay As You Earn) as the employer collects it.

- It is generally convenient for the taxpayer. With PAYE, it is deducted at source from salaries and wages.

Disadvantages:

- High marginal rates of tax act as a disincentive to effort. People who are self employed and can control their level of work, may reduce their work effort if marginal rates of tax are high. Wage differentials may be reduced and this will be a disincentive to effort on the part of workers and may deter them from seeking promotion or education.

- High rates of direct tax may be a disincentive to investment. It is the after tax return on investment that is looked at when deciding on where to invest.

- If tax rates are high, savings will be lower.

- Finally, high of tax rates tend to encourage tax evasion. People working without paying tax are able to under sell those in legitimate businesses and paying taxes.

Indirect taxes:

These are levied on goods and services and the tax is included in the price of the good. Indirect taxes largely fall on goods and services and the main burden will not necessarily fall on those who formally pay the taxes as there is an attempt to shift payment onto the customer.

Advantages:

- These taxes produce revenue and if they are on relatively price inelastic goods, the yield can be fairly accurately calculated. Collection costs are small.

- Direct taxes are based on income while indirect taxes are based on expenditure. It is difficult to accurately determine income and as expenditure is related to income, a tax on it may be fairer.

- Payment of the tax is immediate on purchase. The buyer knows the tax-inclusive price of the good and can decide as to whether he/she can afford it now or not.

- It is flexible and can be used by the government in a discriminatory way in that it can put a lower rate of tax on necessities and a higher rate on imports or luxury goods in theory.

- Indirect taxes are not perceived as a disincentive to work. In fact, people may work harder to maintain their purchasing power when an indirect tax is imposed or increased.
- If an indirect tax is levied on goods with a high-income elasticity of demand, as income increases, so too do the tax proceeds. Conversely, if income falls, so will the yield. This has a stabilising effect on the economy.

Disadvantages:

- If indirect taxes are levied equally on rich and poor, they are regressive.

- Indirect taxes increase the price of goods and services and can increase the cost of living and may be inflationary.

- Depending on elasticity of demand, indirect taxes may affect employment and viability of industries. For example, if there is a tax on tobacco, employment in the tobacco industry may go down and the viability of the industry may be threatened.

- There may be discrimination between individuals. People who do not smoke or drink make a smaller contribution towards revenue than smokers and drinkers so that the latter are penalised.

Reasons for Imposition of Taxes:

- To cover the cost of running the country and the provision of, social and other services.

- To reduce inequalities in income by means of progressive income tax. This involves a transfer of wealth from the "well off" to the "less well off". The degree of redistribution of income will depend on how progressive the tax is.

- To check the consumption of tobacco and spirits, for reasons of health. This is a social rather than an economic reason.

- To improve the performance of the economy by directing investment into certain sectors of the economy by means of a reduced tax rate and other tax-related incentives.

Incidence of Taxes:

The incidence of a tax measures the final tax burden on different people and allowance is made for the direct as well as the indirect effects of the tax. Incidence is on the person who suffers a loss in real income as a result of the tax.

If the government puts a tax on a good, the price will rise for the consumer but it will also cause producer revenue to fall. The distribution of the burden of the tax between consumers and producers depends on the price elasticity of demand and supply of the good. The consumers' burden will be greater and the producers lower the less elastic the demand and more elastic the supply of the good. Total tax for the government will be higher the less elastic demand and supply are.

Government Revenue:

Government revenue is divided into current and capital receipts. Current revenue or receipts consist of money received annually on a continuous basis which does not have to be repaid. These are also known as "above the line" receipts. The main source of government revenue is taxation but other sources are government trading and investment income and the proceeds of the National Lottery.

Trends in Taxation:

Table 14.1 gives a breakdown of current revenue 1995 to 1998. Income tax contributed the greatest amount, followed by VAT and excise duty. In 1998, income tax accounted for 37.1%, VAT 28%, and excise duties 18.3%

Income tax is a major part of government revenue over the years. The burden of taxation is heavy on the PAYE workers due to the fact that Ireland has a very narrow tax base. It is difficult to find new taxes especially on property and wealth. The Residential Property Tax was withdrawn in 1997 because it could not be properly implemented.

The Minister for Finance in his 1999 Budget speech announced that a system of tax credits was to be introduced which would replace the present system of tax allowances. As a result of previous years' budgets some relief such as mortgage interest are only allowable at the standard rate and are classified as tax credits. From the 5th April 1999 the PAYE allowance was increased to £1,000 but was converted into a tax credit so that it is worth £240 to each taxpayer. The basic single and married personal allowances are also standard rated. Credits mean that the individual has a fixed amount (does not apply to high income earners) deducted from what he or she, owes in tax, and if that exceeds the tax due he or she gets a refund. This is better than the allowance which may not be fully used up. The move to tax credits enables more resources to be devoted to those on lower incomes for a given Exchequer cost by equalising the value of the personal tax allowances to all taxpayers at the standard rate of tax. The first £100 of weekly income is not now subject to income tax.

Future Taxation Policy:

Under it's Statement of Strategy, published on the 22th December 1998 the Department of Finance aims to improve the structure of the taxation system so that it will do the following:
- Promote a competitive economy through the reduction of tax rates and the reduction of the impact of taxation on employment and the productive sector;

- Promote greater equity in the tax system through measures to broaden the tax base, reduce the proportion of taxpayers on the higher income tax rate, and reduce the burden of tax on the lower paid;
- Ensure that that tax policy integrates with income support measures so as to maximise the incentive to work and promote social cohesion;
- Support a moderate pay regime; and
- Encourage entrepreneurship, technological innovation and the acquisition of skills.

Table 14.1
Irish Current Government Revenue 1995 to 1998

	1995	1996	1997	1998	1995	1996	1997	1998
Tax Revenue:		£mn.				% of Total		
Excise Duties	2,069	2,100	2,470	2,800	17.2	18.9	18.6	18.3
Income Tax	4,051	3,950	4,926	5,700	32.2	36.4	37.1	37.1
Corporation Tax	1,290	2,350	1,448	2,000	19.2	10	10.9	13.0
VAT	2,927	2,850	3,461	4,300	23.2	25.4	26.1	28.0
Other Taxes	986	1,000	958	540	8.2	9.2	7.3	3.6
	11,193	12,250	13, 2 63	15,34 0	100	100	100	100

Source: Various Budgets.

Government Expenditure:

The public sector of the Irish Economy can be divided into three parts: Central Government, Local Government and Nationalised Industries. We confine ourselves here to central government expenditure as this is by far the largest part.

Government expenditure has been traditionally divided into current and capital expenditure. Current expenditure consists of expenditure on the day to day running of the State. It is undertaken on a regular basis and includes payments made to teachers, civil servants, debt service, transfer payments and payment for other goods and services consumed during the year. Current expenditure can be referred to as "above the line" expenditure. Capital expenditure is expenditure on items that will help production in the future. It adds to the country's productive and social capital, as what it is spent is not consumed during the year of expenditure. The construction of roads, hospitals, houses and telecommunications, transport and schools are some of the forms of capital expenditure. It is also referred to as "below the line" expenditure.

219

The distinction between current and capital expenditure came about because of the opinion that current expenditure should be financed through taxation while capital expenditure should be financed through borrowing. The difference no longer holds as for example, the deficit on current account, has been financed by borrowing in modern times.

Government expenditure is divided as follows: Central Fund, Supply Services and Public Capital Programme. Current expenditure is obtained by adding Central Fund and Supply Services while the Public Capital Programme is government capital expenditure for the year.

Estimates of Government Expenditure:

Each government department prepares an estimate of its likely expenditure for the year. The Department of Finance looks at them to ensure that they are in line with overall budgetary policy and that the amount of expenditure is justified. When the estimates are agreed they are published in the "Book of Estimates" at least one week before Budget day. All likely receipts are calculated and these are included with the estimates of expenditure in the "Estimates of Receipts and Expenditure".

Central Fund: All government revenue goes into this and law controls payments from it. The largest element in Central Fund Services is the annual cost of servicing the National Debt. To remain creditworthy the interest due on loans must be paid. The government cannot cutback in this area and it is considered to be a prior charge on state revenue.

Supply Services:

These services are the day to day cost of providing public services such as education, health and all the social welfare payments. The amount spent on these services has to be voted annually in the Dail. Supply Services are divided up as follows:

- **Transfer Payments**

Social Welfare payments are the biggest item here.

- **Current subsidies**

These are given in order to keep down the cost of a particular good to consumers. Examples are subsidies for housing and to farmers

- **Public Services**

Central government gives grants to local authorities and they provide some of these services.

- **Government Consumption**

The government consumes many goods and services and pays for the provision of services by public sector employees.

Public Sector Borrowing:

To obtain the total for government borrowing, borrowing for capital purposes must be added to the current budget deficit (CBD). Capital borrowing is for capital spending that is not financed by internally generated resources. Overall government borrowing, the Exchequer Borrowing Requirement (EBR), is the amount of money which the government has to borrow each year to finance spending not covered by government revenue. It is made up of current budget deficit plus, exchequer borrowing for capital purposes. Even before Ireland had a current budget deficit, the government borrowed for capital purposes, so that there was an accumulated national debt by 1972.

In order to obtain total government borrowing, borrowing by state sponsored bodies and local authorities must be added to EBR. Since the government is responsible for the borrowing, the resultant total is known as the Public Sector Borrowing Requirement (PSBR). The Primary Budget Balance is equal to EBR less interest paid on the National Debt. A plus sign indicates a deficit while a minus indicates a surplus. A deficit means that the Debt/GDP ratio will rise while a surplus can cause it to fall.

Table 14.2 gives details for CBD, EBR, PSBR and the primary budge for the years 1978 to 1998 and shows all four as a percentage of GNP. CBD rose gradually from 1978 to 1981 and it peaked in 1986 at £1,395 million or 8.2% of GNP. With the advent of fiscal rectitude in 1987, it fell to £317 million or 1.6% of G.N.P in 1988, and was under 2 per cent of GNP until 1994 when there was a small surplus of £15 mn. In 1995 there was a deficit of 1.1% and it is in surplus since. The forecast for 1999 is £2,335 or 4.6% of GNP. The primary budget is in surplus since 1995.

EBR over the same period reached very high figures and peaked in 1981 at 15.9% of GNP. Each year 1989 to 1998 it has been less than 3% of GNP.

PSBR was 20.3% of GNP in 1981 and up to 1987 was in double figures but has been less than 4% of GNP since, then.

Primary budget: Table 14.2 shows the primary budget balance as a percentage of GNP since 1980. From 1980 to 1983 there was a primary budget deficit each year but it has been in surplus since. When there is a surplus Debt/GDP ratio falls.

The Budget:

The budget contains financial data on government business for the previous year and estimated figures for the current year. It is an economic document and it is the main instrument for implementing fiscal policy. It seeks to implement fiscal policy and through it to influence the economic life of the country. To be successful the budget must be properly framed. After the Budget is introduced, the Finance Act is passed and this gives the government permission to collect the money by taxation. An Appropriation Act is also passed and this allows the government to spend the money raised. It includes all financial transactions of the government and departments and agencies of the government. Some public enterprises are excluded since they make their own decisions autonomously.

The main objectives of budgetary policy are as follows:

1. **The efficient social allocation of resources**;
The allocation function consists of policies to achieve efficient allocation of resources between the public and private sector. It is concerned with tax policy, social services, health and education, law and order and defence. It includes policies that have a bearing on consumption and investment decisions in the private and public sector. Movements of resources between different activities and regions are covered.

2. **An equitable distribution of income and wealth**;

This concerns the distribution of income between households. Taxation, transfer payments and government services seek to accomplish equitable distribution, so that the less well off in society are protected.

3. **Stabilisation policies with the aim of achieving full employment, balance of payments equilibrium, and price stability.**

Policy here seeks to achieve a high level of employment and economic activity while at the same time maintaining price stability and balance of payments equilibrium.

All three are interrelated and this must be taken into account when formulating the Budget.

Types of Budget:

The budget can in general terms be surplus, deficit or neutral:

- **Current Budget surplus**

A current budget surplus means that the government is taking more money from its day to day activities than is required to meet its current expenditure. Since money is taken out of circulation, a budget surplus constitutes a leakage type of savings from the circular flow of income and is deflationary.

- **Budget Deficit**

A budget deficit occurs when government expenditure exceeds government revenue, as enough money is not collected to cover day to day business so borrowing covers the deficit. There is an injection of spending into the economy and it is considered inflationary. This assumes that the current deficit is greater than that of the previous year and if it is less, then money is taken out of the economy as the government is reducing the deficit. In this case even though there is a budget deficit, there is a leakage from the circular flow of income.

- **Neutral Budget**

This occurs when the budget neither deflates or inflates the economy i.e. current revenue equals current expenditure so that the budget is balanced.

Table 14.2
Trend in the Current Budget Deficit and the Exchequer Public Sector Borrowing Requirement (In Absolute Terms and as a % of GNP) 1977-1998

Year	Current Budget Deficit		Total Exchequer Borrowing		Public Sector Borrowing Requirement		Primary Budget	
	£m	% of GNP	£m	% of GNP	£m	% of GNP	£m	% of GNP
1980	547	6.1	1,218	13.5	1,559	17.3	426	4.7
1981	802	7.4	1,721	15.9	2,204	20.3	668	6.1
1982	988	7.9	1,945	15.6	2,466	19.8	485	3.9
1983	960	7.1	1,756	12.9	2,277	16.7	43	0.3
1984	1,039	7.0	1,825	12.4	2,375	16.1	-75	-0.5
1985	1,284	8.1	2,015	12.7	2,444	15.4	188	-1.2
1986	1,395	8.2	2,145	12.7	2,506	14.8	-75	-0.4
1987	1,180	6.4	1,786	9.8	2,056	11.2	-575	-3.0
1988	317	1.6	619	3.2	751	3.9	-1533	-7.7
1989	263	1.2	479	2.3	667	3.1	-1671	7.7
1990	152	0.7	462	2.0	681	3.0	-1,840	-7.7
1991	300	1.3	501	2.1	816	3.4	-1826	-7.3
1992	446	1.8	713	2.8	861	3.7	-1586	-6.0
1993	379	1.4	690	2.5	925	3.5	-1586	-5.7
1994	-15	-0.5	672	2.2	782	2.6	-1,633	-5.5
1995	362	1.1	627	1.9	826	2.5	-1714	-5.0
1996	-292	-0.8	436	1.2	531	1.5	-1,904	-5.1
1997	-193	-0.5	636	1.6	764	1.9	-1714	-4.2
1998	-2,092	- 3.5*	- 948	1.6*				
1999	-2,335	- 4.6*	-1,175*	1.9*				

*Forecast

Source: Various Budgets. ESRI Quarterly Commentary February 1999

Irish Fiscal Policy:

Current Budget:

The government budget is made up of three items: expected income, planned spending and the difference if any between the two. Initially Ireland did not have a current budget deficit. Deficits started in the 1970's and were in response to deflationary pressure caused mainly by the oil crisis in 1973/74. Government spending was increased, to counteract the severe international recession, without any increase in taxation. This was done on the basis of Keynesian demand management, which was to stabilise demand. Increased spending should have been diverted into capital projects, which would have given a return in the form of greater industrialisation, higher employment and better infrastructure. This did not happen and current budget deficits continued to 1993. The deficit in 1975 was 6.8% of G.N.P declining further in 1977 to 3.6%.

1977 saw Fianna Fail back in government on the basis of their manifesto, which made all sorts of expensive promises later fulfilled in the 1978 Budget. This did not do the deficit any good as it went back up to 6.1%. Again the deficit was seen as a temporary measure on the basis that private investment would rise due to the increase in government spending. It was expected that the growth rate would increase resulting in greater tax revenue. Thus in 1979 when the second oil crisis occurred, Irish public finances were in a very poor state and debt was mounting all the time as was the tax burden due to ever increasing interest on this debt. The deficit was 6.8%.

1981 brought in a Coalition government of Fine Gael and Labour and they introduced a mini-budget in July 1981 in an effort to halt the slide. Tax increase was the method used but the tax take was not enough to prevent the current budget deficit rising to 7.4% of GNP. Fianna Fail was in again for a brief period in 1982 when the Coalition returned. The 1982 deficit was 7.9%

Over the period 1982 to 1986 the Coalition increased taxes and reduced public expenditure but made no progress towards restoring order in the public finances with the current budget deficit at a new high of 8.2% (Table 14.2) in 1986.

In 1987 Fianna Fail were back again, this time as a minority government, Fiscal rectitude started. Cuts were made in current government spending. Fiscal targets were achieved helped by the collapse in oil prices among other things. 1988 saw the current budget deficit down to 1.6% of GNP.

In the 1990's fiscal policy was based on Ireland's endeavour to qualify for membership of the EMU. One of the convergence criteria in Maastricht is that the fiscal budget deficit must not be greater than 3% of GDP, unless for a temporary or exceptional case, such as adverse conditions not usually associated with the country's general performance. Debt/ GDP ratio had to be 60% or to be falling quickly. Ireland succeeded in qualifying for, and is since January 1st 1999 a member of EMU.

On the 1st of September 1998 the Department of Finance made a Strategy Statement in accordance with the Public Service Management Act 1997. In relation to Fiscal Policy it will promote tax reform, reduction of debt, effective management of public expenditure and price stability. Multi-annual budgets are now prepared to plan for more effective medium-term management of public finances.

Table 14.3
Summary of Current and Capital Budgets, 1998 and 1999

	1998 Estimated Outturn £m	1999 Post Budget Estimate £m
Current Budget:		
1. Current Expenditure		
Gross Voted(Dail)	12,230	13,332
Non-Voted	3,436	3,407
Social Welfare Fund	2,033	2,161
Gross Current Expenditure	17,699	18,900
Less appropiations	(3,219)	(3,479)
Less Departmental Balances	(10)	(20)
Net Current Expenditure	14,469	15,401
Current Receipts:		
Tax Revenue	16,093	17,335
Non-tax Revenue	1,985	2,335
Total Current Receits	16,454	17,736
Current Budget Surplus	1,985	2,335
Capital Budget:		
Capital Expenditure		
Gross Voted	1,950	2,308
Non-Voted	188	52
Less Appropriated	(85)	(113)
Net Capital Expenditure	2,053	2,247
Capital Resources	737	836
Capital Budget Deficit	(1,316)	(1,410)
Exchequer Surplus with Contingency	668	925
General Contingency	-	-
Exchequer Surplus with Contingency	668	925
General Government Surplus	951	1,057
GGSurplus as % of GDP		
Including contingency	1.7%	1.7%
Before contingency	1.7%	1.7%
GDP Value (ESA 95 BASIS)	56,675	62,125

Source: Budget1998 and 1999.

1999 Irish Budget:

The aims of the 1999 budget were as follows:
- To effect major personal tax reform;
- To plan for the longer term;
- To sustain a growing economy; and
- To maintain social inclusiveness.

The Minister of Finance brought in a budget package which in the light of the unprecedented growth and falling interest rates would seem to be inflationary. However this type of budget was necessary to curb wage and price pressure. It is aimed at achieving a new wage agreement to succeed Partnership 2000. Demand for labour in particular for skilled labour, is putting pressure on labour costs and this is a trend that will continue irrespective of what new deal is negotiated.

Main Targets of 1999 Budget:
- Current budget surplus of £2,335 million;
- Capital budget deficit of £1,410 million;
- An exchequer surplus of £925million; and
- A general Government surplus of 1.7% of GDP.

There was a cut of 4% in the non-manufacturing corporation tax rate from 32% to 28% in line with the objectives of reducing it to 12.5 % by 2003. The income ceiling on 12% employer's PRSI increased from £29,000 to £35,000. This results in an incremental cost to business of £720 per employee per annum.

Table 14.3 gives details of the estimated out-turn for 1998 and estimate for 1999. An estimated surplus of £1,985 million in the Current Budget was achieved in1998. The surplus was in fact £2,092 (Table14.2). The general government surplus was 1.7% and the estimate for 1999 is also for 1.7%. 1998 was the first time in over fifty years that the Irish budget was in overall surplus. The General Government Deficit/Surplus measure that adjusts for items such as privatisation receipts that affect EBR was first used in Ireland in the 1993 budget.

Irish Fiscal Policy in the EMU:

The EMU has no central fiscal authority therefore budgetary decisions remain with individual member states. Since monetary policy is the province of the EMU, it is possible for member states to pursue fiscal policies in conflict with it. Germany tried to avoid this when it sought but did not get agreement on national fiscal policies.

Under EMU Ireland no longer has the option to independently devalue its exchange rate or set interest rates. This leaves fiscal policy as the only means of macroeconomic intervention in the economy. As already stated monetary policy now rests with the ESCB and decisions made may not necessarily suit Ireland. It is important therefore that when monetary policy suited to other members is likely to be destabilising for Ireland, fiscal policy is effectively used. We must also ensure that we avoid budgetary imbalances and keep within the rules of The Pact for Stability and Growth detailed below.

The Pact for Stability and Growth:

This pact was agreed in Dublin in December 1996 and ratified in Amsterdam in June 1997. Euro zone countries must not run budget deficits greater than 3% of GDP. Any country, running a deficit greater than 3% may be fined. If the economy shrinks by more than 2% there is an automatic exception. Over the past 25 years the economies of the EU 15 have shrunk by 2% only nine times as shown in Table 14.4. The Irish economy has not shrunk at all over the same period. The country concerned can also plead exceptional circumstances if they shrink at all, thought a resolution says that GDP should drop by more than ¾ of 1% before leniency is sought. Fines may be up to ½ % of GDP and must be approved by the Council of Ministers.

Table 14.4
Number of Years in the period 1970-1996 when GDP fell
Fall in Real GDP

Country	>2%	0.75-2%
Austria	0	0
Ireland	0	0
Netherlands	0	0
Spain	0	1
Denmark	0	2
France	0	2
Belgium	0	3
Germany	0	3
Luxemburg	1	0
Greece	1	1
Italy	1	1
Portugal	1	2
Sweden	1	3
Finland	2	1
UK	2	2
Total	9	21

Source: OECD

Irish Stability and Growth Pact Programme 1999-2001:

This programme sets out the Irish government's budgetary objectives for the period 1999 to 2001. An average General Government Surplus of 1.6 per cent of GDP is projected for the three years compared to 1.7% for 1998. This meets the medium-term objective of the Pact for Stability and Growth of keeping the budget "close to balance or in surplus" in normal economic circumstances. This means that cyclical factors and their effect on the Budget must be taken into account when assessing the budgetary position. The increase in the deficit in the capital account is projected in the expectation of a drop in EU transfers and greater public sector investment over the period.

As seen in Table 14.5 the policy is to run budget surpluses in the light of the strong growth in the Irish economy and the prospect of a continuation of this strong growth over the next three years. It is however extremely difficult to measure the extent to which the economy is above or below the trend or estimated output gap. The magnitude of the cyclically adjusted budget balance is also difficult to estimate.

Table 14.5
Budgetary Projections 1999-2001 (%GDP)*

	1998	1999	2000	2001
Current Account Surplus	3.7	4.0	4.6	5.1
Capital Account Deficit	-2.0	-2.3	-2.8	-2.7
Contingency			-0.4	-0.8
General Government Surplus	1.7	1.7	1.4	1.6
Of which Primary Surplus	5.4	5.1	4.2	1.8
Change in Cyclically Adjusted	-	-	-0.3	+0.5
General Government Balance	-	+0.1	+0.2	+0.8

+ = Tightening
*These figures are given on a European System of National and Regional Accounts (ESA95) basis for comparative purposes.
Source: Irish Business Digest, November/December 1998.

Table14.5 shows that the budget surplus on an ESA95 basis and including the contingency provision is forecast to fall from 1.7% of GDP in 1998 to 1.6% in 2001. This reflects lower EU transfers, slower growth and greater capital investment. In spite of the expected slow down in the economy, budget surpluses are forecast as shown in Table 14.5. Excluding the contingency provision, the budget surplus is forecast to increase from 1.7% in 1998 to 2.4% in 2001.Under the cyclically adjusted methodology of the EU this is a tightening of fiscal policy.

National Debt:

National debt is the cumulative total of borrowing raised by government over a period of years. The term national debt is misleading as over two thirds of the debt is owed to one part of the nation by another part of the nation. National Debt is the remaining one third as it is owed to foreigners. A more accurate term would be Government Debt.

External versus Internal Debt:

Foreign Borrowings: The external portion of the National Debt represents government borrowing abroad from foreign governments or international institutions and foreign banks together with Irish bonds and bills held by non-residents. This involves a net subtraction from the resources available to Ireland.

Domestic Borrowing: Internal debt is the total of government stocks and bonds held and savings through the Post Office of people living in Ireland. It can be divided into short and long –term borrowing. Short -term borrowing is for periods up to three months, usually by means of exchequer bills bought by financial institutions. It could also be gilts that are short dated. Insurance companies banks and others buy these. Long –term borrowing is the national loan and is made up of long-term securities repayable after a long period at a fixed rate of interest. The purpose of these is to finance the capital budget.

Burden of National Debt:

The national debt is a burden for the following reasons:

- The general level of taxation is higher than it need otherwise be.

- External debt involves the transfer of resources out of the country and foreign exchange is used which could otherwise be used to buy goods and services. If the initial foreign borrowing is not self liquidating then the burden is on future generations since they must provide the foreign exchange required to service and repay this debt.

- There is no tax deducted from interest paid on the external debt. Tax is paid on internal debt interest so that it is cheaper to service than the foreign debt element.

- Since the external debt and interest on it must be paid in foreign currencies there is an exchange risk. If the currency in which the loan is denominated appreciates as it did in January 1993, then the interest costs are higher and more than the amount borrowed must be repaid.

- A sizeable debt displaces capital since as the government debt grows people will purchase it and this will displace private capital.

- A large debt retards a country's growth due to displacement of private capital and the increased inefficiency it brings about in taxation. Government investment in infrastructure may be less than it need otherwise be.

- Internal debt is rarely repaid and it is usually 'rolled over'. This means that it is converted into more long-term debt, when it matures. This can also be done with foreign debt but not as easily. It depends on how our foreign lenders view our credit-worthiness. Their assessment of this would be based on our external reserves, political climate and size of our existing debt related to their assessment of what we can manage.

Borrowing which leads to debt can be used for productive or for social or non-productive investment. Until 1973 the Irish Budget was balanced in the sense that revenue equalled expenditure. At the same time we borrowed for productive purposes on the basis that such borrowing was self-liquidating. However there was investment in schools, hospitals and many other non -productive or social areas, a style of investment resulting in dead-weight debt which is not self -liquidating.

Table 14.6
Irish National Debt 1977-1998

Year£m	Foreign debt Outstanding % of Total		Domestic debt Outstanding £m % of Total		Total National Debt £m
1977	1,039	24.6	3,190	75.4	4,229
1978	1,064	20.6	4,103	79.4	5,167
1979	1,542	23.6	4,998	76.4	6,540
1980	2,207	28.0	5,689	72.0	7,896
1981	3,794	37.2	6,401	62.8	10,195
1982	5,248	45.0	6,421	55.0	11,669
1983	6,899	47.9	7,493	52.1	14,392
1984	7,910	47.0	8,911	53.0	16,821
1985	8,114	43.8	10,388	56.2	18,502
1986	9,220	42.7	12,391	57.3	21,611
1987	9,693	40.9	14,001	59.1	23,694
1988	9,498	38.6	15,113	61.4	24,611
1989	9,123	36.7	15,705	63.3	24,828
1990	8,848	35.3	16,235	64.7	25,083
1991	8,872	34.9	16,519	65.1	25,391
1992	10,122	38.4	16,223	61.6	26,345
1993	11,400	40.0	17,100	60.0	28,500
1994	11,000	37.5	18,300	62.5	29,300
1995	11,518	38.0	18,541	62.0	30,059
1996	8,718	28.5	21,971	71.5	30,689
1997	8,288	28.1	21,252	71.9	29,540
1998	7,375	25.0	22,125	75.0	29,500

Source: Central Bank Various Bulletins and National Treasury Management Agency direct communication May 1999.

Irish Debt:

Table 14.6 gives details of Irish National Debt 1977 to 1998. This is broken down into foreign and domestic debt. The debt was £4,229 million in 1977. It increased rapidly during the 1980's and reached £30,689 million in 1996, and it decreased to £29,500mn in 1998. This is an average of £7,973, per head of population based on the CSO estimate of population in 1998 of 3.7 million. From the start of the 1980's the debt increased substantially each year until 1988 when the rate of increase slowed down due to the policy of fiscal rectitude introduced in 1987.

In the early years of the period covered domestic debt was a large part of the debt, being over 75 per cent in 1977. In 1983 it was down to 52 per cent when the amount of foreign debt as a percentage of the total debt peaked. In 1998 it was 25.0 per cent foreign the lowest in GDP terms since 1980 and 75.0 per cent domestic.

Service of Public Debt:

Service of the public debt takes up a large proportion of government resources and budget flexibility is constrained by this. The high share of taxation required makes the exchequer vulnerable to unfavourable interest and exchange rate movements. This was borne out in the second half of 1992 and early 1993. Interest payments on the national debt as a percentage of income tax is now at its lowest level since 1976.

Table 14.7

Trend in Service of Public Debt as % of Current Expenditure, as % of Overall Taxation and as % of Income Taxation 1976-1998

Year	Service of Public Debt £mn.	As a % of Current Expenditure	As a % of Tax Revenue	As a % of Income Tax	As a % of GNP
1976	278	16.6	22.0	60.2	8.2
1977	334	17.1	22.5	64.0	6.3
1978	418	17.3	24.2	69.1	6.4
1979	514	17.7	25.6	70.2	6.7
1980	661	17.9	25.2	65.2	7.3
1981	885	18.5	26.7	71.2	8.2
1982	1,249	21.2	30.8	85.6	10.0
1983	1,456	21.8	31.1	87.5	10.7
1984	1,705	24.5	32.1	86.7	11.5
1985	1,967	25.8	35.2	93.5	12.5
1986	1,989	24.5	32.6	83.3	11.4
1987	2,118	25.4	32.6	78.1	11.3
1988	2,142	26.6	31.2	76.8	9.5
1989	2,140	26.7	28.8	76.2	9.8
1990	2,300	27.3	29.1	69.7	8.8
1991	2,351	25.9	28.2	66.0	8.5
1992	2,355	24.0	26.4	61.7	7.8
1993	2,390	21.7	23.0	55.9	7.2
1994	2,827	25.2	26.0	54.4	6.6
1995	2,400	19.9	21.1	48.8	5.6
1996	2,360	18.5	19.1	51.7	5.6
1997	2,755	16.1	15.0	43.6	5.4
1998	02,559	18.0	13.0	40.7	5.0°

Note: The 1988 figures exclude the exceptional once-off effects of the tax incentive scheme (amnesty)

°Estimate

Source: Budget Books and Income and Expenditure Accounts NTMA

Table 14.7 shows the trend in public debt as a percentage of current expenditure, overall taxation and income tax from 1977 to 1998. As the total debt increased, the cost of servicing it increased. In 1995 the amount of debt service was £2,400 nearly double that of 1982 when it was £1,249. The percentage of current expenditure going towards servicing debt grew steadily up to 1990 when it was 27.3% of GNP. It declined since then and was 18.0% for 1998. As a percentage of tax revenue, debt service as a % of GNP peaked in 1985 at 35.2% and is expected to account for 13.0% of tax revenue in 1998. In 1985, 93.5% of income tax went on debt service payment compared to 40.7% in 1998.

Finally debt service is estimated to take 5 per cent of GNP in 1998 while in 1985 it took 12.5 per cent, the highest for the period under consideration and also the highest ever recorded.

Debt GNP Ratio:

Table 14.8 shows the evolution of Debt/ GNP ratio from 1983 to 1998. It went over 100% for the first time in 1983 and increased steadily to 1987 when it peaked at 126.2 %. When the ratio exceeds 100 it means that debt is greater than annual income. The increase in the ratio over the period 1983 to 1987 damaged confidence in the Irish economy. When corrective action was taken in 1987/88 it began to fall and is expected to continue its downward trend in 1999.

Table 14.8
Irish Debt/GNP Ratio 1983/1998.

Year	Debt/GNP Ratio	Year	Debt/GNP Ratio
1983	105.9	1991	102.0
1984	113.7	1992	100.0
1985	117.9	1993	99.3
1986	129.2	1994	94.3
1987	126.8	1995	90.0
1988	124.4	1996	81.2
1989	114.1	1997	70.5
1990	106.0	1998°	62.8

°Estimate ESRI.

Source: National Income and Expenditure Accounts. Central Bank Bulletins. NTMA 1999

Gross General Government Debt/GDP Ratio:

Gross General Government Debt is wider than Exchequer Debt because it includes borrowing by local authorities and grant aided bodies. It is the criterion used in the Maastricht guidelines. In 1994 Irish Debt/GDP was 88.2 %, went down to 63.4% in 1997, 53.3% in 1998 and is forecast to go down each year to 2000 when it is expected to be 34.4% as shown in Table 14.9. The fall in the ratio is due to a relatively low EBR together with good growth in national income. The rate at which Ireland's debt ratio can be reduced depends on the rate of economic growth and the level of real interest rates. Over the period 1994 to 1998 Irish growth rates were exceptionally high and interest rates were relatively low. The outlook for 1999 and 2000 is that these trends will continue. The ratios of Belgium, Greece and Italy were 121.9%, 109.5% and 121.6% respectively in 1997. They are forecast to be 110.1%, 104.2% and 111.7% per cent respectively in 2000.

Table 14.9
Gross General Government Debt as a Percentage of GDP 1994 - 2000

	1994	1995	1996	1997	1998	1999	2000
Germany	50.2	58.3	60.8	61.5	61.3	61.0	60.7
France	48.5	52.7	55.7	58.1	58.3	58.6	58.3
Italy	124.9	124.2	124.0	121.6	118.8	115.3	111.7
UK	50.4	53.9	54.7	53.5	51.5	49.9	48.5
Belgium	133.2	131.0	126.8	121.9	117.2	113.7	110.1
Denmark	77.8	73.1	68.4	64.1	58.8	54.3	49.8
Greece	109.3	110.1	112.2	109.5	108.7	107.0	104.2
Ireland	88.2	80.9	71.4	63.4	53.3	44.1	34.4
Netherlands	77.9	79.2	77.1	71.4	68.6	66.6	63.7
Norway	62.6	65.6	70.2	68.9	67.7	66.0	63.6
Spain	79.3	78.0	77.2	76.9	74.0	69.5	63.8
Luxembourg	5.7	5.9	6.6	6.7	7.1	7.5	7.7
Austria	65.4	69.2	69.6	64.3	64.0	63.6	62.8
Portugal	63.8	65.9	64.9	61.5	57.4	55.3	53.7
EU 11	69.7	72.8	75.2	75.0	73.8	72.5	70.9
EU15	68.0	71.0	72.9	71.9	70.3	69.0	67.3

Source: European Economy, Supplement A Economic Trends No 10 1998.

The National Treasury Management Agency (NTMA).

This agency was established by the National Treasury Management Agency Act 1990, "to borrow moneys for the Exchequer and to manage the National Debt". It took over the functions of the Minister for Finance in the areas of exchequer borrowing and management of the national debt. It is under the general supervision of the Minister for Finance and is controlled by him/her. Obligations and functions undertaken by the Agency have the same authority, force and effect as if taken by the Minister.

Neither the chief executive nor any other staff member of the NTMA can be a civil servant. The chief executive reports directly to the Minister and is the accounting officer for the purpose of expenditure by the agency. Debt management includes the changing of loans from one currency to another and obtaining the most attractive interest rates. Foreign debt is now in the form of commercial paper, bonds and medium term loans.

Under the management of the NTMA, interest payable on our national debt is less and sums repayable may also be less due to appreciation of currency in re/lation to the foreign currencies, which make up the loans. The Agency's first priority is to obtain the money needed to meet the Exchequer borrowing requirement each year and to meet the repayments on existing debt.

The general aim of the agency is to raise as much money as possible in Irish pounds at the lowest possible rate of interest. Irish banks previously had to maintain a substantial part of their increase in resources each year in Irish government Gilts and Exchequer Bills.

Economic and Monetary Union and NTMA:

EMU gives opportunities as well as challenges for the NTMA in its borrowing and debt management activities. As in the past it is in a position to manage the debt in the most cost-effective manner within the EMU.

Questions

1. What do you understand by the Government's budget deficit? What in your opinion was the strategy of the 1999 Budget?

2. "Not all economists agree that the best means of stabilising the economy is through the use of fiscal policy." Discuss this statement outlining common areas of controversy and their importance in Ireland.

3. State what is meant by the Public Sector Borrowing Requirement and discuss the problems that may follow from its growth.

4. "Fiscal policy in Ireland is directed at Ireland's membership of the European Monetary Union." Discuss.

5. To what extent can fiscal policy contribute towards the achievement of government macro-economic objectives?

6. Distinguish between and outline the characteristics of direct and indirect taxes. Why may a government prefer to raise more revenue from one rather than from the other?

7. What is the National Debt? To what extent does it form a burden on society?

CHAPTER 15

INTERNATIONAL TRADE

Introduction:

This Chapter describes and explains the reasons for the international specialisation of production between countries. We discuss the pattern of international trade and the direction of Irish trade. It includes a critique of the free trade argument and an examination of the case for protection. Free trade areas and customs unions are surveyed. The Single European Market (SEM) is described and its impact on the Irish economy is assessed. The work of the General Agreement on Tariffs and Trade (GATT) now the World Trade Organisation (WTO) is assessed particularly the Uruguay Round. Finally the impact of the Common Agricultural Policy (CAP) and the 1992 and 1999 reforms of it on Irish trade is examined.

Ireland and Protectionism:

In the first decade after Independence Ireland adopted a free trade policy. The Irish economy at that time was very dependent on agricultural exports and the market in the UK was very competitive since there was a world over supply of agricultural goods. Policy changed to protectionism in 1932 and the main aim was to reduce dependence on the U K. The Control of Manufactures Acts, 1932-1934 were introduced to ensure that manufacturing businesses set up with the aid of protection would remain in Irish control. Ad valorem duties ranging from 15% to 75% were introduced. In the same year the Economic War between Ireland and the UK started over the non-payment by Ireland of land annuities to the UK. As a result the UK imposed Ad valorem duty of 20% on imports of Irish agricultural goods and also revoked Ireland's exemption from a general import duty of 10% imposed in 1932. Ireland, in return, imposed duties on UK coal, steel cement and other goods. The Economic War lasted until 1938.

The Economic War finished in 1938 with the Defence, Financial, and Trade Agreements. Under this agreement Ireland regained its UK export market for agricultural goods while discontinuing its export subsidies and bounties. It retained most of its protective duties on imports. During the war years practically all Irish exports were to the UK so that Ireland was still very much dependent on the rest of the world. The Trade Agreement with the UK allowed most Irish manufactured goods free entry to the UK. At the same time Ireland kept most of its own protective tariffs in place.

There was a movement towards free trade in Europe with the setting up of the Common Market in 1958. Ireland applied for membership in 1961 but was unsuccessful, but continued to free trade with two unilateral reductions in 1963 and 1964 of 10% each. The Anglo-Irish Free Trade Area Agreement of 1966 gave Ireland greater access to UK markets for agricultural goods and all remaining restrictions on industrial exports were removed. Ireland removed tariffs on UK goods with a few exceptions over a ten -year period.

In 1973 Ireland joined the EU and by so doing, agreed to establish free trade with member countries. Since the 1960's Ireland has made great efforts to diversify away from excessive dependence on the UK market by increasing exports to other countries. This is particularly important since Ireland broke the link with sterling in 1979. Successive GATT rounds have practically eliminated tariff protection in the developed world.

Openness of Irish Economy and Importance of Trade:

Ireland is a small open economy very dependent on trade with other countries. Since it is a small country with a small home market it specialises in some goods and imports the others. One measure of its openness is the ratio of its exports and imports to GNP as seen in Table 15.1. In 1997 exports amounted to 83.5% of GNP while in comparison the figure was 22% in 1958. Imports for the same years were 81.6 and 32% respectively. The estimated ratio for exports in 1998 is 107.4 when the value of exports exceeded GNP while imports are 91.0%. The smaller the country the more likely that it will specialise in some goods and import others. For example, from Table 15.1 the ratio of exports to GNP in Ireland in 1990 was 59.8% compared to 7.9% for the US and 23% on average for the EU (Eurostat 1994). In 1990 imports were 52% of GDP when the EU average was 24% (Eurostat 1994). This shows that Ireland is very dependent on foreign trade and that it is very important due to the openness of the Irish economy and the small size of the domestic market.

Table 15.1
Ratio of Exports to GNP 1958 and 1988 - 1998

Year	GNP (£mn)	Exports (£mn)	Exports (% GNP)	Imports (£mn)	Imports (% GNP)
1958	600	131	21.8	190	31.6
1988	19,995	12,305	61.5	10,215	51.0
1989	22,161	14,597	65.8	12,284	55.4
1990	23,962	14,336	59.8	12,468	52.0
1991	25,324	15,019	59.3	12,851	50.7
1992	26,693	16,629	62.2	13,195	49.4
1993	27,700	19,450	70.2	14,621	52.8
1994	30,614	22,435	73.2	16,903	55.2
1995	34,807	27,825	79.9	20,619	59.2
1996	37,790	30,407	80.4	22,429	59.3
1997	41,919	40,614	83.5	34,220	81.6
1998*	46,793	50,263	107.4	42,628	91.0

*Preliminary

Source: Economic Series 1998 Central Bank Reports and Irish Trade Bulletin 1961.

Exports:

The Irish home market is small being less than three and a half million consumers. Export markets make it possible for Irish firms to grow so as to achieve economies of scale. Economic growth is made possible and employment is provided. Exports earn the foreign exchange to pay for the importation of goods that are not or cannot be produced at home. They also provide the foreign exchange required to service foreign debt. Ireland is a part of world trade through exports and it is through expansion and diversification of this trade that growth in the Irish economy, can be achieved.

In the early years after Independence and up to the early 1950s, there was a policy of self - sufficiency and protectionism. Infant industry was fostered and was protected by high tariffs. World markets were also protected over this period. Ireland entered the 'Economic War' with Britain, as already stated thus closing off access to its main export market.

There was a relaxation of protectionism in the 1950s and early 1960s, as outlined above and tariffs began to disappear especially after the 1966 Anglo Irish Trade Agreement. Entry to the EU in 1973 intensified the export drive and many foreign firms were attracted and their output is mainly exported. Since 1973 Ireland has sought to be less reliant on the UK as a market for exports and therefore has tried to diversify markets for Irish goods.

Role of Multinationals in Irish Exports:

Export performance in Ireland has improved over the past thirty years and has assisted in increasing output and employment. This growth includes growth in manufactured goods which has come mainly from multinational or trans-national firms. These firms set up in Ireland because of IDA incentives, plentiful labour supply and suitability as a base from which to export into the EU market. This has resulted in a shift in export dependence away from the UK market towards other EU countries.

Table 15.2
Export Trade by Areas 1996 and 1997

Area	Exports (£millions)					
	1996	% of Total		1997	% of Total	% C
United Kingdom	7,477	24.6	8,510		24.2	+14
Germany	3,987	13.1	4,354		12.4	+9
France	2,503	8.2	2,763		7.8	+10
Netherlands	2,043	6.7	2,386		6.8	+17
USA	2,814	9.2	3,995		11.4	+42
Japan	860	2.8	1,124		3.2	+31
EU Total	20,804	68.4	23,276		66.5	+12
Non EU	9,603	31.6	11,751		33.5	+22.4
Total Exports	30,407	100.0	35,027		100.0	+15

Source:Statistical Abstract 1998

Direction of Irish Trade:

Table 15.2 shows the direction of Irish exports 1996 and 1997. Trade with the US and Japan increased substantially in 1997 over 1996. Trade with non-EU countries shows an increase of over 24% for the same period.

Ireland's Trade with the UK:

When Ireland became independent, almost 90% of Irish exports were to the UK. This percentage fell to approximately 75% in 1960. Since then there has been a sharp decline as seen in Table 15.2 that shows that 24.2% of exports went to the UK in 1997.

Trade dependency on the UK causes problems for Ireland. Exports are sensitive to income growth there and this has been slow over the past number of years. This dependence on the UK also hampers Ireland's efforts to establish an independent exchange rate policy. The higher the trade share and the more price sensitive trade is, the greater the cost of a change in the Euro/Sterling exchange rate. This was apparent during the exchange rate crisis 1992/1993 as it is in 1999 to a lesser extent. Irish indigenous industry is very dependent on the UK market. During the currency crisis 1992/93 these industries lost competitiveness when the IR£ appreciated against sterling. At the time the Irish Government reacted by setting up a fund to help these firms. This, of course, causes further problems in that Government spending increases, as does debt.

Table 15.3
Irish Imports and Exports by Section 1996 – 1997 (%)

Type of Product	Exports		Imports	
	1996	1997	1996	1997
1.Food and Live Animals	13.6	10.2	6.9	6.4
2.Beverages and Tobacco	1.7	1.8	1.1	1.1
3.Crude materials inedible except fuels	1.8	1.7	1.8	1.7
4.Mineral fuels, lubricants	0.3	0.4	3.7	3.6
5.Animal and vegetable oil	0.1	0.1	0.4	0.03
6.Chemicals	21.1	25.5	12.3	12.4
7.Manufactured goods classified by materials	4.4	3.9	10.8	10.2
8Machinery and Transport	35.0	37.5	42.2	45.3
9.Miscellaneous, Manufactures goods	15.1	13.6	12.7	11.9
6,7,8 & 9.	75.8	80.6	78.1	79.8
10.Commodities not classified elsewhere	4.1	4.2	8.1	7.2
	100.0	100.0	100.0	100.0

Source: CSO Trade Statistics

Structure of Irish Trade:

Table 15.3 shows imports and exports of visible or merchandise goods by section for 1996 and 1997. Manufactured goods are our biggest imports and our greatest exports. Columns 6,7,8 and 9 are manufactured goods and in 1997, 79.8% of our imports were such goods. Exports of manufactured goods were over 80% for 1997.

Free Trade Area:

In a free trade area members remove all tariffs, quotas and intra-area obstacles to free trade while still having barriers to trade against non members. There is therefore free movement of goods and services between countries. The North American Free Trade Agreement(NAFTA) between the US, Canada and Mexico is an example of this and it is discussed later.

Customs Union:

A customs union is established between two or more countries when all obstacles to free trade between members are removed. A common external tariff against non- members is also put in place, whereas in a free trade area each country retains its own tariff vis-à-vis non members. The European Union is a customs union and Ireland is a member.

Common Market:

This is similar to a customs union but in addition there is free movement of factors of production, labour and capital between member countries. The EU became a common market (the so called "single market") in January 1993 and Ireland is part of this market.

Economic Union:

This consists of a common market plus harmonisation of national economic policies. Countries surrender their national control over agriculture, exchange rate, taxation, transport and monetary policy. At present the United States is an economic union while the E.U. has achieved some degree of economic union and is set to make further progress now that a single currency is in place in eleven member states.

Reasons for Trade:

International trade arises because countries differ in their demand for goods and in their ability to produce them. Countries trade with each other so that their inhabitants can enjoy a higher standard of living. Trade takes place for the following reasons:

- Goods that cannot be produced in Ireland are available from another country e.g. petroleum products from Russia and the UK.

- Other countries are more skilled in the production of certain goods e.g. motor vehicles, so that it makes sense for Ireland to import them from countries such as Japan.

- Excess demand for a home produced good may cause imports to be bought to overcome the shortage.

- In a free market economy, consumers are free to choose and many decide on a foreign produced good in preference to a home produced good. The foreign good may not be cheaper so that the purchase reflects the buyer's taste e.g. demand for French cheese in Ireland.

- Ireland can take advantage of growth in the world economy by increasing her exports.

- Exports earn foreign currency needed to pay for imports and interest on foreign debt.

Absolute Advantage:

If a country is 'best at' producing a good or service it possesses absolute advantage. If it is not the best at producing it, the country has an absolute disadvantage.
The UK has an absolute advantage in the production of both cars and butter in the example used below to outline comparative cost. The production of a unit of cars and butter uses fewer resources in the UK than in Ireland.

Principle of Comparative Advantage:

Adam Smith (1723-1790) saw clearly that a country could gain by trading and he put the argument as follows: "It is the maxim of every prudent master of a family, never to attempt to make at home what it will cost him more to make than to buy. The tailor does not attempt to make his own shoes, he buys them from the shoemaker. The shoemaker does not attempt to make his own clothes, but employs a tailor … What is prudent in the conduct of every private family can scarce be folly in that of a great kingdom." This quotation is from Smith's, book An Enquiry into the Nature and Causes of the Wealth of Nations.

David Ricardo (1772-1823), an English economist, inspired by Smiths book developed the Law of Comparative Advantage as we know it today and it forms the basis of international trade theory. The Law states that even if one country is more efficient than another in the production of two commodities, it will benefit the original country to concentrate on the commodity in which its efficiency is comparatively greater and import the commodity in which its comparative advantage is not so good. A country has a comparative advantage with respect to another country in the production of a given commodity if the opportunity cost of the commodity in question is lower in that country than in the other country.

To explain this principle we will take a model of the 'world' economy with just two countries, Ireland and the UK. Each country has just two units of resources that can produce just two commodities cars and butter. Each unit of resource can be switched from one industry to another. Suppose the production possibilities in each country are that one unit of resource can produce:

      In UK 4 cars or 2 tonnes butter
      In Ireland   1 car or 1 tonne butter

The UK is best at or has an absolute advantage in producing both cars and butter, but has comparative advantage in car production. Comparative advantage is measured in terms of opportunity cost i.e. what a country gives up when it increases output in one industry by one unit.

The country that gives up least when increasing output of a commodity by one unit possesses comparative advantage in that good. How many cars would the UK have to give up in order to increase its output of butter by one tonne? The answer is 2 cars but Ireland would have to give up one car to produce an extra tonne of butter. Ireland therefore has comparative advantage in butter even though it has an absolute disadvantage in both products.

Suppose the UK and Ireland do not specialise and they each devote one unit of resource to each industry, total world production will be 5 cars and 3 tonnes of butter.

If complete specialisation starts, they produce only the good in which they have comparative advantage. World production is 8 cars and 2 tonnes of butter. Production of cars is up but butter is down. However, we are not comparing like with like therefore this does not necessarily represent a net gain in output.

Suppose Ireland completely specialises but the U.K. with absolute advantage in both goods puts a half a unit into butter so that world production is 3 tonnes. This means the U.K. is partially specialising putting 1.5 units of resource into cars and producing 6 cars. Total world production will now be 6 cars and 3 tonnes of butter. More cars and the same amount of butter are produced therefore output has increased in line with the principle of comparative advantage.

Terms of Trade:

In the UK the opportunity cost of one tonne of butter is 2 cars. In Ireland the opportunity cost of one car is 1 tonne of butter. The terms of trade will lie between 2 to 1 cars per one tonne of butter. The final price at which the goods are exchanged will be determined by demand patterns in the two countries.

Assumptions Underlying the Principle of Comparative Advantage:

A number of assumptions must be made to show that benefits are likely to accrue from specialisation and trade in accordance with the principle of comparative advantage. These include:

- One unit of resources is assumed to produce 4 cars or 2 tonnes of butter in the U.K. whether it is the first unit of resource employed or the millionth unit.

- The law assumes that there are no transport costs.

- Each country's endowment of factors of production including capital and labour is assumed fixed. Capital and labour are treated as being non- transferable between the countries. Finished goods are however mobile between countries.

- .It assumes that the benefits of trade will flow throughout the economy.

- The principle of comparative cost implicitly assumes relatively stable demand and cost conditions.

Comparative Advantage can be attributed to:

- A country may have comparative advantage in the production of a good because of its land and climate. Ireland has a comparative advantage in the production of meat and dairy products for this reason.

- A country may have mineral deposits;

- When people work hard, they have an advantage over those who lead a more indolent way of life;

- The presence of 'technological know-how; and

- The availability of necessary infrastructure and capital. If there is plenty of capital in a country it will have comparative advantage in an industry that is capital intensive.

Qualifications of the Principle of Comparative Advantage :

Transport Costs:

These reduce the possible gains from trade and it is conceivable that they could offset Ireland's superiority in making butter, in which case, UK may find it better to produce her own butter.

Opportunity Cost Ratios:

The theory outlined above is based on the unrealistic assumption that the opportunity cost ratios remain the same as resources are moved from one industry to another.

Availability of Alternative Employment:

It is assumed that when resources are released through not producing a good, they are employed elsewhere. It is possible that they might be unemployed.

Shifting Nature of Comparative Cost:

The shifting nature of comparative cost advantage points to a danger of over-specialisation, as well as the danger of over-dependence on foreign trade. When economic change occurs, countries in this position are very vulnerable due to the narrow range of production possibilities or industries.

Efficiency and Competition:

International trade leads to greater markets and increases competition that must result in increased efficiency.

Trade Theories:

In general, nations benefit from trade via specialisation and exchange.

The Heckseher-Ohlin Theory:

In the 19ᵗʰ and early 20ᵗʰ centuries the earliest countries to industrialise did so because they had manufacturing comparative advantage. These countries of the North exported manufactured goods to the less developed South and imported primary commodities from them.

In the 1930's, Heckscher and Ohlin came up with a theory, which attempted to explain this exchange between North and South in terms of factor endowments. Basically their theory is an extension of the principle of comparative advantage in that if a country possesses a great deal of capital relative to labour it will industrialise and export manufactured goods. If capital is scarce relative to labour a country will export primary products which are labour intensive.

The Heckscher-Ohlin Theory has been called a dependency theory. The basis for this theory is that less developed countries have little capital because the developed countries have ensured that the pattern of trade and payments brings this about. The terms of trade have generally moved against the less developed countries, meaning that the developed countries are able to import a great quantity of primary products for the same amount of exports of their manufactured goods. Multinationals of the developed world transfer wealth and resources to their home countries in the form of profits and dividends from their operations in the less developed countries.

Leontief showed that the US exported labour-intensive rather than capital-intensive manufactured goods. This paradox seemed at first sight to be a contradiction of the Heckscher-Ohlin theory. However when labour is regarded as human capital the paradox can largely be explained away. This can be used to explain why developed economies export labour- intensive manufactured goods.

The Technology Gap Theory:

This theory holds that much of the trade among developed countries is based on new products and new methods of production. This gives them a temporary monopoly in the world market. This advantage is reinforced by economies of scale due to the monopoly position of the firm. The advantage will go when other countries adopt the new technology. It may happen that foreign producers eventually can supply to foreign markets due to their lower labour costs. In the meantime the developed countries come up with new products and more technologies. This technological gap explains much of the pattern of world trade in manufactured goods. The theory however does not explain the size of the technological gap, how it arises or how it goes away.

Trade Based on Differentiated Products:

A great deal of international trade involves the exchange of differentiated products of the same industry, i.e. intra-industry trade. For instance Ireland exports Ballygowan water and imports French Perrier water. Irish cheddar cheese goes to France and French brie comes to Ireland. Germans buy French cars and the French buy German cars. The general flow of similar products between developed countries is due to three forces:

- Consumers like a wide choice of brands. They do not want exactly the same product as everyone else. In Germany most drivers go for Volkswagens but some buy Renaults to be different.
- Since economies of scale require a large output it would not make sense for say Germany to produce every make of car as the numbers required would be too small.

- Countries tend to specialise in brands suited to the countries with relatively low transport costs. Germany would have greater intra-industry trade with say Norway than with Japan.

The more closely markets are integrated and the lower the obstacles to trade in terms of tariffs and transport costs the greater the level of intra-industry trade. While the Heckscher-Ohlin Theory that states trade will lower the return to the nation's scarce factors, intra-industry trade based on economies of scale makes it is possible for all factors to gain.

Advantages of Free Trade:

• Sale of 'Surplus' Product

Countries have products that are surplus to their requirements. In the absence of international trade, Ireland could not sell all the cattle produced by the farmers in excess of domestic demand.

• Enables Specialisation

Specialisation improves the standard of living of countries engaging in international trade. It also brings about economies of scale which could not be achieved in Ireland without trade due to its small domestic market.

• Imports Are Possible

Without international trade, many countries would have to go without certain products. Ireland would have to go without petroleum products.

Improved Efficiency

There is competition and less likelihood of dominant firms arising. Competition may stimulate greater efficiency at home and lead to greater research and development.

- **Greater International Co-operation**

Trade promotes closer links between countries and can introduce new ideas into a trading country. There may be political, cultural and social advantages to be gained by promoting international trade e.g. between the Republic and Northern Ireland.

Arguments against Free Trade:

- **To Protect Home Industries Particularly an 'Infant' Industry**

The idea is that new industries may need protection in their early years against foreign firms already established and enjoying economies of scale. The danger is that over time these firms may become dependent on this protection and Government money so that they never become competitive. This is true of some of the semi-state bodies in Ireland, for e.g. CIE

- **Countries Seek to Maintain Home Employment in a Period of Depression**

Placing restrictions on imports to promote employment in the manufacture of home-produced goods does this. The difficulty is that other countries are likely to retaliate.

- **To Prevent Dumping**

Goods may be sold abroad at a lower price than in the home market. This may be possible because (a) producers receive export subsidies and (b) price discrimination by a monopoly is possible. In either case price no longer reflects comparative costs of production. Ireland sold butter to the UK for many years at prices lower than in the home market.

- **To Enable an Industry to Decline Gradually**

Fundamental changes in demand for a good may hit an industry. If imports are restricted it can allow the industry time to contract gradually thus preventing a sudden large increase in the number of people made unemployed.

- **To Encourage the Production of a Good of Strategic Importance**

When a country is dependent on another for a good of strategic importance, there is the danger of supply being stopped. This is often true in the area of food supply. During the Second World War, Ireland had to encourage the production of wheat.

To Pursue Political Objectives:

Trade can be a weapon of foreign policy. An example of this is the sanctions by the UN against Iraq as a result of the invasion of Kuwait. During the Economic War Ireland refused to buy UK coal.

- **To Promote Social Policies**

Countries give subsidies on food in order to avoid depression in rural areas and among the unemployed in urban areas.

- **Senile Industry Argument**

This is where an industry with a potential comparative advantage has been allowed to run down. It cannot make sufficient profit to compete without some measure of protection on a temporary basis. The US has used this argument to protect the automobile industry.

- **Non-Economic Arguments**

Farmers argue for protection for agriculture to maintain rural communities. This argument is also used to encourage the production of a good of strategic importance, the supply of which could be cut off by the supplier in time of war.

Government Intervention in International Trade:

All countries follow policies that impede to some extent the free flow of goods to protect home industries against foreign competition. Some of the methods used are outlined below.

Tariffs (Customs Duties):
Tariffs are taxes on imports and are usually ad valorem: i.e. a percentage of the price of the imported good. Import duties increase the price of imports and as a result domestic consumers will purchase more home produced goods and imports will fall. Tariffs produce revenue for the government.

If import duties are used with excise duties, then it is a revenue tariff and as such, is not a protective measure. Tariffs place a cost on consumers by both increasing the cost of imports and allowing the domestic producer to be inefficient or to earn extra profit. There are no tariffs between EU member states.

- **Quotas**

With an import quota, only a certain quantity of goods may be imported, therefore it is a physical restriction on the movement of goods. Compared with duties, quotas have disadvantages:

- Due to artificial shortage of supply, the price may be increased by the foreign supplier or by the importer. Government must bring in price control to prevent this happening.
- Quotas are normally based on past imports and efficient firms in the exporting country are penalised since they cannot increase their supply. There is no tariff revenue but the authoriser will gain through higher profits. Quotas have been eliminated for intra- EU trade but have been imposed by individual members on imports from outside the EU e.g. by the UK on Japanese cars.

- **Subsidies**

These are payments given by the Government to domestic producers to enable them compete with foreign producers at home and abroad. This brings about a reduction in imports. The subsidy can be in the form of services supplied by the government at no charge to the exporter. Preferential interest rates on money borrowed for exporting or subsidised insurance on exports so as to cover the possibility of non-payment by the purchaser, are also forms of subsidies. Subsidies are a form of protection for inefficient firms. The cost to the consumer is the payment of taxes then given as subsidies. If the subsidy is on exports, trade is artificially increased and it is known as dumping.

- **Administrative Barriers**

The government may have a policy of making it difficult to import certain goods and this is done by the imposition of a long and costly procedure before importation and again after it. The result is that importers will find it too costly and it may also mean that domestic prices are lower than the imported goods' prices after the addition of the extra costs. Japanese customs procedures are very complex and as a result expensive. The Germans ban lagers that fail to meet certain purity standards, effectively excluding foreign lagers.

- **Physical Control**

There may be a complete ban or embargo as may be the case if animal disease exists in the country of origin, e.g. foot and mouth disease. It also happens in cases of accidents such as radiation contamination, e.g. Chernobyl. Health and safety standards can be used to protect domestic industry against imports.

- **Exchange Control**

This means that it is not possible to purchase foreign exchange freely. All foreign exchange must be exchanged for local currency. Applicants for import licenses, if successful, obtain foreign exchange and the government can give priority to certain goods.

- **Voluntary Export Restraints (VERs)**

The VER is a relatively new but increasingly popular method of restricting imports. They became popular in the 1970's when countries wished to protect their industries while keeping to GATT rules. The importing country negotiates with its foreign suppliers quantitative restrictions on the amount of exports they will supply to the domestic market. Agreements may be between two countries or other bodies acting with government approval e.g. association of manufacturers whereby the country voluntarily agrees to restrict the volume of a product that is exported to the other country. Agreements cover cars and electronics products like televisions. For example the Japanese agreed to 'voluntarily' curb their sales of cars in the UK to 11 per cent of the market. As a result the consumer has to pay higher prices.

Single European Market (SEM):

The SEM is an effort by the EU to create a single market so that all producers and consumers can carry on business on equal terms anywhere within the Union. In Western countries the 1980's was a decade when things went against big governments who relied on very extensive regulation of their economies. The emphasis then changed to competition, market forces and deregulation. The Single European Act (SEA) 1987 set the end of 1992 as the date for the removal of physical, technical and fiscal barriers.

Single European Act (SEA) 1987:

Even though the EU was a 'Common Market' in the years prior to 1993 and tariff barriers were removed there were still physical, technical and fiscal barriers to trade in place. The Single European Act 1987 changed all that by removing all non- tariff barriers as and from January 1993. Non tariff barriers are differences in national practices that prevent the free movement of goods, services as well as factors across countries.

The Single Act defines the Internal Market as "an area without internal frontiers, in which the free movement of goods, labour, services and capital is ensured in accordance with the provisions of the Treaty." Three categories of barrier i.e. physical, technical and fiscal were removed by January 1993.

- **Physical Barriers**

Physical barriers are such things as customs controls with a great deal of paper work and delay. These cause queues. The Cecchini Report 1992 estimates the cost at ECU 8 billion per annum. Removal of these entailed:
- The removal of customs controls imposed by member states at borders.
- The harmonisation of public health standards.
- The removal of immigration and passport controls between member states.

The removal of costs associated with customs and delays at borders will lower the cost of trade.

- **Technical Barriers**

Technical barriers were many and varied and ranged from safety requirements to restriction of competition for government contracts to differences in business law.

- Technical barriers to the now free movement of goods, due to national technical regulations and product standards, are now removed.

- Public procurement of resources by government will now allow all member states to compete on equal grounds with favoured domestic suppliers, who will have to be more competitive. This will result in cost saving to major public utilities.

- Allowing freedom of establishment and the provision of services facilitates free movement of people.

- In the financial services area, institutions from one member state are allowed to provide cross-frontier services without the need to set up offices in the other member state and there has been a measure of harmonisation of national regulatory systems. Regulation is by the home country. Free movement of capital is also allowed.

Fiscal Barriers:

These are barriers that apply to the capital markets and those that came about because of differences in the rate of taxation such as Value Added Tax. As a result of the S.E.A. there is now an approximation of indirect taxes, VAT and excise duties. Fiscal checks at frontier posts are also gone. A minimum VAT rate was introduced in January 1993 but no maximum was set.

Economic Theory and SEM:

The Single Market is a supply-side measure and the intention is to allow markets to work more efficiently. There are four main areas of economic theory that can be used to explain the advantages of the internal market and these are as follows:

- **Comparative advantage**

The SEM will allow member states to specialise in areas where they have comparative advantage and this will benefit the consumer as prices will fall.

- **Greater Competition**

Now all firms can compete across Europe and this will mean that protection in domestic markets will go and prices will be competed down. Cost will decrease as a result of greater competition.

- **Economies of Scale**

As industries can be based on a Europe - wide scale, firms can reach a size that will give the full benefit of economies of scale. This will bring about a reduction in prices.

- **Increased demand**

As the trend in the price level is downward in the three effects mentioned above this should lead to increased demand as consumers will buy more. Greater output will be required and employment will increase. European industry will be better able to compete with the rest of the world. However, some of the less efficient firms will go out of business causing structural or regional unemployment and particular regions will need assistance.

Estimating the Effects of 1992:

The Cecchini Report entitled "The European Challenge 1992 - The Benefits of a Single Market" published on behalf of the European Commission identified the benefits of the Single European Act. It looked at the micro and macro economic gains and these are now examined.

Microeconomic Gains:

1. The removal of non-tariff barriers results in a reduction in costs and increased competition as domestic markets are exposed to a greater number of potential sellers.

2. This increased competition has three effects:

- Profit margins are squeezed and prices brought into line with costs.
- Encourages firms to become more efficient in their use of resources. There will be a reduction in the so-called X inefficiency associated over-manning and excess overhead costs that allows for recovery of some of the margins lost.
- Competition may cause firms to restructure. Firms may have to stop production altogether, others may have to move to a new site and look for new products and methods of operation. This means that they can more fully exploit economies of scale even though this latter effect may take a considerable period of time to achieve. Prices fall and demand increases contributing to the exploitation of economies of scale. Cecchini estimates the microeconomic gains as equivalent to 5.3% of EU GDP.

- **Macroeconomic Gains**

1. Elimination of border controls

This causes a direct improvement in the balance of trade for SEM members and is estimated to save approximately £6 bn for the EU. Therefore, gains for intra-EU imports, at the expense of imports from outside the EU will occur resulting in an increase in EU GDP.

2. Liberalisation of Financial Services

Firms can invest more easily in EU states using the cheapest financial services, the cost of which will be competed down anyway. This investment will in the long-run have a beneficial effect on employment and output.

3. Supply Side Effects

Free movement of capital and labour means that resources are more efficiently allocated resulting in increased economic growth. Firms are more efficient since competition is greater and they need to keep ahead of their competitors.

4. Opening up of Public Procurement

Cost cuts in the public sector will result and member governments' budget deficits will fall or surpluses will rise. This gives scope for tax reductions or greater investment, and may also assist in reducing unemployment and therefore the benefits paid out.

The Cecchini Report estimates the macroeconomic gains as:

- A downward effect on inflation of 6.1%;

- An increase in employment of 1.8 million people; and

- A rise in EU GDP of 4.5%.

Table 15.4 shows the macroeconomic gains estimated to result from the SEA. These include a disinflationary effect of 6.1%, a rise in employment of 1.8 million and a rise in EU GDP of 4.5%. The estimate shown under microeconomic gains ginen earlier is greater at 5.3%. The rise in real GDP will not be immediate but will make the EU more efficient and more competitive on world markets. The move to set up this market was motivated by the necessity to compete on a more realistic basis with Japan and the US. It will take some time before it is established that the EU is successful in this regard. It is up to EU firms to move quickly to take advantage of the new situation. Even in 1993 some non-EU countries had lower costs than EU countries. They have the protection of tariff and non-tariff barriers but these were reduced further by the GATT agreement (1993) and even now are at a relatively low level.

Table 15.4
Macroeconomic Consequences of EU Market Integration in the Medium Term

Customs	Public Facilities	Financial Procurement	Supply Services	Side Effects	Total	Average Spread
Relative Change GDP(%)	0.4	0.5	1.5	2.1	4.5	(3.2 to 5.7)
Consumer Prices (%) Change	-1.0	-1.4	-1.4	-2.3	-6.1	(-4.5 to 7.7)
Absolute changes in Employment 000's	200	350	400	850	1800	(1300 to 2300)
Budgetary Balance (% of GDP)	0.2	0.3	1.1	10.6	2.2	(1.5 to 3.0)
External Balance % of G.D.P.	0.2	0.1	0.3	0.4	1.0	(0.7 to 1.3)

Source Hermes (EU Commission and National Teams)
and Inter-link (OECD) economic models.

Increase in Trading of Goods and Services into the EU:

When the Single Market is fully completed, it will become the single biggest market in the world and this will make the EU a major attraction for foreigners to export to because of the buying power it has. Foreign companies will be forced to take a look at the EU market because of the huge opportunities that lie there.

More Exporting by the EU to Foreign Countries:

The Single Market should improve EU terms of trade, particularly with the US and Japan. There is a great fear among non-members that the Single Market will create a "fortress" Europe, placing obstacles in the way of foreign imports. If the EU threatened to do that, previously closed markets like Japan could become open to it. For example if the EU as a whole put a quota on the number of Japanese cars that could be imported, this would seriously affect Japanese exports. The quota could then be removed provided the Japanese allow EU exporters greater access to their market.

More Foreign Subsidiaries in the EU:

For industrial nations outside the EU, the implications of the SEM will differ depending on whether companies operate through subsidiaries inside the EU or have their subsidiaries entirely outside the member states. Under EU legislation, companies operating in any of the member states are regarded as EU entities, regardless of ownership. This should encourage more foreign companies to establish subsidiaries in the EU. and this could benefit Ireland if firms locate here in order to gain access to the Single Market.

More Trading Agreements with the EU:

Due of the fear among non-EU countries that the Single Market will lead to a "fortress" Europe, many foreign countries would be eager to secure trade agreements with the EU to protect their exports. In return, the EU will secure access to their markets.

Reduced Costs of Exports to the EU:

If, for example, a Japanese company was exporting to more than one country in the EU, it must bear the cost of entering the EU. It also has to bear the cost of moving goods between member states, and it must satisfy different national technical regulations. The Single Market aims to eliminate all these different costs and technical differences. Thus the cost of exporting to the EU is reduced if a company is exporting to more than one member state which, in theory, should lead to a reduction in prices for the consumer.

More Free and Open Trade:

If the Single Market is a success and leads to increased trading and wealth and reduced costs, it should encourage more open trade. If it is a success, it will demonstrate the benefits to be derived from this and the removal of all barriers to trade.

Implications of SEM for Ireland:

Even if the EU as a whole benefits from the SEM, these benefits will not be equally distributed. We look at Ireland's position under a number of headings as follows:

- **Removal of Barriers**

This will create easier access for Irish exports to EU markets with 320 million customers. Irish exports will be more competitive due to a reduction in costs because of the removal of barriers, and customs charges in particular. Increased exports will mean more jobs. It is no longer necessary to complete forms when exporting and importing.

Increased competition will facilitate growth in order to take full advantage of economies of scale and businesses will seek to grow by way of merger. Small Irish firms will have difficulty competing and even firms considered large may not be able to compete. These adverse changes necessarily involve some redundancies arising from bankruptcies, take-overs and the introduction of new technology. The severity of this technological and structural unemployment depends on the pace of change and the mobility of labour on an occupational and geographical basis.

Firms will tend to locate near the centre of activity of their markets and sources of supply. Large centres in Germany, France and UK may attract very large industries to the detriment of Ireland a peripheral region. Research and development will take place in these major centres enhancing the competitive edge of these firms. Ireland is distant from other member states and consequently transport costs are higher. Since Ireland is a small open economy it relies on these markets and is also subject to competition in its small domestic market. However, since the "Celtic Tiger" fears about Irelands peripherality have greatly diminished.

In an ideal market situation Ireland should attract resources from other parts of the EU since Irish wages and land prices are relatively lower. These lower costs should encourage industrial location here, but it is possible that capital and labour will leave for the bigger centres thus further depressing Ireland. Infrastructure will be neglected if this should happen and it will become even less attractive to industry.

Irish people will be able to move freely in Europe to set up business and to obtain employment. Unemployment in Ireland should decrease.

- **Access to European Financial Institutions and Services**

Irish business and individuals have access to financial institutions and services within the EU. Insurance, building construction, building societies and banking are industries likely to be most affected. Insurance companies have until 1999 to get in line with their European counterparts. This exposure to foreign competition will benefit the consumer. The free movement of capital may lead to giant 'Euro firms' with higher not lower prices and less choice for the consumer.

- **Manufacturing sector**

Within manufacturing there will be losses and gains. Areas like textiles will lose as the multi- fibre agreements are phased out under GATT. It is possible that some foreign firms may close their Irish operations in order to rationalise.

- **Fiscal Policy**

Removal of exchange controls means free capital movement that will constrain Irish fiscal policy.

- **Harmonisation of VAT rates**

Taxes especially VAT will be made more even throughout the E.U. This will improve trade between countries and will spread the burden of taxation more equitably. VAT at point of entry is now abolished.

- **Agriculture**

Border taxes such as monetary compensatory amounts (MCA) can no longer be imposed.

- **Inflation**

Since prices will fall due to VAT harmonisation and increased competition, inflation should be kept to a minimum.

The Direction of Trade as a result of the Single Market:

With the completion of the Single Market, the EU will be the most attractive market in the world. Undoubtedly there will be a lot of trade done with it particularly imports into the EU because of the great opportunities there. Foreign companies will realise that this market cannot be ignored.

If the Single Market is a success, it should improve the economic position of the EU. If it can show some unity, this may allow it to penetrate previously closed markets like Japan by asserting its interests more strongly. It could threaten to put up barriers if it cannot gain access to foreign markets, and this would have the effect of switching the direction of trade from the EU to previously closed markets like Japan.

Finally, trade should intensify as companies from each member state try to gain access to new markets opening up in the EU. Before the completion of the Single Market, non-tariff barriers existed between member states, but these have been abolished since the 1 January 1993. Competition intensity will increase because the criteria for the SEM are for member states to deregulate their economies, so as to allow foreign competition to enter their markets.

Table 15.5 shows that the EU, even with a much larger population than either the US or Japan, has a GDP per head (income per head) much lower than these two countries, particularly the US. The EU as a whole has suffered trade deficits with both the US and Japan, while their economies have the potential to do much well than that.

Table 15.5
Population and GDP per Head in Major Trading Areas

	Japan	EU	US
Population (millions)	123	324	246
GDP per head (ECU)	15,155	13,639	21,307

The value of EU external trade is about 20 per cent of its GDP. If the Single Market is a success, it should improve the EU's terms of trade around the world particularly with the US and Japan thus improving their economies significantly due to the crucial role played by trade. EU is more dependent on trade than Japan or the US.

Japanese Competition:

Japanese competition was a major motivating factor behind the creation of the Single Market. Up to about 1970, the EU had very little trade with Japan, but since then, trade between the two has increased dramatically, mainly due to Japan's emergence as an economic force. The EU has a huge trade deficit with Japan. Japan is a closed market with numerous administrative and technical barriers making it very difficult for any exporter to sell its products there.

Japanese companies have the ability to establish themselves in a large number of locations in Europe, from where they enjoy a large share in markets across the world. Yet despite this, only 51 Japanese companies had profits of $200 million or more compared to 58 for Britain and 205 for the US. The reason for this is that Japanese companies reinvest their profits in research and development, quality improvement and market investment to stay one step ahead of the rest.

Technological sectors are expected to gain most from the Single Market and Japan is very strong in these areas.

Progress since 1993 to 1999:

It is extremely difficult to assess the impact of the SEM. It has resulted in increased competition in many areas of the EU economy. The number of European mergers has increased. The harmonisation of standards and economic indicators has not occurred as envisaged and the following are some examples:

- **Company taxation**
Tax rates are varied between member states and this can affect the viability of investment plans.

- **Indirect taxation**

Some progress has been made towards harmonisation but there are still differences between rates imposed by member states.

- **Infrastructure**

Some member states have better infrastructure e.g. roads and rail than other member states. Since accessibility to markets is important to Ireland, poor infrastructure adds to the cost of distribution.

- **Different Levels of Development:**

There are substantial differences in the level of development between the most prosperous EU country, Germany and the least prosperous, Greece. Ireland is somewhere in the middle. Grants are available to the less well off regions and this affects investment decisions.

- **Level of Skills:**

The level of workforce skills can have a significant effect on investment decisions. Germany has the most skilled work force in the EU and therefore can attract high value industries.

North American Competition:

Almost 40 per cent of the world's top 1,000 companies are North American, and most of these companies operate in the EU. North American companies such as IBM and Procter and Gamble have operated in Europe since the end of World War II. American companies need to operate globally in order to achieve the level of economies of scale to compete at home and the SEM is the perfect opportunity for that. In some cases, American companies are able to operate more effectively than their European competitors, as they are much larger. With the free movement of goods, the Americans should enjoy the full benefits of economies of scale. They know the value of the European market and in the future even more US firms will look to Europe for expansion possibilities.

North American Free Trade Agreement (NAFTA):

Canada and the US implemented a free trade agreement in 1989. In November 1993 the US Congress voted to admit Mexico and NAFTA was formed. This area covers a population of approximately 360 million. Some of NAFTA's more important decisions are as follows:-

- U.S. and Canada to phase out tariffs on textiles and apparel over ten years. Mexico is to eliminate many tariffs in this sector immediately.

- All tariffs on cars and car parts must be eliminated over a period of ten years. Overall the provisions of NAFTA are in line with GATT and do not directly raise any new barriers to goods from third countries. The North American market should be much bigger and more accessible to other countries' product.

Opposition to NAFTA in the US was based mainly on the fear that jobs would be lost, because firms would relocate in Mexico due to lower labour costs. Mexico's economy is only 5 per cent of the combined Canadian and US economies.

Competition from the Pacific Basin:

The Single Market also faces competition from Far Eastern countries such as Korea, Taiwan, Singapore and Hong Kong. For example, Korea has the most efficient steel making industry in the world for its rapidly expanding automotive industry. The major impact of competition from the Far East will be to attack vulnerable low-technology European industries and these will need to improve on cost, quality and reliability in order to compete, otherwise they will not succeed.

General Agreement on Tariffs and Trade (GATT) and World Trade Organisation (WTO):

GATT was established in 1947 and came into effect in 1948 as a complex set of trade agreements. It is the widest scheme for encouraging liberalisation of trade in operation and Ireland became a member in 1967. GATT with 116 members accounted for almost 90 per cent of world merchandise trade when it changed its name to World Trade Organisation (WTO). It was set up on 1st January 1995 and it is a permanent body with a set of rules and a mandate to regulate international trade.

The basic functions of WTO are as follows:
- The implementation of the multilateral and plurilateral trade agreements.
- seeking to resolve trade disputes;
- acting as a forum for multilateral trade negotiations; and
- to co-operate with other international organisations.

Principles of WTO:

It adheres to the same fundamental principles of the multilateral trading system established by GATT.

- **Trade without Discrimination**

This is known as the "most favoured nation clause" and means that trade must be conducted on the basis of non-discrimination. It is designed to eliminate any preferential agreements between nations. Exceptions are allowed in special circumstances, e.g. developing countries and regional trading arrangements. The principle is that if a member state reduces tariffs for any particular state it must extend the concession to all members.

- **Protection through Tariffs**

Where protection is given to domestic industry it should be in the form of a customs tariff and not other protective measures such as import quotas. A customs tariff is a percentage added to the import price. The aim of this principle is to make the extent of protection clear.

- **A Stable Basis for Trade**

The 'binding' of the tariff levels, negotiated among members of WTO provides this. There is, however, provision for re-negotiation of bound tariffs, and a return to higher tariffs is discouraged by virtue of the fact that any increase must be compensated for.

- **The 'Waiver' and Emergency Action**

A member when its economic or trade circumstances warrant it, can seek derogation from particular WTO obligations. Emergency action can be taken in defined circumstances such as when imports increase in such quantities as to cause very serious difficulties for competing domestic production.

- **Consultation, Conciliation and Settlement Differences**

Countries can call on WTO if they feel that their rights are being withheld or compromised by other members.

- **Quantitative Restrictions on Imports:**

These are prohibited under WTO rules. They are now less widespread but are still numerous particularly in the area of agricultural goods, textiles, steel and some other products of interest to developing countries. Members are allowed to use quantitative restrictions when they experience balance of payment difficulties. There is also an exception where domestic production is subject to quantitative restriction.

- **Regional Trading Arrangements:**

WTO rules permit trading arrangements in which a group of countries agree to abolish or reduce barriers against imports from one another. It thus allows such groupings, as an exception to the 'most favoured nation' rule, provided certain strict criteria are met. These rules are to ensure that the agreements facilitate trade among the countries concerned, without raising barriers to trade with the outside world. Examples are EU and EFTA.

Trade ' Rounds':

Trade liberalisation has taken place under GATT, using the "Round" system. This is a system of multi-lateral trade negotiations. There have been eight "Rounds" to date. The early "Rounds" were mainly to do with reductions in tariffs while the later ones have looked again at the articles of GATT. Much has been achieved in the area of tariff reductions since average global tariffs have fallen from 40 percent in 1947 to 4.7 percent after the Tokyo (1979) "Round", in the nine foremost industrial markets.

Protectionism still exists and there are a number of large trading groups such as EU, NAFTA, Cairns Group, Asian Pacific Economic Co-operation (APEC), and Japan involved in negotiations of trade 'Rounds'.

Three important "Rounds" were:

1. **Kennedy "Round"** (1964 -1967) which led to tariff reductions averaging 35% and it looked at anti-dumping also.

2. **Tokyo "Round"** (1973 - 1979) considered tariffs and non-tariffs. Tariffs were to be reduced by about 33% but were subsequently less than agreed.

3. **Uruguay "Round"** (1986 - 1993) considered in detail below.

Uruguay Round:

This round began in September 1986 in Punt de Este in Uruguay. It is the eight and most ambitious of all rounds to-date. The GATT deal under the Uruguay Round was signed on April 15th 1994 at Marrakesh, Morocco.

Some of the negotiating goals of the round were:
- to cut overall tariffs by one-third;
- to reduce some and remove other non-tariff measures;
- to remove tariffs, taxes and other subsidies on a large number of agricultural products and open up domestic markets so as to eventually have free trade in agriculture; and
- to phase out the multi-fibre arrangement (MFA) and bring textiles within the normal GATT rules. The aim is to abolish the western world's 16 year old controls on third world textiles and clothing imports through the MFA.

Agriculture:

Agricultural free trade was perhaps the main aim of the Uruguay round and the US entered negotiations very much against the EU's Common Agricultural Policy. The latter kept food prices high by subsidising its 10 million or so farmers by up to 50 per cent of their incomes in some cases. Farmers received fixed guaranteed prices and surplus production was bought into intervention and sold cheaply to non-EU countries e.g. Russia. Exporters got refunds for selling goods outside the EU and this resulted in trade distortion. President Bush felt that CAP was an "iron curtain of protectionism" and the EU in turn pointed to US farm subsidies but little notice was taken of this.

The main aim of the US was to achieve a substantial reduction in EU export subsidies. This would enable its farmers to sell cereals and other food products in third world and new markets in the newly shaped Europe. Therefore, the US, which up to the Uruguay round was subsidising its farmers by up to 40 per cent of their incomes, could cut back on this.

Between 1986 and 1989 negotiators had failed to reach agreement and in April 1989 at a meeting in Geneva a compromise on the objectives was reached. This was known as the Geneva Declaration and was to bring about reductions in agricultural support and protection. The different groups including US, EU and Cairns Group (Latin American and Asian exporting countries plus Australia, New Zealand, Canada and Hungary) put forward proposals on how to achieve the objectives of the Geneva Declaration. The US proposal called for cuts of 75 per cent in farm supports over 10 years. Together with these cuts it wanted the three areas of agricultural support policy i.e. internal support (intervention, deficiency payments), export competition (export refunds and enhancement) and border protection (import levies) dealt with individually and all three subject to specific reductions.

The final agreement was to be reached by December 1990 but this didn't materialise. It was not until November 1991 at a meeting in The Hague between President Bush and Mr. Mc Sharry that negotiations got going again. President Bush was willing to tolerate the CAP compensation payments, provided the EU made a large cut in export subsidies. Discussions however broke down in November 1992 due to a dispute over oilseeds. The US threat of a trade war and the imposition of tariffs of up to $300 million worth of EU food and wine exports brought the parties together again.

Blair House Agreement:

Agreement was reached at the Blair House meeting in Washington in November 1992. The overall deal consisted of 28 separate agreements and is estimated to add $200 billion per annum to the world economy and to run for six years coming into effect in January 1994.

The main points of the Uruguay Agreement:

- The EU to cut farm subsidised exports in volume terms over six years from the average base period 1986 to 1990 by 21 per cent resulting in EU food prices falling and drawing nearer to world food prices.

- An overall cut in all tariffs of 30 per cent to take place. This has major repercussions for developing countries as their current tariff levels are up to 80 per cent. It will have very little effect on the advanced countries as their tariffs are now down to about 4.7 per cent.

- Services came under GATT rules. There are agreements covering, insurance, tourism, transport, consultation and telecommunications. This means that a free pattern of global investment can emerge.

- Stricter laws regarding copyright were introduced.

- Holders of these copyrights and patents will be encouraged to invest in developing countries once they know their property will not be stolen. In September 1993 the OECD estimated that the conclusion of the Uruguay round would add $213 billion to the world economy from manufacturing and agriculture alone. This was an effort to bring the Uruguay Round negotiations to a successful conclusion.
- Establishment of WTO.

Opposition to Blair House:

France and Ireland and to a lesser extent Spain, Netherlands and Italy had reservations about the Blair House Agreement. France was opposed to the 21 per cent cut in farm export subsidies since it is the world's second largest food exporter. The main fear was that many of the markets, some in the US, that France had gained over the years under CAP would now be lost. There was much political pressure on the French government by farmers. France was in disagreement with the US over proposed changes in the audio-visual sector.

Ireland was also opposed to the 21 per cent cut since it was estimated that £260 million would be lost up to the year 2000. Approximately £1.2 billion is earned from the beef sector annually and almost 85 per cent of this is from exports. It was not until December 15th 1993 that the Uruguay Round was finally concluded.

Outcome of the Uruguay Round:

The following was the outcome by the main sectors involved:

Agriculture:

- Agriculture was included for the first time under GATT;

- Subsidies for agriculture were to fall in the EU and the US;

- EU export subsidies were to fall in volume terms over six years to 2000 from the average base period 1986 to 1990 by 21 per cent; and

- Domestic farm subsidies were to be cut by 20 per cent but this had already been done by the E.U. in 1993. EU food prices were expected to fall and approach world prices.

Trade Barriers:

- Members agreed to cut their average tariff rate from 4.7 per cent to 3 per cent, i.e an average reduction of 36 per cent. This had major repercussions for developing countries as their current tariff levels were up to 80 per cent.

- Quotas and other import restrictions were also reduced; and

- Under new rules concerning dumping, it was to be more difficult to make up claims and to use them as an excuse to introduce trade barriers.

Services:

Services came under GATT and the Uruguay Round established a framework to cover software, tourism, insurance, transport, consulting and telecommunications.

Textiles:

Multi- Fibre Agreements were to be phased out over the next ten to fifteen years. These restricted imports from low cost countries such as Taiwan. EU markets were to be made more open.

Copyright or Intellectual Property:

The Uruguay Round brought in protection for copyright for 50 years and trademarks and patents for 20 years.

Aviation:

EU wanted and got agreement for the US, EU agreement of 1992 which limits the amount of direct and indirect subsidies granted for research on aircraft with more than 100 seats. The general subsidies code applies to all other aircraft and it is up to the attacker to prove that it has suffered harm.

Unfinished Business; Audio Visual Sector:

Changes in the audio-visual sector led to disagreement between the US and France. The dispute centred on measures to protect the French film industry from US movies. The quotas, subsidies and rules applied by the EU were retained. However the audio-visual sector was included under the Uruguay Round and was therefore subject to rules for industrial trade. This is true especially relating to transparency and settlement of trade conflicts at GATT level. The US therefore cannot make a unilateral attack on the French or any other EU state.

The Uruguay Round and Ireland:

Impact on Agriculture:

Agriculture was seen to be the main loser with the most serious problem arising in the beef sector. Ireland then accounted for 24 per cent of EU beef exports to world markets and was subject to the 21 per cent cut in export subsidies. This made Ireland very vulnerable to price falls. As already stated, Irish farmers expected to lose £260 million to the year 2000 and a fall of over £40 million in gross farm output. Some farmers perhaps as many as 3,000 were expected to be pushed out of business as a result. The cut in subsidies for EU farm exports was spread more gradually than at first suggested over the six years of the deal. The actual agreement did not come into effect until 1995. Support for agriculture was cut by 20 per cent.

Impact on Textiles:

Irish textiles had to compete with cheap labour intensive supplies of textiles from low cost, low labour economies such as Taiwan. Approximately 2,000 people were employed in the Irish textile industry accounting for approximately 13 per cent of all manufacturing employment.

World Markets:

A large surge in world markets was expected, as a result of the Uruguay Round. This would result in higher economic growth that should come on a gradual basis over the next ten years.

It was however difficult to establish the exact contribution to growth since other factors would also contribute over the next ten years. The Fitzpatrick Report estimated that some 4,500 to 13,000 jobs would be created in manufacturing and 12,000 or so in services. Barriers to the drinks industry should fall and Ireland should obtain access to markets in Asia and Latin America.

Electronics industries were hopeful that their superiority in technology would enable them compete with cheap labour countries particularly in the Far East. Chemical and pharmaceutical sectors were expected to benefit.

Prices:

The Fitzpatrick Report estimated a drop of 2 per cent in prices on average and a gain to consumers of £175 million. The effect of these reductions is over a ten-year period. Consequently, it will be so gradual it will be barely noticeable. It is however possible that as prices are reduced due to tariff reductions, that the government will seek to replace lost revenue by increasing VAT and/or other taxes.

Impact on Employment:

As expected, employment was lost in agriculture and textiles. It was expected to increase in other areas due to the increase in production and greater market opportunities. However an increase in production can be achieved by using additional machinery. Some multinationals have since relocated in low cost countries and in countries where environmental controls are less than in Ireland.

Enlarging the EU:

Different countries wish to join the EU. Turkey applied for membership in 1987 but was turned down. The main reasons are that it is economically backward and it poor civil rights record. Malta and Cyprus applied in 1990. Poland, the Czech Republic, Slovakia and Hungary known as the Visegrad Four, applied after a meeting in that town. Romania, Bulgaria, Slovenia, Albania have expressed a wish to join.

There would be some advantages to the EU in the form of increased trade but new members would gain most. Those seeking to join would have a competitive advantage in the form of low wages while entering a large market of relatively rich consumers. Workers in the EU producing goods that would then be no longer competitive will lose out.

Approximately half of the EU budget goes to agriculture and countries applying to join have large agricultural sectors e.g. Poland. Unless the rules for CAP are changed their entry would cause a massive increase in spending. On the other hand, the applicants are relatively poor so that they will be unable to contribute much to the EU budget.

Common Agricultural Policy (CAP) and Trade:

The Treaty of Rome (1957) has 10 of its 248 Articles devoted to agriculture (Articles 38 - 47). Although there was diversity in the agriculture of the founding member states, they still created the CAP. It provides a common market for approximately 99% of final agricultural production within the EU. Policy is based on three principles as follows:

- **Market unity:** Europe is one market for food and it can be sold in any part of the market.

- **Community Preferences**: Food will not be imported until production within the EU has been used up.

- **Financial Solidarity:** The cost of the policy is borne by all the countries within the EU

Objectives of CAP:

Objectives of CAP are set out in Article 39.1 and are as follows:

- To stabilise markets;
- To increase productivity;
- To ensure a reasonable standard of living for the agricultural community;
- To provide consumers with food at reasonable prices; and
- To assure the availability of supplies.

Reform of CAP:

When Mr Ray Mc Sharry became EU Commissioner for Agriculture in 1989 he set out to reform the CAP. However, it took until June 1992 before the reforms were accepted.

Objectives of 1992 CAP Reform:

- To maintain the EU position as a major producer and exporter of agricultural goods by making its farmers more competitive on home and export markets.

- To bring production down to levels more in line with market demand and to focus support for farmers incomes where it is most needed. It also encourages farmers, to remain on the land.

- To seek to protect the environment and to develop the natural potential of the countryside.

Measures were taken to regulate trade as follows:

- **Restrictive Measures:**
These measures are intended to have the system geared to market trends and to cut back on the mechanism in force up to the time of reform. These measures are introduced by means of:

- Guaranteed ceilings for different products above which price reductions of varying degrees of severity come into effect, the purpose of which is to stabilise expenditure.

- Reducing prices in order to bring them into line with world prices for some products such as cereals.

- To make access to intervention more difficult and making prices less attractive. Safety net intervention levels are lowered for Irish farmers and will now operate when prices fall below 60% rather than 72% up to 1992.

- **Conversion to Organic Farming and Extensification of Production:**

EU Regulation 1760/87 brought in a scheme for the conversion and extensification of production, which entailed action at a structural level. This action was a response to huge surpluses within the EU. The action was however limited to extensification and neither the list of products subject to conversion nor the arrangements for conversion to take place were defined. Extensification is basically assistance for farmers reducing output of surplus products, over a period of not less than 5 years by at least 20% without at the same time increasing output of other surplus products. Member states are allowed great flexibility in the exercise of these measures.

Supply Controls:

Supply controls were already in place for milk and sugar beet but now cereals, beef and sheep meat are added. About 83% of EU gross agricultural output is now covered by supply controls.

For beef, the emphasis on the market support system shifted away from intervention purchasing towards direct payments to farmers under the Livestock Premium arrangement. Supply control operates through a ceiling on the number of animals eligible for premia.

First Results of 1992 CAP Reform:

There were positive results after the first three years:
- Market balance has been restored in the cereal sector.
- Control of production has been achieved.
- The application of farm inputs has been reduced.
- In many sectors, EU prices have been reduced so that they are nearly on a par with world prices.

CAP Reforms 1999:

EU Heads of Government at their meeting in Berlin on March 26th 1999, agreed a number of further reforms to the CAP.

The main points agreed are as follows:

The agricultural budget is stabilised at € 40.5bn annually (plus 2 per cent inflation) for the years 2000 to 2006. There is €14bn over the period for rural development. This is €1bn less than agreed by the agricultural ministers at an earlier meeting.

"Degressivity" -a proposal by the French to cut direct aid payments annually -was rejected as a cost-saving option. In its place reforms are delayed as a means of saving money. Degressivity if introduced, would have cost Irish farmers €220 million over the seven-year period.

Reform of the dairy sector is postponed from 2003, agreed by the agricultural ministers, until 2005/2006. It has been agreed to continue the milk quota system until 2006 and to review its operation in 2003. An increase in quotas of 2.4% for the EU was also agreed. A 1.5% national quota increase will apply to eleven member states. Special increases for four countries will come into force from the first year of the reforms: Greece 11%, Spain10%, Italy 6% and Ireland 2.9%. The overall increase in the milk quota for Ireland is 32 million gallons i.e. 20.5 million gallons from April 1ST 2000 and 11.5 million in 2001. There is a delay of three years to 2005 in guarantee price cuts of 15% for butter and skimmed milk powder. Cuts in the prices of butter and skimmed milk powder will work their way through to cuts in milk prices paid to farmers.

The European Council (Heads of Government) diluted reform in the cereals sector decided by the Ministers. The original one step support price cut was reduced from 20% to 15% in two equal steps of 7.5%. The Area Aid payment was reduced from €161/acre agreed by the ministers to €154 per acre. A decision on a final reduction in the intervention price to be applied from 2002/2003 is to be taken in the light of market developments. This means that the cereals sectors reforms are not complete. The basic compulsory set aside rate is 10% for the period 2000 to 2006 instead of the first two years of the reform as originally envisaged.

The beef sector will have a 20% cut in guarantee price that will be made in three equal annual stages from 2000. The present remit for the Commission to open and close intervention buying according to its own market judgement remains. The proposed safety net intervention system is not now materialising. The so called 'Herod' premium that was designed to encourage a cut in beef production is to continue on a voluntary member state basis. A new slaughter premium of €80 on adult calves is to be paid out of the discretionary 'national envelope' which in Ireland's case amounts to €31.5 million. There is also an improvement in payments for farmers engaged in extensive production. The Commission has been asked by the European Council to follow closely developments in the European beef market and if necessary, implement relevant measures to support the market.

Achievements of the CAP:

Stable markets have been achieved for most products and this is borne out by the fact that the EU has remained untouched by the periodic surges in world prices for sugar and cereals.

The EU is now safe from all risk of food shortage and has achieved complete security of supply. It is the worlds largest importer of farm produce and animal feed stuffs such as soya bean and maize.

Reasonable consumer prices have been achieved while the average price paid to producers has increased less rapidly than prices as a whole and more slowly than food prices, which also cover the cost of marketing and processing. Some argue that CAP has kept food prices permanently high in the EU.

Criticisms of CAP:

The system of intervention in the markets leads to huge surpluses variously described as a butter mountain, wines lake, cereal mountain and beef mountain. Some of the surplus has been stored at great expense while more has been sold at a loss. The consumer does not benefit from lower prices from excess production as it is bought into intervention. These huge surpluses have depressed world prices and led to great rivalry between the EU and the US in particular. This caused the US to insist on a reduction in support for EU produce when it is sold in markets outside of the EU. External demand isn't unending and Third World countries have increased their own output of food while others are unable to pay. The latter markets can only be supplied with the aid of substantial subsidies. The prohibitive cost to the EU budget of the CAP was one of the main reasons why reform was inevitable.

Levies on imported food reduce the amount of food that other countries can export to the EU.

CAP has become a huge budgetary cost to the EU particularly over recent years and this hasn't substantially or comparably improved farm incomes. It was not possible to continue on this path and it was for this reason that the CAP was reformed in 1992 and 1999.

CAP caused problems in the Uruguay round of GATT due mainly to subsidies on produce exported to non- EU markets.

Irish farmers were encouraged to intensify grass growth by use of new fertilisers. This was supposed to increase the stocking rate (the number of animals) per hectare and productivity generally, all of which it did but it also led to surplus output.

Although it is common, policy individual countries have flouted the regulations by subsidising their own farmers or by reducing imports from other EU countries.

Intervention moderates the impact of market forces and this continues to operate but there is government regulation forcing adjustment to policy. If market forces were allowed to operate fully then farmers would have to adjust and find their own markets.

Challenges for the future:

- Internally, environmental sustainability is a major concern.
- Agricultural and rural policy must be more clearly integrated.
- The complexity of CAP management must be reduced.

- It must ensure that production has fallen sufficiently to meet the restriction on export subsidies by 2000.
- Trade liberalisation with WTO negotiations starting in 2000 when the EU will come under pressure to cut agricultural subsidies.
- Enlargement to the East will double the farm population of the EU and the new members will come from farms with low levels of productivity. The reforms of 1999 must be in place before this takes possibly in 2003 so as to minimise the cost to the EU budget.
- Enlargement will increase agricultural area of the EU by more than 40%.
- It must address the implications for demand and supply of new technology especially the bio-technological revolution.

Questions

1. "The direction of Irish trade has changed substantially over the past twenty years or so." Evaluate this statement and outline the reasons for this change.

2. Outline the advantages and disadvantages to Ireland from the development of the Single Market in the EU?

3. The following is a table showing the production of food and machinery:

	Food (Production per man hour)	Machinery (Production per man hour)
Country A	20 kg	4 units
Country B	30 kg	16 units

a) In the above situation would international trade be justified under the Law of Comparative Cost?

b) What factors other than comparative advantage might determine whether or not international trade takes place?

c) Comment on the possible terms of trade should trade take place.

4. Give arguments for and against the imposition of import restrictions by the Irish government.

5. What is GATT? Evaluate and critically examine the outcome of the Uruguay Round and assess its impact on Ireland.

6. Outline the reforms to CAP agreed at the Berlin Summit meeting in March 1999. Critically evaluate their impact on Irish agriculture.

7. What are the challenges facing CAP over the next five years?

CHAPTER 16

BALANCE OF PAYMENTS AND EXCHANGE RATES

Introduction:

In this Chapter we examine the structure of and the trends in the Irish balance of payments and policies the government can use to reduce or eliminate balance of payments disequilibrium. Arguments for and against fixed and floating exchange rates are outlined. The mechanisms through which fixed and freely floating exchange rates may restore equilibrium in the balance of payments are described. A brief account of the evolution of the world monetary system is given. The European Monetary System (EMS) is explained and reasons for its collapse are suggested. The Maastricht Treaty including the criteria for the introduction of the single currency is examined. Irelands membership of Economic and Monetary Union is documented and the advantages and disadvantages of this membership are assessed.

Balance of Payments:

The Balance of Payments (BP) is a statistical record of the economic and business transactions between residents of one country and the rest of the world for a given time-period, usually a year. It gives details of Ireland's current income and expenditure transactions with the rest of the world. Appendix 16.1 shows the layout of the BP accounts together with details for 1996 and 1997. Transactions include those arising from trade in goods and services or transfers of capital.

The word 'balance' implies a kind of equality and in the accounting sense the balance of payments must balance. If Ireland has 'over spent it must have obtained the finance for this from somewhere (by running down reserves or increasing foreign debt or the sale of foreign assets) and when this item is included in the accounts, they will balance. When we refer to deficit or surplus in balance of payments we only include transactions in goods and services and this is known as Balance of Payments on current account. A balance of payment's deficit on current account must be balanced by a balance of payments surplus on capital account. Similarly a balance of payment's surplus (or inflow) on current account must be balanced by an outflow (or deficit) of the same magnitude on the capital account.

Current Account:

This records earnings from exports and invisibles and payments for imports and invisibles. It is an effort to calculate the external trade flows of the economy. Merchandise trade (physical goods) in 1997 was £61,928mn (Appendix1) and when measuring the openness of the Irish economy we get the ratio of this to GNP. In 1997 this ratio was 1.5:1 i.e. £61,928: £41,919. It can be subdivided into:

Merchandise Trade: This consists of exports and imports of goods that can be seen crossing national borders over a given period usually a year. The difference between exports and imports is known as the 'balance of trade'. It is also known as the 'balance of visible trade'. Examples are export of meat and dairy produce and the import of oil. It is unusual for merchandise imported to equal merchandise exported so that there is either a surplus or a deficit. When there is a surplus there is a 'favourable' balance of trade whereas it is 'unfavourable' when there is a deficit. Ireland has had a relatively large surplus over the past number of years and in 1997 it was £11,084 million and £14,606mn in 1998. A large part of the sizeable surplus is due to multinational companies. The multinationals are accused of transfer pricing which occurs when they depress the price of intermediate goods from say Germany for their plant in Ireland and this gives the Irish plant very large profits. There is only a 10% corporation tax on these in Ireland that is small in comparison to the rate in Germany. This practice distorts the pattern of merchandise trade and exaggerates the magnitude of it.

Services: These are referred to as "invisibles" and include tourism, civil aviation, banking and insurance. For example, when foreigners stay in an Irish hotel they buy services and this is called an invisible export, but if Irish people go on holiday to France this is an invisible import. Ireland has recorded a surplus over the past number of years, due mainly to the performance of tourism and transport.

Trading and Investment Income: This refers to income earning assets owned by non- residents in Ireland and by Irish people abroad. Investment income records profit, dividends and royalties paid out to foreigners and received by Irish residents. Interest paid on the foreign element of national debt is also included. Over the past number of years we have had a substantial deficit on this account due mainly to repatriation of profits, by multi -national companies and interest payments due on the national debt to foreigners. In 1997, the deficit was £6,494 million and this is the difference between GDP and GNP. Of the £6,494, £6,708 was due to outflow in the form of gross profits, dividends and royalties repatriated by multinationals. As shown in Appendix 1 this has grown substantially over the period 1994 to 1997.

International Transfers: Here, neither goods nor services are involved. Transfers to Ireland are mainly in the form of EU aid under different funds. Money sent home by emigrants is included. Aid given by Ireland to Third World countries comes under this heading. Ireland invariably receives more than is given under this heading.

Capital Account:

The capital account is a record of transactions arising from capital movements into and out of Ireland. It is comprised of four main categories: private capital, official capital, banking transactions and official external reserves. Inward flows carry a plus sign while outflows carry a minus sign.

Private Capital: This consists of direct investment in Ireland by non- residents, for example in new factories and abroad by Irish residents. Foreign borrowings by semi-state companies such as ESB are included. There is a large net outflow of funds as shown in Appendix 16.1 indicating increasing investment in foreign assets.

Official Capital: This is made up of Exchequer foreign borrowing by the National Treasury Management Agency which is the main item plus sales and purchases of government securities and other transactions.

Banking Transactions: This records the net external position of the licensed banks, other financial institutions such as building societies and hire purchase companies i.e. the Irish Banking System.

External Reserves: Ireland's external reserves consist of holdings of foreign reserves by the Central Bank. These are made up of gold, special drawing rights (IMF), reserve position in IMF and by far the greater part is made up of foreign exchange (Appendix 16.1). In 1997 there was a decrease in external reserves to the value of £754mn.

Net Residual:

Overall the balance of payments must balance. The surplus of £1,362 on the current account in 1997 must be equal to the deficit in the capital account. The deficit in the capital account in 1997 was -£3,812.The figures do not agree due to inaccuracies. A balancing item or net residual appears in the balance of payments. In 1997 this was £2,450 million(Appendix16.1).

Balance of Payments Deficit:

Recall the following identity:

$$Y = C + I + G + X - M$$

$$\Longrightarrow Y - (C + I + G) = X - M$$

A BP deficit arises when expenditure is greater than income. Excess expenditure is financed by capital inflow. C and I are treated in the same way. A deficit means a fall in external reserves. In 1997 reserves fell by £754mn.so Ireland had a deficit in its balance of payments. We can specify the balance of payments from the above identities.

1. $Y = C + I + G + X - M$

2. $Yd = C+S$

3. $Yd = Y-T$ (or $Y= Yd +T$)

4. $Y = C+S+T$

5. C + S + T = C + I + G + X - M
   (Income)   (Expenditure)
6. S + T +M = I + G + X
   (Leakages)   (Injections)

7. S - I + T - G = X - M

8. (S + T - G) - I = X - M

Current account balances are X and M. If the right hand side is negative i.e. a balance of payments deficit (X>M), then it would seem that it reflects an excess of domestic investment (I) over savings (public and private). In the long run investment (I) should yield a return unless it is unproductive investment.

When current income into Ireland is greater than expenditure abroad during the year there is a balance of payment surplus on current account. After years of deficits in this account we have had a surplus since 1990 when it was small. Up to 1988 the deficits in current account were very substantial, for example in 1981 the current deficit was £1,595 million. Appendix16.1 shows the Irish current balance of payments position 1994 - 1997. In all these years exports have exceeded imports. To obtain the overall trade balance, Ireland's trade balance in services must be added, to the merchandise trade balance. In 1997 the balance on current account was £1,362 or 3.2% GNP.

Policies to Cure a Balance of Payments Deficit:

The correct measure to remedy a deficit will depend on what is causing it and the exchange rate regime in operation at the time.
Measures to correct a deficit can be divided into two categories:

1. Expenditure reducing measures such as domestic deflation that cuts expenditure.
2. Expenditure switching measures such as import controls and devaluation of the national currency.

The two measures can be regarded as complements. To cure a persistent deficit due to an overvalued exchange rate (makes exports dear to foreigners and exports cheap to us). The government can use three policy measures as follows:

1. Deflation:

Fiscal and monetary policies can be used to restrict the total level of demand in the country. Increasing interest rates and/or taxes can reduce aggregate demand. This is an expenditure reducing policy, which cures a deficit, by reducing the demand for imports. Irish GNP will fall and unemployment will rise. A country may choose to adopt this method when:

- Under WTO, EU and other treaties it may not be able to use import controls and other protective measures; and

- Protective measures invite retaliation.

This policy is one of maintaining the external exchange rate and may result in unemployment at home. The depression of demand may cause the domestic inflation rate to fall relative to that of competitor countries. This results in increasing the competitiveness of exports and reducing competitiveness of imports. Foreigners may switch their demand to the country's exports and residents may change away from imports to buy home produced goods. But all this takes time.

2. Import Controls or Protection:

These have an immediate expenditure switching effect on the balance of payments. Import duties and tariffs put people off imports while quotas and embargoes directly reduce expenditure on imports. They do little or nothing about the underlying causes of the deficit but try to cure it by cutting off imports. Protection invites retaliation and as mentioned already, countries may be prohibited by treaty from using such measures.

3. Devaluation or Depreciation:

A decrease in the official price of a nation's currency as expressed in the currencies of other nations is a devaluation. The unavailability of import controls has meant that Ireland is left with a choice between deflation and devaluation. If a country has a 'floating' exchange rate and it allows the external value of its currency to drop, this fall in the external value of the currency is referred to as depreciation.

Devaluation and depreciation have the same effect in that exports will now seem cheaper to foreigners while imports will appear dearer to domestic consumers. For example a bottle of French perfume costs €15. This is worth $15 when €1=$1 and $19.5 when €1=$1.3 These measures are expenditure switching. To assess devaluation or depreciation as a method we need to examine the elasticities of demand for exports and imports.

Marshall- Lerner Condition and Exchange Rate Stability:

The Marshall Lerner condition is such that depreciation or devaluation of a currency will improve the balance of payments (i.e. reduce the BP deficit) only if the sum "as a weighted average" of the price elasticities of demand of exports and imports is greater than one. Conversely a BP surplus could be reduced by revaluation if the same criterion is fulfilled. If export and import elasticities are highly inelastic adding up to less than one a fall in the exchange rate may cause a deficit to become worse and a revaluation may increase the surplus.

In Ireland's case suppose demand is elastic and the Irish pound is devalued by 10 per cent. (The price of imports should increase by 10 per cent.) Imports will fall by more than 10%. If, on the other hand, demand is inelastic the quantity of imports purchased may decrease by only 2 or 3 per cent. The result is that we are buying substantially the same amount of imports but at a much higher price and as a result the deficit in the Balance of Payments increases. Imports into Ireland that are inelastic are petroleum products and many raw materials. Costs to Irish business go up as a result of dearer imports so what is gained by exports being cheaper is eventually lost.

Expenditure Reducing Versus Expenditure Switching Policies:

Marshall - Lerner condition while it is a very necessary condition is not a sufficient condition for a fall in the exchange rate to reduce a balance of payment's deficit. If devaluation is to be successful domestic supply must come up to the level necessary to meet the increase in demand as a result of the drop in the exchange rate. Spare capacity is required which can be used to increase supply to meet the switch of international and home demand away from foreign produced goods and towards home produced substitutes. Expenditure reducing deflation and expenditure switching devaluation are complementary policies in seeking to reduce balance of payments deficits.

The J Curve:

From observation, measures to rectify a BP deficit have often led to an immediate deterioration in the payments position followed by a recovery. This gives a J Curve effect as seen in Diagram 16.1.

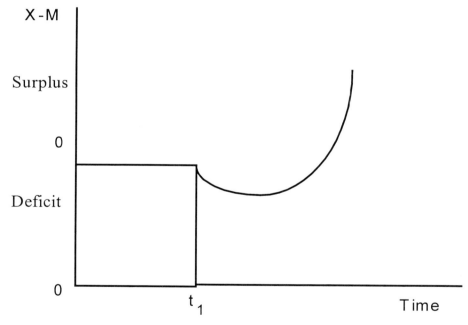

Diagram 16.1 J. Curve Effect

274

There are a number of reasons for this:

- If the economy is at or near full capacity, expenditure switching policies will not have an immediate effect and will not be successful until capacity is increased.

- Money may flow out of the country when measures to rectify a balance of payment's deficit are taken. Confidence may return and recovery will then take place.

- The price elasticities for exports and imports may be less than one so that the Marshall Lerner condition is not fulfilled. Immediately after devaluation exports may not rise and more has to be paid for imports that do not have immediate substitutes the BP gets worse before it improves. In Diagram 16.1 devaluation takes place at t_1 and the curve is J shaped.

Absorption Approach to Balance of Payments:

The Keynesian approach to the balance of payments is to look on it in terms of whether aggregate demand is sufficient to absorb national output. The equilibrium equation for national income in the Keynesian income expenditure model is;

$Y = C + I + G + (X - M)$ which can be written as $X - M = Y - (C + I + G)$

This indicates that the balance of payments (X-M) will be in deficit if the economy absorbs or consumes more goods and services than it produces. C+I+G is equal to total domestic expenditure and if this exceeds Y national output the balance of payments will be in deficit. Devaluation will be successful only if total domestic expenditure does not absorb the whole of Y. Spare capacity is a necessity if output is to rise to meet the increased demand for exports.

An increase in the value of exports due to devaluation and via the multiplier will bring about an increase in national income, resulting in a greater demand for imports. Even if there is spare capacity absorption will reduce the effect of devaluation. This approach points to the need to have spare capacity before devaluing the currency, showing that it may be necessary to undertake expenditure reducing polices, before expenditure switching depreciation.

The Keynesian approach concentrates on the current account.

Balance of Payments Surplus:

It is usual to discuss deficits but not surpluses that also cause problems. A surplus is generally looked on as a sign of the country's competitiveness in exporting. A small surplus is desirable but there are a number of reasons why a large payment's surplus is undesirable.

Arguments against having a large surplus include the following:

- **One country's surplus is another country's deficit:**

Since the balance of payments must balance for the world, it is not possible for all countries to have surpluses at the same time. There is also the problem that deficit countries cannot reduce their deficits unless the surplus countries reduce their surpluses. If the latter are unwilling then other action must be taken by the deficit countries and this will cause a reduction in world trade and even a world recession. In the early 1970's oil-producing countries had large surpluses and these caused problems for other countries. In the 1980's and early 1990's the problems were being caused by a Japanese surplus and US trade deficit. Pressure has come on the US from its manufacturing industry to introduce import controls. If this happens then world trade will suffer. Another major problem caused by world trade imbalance is the chronic deficits of the less developed countries due to developed country surpluses.

- **Dutch Disease Effect:**

'Dutch disease' is the name given to the phenomenon of the contraction of the traditional manufacturing sector (exporting) due to the rapid expansion of the extractive sector of the economy. It is called 'Dutch' because this phenomenon arose in Holland when natural gas extraction grew rapidly there and 'disease' because other sectors of the economy were adversely affected. Production and employment in the extractive sector will increase while they will decline in the traditional sector. In the non- traded sector (commodities for which transport costs are so high that no international trade can take place) production and employment may either contract or expand. The price of non-traded goods rise and the prices of traded goods are constrained by the terms of trade. The result is the venting of the boom through the inflation of domestic goods.

Another example is that of the UK when it started to produce petroleum from the North Sea in 1976. The UK oil trade surplus in 1980 and 1981 caused an inflow of hot money that caused the £'s exchange rate to rise to a level greatly overvalued in terms of trading competitiveness of her non-oil manufacturing industries. UK manufacturing industry lost world markets and suffered from intense import competition. This caused de-industrialisation and large-scale unemployment and as a result much of the benefit of North Sea oil revenue was lost in financing imports and supporting the unemployed.

A Balance of Payments Surplus is Inflationary:

A balance of payment's surplus can be a cause of domestic inflation. This can be explained in Keynesian and monetarist terms.

- **Keynesian terms:**

This explanation is an extension to the absorption approach already discussed. A surplus is an injection into the circular flow of income and through the multiplier it will increase the equilibrium level of money national income. The effect is inflationary if there is no spare capacity in the economy.

- **Monetarist Terms:**

If the exchange rate is fixed in an open economy the domestic money supply is affected by the balance of payments. A surplus increases the money supply. The country's currency is scarce on the foreign exchange markets and the exchange rate rises. To prevent the exchange rate rising the country with the surplus must sell its own currency and buy others that it adds to its official reserves. Since more of the country's currency has been issued the money supply has increased. If this increased supply of money is invested in the purchase of the country's capital assets or spent on exports the domestic price level may go up, causing inflation.

Determination of Exchange Rates:

The exchange rate is the price of one currency in terms of another, e.g. Euro for £Stg for US$ and so on. Price is determined by supply and demand for a currency and this depends on:

- **Balance of Payments**

When Ireland exports goods to the UK the importer buys Euros. This creates demand for Euros and an excess supply of sterling. Sterling falls in value against the Euro. A country exporting more than it imports will therefore have a strong currency, while if it is the other way around the value will fall against other currencies.

- **European Central Bank**

If there is pressure on the Euro the European Central Bank can buy Euros thus increasing demand and halting or at least slowing down the fall in value against other currencies.

- **Speculation:**

Speculators buy up currencies they expect to rise in value and sell those they expect to fall in value, so as to make a profit. In 1992/93 the IR£ came under speculative pressure. This can cause uncertainty and adversely affect international trade. It can take a number of forms:

- Multinationals can deposit large amounts of cash say in Ireland and cause the exchange rate to rise. When this happens they remove the cash making a profit, all of which can happen in a few days or even less than this.

- Importers expecting the value of a currency to fall will buy in large quantities in advance so that the market value of the currency will fall.

- A rise in the rate of inflation above international rates; Assume for example that there is a rise in Irish inflation above international rates. This causes a fall in demand for Irish exports and as a result a fall in the demand for Euro (assuming a price elasticity of demand greater than 1) and a rise in imports and thus a rise in the supply of the Euro. The exchange rate depreciates and speculators can react in one of two ways. The first is stabilising speculation and occurs when speculators think that any exchange rate change will be reversed. If they think the exchange rate will appreciate they buy more Euro and sell fewer. They thus cause the exchange rate to appreciate as they had anticipated it would. The second is destabilising speculation and this occurs when speculators believe that exchange rate movements will continue in the same direction i.e. down. They sell more Euros now before the exchange rate falls further. Eventually this could cause overshooting with the exchange rate falling well below the purchasing power parity rate. At this point speculators think the rate will rise so they buy € thereby causing the rate to rise.

During the 1992/93 currency crisis speculation brought about the devaluation of the IR£.

- **Expansionary Fiscal and Monetary Policies**

If expansionary fiscal and monetary policies are introduced in Ireland they will lead to increased imports thus putting downward pressure on the exchange rate for the IR£.

- **Level of Irish Interest Rates**

When Irish rates are relatively high money flows in, whereas when they are relatively low money flows out. An inflow strengthens the Irish currency and this type of money is called "hot" or "funk" money.

- **Purchasing Power Parity Theory (PPP)**

This theory developed in the 1920's explains the equilibrium exchange rate between two currencies in terms of the price levels in the two countries. It states that the value of one currency relative to another depends upon the relative purchasing power of the two currencies in their domestic economies. This theory can be expressed as follows:

The price of the € in US $ = $\dfrac{\text{US Price Level}}{\text{Eurozone Price Level}}$

In a free market the exchange rate will settle at that level where the purchasing power of a single unit is the same no matter where it is spent. It implies that floating rates will automatically change, to reflect differences in inflation between countries. If the Irish inflation rate is 3% higher than the US rate then the € will depreciate by 3% to maintain the competitiveness of Irish goods.

Suppose there is only one good, which costs €110 in Ireland and US$220 in the US. The exchange rate is € = US$2. If as a result of inflation the cost of the good in Ireland increases to €120, the exchange rate adjusts as follows:

$$2 \times \dfrac{110}{120} \times € = US\$1.83$$

PPP predicts that the value of the Euro will fall by an amount required to restore the competitiveness of Irish goods.

Problems with Purchasing Power Parity:

- It is difficult to select the appropriate price index for calculating PPP rates. A base year must be chosen for a year when exchange rates were in equilibrium;

- transport costs, tariffs and other trade restrictions prevent price equality in different countries;

- some goods and services cannot be very easily exported (i.e. non-traded goods) so that if they are cheaper in one country supply and demand cannot bring about equality; and

- the real exchange rate may change due to changes in the growth of real income, technology and tastes in different countries. As a result the equilibrium exchange rate will not be the same as the PPP rate based on relative inflation rates.

Though short run deviations from PPP are possible, in the long run the theory probably does hold true. The price of a currency is determined by supply and demand and this is shown in Diagram 16.2

Suppose there are just two countries, Ireland and US. When Irish firms wish to buy goods in the US or investors wish to invest there, they will supply €s for US dollars. The higher the exchange rate the more dollars they will obtain for their €. US goods will be cheaper and investment there more profitable so that more € will be supplied. Supply curve for the € will slope upwards, as in Diagram 16.2.

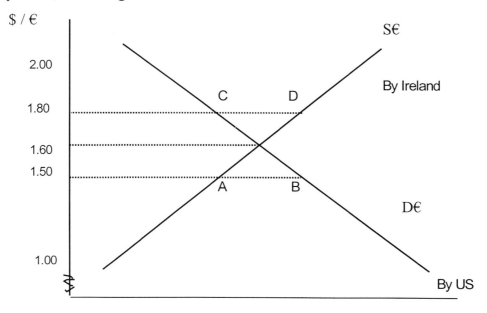

Diagram 16.2 Determination of the Rate of Exchange

Americans wishing to buy Irish goods or to invest will need €. They demand by selling US$'s. The lower the price of the € the cheaper it will be for them to buy Irish goods, and the greater the demand for Euros. The demand curve will slope downwards. In Diagram 16.2 the equilibrium exchange rate is $1.60 per €1. What brings about this equilibrium? If the rate was below $1.60, say at US$1.50 per €, there would be a shortage of Euros (AB). Banks would have too few Euros and too many dollars and they would increase the rate until demand equalled supply, at $1.60. If the rate were above the equilibrium of US $1.60 supply of Irish pounds would exceed demand. If the exchange rate was €1= US $1.80 there would be an excess supply of Euros (CD). Banks would lower the rate until supply equals demand at €1= US$1.60. Equilibrium in practice is reached quickly since the banks are continuously adjusting rates, as due to competition they must keep in line with one another.

Trade Weighted Indices:

The trade weighted exchange rate index is the average cost of foreign currency. It is also known as the effective exchange rate index. Weighting is done according to the foreign countries' importance to the home country, whose currency is being measured. Weights are given in order of magnitude of trade with the particular country and the total is 1. The UK has the highest weight as it is our biggest trading partner.

Fixed Exchange Rates :

If a country does not allow any short-term variations in its exchange rate, it is said to be on a fixed external standard. This is done by using foreign exchange reserves of the Central Bank to buy up any excess selling of a country's currency, thus keeping price steady or issuing more of its own currency when there is excess buying of it, thus holding price steady by increasing the country's money supply. Under the fixed exchange rate regime, the exchange rate can be altered only when balance of payments is in a state of fundamental disequilibrium. The disequilibrium is not automatically corrected and must be controlled by devaluation, increased exports, decreased imports or import controls. The government sets the fixed exchange rate and the Central Bank maintains it.

Advantages of a Fixed Rate System:

- It makes international trade more stable as it gives more certainty to traders about what the exchange rate is going to be and it encourages international trade.

- Countries must take action to cure a balance of payments deficit and the IMF has traditionally insisted on this.

- A country is more likely to fight inflation since with a fixed exchange rate it is damaging to the Balance of Payments. This is not so when the rate can automatically depreciate.

- Overseas investment is encouraged since firms will be more willing to set up business in foreign countries if the uncertainty of exchange rate fluctuations is removed.

Disadvantages of Fixed Exchange Rates:

- As devaluation must be avoided, countries with a deficit are obliged to take damaging deflationary measures.

- When there is a high and differential rate of inflation between countries, the fixed exchange rate is inappropriate.

- If a devaluation/revaluation is expected, speculation intensifies as great gains can be made. Money leaves the country that is expected to devalue and this results in a loss of foreign exchange reserves, as the central bank has to maintain the par value of the currency.

- Capital flows into a country mean that the central bank has to create more money to meet demand for its currency and money supply, therefore, increases.

- There is a loss of flexibility in economic policy making.

Freely Floating Exchange Rate:

The forces of supply and demand on foreign exchange markets determine the external value of a country's currency without the need for official financing or external reserves. In this type of market, the value of the Irish pound in terms of the dollar would depend on the demand for Irish pounds from holders of dollars and the supply of Irish pounds from holders of Irish pounds wishing to buy dollars. The foreign exchange value of a national currency is closely related to that country's balance between exports and imports. It will also be affected by the capital transactions between that country and the rest of the world.

Advantages of a Floating Exchange Rate:

- The exchange rate moves up or down to correct a balance of payments imbalance and in theory, the rate should never be under or over valued.

- It is not necessary to work out the new exchange rate, as it will be established by supply and demand.

- In a situation of rapid inflation, the exchange rate will automatically depreciate thus preventing damage to exports. It helps to shield a country from inflation elsewhere because if a country is on a fixed exchange rate it imports inflation by way of higher import prices.

- Capital inflows do not create more money in the economy as the Central Bank of the country does not have to create money with which to buy the foreign currency. A country's monetary policy (and also its fiscal policy) can in principle be completely independent of external influences.

- There is a smooth, automatic adjustment in the exchange rate so that there is no mass speculation.

- There is less need to hold large reserves to defend the currency, since there is no Central Bank intervention in the foreign exchange market.

Disadvantages of Floating Exchange Rates:

- A major objection to floating exchange rates is the uncertainty that exchange rate volatility generates for traders. Hedging which is the avoidance of foreign exchange risk can reduce the effects of volatility but forward planning is more difficult.

- Uncertainty may discourage foreign investment.

- Capital movements can change the exchange rate with damaging effects to the economy. If there is an increase in demand for the country's currency, it will appreciate and will make exports less competitive.

- Speculation in the currency could cause the exchange rate to become unstable and to fluctuate excessively.

- Since there is no need to maintain discipline in the economy; problems like inflation may be ignored until they have reached very damaging proportions.

Dirty or Managed Floating:

'Dirty' or 'managed' floating occurs when the exchange rate is 'officially' floating but the authorities intervene "unofficially". If the intervention is just a smoothing operation, it can be described as freely floating. If, however, the Central Bank seeks to have an unofficial exchange rate target, it is 'dirty' floating. Since the breakdown of The Bretton Woods System in 1971/72, many of the world's trading currencies floated in this way. The forms of intervention include central bank purchases and sales of currencies, changes in interest rates and exchange controls.

Problems with Dirty Floating:

- It is difficult to predict long term equilibrium exchange rates;

- Due to the growth in "hot money" since the early 1970's, it is very difficult for an individual country to counter inflation by itself; and

- The use of high interest rates to prevent short term capital outflows may bring about begger-my-neighbour policies with other countries raising their interest rates.

Exchange Rates and the Balance of Payments: No Government Intervention.

In a free foreign exchange market the balance of payments will automatically balance. In Ireland's case the supply of Irish pounds arises from imports to Ireland or the purchase of foreign assets by Irish residents. Conversely the demand for Irish pounds arises from exports and the purchase of Irish assets by foreigners. With a floating exchange rate the supply and demand of Irish pounds is equalised by appropriate movements in the exchange rate.

The balance of payments is the sum of the current and capital account. With a floating exchange rate a current account surplus must be matched with a capital account deficit and vice versa. A current account surplus must be matched by an increase in the country's holding of foreign assets. Since the government is not adding to the foreign exchange reserves this must show up in the capital account as a deficit equal exactly to the current account surplus, as previously stated.

If the supply and/or demand curves of the Irish pound shift, the exchange rate will alter. This is shown in Diagram 16.3. Again we take the US$- € exchange rate. Assume that the supply curve shifts to the right and the demand curve to the left, then the exchange rate will fall from €1 = US$1.8 to €1 = US$1.60.

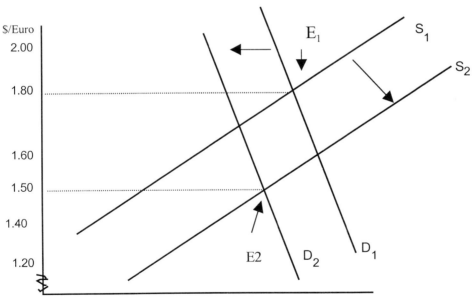

Diagram 16.3 Floating Exchange Rate - Movement to New Equilibrium

The above outcome happened because one or other of the following factors were at work.

- If inflation is higher in Ireland than it is in the US then Irish exports will become less competitive and demand for Euros will fall. Imports from the US will become cheaper therefore the supply of Euros will rise.
- If interest rates in Ireland fall relative to say US, Irish residents will deposit their money abroad, as they will earn more. The supply of Irish pounds rises while demand falls due to reluctance by foreigners to deposit their money in Ireland.

- Should investment prospects in the US become better than those in Ireland due to more attractive incentives, demand for the Euro will fall and supply will rise.

- If Irish incomes rise the demand for US imports will rise as will the supply of Euros. Demand for Irish exports falls and demand for Euro falls.

- When speculators feel that the value of the Euro is going to fall they sell Euros now. The supply of Euros goes up and people wishing to buy them will wait for the value to fall fully and as a result demand will fall.

In the cases given above the exchange rate has depreciated. If the exchange rate rises there is an appreciation of the € against the US$.

Government Intervention -Floating Exchange Rate:

The government will not wish to have supply and demand changing frequently and can intervene in the foreign exchange market. The objective may vary but could be as follows:

Short Term Fluctuations:

Suppose the Central Bank thinks that € = US$ 1.80 is the long- term equilibrium rate, it can intervene to stop excessive fluctuations. In Diagram 8.3 demand and supply curves shift to D2 and S2 respectively. The government has three means of preventing the rate from falling to US$ 1.60.

1. It can use its reserves to buy Irish pounds, a move that will shift the demand curve to the right. Some say this does not cause D to shift but just closes the excess supply gap at $1.80.

2. Interest rates can be increased so as to encourage people to invest in Ireland. The rate of Deposit Interest Retention Tax (DIRT) was reduced to 10 per cent on special accounts in order to attract deposits but is now 15%. The demand curve shifts to the right.

3. Foreign currency can be borrowed from another country or from the IMF or another international financial institution. This money can be used to buy Irish pounds and in this way demand for Irish pounds is moved to the right.

Foreign Exchange Market:

This market is the intermediary through which one currency is converted into another and it does not have an exact place of business unlike other markets. Dealing in foreign exchange is done mainly by telephone and telex networks. Banks and money brokers have dealing rooms. The products being traded are homogeneous so that this market fits the classical economist's model of perfect competition.

Broadly speaking there are two markets-spot and forward-in which foreign currency is bought and sold:

- **Spot Market**

In this market the transaction takes place immediately and delivery takes about two days. The spot rate is the price that must be paid for immediate delivery, and it is determined by supply and demand. Thus an Irish firm might receive US$1,500 from a US customer and sells it 'spot' to a bank to obtain Euros immediately (usually within two days). If the exchange rate is $1.5 to the €, the Irish firm will receive €1, 000.

- **Forward Market**

This is a market where currency can be bought and sold at a rate of exchange agreed today for delivery at a specified future date. Rates are quoted continuously for 30, 60, and 90 days delivery but deals can be arranged for longer periods also. Traders try to eliminate risks due to fluctuation in exchange rates by using the forward market. The forward rate is the spot rate plus a premium or minus a discount.

After the break with sterling in 1979, the Central Bank determined forward discounts/premia on the € by quoting swap rates. This arrangement was phased out between July and November 1980. Now the market determines forward discount/premia.

- **Dublin Foreign Exchange Market:**

Up to 1979 Ireland's monetary union with the U.K meant that the exchange rate for the Irish £ was identical to that of sterling and Irish interest rates moved in line with UK rates. There was therefore no need for an Irish foreign exchange market. There was an inter-bank market in foreign exchange in the 1960's when business was between the Central Bank and the commercial banks. In an effort to expand the inter-bank market, the Dublin Banks Foreign Exchange Committee was set up in 1977 to regulate and supervise business. There was an increase in business but the exchange rate was determined in London due to the sterling link. With EMS membership and the break with sterling, the Dublin market had to trade a "small" currency when the exchange rate was determined by supply and demand, albeit within EMS limits. It took the market some time to adjust and to become fully involved in the day to day movements in the IR£ exchange rate.

Central Bank and the Exchange Rate:

After the break with sterling, the Central Bank administered the exchange rate within EMS limits. It had a fixed spread of 0.25% between its buying and selling rates. However, inter-bank dealings remained small so that the spread was increased to 0.8 per cent to encourage inter-bank business. In 1980 the Central Bank introduced a mini-band of $\pm$ 1.65 per cent within the EMS band of $\pm$ 2.25 per cent. Later in 1980 the full $\pm$ 2.25 was used. There were overnight limits on each bank's holdings of foreign currencies against the Irish pound (open limits). This was discontinued in 1992, but doesn't mean the banks have unlimited open positions as the Central Bank supervises them.

The Gold Standard:

Under the Gold Standard the government of each country fixed the price of gold in terms of its own currency. It maintained convertibility of its currency into gold and linked its money creation to its supply of gold. Under the Gold Standard Ireland was linked to sterling. If for example an ounce of gold was convertible in Stg £5 and US $10 then the dollar–Sterling exchange rate must always be US$ 2 to Stg£1. This was known as the gold parity rate.

Convertibility into gold was suspended in 1914, reintroduced by the UK in 1925 and most major currencies were again convertible into gold by 1927. The system proved impossible to sustain as the countries with overvalued currencies against gold had to deflate and this led to high unemployment. It is often suggested that the Gold Standard was what triggered the slump of the 1930s. In September 1931 the system came to an end when the UK then the world's leading trading nation, suspended the gold convertibility of sterling.

Advantages of the Gold Standard:

- The majority of world currencies had fixed exchange rates therefore there was little uncertainty and world trade grew.

- It provided a self-adjusting mechanism and it tended to correct trade surpluses and deficits.

Disadvantages of the Gold Standard:

- Countries with deficits lost gold and suffered from unemployment, falling incomes and investment.

- Countries with trade surpluses should have expanded their money supply but often did not thus preventing the self- adjusting process from working.

The Adjustable Peg and the Dollar Standard:

After the collapse of the Gold Standard, there was a period of fluctuating exchange rates. With the out-break of World War Two most countries pegged their exchange rates. In 1944 at Bretton Woods in New Hampshire in the US, a system called the Adjustable Peg System was established under which rates were fixed. Rates could be adjusted in the case of fundamental disequilibrium or continuous excess of demand or supply of a currency on the foreign exchange market. Market forces were free to determine the day to day exchange rate of a currency 1% either side of an agreed par value or "peg". A member could propose a change if it had a fundamental disequilibrium in its balance of payments.

The International Monetary Fund (IMF)

The objectives of the Fund are set out in its articles of agreement which state that the purpose of the fund is:

- To promote international monetary co-operation though a permanent institution that provides the machinery for consultation and collaboration on international monetary problems. This has been achieved over the period since 1947 certainly in the richer countries.

- Promote stable exchange rates, maintain orderly exchange arrangements and avoid competitive exchange depreciation.

- To facilitate the expansion and balanced growth of international trade.

- To reduce periods of disequilibrium in the balance of payments of member countries.

- To encourage full convertibility between currencies and an ending of exchange controls. This has been achieved over the period since 1947 certainly in the richer countries. The same cannot be said for less developed countries.

IMF can be said to have had three main roles:

1. Acting in an advisory capacity to member countries;

2. Overseeing the exchange rate system until it broke down in 1971. 'Dirty Floating' then took over and the IMF tried to limit the freedom of deficit members. Less developed countries have been badly affected by deflationary policies forced on them, by the IMF.

3. It has a banking role and is supposed to ensure that there is an adequate supply of international liquidity. It acts as a monitor of the world's currencies by helping to maintain an orderly system of payments between countries. The dollar provided the main source of liquidity but its own weakening in the late 1960's and early 1970's contributed to the collapse of the Bretton Woods exchange rates. Specially created reserves of the IMF were to provide secondary liquidity. When it started, each member paid a quota ie 75 per cent in

its own currency and 25 per cent in gold, into an IMF 'basket' of currency reserves; which were made available to members with a temporary BP deficit. The first part of this drawing is automatic but after that, conditions are attached. Quotas have been increased from time to time.

It also lends through stand-by credits created in the 1950s and currency swaps and General Agreement to Borrow (GAB) introduced in 1962. Under this system ten leading industrialised countries, the Group of Ten, agreed to support each other's currency through a supplementary IMF pool. In 1970, the Special Drawings Rights (SDR) scheme was introduced as a substitute for gold in international payments.

SDRs are basically bookkeeping units of account allocated to member countries in proportion to their quotas. Before they were introduced, IMF lending ability was restricted by the size of its currency reserves, many of which were too soft to be acceptable for trade. Now the IMF has a role similar to a domestic bank within a country and can expand its lending beyond the size of the currencies deposited with it by members. SDRs have not been really acceptable and are not trusted by many countries. For this reason, they have not solved the problem of world liquidity.

The devaluation of the pound sterling in 1967 even after support from the US and other countries is seen as the start of events leading up to the breakdown of the Bretton Woods system. There was a flight from dollars into gold in 1968 when there was doubt about the US commitment to maintaining the dollar price of gold. A two tiered gold market developed with central banks holding gold at $35 an ounce while the private market price of gold was allowed to be free at a much higher level. There was movement of gold from the public to the private sector so that its importance as a reserve asset diminished sharply. In August 1971 the US severed the link between the dollar and gold and the system then collapsed.

There is little doubt but that the recent (since 1997) financial crises in Brazil, Russia and South East Asia have stretched the resources of the IMF and reduced its ability to support economies in financial difficulty. Due to the mounting debt crisis involving less developed countries, the IMF is wary of lending to them. It has been criticised for not trying to stop the Asian crisis and later for not doing enough to stop it spreading.

In the early 1990s it helped countries of Central Europe, the Baltic countries, Russia and other countries of the former Soviet Union in the difficult shift from centrally planned to market economies.

The "Snake"(1973 – 1979):

This was a currency co-operation system set up in 1973 between the then members of the EU. It required each central bank to maintain its currency within a band of +/- 2.25% against the US dollar. This reduced uncertainty but restricted the use of the exchange rate as a policy instrument for adjusting trade deficits and surpluses between members.

The 1973/74 first oil crisis caused fluctuations in balance of payments and made it difficult for members to stay within the narrow bands of the "Snake". The UK, Ireland and France remained in for only a few months but continued as 'outside' members.

European Monetary System:

Members of the EU (including Ireland) founded the European Monetary System in March 1979. Ireland broke the link with Sterling as the UK did not join the Exchange Rate Mechanism (ERM) at that stage. The ERM was the central feature of the EMS. To maintain a common market it is necessary for the members to have similar rates of inflation and to maintain fixed exchange rates against each other.

It was intended to maintain a 'zone of monetary stability', meaning stability of exchange rates and a common effort at achieving common and lower rates of member inflation. It was also set up to co-ordinate credit policies of members and to promote trade among them.

Exchange Rate Mechanism (ERM):

The means by which exchange rates were maintained within agreed limits was known as the ERM of the EMS. To do this the members had to ensure that domestic conditions did not differ substantially from those of the countries with which they had aligned their currencies. Currencies of ERM members floated against the US dollar. For example the Irish pound traded against the deutschmark within defined bands but floated freely against the US dollar.

To maintain the agreed exchange rate with Germany, the Irish had to maintain inflation and interest rates in line with those of Germany otherwise the Irish Pound would go outside the limits. Investors outside the ERM could find the deutschmark more attractive than the IR£ and this would cause further movements. The IR£ had to move in much the same way against the US dollar as the deutschmark. Ireland had to pursue similar monetary policies to those of Germany.

Basically the ERM was the deutschmark as it was the strongest currency in it. Germany was a low inflation country and Ireland having tied the IR£ to the deutschmark was expected to keep the inflation level at that of the Germans. From the start of ERM inflation rates of members fell. Our inflation and interest rates took a long time to fall.

European Currency Unit (ECU):

The EMS was based on a hypothetical unit of account called the ECU. Each country's central rate in the EMS was set in ECU's. The value of one unit was determined by taking a weighted basket, of all member currencies and the value of the weight is determined by the relative size of the members GDP.

The ECU contains specific amounts of the currencies of each member depending on their economic importance, determined by the share of each country in EU GNP, intra EU trade and importance of currency reserves. The amount of each currency remained fixed for five years. Due to changes in countries' economic importance and new members joining, the weights were changed in 1984 and 1989 and were frozen in 1993. The weight given to each of the 12 currencies is shown on Table 16.1

Table 16.1
European Currency Unit (ECU) Composition November 1993

Currency	Units in ECU	Weight %
Belgian Franc	3.3010	7.60
Luxembourg Franc	0.13	0.30
Danish Krone	0.1976	2.45
German Mark	0.6242	30.1
Greek Drachma	1.440	0.8
Spanish Peseta	6.885	5.3
French Franc	1.332	19.0
Irish Pound	0.0086	1.1
Lira	1.8	10.15
Dutch Guilder	0.2198	9.4
Portuguese Escudo	1.393	0.8
UK Pound Sterling	0.08784	13.0
	1 ECU	100.00

Source: European Economy No. 54 Table 51 1996

Parity Grid: 1979 - August 1993:

Each currency had a central rate against the ECU that was translated into cross rates for each pair of currencies. This information is shown for 1979 to 1995 in Spring 1995 Bulletin of the Central Bank. The ECU was the unit of account for the EU. It was used for all member state transactions. Currencies' fluctuations were limited to ±2.25 per cent either side of the central rate against any other ERM currency (6 per cent for Italy initially, UK and Spain for example) up to August 1993 when they changed to ±15%. Central banks had to intervene once their limits were reached. Member governments had to lodge 20 per cent of their dollar and gold reserves with the European Monetary Co-operation Fund (EMCF) and receive ECU in exchange. The EMCF provided credit facilities to support the agreed exchange rate between members. It was set up in 1973 but was more or less dormant until the start of the EMS and never played the major role it was intended to play.

Divergence Indicator:

To avoid frequent intervention the ERM had a divergence indicator or early warning system. Each currency had a divergence threshold of 75 per cent of the maximum allowed difference between its actual ECU rate and its central ECU rate. Since the value of the ECU changed when its component currencies changed this divergence threshold was different or separate

To avoid frequent intervention the ERM had a divergence indicator or early warning system. Each currency had a divergence threshold of 75 per cent of the maximum allowed difference between its actual ECU rate and its central ECU rate. Since the value of the ECU changed when its component currencies changed this divergence threshold was different or separate from the 2.25 per cent band of the parity grid. If the exchange rate diverged by more than three quarters of the 2.25 per cent of its central rate up to August 1993, all EMS members needed to consider whether realignment was necessary and what internal policies needed to be adopted by the divergent country.

Some of the likely internal policies were:

- Try to stabilise its exchange rate by using its official reserves;

- If pressure was downward on the currency, extra reserves could be obtained from the EMCF, and could be used to support the currency on foreign exchange markets;

- Deflationary policy to bring domestic costs and finances into line with other members had to be used if the weakness in the currency continued for long; and

- Failing the above measures to rectify the position the country could realign its currency provided it had the permission of all members of ERM.

Ireland and the EMS/ ERM:

Prior to joining the EMS/ERM in 1979, Ireland was in a full currency union with the UK, therefore there was a one-for-one exchange rate between the IR£ and Stg£. During the 1970's in particular the UK had a relatively high rate of inflation and Ireland, as a small open economy linked to it, imported the high inflation rate. There was very little Ireland could do to reduce the rate of inflation below that of the UK. What was required was a break with sterling and the pursuit of a "harder currency" policy and in 1979 with the establishment of the ERM the opportunity to do this presented itself. The other members of ERM, had lower inflation rates and it was expected that the Irish rate would decrease to their level.

The experience of the early years of EMS membership did not work out as expected. Ireland's inflation rate increased to over 20 per cent in the two years after joining. There were a number of reasons for this.

At the time of joining in March 1979, the major ERM currencies were relatively weak. Sterling appreciated in value as a result of a tight monetary policy in an effort to reduce inflation. It was helped by its status as a Petro-currency. The Irish pound avoided an artificial appreciation in its value that it would have incurred if still linked to sterling. However, since the UK was our major trading partner, our exchange rate was depreciated in trade weighted terms.

and loose fiscal policy in the US. This manifested itself in high US interest rates and an appreciation of the US dollar against ERM currencies.

Given the importance of our international trade it is important to maintain a rate of inflation that is lower than our trading partners. In the early 1980s wage and price inflation undermined our competitive position. After 1981 the Government reduced its investment spending.

From the commencement in 1979 to 1982 inflation worsened, unemployment rose and output declined. Some of the causes, such as the oil crises, were out of our control but even so there were question marks over the value of being a member of the ERM.

The fact that the UK was not a member of the ERM caused problems for Ireland when sterling weakened because of the magnitude of trade flows with the U.K. In 1983 the Irish pound was devalued by 3.5 per cent due to sterling weakness and its depreciation relative to ERM currencies. Large amounts of IR £s were converted into sterling and other foreign currencies in the expectation that the IR£ would be devalued. This large capital outflow caused Irish external reserves to fall and the Central Bank increased the short- term interest rate in an attempt to stop the outflows. Eventually the IR£ had to be devalued by 3.5%. A further and larger devaluation of 8 per cent took place in 1986 for similar reasons. By 1987 the Irish government had seen the necessity for fiscal rectitude, prices and wages had come under the discipline of ERM membership and Irish inflation drew nearer the rate of other ERM members. Exchequer Borrowing Requirement fell from 13 per cent of GNP in 1983, to 2.8% in 1992 and went as low as 2.0 per cent in 1990.

Reduction in government borrowings didn't essentially retard the rate of growth of the economy and total output increased rapidly and inflation was down to less than 3 per cent in 1992. The basic objectives of the EMS were being achieved.

Exchange rate policy between 1987 and 1992 was expressed clearly in terms of ERM commitment. Over this period, financial markets in Ireland had become more closely integrated with European markets and capital flows had increased. This encouraged international investment and trade due to lack of risk of currency changes because of the consistent economic policies followed by the narrow band countries. Irish interest rates approached German rates towards the end of the 1980's and in 1991 there was less than 1 per cent between them. However, due to the currency crisis the difference was 10 per cent by December1992 and 14 per cent by January 1993.

The crises in the ERM intensified during the third quarter of 1992. A great deal of adjustment was required as a result of German economic and monetary union in 1990. In early 1990 the Germans looked for a revaluation of the DM but France and the UK did not agree. When Ireland was in trouble in 1992/1993 the Germans did not accept that they should give unlimited assistance to the Punt since they were refused a revaluation themselves. The Germans maintained high interest rates to counter inflation. Unemployment increased above its already high level due to world recession. Nations started to look to their own interest and the Danes voted no to the Maastricht Treaty in June 1992 creating uncertainty. Speculators saw a weakening in commitment to the ERM and began to look for currencies to attack. By this time they knew that the last of the exchange controls were going in January 1993 with the completion of the SEM. Due to this they were in a position to move large amounts of currencies.

When pressure came on initially, higher short-term Irish interest rates and Central Bank intervention were used, to uphold the existing parities. UK interest rates were raised from 10 to 15 per cent, and approximately £10 billion Sterling worth of reserves was spent on supporting sterling. So long as sterling remained tied to the Deutsche Mark, interest rates could not fall, therefore the UK could not get out of the recession it was in. Speculators expected the UK to devalue and in September 1992 sterling left the ERM.

The Lira left the ERM as a result of attacks on it and depreciated in value cosiderably. Spain and Portugal followed these in devaluing their currencies. Even though these upheavals took place, the initial structure of the ERM remained until August 1993 when the bands were widened to ± 15 per cent, except between the German duetschmark and the Dutch gilder. The Germans could have helped by reducing interest rates, but they did not. After this things settled down and fluctuations were small. All of this dealt a major blow to the EMS and its main weakness was seen to be its inflexibility.

Irish Pound Devaluation 1993:

When the UK joined the ERM in 1990 it picked its own exchange rate and the band of 6% without reference to the other ERM members, as was normal practice.

One of the criteria for Monetary Union under the Maastricht agreement in December 1991 was that there must be no realignment of the exchange rate in the two years preceding 1997. January 1997 was to be the starting date for European Monetary Union and this meant that the last date for realignment was December 1994. Realignments were therefore expected and the UK expected Germany to revalue the DM against all ERM currencies but this didn't suit the Germans. Italy however devalued the Lira within the ERM in September 1992. Sterling did not follow and due to selling of sterling over a few subsequent days the UK pulled out of the ERM and allowed its exchange rate to be determined by market forces. Sterling depreciated by 15% and as a result funds left Ireland in anticipation of a devaluation. Again the UK attempted to solve its exchange rate problem by itself and this led to lack of confidence in the System. The day of UK withdrawal from the ERM is known as Black Wednesday, September 16th 1992. At this stage the Irish position was unclear as the authorities did not know how far sterling would fall or to what extent the EU would assist in resolving the crisis. Irish exchange rate policy at that time consisted of strict adherence to the Deutschmark parity, so devaluation, was not a ready or easy option.

The UK is one of Ireland's main trading partners and over the latter part of the 1980s and early 1990s Ireland had a surplus in international trade. This was taken as a sign that the Irish currency was not overvalued and that speculators should be prevented from destroying the

ERM. Also over this period the inflation rate was below the European average. In other words Irish 'fundamentals' were right and a realignment was not sought. This decision was based partly on the fact that the inflation rate was lower than that of the UK. Opinion was that the IR£ could reach parity with sterling and that Ireland could still be competitive. When the UK left the ERM Irish Currency appreciated approximately 17 per cent against sterling. This appreciation of the IR£ led to large sales of Irish securities and large outflows of funds. Irish business people bought sterling now that it was cheap for future use in trade with the UK. Devaluation was expected and treasury managers sold IR £s and purchased stronger currencies to cover this risk. Speculators worked in a similar way. Approximately £1 billion left Irish financial markets and external reserves fell by over £2 billion.

Over this period the Irish authorities insisted that the exchange rate within the ERM would be maintained. Due to devaluation of other currencies as well as sterling, Irish business suffered a loss of competitiveness and if the exchange rate was to be maintained, a reduction in costs and domestic prices was needed. To this end a £50m market development fund was introduced to help selected industries. Over the period high interest rates (25%) pushed up costs.

In January 1993 the exchange risk on relevant transactions was covered by the Central Bank but this did little to reduce speculation and the Irish Pound was devalued by 10 per cent in January 1993, and was then around parity with sterling. Irish interest rates fell and money returned to Ireland.

Devaluation:

The following are some of the advantages and disadvantages of devaluation with reference to the Irish 1993 devaluation.

Advantages of Devaluation:

- Irish goods became more competitive on export markets particularly in the UK, Germany and France. With the exchange rate of 110 pence sterling, competitiveness was severely reduced and the devaluation brought about a change for the better;

- Reduced pressure on firms exporting goods protected jobs in the export sector of the economy. The employment forecast for 1993 before devaluation was for a drop of 10,000 jobs whereas after it, employment was to remain static;

- An overvalued currency means that economic activity is depressed so that government finances are down. With regard to servicing national debt it is important that the country is in a position to meet this commitment. Consequently it may be better to devalue, so that the revenue required to meet the debt is available. As a result of the devaluation tax revenues were higher due to both price and volume effects. Ability to service the debt would be in question had devaluation not taken place. Devaluation measures the real cost of foreign servicing of the debt;

- In the Irish case in 1992/93 high interest rates were a consequence of an overvalued Punt against sterling so that devaluing also solved the problem of high interest rates. At the time this was the great unknown but as it turned out rates went down;

- Foreign borrowing should mean a one-for-one increase in external reserves but in Ireland's case foreign borrowing increased by £11,926 million between 1979 and 1991 while external reserves for the same period increased by just £2,004 million. The reason for this is that the Central Bank purchased Irish pounds with the reserves in order to keep the exchange rate artificially high. In the absence of foreign borrowing external reserves would have disappeared and the punt would have been devalued. The only option in this case was to devalue;

- The Peseta and Escudo were devalued by 6% on November 22nd 1992. At that stage over 40 per cent of Irish exports were going to countries whose currencies were recently devalued or depreciated. It made sense to devalue in this situation;

- Mortgage holders were under very severe pressure due to high interest rates and a devaluation postpones further increases. It also obviated the necessity for government to subsidise them;

- The tourist industry gained from the devaluation as holidays in Ireland are cheaper in foreign currency terms.

Against Devaluation:-

- If economic "fundamentals" are right (low inflation and large balance of payments surplus) speculation against a currency is unwarranted, and would fail. In the interim high interest rates to protect the IR£ had to be endured;

- By maintaining the exchange rate it stops people expecting a devaluation of the IR£ every time sterling weakened. This caused private capital to flow into Ireland, allowing interest rates to fall and external reserves to rise. There is no guarantee that devaluation will be fully accepted by the markets. If it isn't, it will fail to generate the inflows necessary to bring about a reduction in interest rates;

- Irish interest rates were linked to German rates. Germany was in recession and it was expected that interest rates in this case would fall leading to a fall in Irish rates also. There was then no need to devalue;

- Exchange rate policy prior to devaluation brought about lower rates of inflation and prices were reduced in shops. The drawback of this situation was that businesses exporting to the UK were forced to close resulting in higher unemployment. Labour costs and Employers PRSI would have to be reduced. A devaluation increases the cost of imports and this pushes up inflation. It also leads to higher wage settlements. This in turn reduces our competitiveness over the medium term with an adverse effect on investment and jobs. An increase in inflation increases government expenditure on social welfare, as there is need to protect recipients' standard of living;

- Devaluation was estimated in 1993 to raise the interest costs of our national debt by about £80 million per year.

- Devaluation leads to a rise in the value of the State's foreign debt. The foreign element of the national debt in December 1992 was £10.8 bn. The 10 per cent devaluation immediately added over £1bn to this.

- The significant foreign debt of State bodies increased in terms of Punts as did the cost of servicing it. This led to price increases being passed on to the consumer by e.g. ESB, and Telecom.

- Devaluation benefits some sectors in the short term. Exporters and employers would be helped. However by maintaining the rate of exchange, benefit may have accrued when the recession ended as Ireland had low inflation, low wage costs and a stable currency.

- Over a period 1987 to 1992 there was a high rate of non-resident investment particularly by the Germans in the Irish gilt market and this led, to a progressive reduction in Irish interest rates. This was a vote of confidence in the Governments overall strategy and didn't point to the necessity of devaluing.

- When the UK left the ERM only about 1 per cent of the Irish foreign currency debt was in Sterling, while almost 50 per cent was in other ERM currencies. Due to this Ireland had built a strong relationship with the ERM and devaluation was being avoided due to the wish to continue this close relationship.

- A unilateral devaluation leads to higher interest rates with international investors likely to withdraw funds. International investors then have to get a 'risk premium' for investing here, and this means an increase in interest rates. If devaluation is considered large enough investors may feel that the IR£ is undervalued and may leave funds here thus reducing pressure on interest rates.

- Foreign holidays for Irish people became more expensive.

Lessons from the January 1993 Devaluation:

It is not possible to lay the blame for pressure on the currency at the door of speculators. There were many sections in the foreign exchange market including fund managers, seeking to obtain the highest return possible on the funds. These could not be expected to act patriotically with these funds. Others involved were companies and private individuals and again these had to be expected to act in their own best interest. There were no exchange controls and even if there were, in the long run they would have put investors off investing in Ireland, as they feared that their assets weren't liquid enough. This necessitated a premium on Irish interest rates to offset this effect on liquidity. Private resources were much greater than those of the Central Bank and this gave them the right to have a say in what a sustainable level of currency was. The Irish authorities insisted right up to devaluation that they would not devalue. This insistence was in the face of sterling having fallen nearly 20% and there was no sign that our EU partners were going to help Ireland. There was therefore a lack of credible policy.

The stand against devaluing was not backed up by action on a scale that was required. The action required included pay cuts, reduction in PRSI and business charges such as Telecom and ESB to give business a chance to compete. Also an exchange rate guarantee was needed and a commitment by the authorities to borrow foreign exchange in order to meet demand. This goes back to credibility again in that no action was taken even though the exchange rate was being maintained.

The decision to resist devaluation for so long was political, as the authorities did not want to be relegated to the second tier of development within the EU by devaluing. Policy pursued was incorrect and should be a lesson for the future.

In the period prior to devaluation, assistance was sought from our EU partners without any plan of action, which if there was one in place, may have encouraged them to deliver such assistance.

The Irish authorities used high short- term interest rates to defend the currency and this method of curbing inflation did damage to the domestic economy. These high interest rates led to high retail rates and caused very severe hardship especially to mortgage holders. The Central Bank helped the banks by giving them money at lower rates for what they called 'normal' purposes, when overnight rates went to 100 per cent.

EMS 1993 to 1998:

The ERM after 1993 was basically a system of floating exchange rates as they could fluctuate
15%. In 1995 Austria joined followed by Finland in 1996. Greece and Sweden were never in the EMS.

Denmark, UK, Sweden and Greece are not in the Euro zone, the first three by choice while Greece did not meet the criteria for membership. There is a formal exchange rate mechanism (ERM2) between the Euro and the currencies of Denmark and Greece. The UK and Sweden opted out of this formal arrangement.

Economic and Monetary Union (EMU):

The SEM came into effect on January 1st 1993 and removed all trade barriers within the EU. In the opinion of many this does not constitute a single market that will not come about until the remaining barriers that separate the national economies of the EU are removed. A monetary union has permanently fixed exchange rates within the Union, free movement of capital and a single monetary authority responsible for the Union's money supply.

European Monetary Union would involve the complete economic and financial integration of the EU countries: a United States of Europe. The initial steps toward EMU were taken in 1970 when the Werner Report put forward a plan for economic and monetary union. The EMS was a major step on the way.

The two components, i.e. Economic Union and Monetary Union, were advocated in the Delor Report of 1989, where Economic Union is defined to include:

- a single market with free movement of persons, goods and capital;

- a common competition policy;

- common policies for regional development and structural change; and

- macroeconomic policy co-ordination including binding rules for budgetary policy.

Monetary Union is defined as:

- complete convertibility of all member currencies;

- irrevocable locking of exchange rates; and

- complete liberalisation of capital transactions.

The UK was opposed to monetary union and in 1990 John Major suggested an alternative in the form of a "hard ECU." This was to be a separate currency used in addition to existing currencies. It would replace existing currencies for intra-EU trade and international trade. The other eleven EU states were not receptive to this.

The European Council set up an Inter-Governmental Conference in 1990 to set out the stages needed for EMU and to establish the changes needed in the Treaty of Rome. The Conference drew up the Maastricht Treaty and this was signed in December 1991. It laid down a timetable for EMU.

The stages in EMU:

EMU was achieved in three stages as follows:

Stage I:

This stage began on July 1st 1990 and the Single Market was to be completed by January 1993 and it was. Economic and monetary convergence was to take place, to include increasing co-operation within the ERM. A single financial area giving free access to banking services, stock exchanges and other financial services across member states was created by January 1993 as per timetable. During this stage negotiations were to take place about Treaty amendments required to establish EMU and they did. Multilateral surveillance of national macroeconomic policies is in place and is done by the Commission. Structural funds were to be increased and they were as was reform of the administration of these funds. All members must join the ERM (Greece and Portugal were not in by 1993 and UK and Italy were out) and until all are in, Stage II was not supposed to start but it did.

Stage II:

This stage was to commence in January 1994 and to finish in 1997 and it did. Monetary policy was to be harmonised across the Union with the objective of establishing a European System of Central Banks (ESCB or Eurofed). Precise though not yet binding ceilings were set for the budget deficits of member states. Exchange rate realignment could take place only in exceptional cases.

ERM bands were to be narrowed and a further 10% of member states' external reserves were to be pooled and managed by the ESCB. From August 1995 the ERM bands were widened to $\pm$ 15%.

At Maastricht in 1991 it was decided that a European Monetary Institute (EMI) rather than a Central Bank be established but with limited powers. The President was to be elected by the governors of member state Central Banks. The EMI came into effect in January 1994 and located in Frankfurt in Germany.

Stage III:

The transition to this stage started in 1996 and exchange rates were to be totally and irrevocably locked and they were on January 1st 1999. Rules regarding macroeconomic and government budgets will become binding and monetary financing of budget deficits will not be allowed. A single European currency was to be created. The ESCB was to be responsible for implementing a common monetary policy. All the external reserves were to be pooled and managed by the ESCB.

It was decided at Maastricht in December 1991 that in 1996 the member states should examine whether to move ahead with a single currency. Convergence criteria were laid down and they are as follows:

- Inflation in the year before union must be within 1.5% of the three lowest inflation rates in the Union.

- Nominal long -term interest rates should be within 2% of the two lowest interest rates in the Union.

- The member's currency must not have been devalued unilaterally within the ERM, for at least two years and must be within the narrow band of the ERM.

- Public debt/G.D.P. ratio must not exceed 60% or be tending towards this level.

- Government fiscal budget deficit must not be greater than 3% of GDP unless for a temporary or exceptional cause.

Dangers associated with a weak economy joining with the currency of a strong economy were seen when Germany was united. Unemployment rises, firms close down and inefficiencies are exposed. These were the reasons for convergence conditions or criteria.

The Changeover Scenario:

The scenario had certain characteristics:
- It must allow sufficient time to win popular acceptance.
- It must be flexible enough to allow different speeds of adjustment between currency users and to allow market forces to operate.
- It must be efficient and not impose unnecessary costs.
- It must respect the legal provisions of the Treaty.
- .It must be credible and incapable of being reversed by unforeseen events.

It was considered that a scenario in three phases satisfied these characteristics as follows:

Phase A:

In the twelve months before moving on to Phase B, decisions were taken on the measures needed for moving to EMU, particularly the establishment of the European Central Bank (ECB) and the European System of Central Banks.(ESCB). The European Council then decided to launch the single currency and identified the countries which are now participating.

Two official reports were issued at the end of March 1998 under the Maastricht Treaty requirements for EMU. The purpose of these was to assess member states' progress in achieving the five convergence criteria on inflation, public deficit and debt, stability of exchange rates, long term interest rates, and having appropriate legislation in place.

On March 25th 1998 the EU Commission stated that eleven of the twelve member states wishing to join the single currency (all except Greece) had obtained " a high degree of sustainable convergence". The key conclusion of the report was that only three of the eleven states had actually achieved a fiscal position "that can be unreservedly classified as "sustainable" i.e. Ireland, Finland, and Luxembourg. The following states were in at the start in January 1st 1999: Austria, Finland, Germany, Italy, Netherlands, Spain, Belgium, France, Ireland, Luxembourg and Portugal. The three states apart from Greece not in, at the start are Denmark and the UK, that have treaty-sanctioned opt-outs, and Sweden which has chosen to stay out by failing to have legislation in place and failing to join the ERM.

Table 16.2
Convergence Results for Inflation, Interest Rates, ERM and Legislation.

Country	Inflation HICP	Long Term Interest Rate	Exchange Rate and ERM	Legislation in Place for Membership
	%	%		
National Bank				
Reference Value	2.7	7.8		
Austria	1.1	5.6	YES	YES
Belgium	1.4	5.7	YES	YES
Denmark	1.9	6.2	YES	YES
Finland	1.2	5.5	YES	YES
France	1.2	5.5	YES	YES
Germany	1.4	5.6	YES	YES
Greece	5.2	9.8	NO(b)	YES
Ireland	1.2	6.2	YES	YES
Italy	1.8	6.7	YES	YES
Luxembourg	1.4	5.6	YES	YES
Netherlands	1.8	5.5	YES	YES
Portugal	1.8	6.2	YES	YES
Spain	1.8	6.3	YES	YES
U K	1.8	7.0	YES	YES

Source: EMI Convergence Report 1998

Meeting the Convergence Criteria:

- **Inflation**: A rate that is within 1.5% of the arithmetic average of the three best states. The values are the percentage change in the arithmetic average of 12 monthly indices over the period February 1997 to January 1998, compared to the same average for February 1996 to January 1997.The three best states were Austria (1.1%), Ireland (1.2%) and France (1.2%). Table 16.2 gives details and shows that Greece alone was over the Reference Value.

- **Interest Rates:** A rate for the 10 year benchmark Government bond which is within 2% points of the arithmetic average of the three States with the lowest inflation (not for interest rate) over the period February 1997 to January 1998. The three lowest States were Austria (5.6%), Ireland (6.2%) and France (5.5%) giving a reference value of 7.8%. Again Greece was the only state over the Reference Value (Table16.2).

- **Membership of ERM:** The member's currency must not have been devalued over the two year period March 1996 to February 1998. To allow Finland and Italy to meet the criterion the Commission decided that the full two years was not required provided all other conditions were met. The UK suspended membership of ERM on August 16th 1992. Sweden was never in the ERM and Greece is only in ERM since March 1998. Greece did not have the exchange rate stability required (Table16.2).

Table 16.3
Government Budgetary Positions

Country	Deficit % of GDP In1997		Debt % of GDP Change from previous year			Existence of Excessive Deficit
			1997	1996	1995	
Ref. Value	3.0			60.0		
Austria	2.5	66.1	-3.4	0.3	3.8	YES
Belgium	2.1	122.2	-4.7	-4.5	-2.2	YES
Denmark	-0.7	65.1	-5.5	-2.7	-4.9	NO
Finland	0.9	55.8	-1.8	-0.9	-1.4	NO
France	3.0	58.0	+2.4	+2.9	+4.2	YES
Germany	2.7	61.3	+0.8	+2.4	+7.8	YES
Greece	4.0	108.7	-2.9	+1.5	+0.7	YES
Ireland	-0.9	66.3	-6.4	-9.6	-6.8	NO
Italy	2.7	121.6	-2.4	-0.2	-0.7	YES
Luxembourg	-1.7	6.7	+0.1	+0.7	+0.2	NO
Netherlands	1.4	72.1	-5.0	-1.9	+1.2	NO
Portugal	2.5	62.0	-3.0	-0.9	+2.1	YES
Spain	2.6	68.8	-1.3	+4.6	+2.9	YES
Sweden	0.8	76.6	-0.1	-0.9	-1.4	YES
UK	1.9	53.4	-1.3	+0.8	+3.5	YES

Source: EMI Convergence Report 1998.

Government financial position: Sustainability of the financial position as decided by the European Council took into account the following:

Deficit: The Government deficit in 1997 or planned in 1998 was not to exceed a Reference value of 3% of GDP unless either the ratio had declined substantially and continuously and reached a value near the Reference Value. It could also be exceeded if the excess over the Reference Value was exceptional and temporary and came close to the Reference Value. Details are given in Table16.3. Greece with a budget deficit of 4% failed this test.

Debt: Total cumulative Government debt at the end of 1997 was not to exceed 60% of GDP unless the ratio was sufficiently diminishing and approaching the Reference Value at a satisfactory pace. Germany failed this test at 61.3% and rising but claimed exceptional circumstances and got in. Italy was nowhere near 60% at 121.6% of GDP, Belgium was at 122.2%

but both said they were making progress towards reducing it and they also qualified! (Table16.3)

- **Legislation:** This necessitated compatibility between the State's national legislation, including statutes for its national bank, the Statute of the ECB and the requirements of the Maastricht Treaty. The outcome is shown in Table16.2.

Five of the eleven member States, Ireland, Denmark, Netherlands, Finland and Luxembourg did not have excessive deficits on the 25th March 1998. Eleven of the twelve applicants met the inflation, interest rate, ERM, and legislation criteria with Greece failing most of them. Even though Denmark, Ireland, and Netherlands were over the 60 % maximum of the Debt /GDP ratio criterion they were judged by the European Commission not to have excessive debt.

Phase B: Introduction of the Euro:

Phase B opened on January 1st 1999 with exchange rates between the national currencies of the eleven countries in the EMU irrevocably fixed. The Irish pound was converted into euros at the conversion rate of 1Euro = £.787564. The Punt will no longer be quoted on international money markets as it is submerged with the other ten currencies into a single unit. The actual exchange rate fixings on a bilateral basis against other in-currencies was at the central ERM rate but the fixing of each against the euro was subject to the spot exchange rate against the dollar at the 31st December 1998.

At this point the ECB and the European System of Central Banks was functioning. The ECU at the start of EMU was equal to one Euro but it no longer exists. The participants' currencies are now units of account based on the Euro. As soon as possible, a "critical mass" of financial activities is to be established in the single currency based on the single monetary policy and the issue of new public debt.

Phase C:
This Phase is to commence not more than three years after the start of Phase B. At this stage notes and coins will be issued to the general public. This is anticipated to be a gradual stage in the move towards the Euro as part of day-to-day economic activity.

Financial Institutions and EMU:

When Ireland entered EMU in January 1999, the financial institutions suffered some negative effects. They lost their ability to earn income on foreign exchange transactions within the euro zone. It is estimated that their foreign exchange earnings will be reduced by £40 million and that this figure will double if and when the UK joins the EMU. To compensate them they were allowed increase their commission on foreign transactions that remain. With reduced interest rates, their traditional lending and deposit taking business margins will come under pressure. As interest rates fall the margin is squeezed, as it becomes more difficult to cut payments to savers. Profit is the difference between what is paid on deposits and charged on loans. There is also a greater possibility that mergers and consolidation will take place. The cost to the Irish banks of the once off conversion of software has been estimated at £100 million over a five-year period to 2002. ECB has laid down new reserve rules for European commercial banks in the euro zone, which requires them to hold reserves, which could otherwise be used to make profit. Benefits to them will depend on the extent to which the single currency speeds up economic growth within the euro zone.

Advantages of EMU:

- A single or common currency reduces transaction costs involved in changing money i.e. commissions. These transactions costs can be very large and were estimated at $30 billion a year for the EU as a whole and 1% of GNP in Ireland's case. This is particularly the case when different parts of the same good are made in different Member States. Ireland is a very open economy and trade relative to GDP is very important so that Ireland stands to gain substantially as a result of reduced transactions costs.

- Uncertainty regarding exchange rates is removed by the single currency and trade will improve. Investment will be stimulated now that risks of currency fluctuation are reduced and fiscal discipline is in place.

- Prices will be denominated in a single currency so that price differentials will become apparent and this should result in price convergence across the member states.

- National markets that have monopolistic elements are exposed to competition.

- Already the single currency has led to a reduction in interest rates. Exchange rate risk is part of the risk premium in interest rates in Ireland and with the removal of exchange rate risk, interest rates have fallen.

- Convergence of fiscal, economic and monetary policies, should maintain price stability and keep inflation rates low. There is a degree of certainty regarding future budgetary policy due to the Pact for Stability and Growth.

- The independent European Central Bank free from political control can pursue anti-inflation policies as and when required. Inflation imported from other member states may disappear.

- The complete macroeconomic package imposed will bring about stability and will raise the growth rate of the EU as a whole.

- The euro has the status of a reserve currency equal to the dollar and yen.

- The ratio of Irish government debt to GDP has fallen and will continue to fall. This will mean that government debt will be reduced as will the cost of servicing it.

- The EMU means that workers in future will have to limit their wage demands to those justified by productivity increases.

Disadvantages of EMU:

- EMU means a loss of sovereignty. Monetary policy is now set by the European Central Bank and governments no longer have the ability to devalue their way out of a crisis. Discretionary exchange rate change is no longer allowed, but this is not of great significance. When the IR£ was devalued in 1986 and again in 1993 it was agreed by most that these devaluations had little effect on output and employment but they did however have an inflationary effect. When Ireland devalued in 1993 import prices rose largely negating the advantage gained for exports.

- The Central Bank lost the limited ability to influence interest rates it had.

- In the EMU to speak of inflation in a single country is meaningless. Monetary policy can only be applied on a Europe wide basis, so that only European inflation could be monitored.

- Member countries will still have the right to use fiscal policy within their own borders but their ability to do so will be constrained by the Stability Pact. There will however be contractionary pressures on Irish fiscal policy as national governments are not allowed borrow from central banks to finance fiscal deficits. With the single currency and integration of financial markets individual country deficits must be financed at the ruling European interest rate at the time.

- Difficulties can arise for Ireland, as the UK is not a member of EMU and can devalue while Ireland cannot. This difficulty is lessened by the continued switch of exports away from the UK as well as the strengthening of non-wage competitiveness which lessens the effect of sterling movements. There is also the risk of capital outflows on a continuous basis in the single currency situation. Another problem is that nominal rather than real convergence may be emphasised.

- Uncompetitive workers can no longer be cushioned by a falling exchange rate and will either lose their jobs or have to accept lower wages.

- The EU has rich and poor areas and the single currency may exacerbate these differences as industry locates to more prosperous, areas.

- The "Cohabitation Problem" or how countries in the EMU will cope with country- specific or asymmetric shocks is a problem. There is no automatic mechanism for assisting areas experiencing difficulty. Funds are available but not for a specific region. If the fishermen in Dingle are doing badly they will get no assistance from the EU so this must come from Irish resources e.g. Social Welfare.

305

Questions

1. Evaluate the impact on the Irish economy of Ireland's membership of the Economic and Monetary Union in 1999.

2. Critically examine the effects on the Irish economy of the UK not being a member of the Eurozone.

3. What are the advantages and disadvantages of fixed exchange rate systems?

4. Why did the ERM with narrow bands collapse in 1993? In retrospect could this in your opinion have been avoided?

5. Describe the different policies a country can adopt in order to correct a balance of payments deficit? Analyse the factors that are likely to determine the success of these policies.

6. Discuss the arguments for and against floating exchange rates.

7. Show how a devaluation of a currency may improve a country's balance of payments position. When is devaluation likely to be unsuccessful?

8. Describe the advantages and disadvantages of devaluation.

9. In relation to the Balance of Payments explain the following:
   a) Marshall-Lerner condition
   b) The J curve; and
   c) Dutch disease effect

Appendix 16.1.
Balance of International Payments 1994 – 1997 £ millions

	1994	1995	1996	1997
Current Account				
1. Merchandise trade	5,396	7,459	8,756	11,084
1.1 Imports	-17,028	-20,239	-21,967	-25,422
1.2 Exports	22,424	27,698	30,723	36,506
2. International freight	83	91	102	105
3, Other transportation	323	331	375	428
4. Tourism and travel	130	109	170	245
5.Royalties licences	-1,218	-1617	-2071	-2,655

6.Other services	-1,297	-1,906	-2,358	-2,813
7. Remuneration of employees	183	181	190	173
8. Investment income	-3,758	-4,689	-5341	-6494
8.1 Direct investment income	-3,490	-4,637	-5,348	-6,708
8.2 Other income:				
of which National debt interest	- 268	-53	7	214
International transfers	1,081	-1,015	-915	-765
9 Current transfers	1,155	1,110	1,354	1,290
10 Net balance on current account	998	1070	1176	1362
Capital and financial account:				
11. Capital transfers	251	511	489	578
12. Private capital	-1375	-1824	-535	-2661
12.1 Semi-state companies	-285	-260	-146	47
12.2 Direct investment liabilities	-1090	-1565	-390	-2708
12.3 Other private capital				
13. Official capital	-1335	24	38	-2180
13.1 Exchequer foreign borrowing	-416	-614	-986	-1055
13.2 Government securities	-421	605	1034	-1122
13.3 Other transactions	-498	33	-10	-4
14. Transactions of credit institutions	140	1798	-1229	-303
15. Official external reserves	102	-1443	55	754
15.1 Reserve position in the IMF	5	-41	-10	-45
15.2 Gold	12	1	11	6
15.3 SDR holding	-4	-4	2	-18
15.4 Other external assets	223	-1387	511	381
15.5 Counterpart to valuation changes	-135	-12	-459	430
15.6 Counterpart to allocation of SDRs	-	-	-	-
16. **Net balance on capital accounts (Items 11-15)**	-2217	-934	-1182	-3812
17. **Net residual**	1219	-136	6	2450

Source: Central Bank Quarterly Bulletins.

CHAPTER 17

POPULATION AND EMPLOYMENT

Introduction:

The statistical study of the characteristics of human population is called demography. Data relating to the population are derived from the census of population. Irish emigration causes and effects are discussed. Economists are interested in the size and trend of the population as well as age distribution, natural increase and areas of economic activity. They are interested in size of the population in relation to the country's land, capital and enterprise. The size and demographic structure of a country's population are an important determinant of both the level and structure of demand within the economy. If the size of the labour supply is too small the country will not achieve the maximum rate of economic growth possible and its people will be poor. If it is too high in proportion to other factors then they will also be poor, as output per head will be low. Changes in the age distribution of the population have economic and social implications. The determinants of labour supply are outlined in this Chapter as is the size and composition of the labour force available for production now and expected in the future. Current trends in employment and unemployment are discussed and in the case of the latter the causes are analysed. Policy issues to reduce unemployment and possible cures are discussed.

Irish Population:

The first complete Irish Census was in 1821 and one was taken every ten years to 1911 in the first year of the decade. There was none in 1921 and the first Census after Independence was in 1926 when it changed to a five yearly Census in 1951 with the next one in 1956. There was no Census in 1976 but there was one in 1979 and every five years since 1981, the latest was in 1996.

Table 17.1 shows the total population, at each census since 1926 to 1996 plus estimates at mid April 1997 and 1998. Population in 1841 was about 6.5 million for an area similar to the Republic of Ireland but it had fallen to 2,971,992 in 1926. Famine and emigration have been the causes and have yielded up demographic trends in Ireland unlike any obtaining in the rest of Europe. This was the first time the population dropped below 3 million where it remained until 1979. Since then it is over 3 million showing an increase in 1986 over 1979 but a decrease of 14,924 in 1991 over 1986, the first decrease in population in over 30 years. The population increased between 1991 and 1996 when it was 3,626,087. Estimates from the CSO for mid April 1998 put the population at 3.7 million, the highest recorded since 1881, when it was 3.87 million. This growth is due to net immigration and a widening gap between the number of births and deaths.

Table 17.1

Population of Ireland 1926 -1996 And Change in Population, Natural Increase and Net Migration per 1000 of Average Population in Each Intercensal Period 1926 – 1996 and April 1997 and 1998.

Year Net	Total	Change in Population	Natural Increase	Estimated Migration Per '000
1926	2,971,992	-	-	-
1936	2,968,420	-0.1	5.5	-5.6
1946	2,955,107	-0.4	5.9	-6.3
1951	2,960,593	+0.4	8.6	-8.2
1956	2,898,264	-4.3	9.2	-13.4
1961	2,818,341	-5.6	9.2	-14.8
1966	2,884,002	+4.6	10.3	-5.7
1971	2,978,248	+6.4	10.1	-3.7
1979	3,368,217	+15.4	11.1	+4.3
1981	3,443,405	+11.0	11.8	-0.7
1986	3,540,643	+5.6	9.7	-4.1
1991	3,525,719	-0.8	6.8	-7.6
1996	3, 626,087	+0.6	0.6	+0.1
1997*	3,660,587	+0.9	0.5	+0.4
1998*	3,704,887	+1.2	0.6	+0.6

* April Estimates

Source: CSO Various Census 1926 to1996 and Population and Migration Estimates Release November 1998.

Factors Influencing the Size of Population:

Population size is affected by four main influences: the birth rate; the death rate; the marriage rate; and net migration i.e. inward less outward.

Birth Rate and Death Rate:

Birth rates are usually expressed as a rate per thousand of the population. Death rates are expressed as the number of people in the country that died in a year per thousand of the population. This is sometimes called the crude death rate as it takes no account of the age of the person at time of death.

The number of births, deaths, and net emigration determines the size of a country's population. If births exceed deaths in a given period the excess is known as the natural increase. A high birth rate with a low death rate will result in a big increase in the size of the population.

Factors affecting the Birth Rate:

- Reduction in family size due in part to deliberate limitation by the parents;

- The desire to improve standards of living which in turn can lead to later marriages and a reduction in the average family size. When the standard of living is very low the birth rate tends to be high;

- Parents wish to do better for their children in the area of education in particular and this increases the cost of bringing up a family so that family size is reduced;

- Emancipation of women and their pursuit of careers leads to a smaller family size;

- When small families are fashionable;

- The birth rate can be high due to custom or religious belief;

- In countries where there is little or no social welfare or pensions a large family is a buffer against loss of income and old age.

Over the years the Irish birth rate has been relatively high being over 21 per thousand until the late 1980's, going as high as 22.3 per thousand in the late 1940's. The trend in the Irish birth rate is shown in Table 17.2. The European Union countries and US rate has been falling from the mid 1960's. Ireland's rate in 1980 was almost 22 whereas the European Union average was 13 per thousand. It fell to nearly 15 in 1991 and was 13.4 in 1994, a dramatic fall since the late 1970's, when it was 21.6%. It was back up to 14.9% in 1998, the highest in the EU, and giving a rate of "natural" population growth six times the EU average. Overall, not including flows of migration or emigration, the Irish population rose by 5.8 per thousand compared to 0.9 per thousand for the EU as a whole.

Table 17.2
Average Annual Marriage Birth and Death Rates per 1000 Population for Each Inter-censal Period Since 1926 and 1997 and 1998

Inter-censal period	Marriages	Births	Deaths
1926-1936	4.6	19.6	14.2
1936-1946	5.4	20.3	14.5
1946-1951	5.5	22.3	13.6
1951-1956	5.4	21.3	12.2
1956-1961	5.4	21.2	11.9
1961-1966	5.7	21.9	11.7
1966-1971	6.5	21.3	11.2
1971-1979	6.8	21.6	0.5
1979-1981	6.3	21.5	9.0
1981-1986	5.5	19.1	9.0
1986-1991	5.1	15.7	9.0
1991-1996	4.6	13.8	8.8
1997	4.3	14.3	8.6
1998	4.6*	14.9*	8.8*

*Estimate.

Source: Statistical Abstract 1997 C.S.O. Table 2.3 Statistical Bulletin 1998 Economic Series 1998

Factors affecting the Death Rate:

- Standard of living is important and if it is adequate, people will have proper nutrition and accommodation and they will live longer;

- Improvement in medicines and medical technology have reduced and continue to reduce the death rate i.e. increase the age at which people die;

- Public health and sanitation improvements lead to a reduced death rate;

- War and the resultant famine increases the death rate particularly in less developed countries; and

- New diseases such as AIDS increase the death rate.

Irish Death Rate:

Up to the end of the 1960's the Irish death rate was above the EU and US rates. It is now more in line with them since falling from 11.7 in 1960, to 9.0 in the 1986/91 inter-censal period. In 1997 it was 8.6. The trend in the death rate is shown in Table 17.2.

Irish Marriage Rate:

As the majority of births are to married women, the number of marriages taking place has an effect on the number of births. The number of the population in the marriageable age determines the number of marriages. From Table 17.2 the marriage rate peaked at 6.8 per thousand in 1971/79 and then decreased in subsequent periods. It was 4.3 per thousand in 1997. During the 1970's emigration slowed down so that people of marriageable age stayed in Ireland and there was a drop in the age at which both male and females married. These two factors combined with urbanisation caused the number of marriages to increase.

Fertility Rate:

Even when population is rising, growth may be due to increasing longevity so that future increase is threatened. The average number of children born per woman of child bearing years gives the fertility rate and it is necessary for the rate to be 2.1 or over if society is to continue to reproduce itself. The fertility rate for Ireland was very high at 3.87 in 1970 but that the rate came down sharply between 1970 and 1991 when it was close to the reproduction rate of 2.0. The trend in Ireland is downward.

Age Structure of the Irish Population:

The participation rate - the number of persons in the labour force as a percentage of the total population over 15 years - measures the proportion of people who are economically active. The age structure of the population will determine the proportion in the economically active age group.

The active age group is composed of those aged between 15 and 65 years of age while those under 15 and over 65 years of age are known as the dependent group. This definition of dependency is not very precise as people now stay longer in full time education and others stay at work after they are 65 years of age. The age dependency ratios are useful measures of the age structure of the population. Expressing young population (0 to14) and the old population (aged 65 and over) as percentages of the population of working age (15 to 64) derives the old and young dependency ratios. The total dependency ratio is the sum of the young and old ratios. In 1996 24.03 per cent of the population was under 14 years of age (Table 17.3) while 11.46 per cent were over 65 years.

This makes a total of 35.1 per cent in the dependent group. The young dependency ratio peaked in 1970s but has since been in decline and was at a low point in 1996. The old dependency ratio having increased steadily between 1926 and 1966 has declined since. Negative migration in the age group 15 to 65 and the fall in the birth rate have effected these ratios over time since the 1980s. The average age has risen by almost three years over the fifteen years from 1981 to 1996. Table 17.7 indicates that the Irish population is growing older, advancing into early middle age. South Dublin had the youngest population at an average of 29.4 years, while Leitrim at 37.3 years was the oldest.

Table 17.3 shows that percentage of the population under 14 years in the EU, Germany and the UK is much lower than it is in Ireland, particularly so in the case of Germany. The percentage over 65 is lower in Ireland than it is in EU, Germany and UK. Overall the dependency rate in Ireland is higher.

Table 17.3
Age Structure of Population Ireland
EU, Germany and UK 1996 (Percentages of Population)

	0-14	15-24	25-44	45-64	65+	Total
			Age Groups			
Ireland	24.03	17.52	27.60	19.39	11.46	100
Germany	16.18	11.19	31.95	25.12	15.56	100
UK	18.50	12.03	28.74	22.40	18.33	100
EU	17.42	13.26	30.24	23.49	15.59	100

Source: Eurostat 1997

Appendix 17.1(Table 17.4) gives projections for elderly dependency ratios for EU15 at ten year intervals 1990 to 2030. Irelands ratio is projected to decline between 1990 and 2010 and to increase thereafter. Ireland has a very young population relative to the other EU countries especially Germany and Italy. In 2030 Ireland's elderly dependency ratio is estimated to be 25.3 per cent compared to 49.2% and 48.3% for Germany and Italy respectively.

Table 17.5 shows the number and percentage of the Irish population under 14 years, and 15 to19 years of age. The decline in the number of children reflects the fall in the birth rate in the 1980's mentioned previously. The annual number of births in Ireland dropped from 74,355 in 1980 to 52,952 in 1990 a decline of 29 percent in a decade. The annual number of births over the period 1991/1996 was 50,000. Over the period under review the 15 to 19 age group increased but the overall percentage aged under 20 years declined to 33.0 per cent in 1996.

The population in the prime working age group, i.e. between 25 and 44 years of age has increased very rapidly over the last two decades. The number in this age category increased in twenty years 1971 – 1991 and it increased each year to 1996. In 1996 the number in the 25 to 44 age group (1,016,091) was greater than the number in the under 15 age group (859424) Table 17.5.

The birth rate as already stated increased rapidly in the 1970's and people born then are now entering the labour force. It is estimated that the labour force will expand by about 2% or 25,000 per annum until next year.

Table 17.5
Ireland's Younger Age Population in Selected Years

Age Group (000's)	1971	1981	1986	1991	1996
0-4	315.7	353.0	324.1	273.5	250.4
5-9	316.9	349.5	350.7	321.9	282.9
10–14	298.6	341.2	350.0	348.6	326.1
	931.2	1043.7	1024.8	943.9	859.4
% of Total Population	31.3%	30.3%	28.9%	26.8%	23.7%
15–19	267.7	326.4	331.1	335.1	339.5
Total under 20	11,989.0	1,370.2	1,355.8	1,279.0	1,198.9
% of Total Population	40.3%	39.8%	38.3%	36.3%	33.0%

Source: CSO Census of Population, Various Years

Table17.6
Projected Labour Force Flows for Different Age Groups, 1990 to 2006

Age Group	1990/91	1995/96 (000's)	2000/01	2005/06
15-24	+59	+58	+56	+48
25–34	-12	-13	-14	-14
35–44	-2	-2	-3	-3
46–64	-10	-11	-12	-14
65+	-10	-9	-9	-10
Total	+25	+23	+18	+7

Note: Assuming Nil Net Migration in all Age Categories
Source: NESC Report No. 90.

Table 17.6 shows the projected inflows and outflows in different age groups for selected years between 1990 and 2006. It is assumed that there is nil migration in all age groups.

Economic Consequences of Changed Age Distribution:

The fall in the number of people in the under 15 group as shown above means that demand for goods purchased by them falls and consequently employment in industries producing these goods.

Facilities such as schools and health services for young people will be under utilised as the population grows older. Schools were established to cater for greater numbers so that they are now underutilised and will become more so in the future.

As more people go into the older categories the cost of pensions, social services and other services increase. This is the current position in Ireland.

Changes in the size of the working population affect the supply of labour which is a factor of production. The Irish labour force has been growing rapidly in recent years.

Density of Population:

Density of population can be judged on the number of people per square kilometre. This method ignores differences in the degree of urbanisation and area suitable for agriculture and can be misleading if international comparisons are made.

Table 17.7 shows Irish population density by province in 1998 and shows that Connaght is very low relative to Leinster. The overall 52 persons per square kilometre is the second lowest in the EU a little over one third of the EU average 145.7.

Irish Emigration:

Emigration is the flow of population out of one country into others. Net migration is the difference between people leaving the country (emigration) and entering it (immigration). This figure must be used together with the difference between births and deaths or the natural increase to explain changes in the population.

Table 17.1 gives details of births, deaths, natural increase, net migration and total population from 1926 to 1996 and estimates for 1997 and 1998. The period 1926 to 1961 shows that except for 1946/51, emigration was greater than the natural increase therefore the population declined. Between 1961 and 1981 the natural increase exceeded net migration and the population grew particularly over the period 1971-1979, when there was net immigration into Ireland of 109,000 people. Net emigration resumed in the period 1986 -1991, but since then there has been net immigration. This reached a historic high in the year to mid April 1998 i.e. the number of immigrants exceeded the number of emigrants by 22,800.

From the Second World War emigration from Ireland was mainly to the U K but in the 1980's and early 1990's there was a change of direction to the US and other countries. Entry to the US in recent years has been restricted and is on a lottery system.

Table 17.7
Density of Population by Province 1998

Province	Persons Per sq kilometre	Area (Hectares)
Leinster	97	1,980,066
Munster	42	2,467,410
Connaght	24	1,771,056
Ulster	29	808,776
Total	52	7,027,308

Source Ordinance Survey 1998

Causes of Emigration:

There are a number of causes and these can be described as push and pull factors.

Push Factors:

- Lack of job opportunities with adequate pay for an individual to settle down. Unemployment assistance is not sufficient for a young person settling down and neither is a low paid job without prospects. This means that people emigrate out of necessity.
- People unemployed within agriculture with no prospects of alternative work in Ireland. As seen in Table 17.10 employment within agriculture continues to decline and those involved must emigrate if they wish to find work.

- Lack of social amenities particularly in the case of the West of Ireland. There is also a lack of males and particularly females of marriageable age in these areas. These factors combine to force people to emigrate.

- Over population with a resultant, low standard of living. This is not the case in Ireland but is true in the case of Third World countries.

- People unhappy with the speed of social change tend to leave the country on the assumption that social conditions are more advanced in the country of their destination.

Pull Factors:

- Youth labour supply is falling in the main European economies so that there is an attraction there for young well-educated Irish people.

- Irish emigrants have tended to go to English speaking countries as there is no language barrier. This has changed to some extent as graduates now usually have a foreign language that enables them to settle in a country where this is the first language. There is also the fact that well-educated labour is in short supply.

- Over the years since emigration began, Irish people have gone to the same destination i.e. UK, Australia New Zealand and US. This trend has continued as relatives or friends there already draw further emigrants.

- Lower levels of personal taxation and higher real disposable incomes abroad attract Irish people.

Economic Effects of Emigration:

Emigration tends to be confined to the16-25 age group who leaves due to lack of skills or having skills but lacking experience. This reduces the working population at home, which in turn increases the dependency ratio. The number unemployed is less with emigration therefore there is a saving in social welfare payments. This means that less government expenditure goes on transfer payments.

There is little return to the state for the money spent on the education and training of people who emigrate. Emigrants' remittances were a form of return but their importance is now greatly reduced. If the emigrant returns at a later stage having gained experience and expertise, it is also a form of return for expenditure on education. A considerable number of net migrants to Ireland nowadays are of this kind, the so-called "homing pigeons".

Highly skilled workers may make up a large proportion of those who emigrate so that those remaining may compete up wages. Real wages cannot be significantly lower than those on offer in places where emigrants go, otherwise they may all go.

When population is reduced in rural areas due to emigration, it is not reproducing itself.

Optimum Population:

The term "optimum population" describes that number of people, which when put together with other resources, gives the maximum output of goods and services per head of the population. In other words it is the level at which per capita national income is maximised.

At low levels of population the productive capacity of the country is not fully used so that any increase in population will increase per capita income. At higher levels of population, capacity becomes fully utilised and when it is, any additional population will cause income per capita to fall. Under-population is rarely a problem in modern times and even if it was, it could be overcome by net immigration similar to what Australia did, when it assisted people wishing to go there.

Advantages of an Increasing Population:

- If the population is below its optimum level, per capita income will go up.

- A growing population increases demand for goods and services and this brings about increased production and investment to meet the demand.

- Employment increases, therefore unemployment decreases.

- If the increase is due in part to net immigration of those in the working age group or increased fertility, the dependency ratio will go down.

- If the population is becoming younger then there will be a smaller dependent population of old people. A younger population will be more enterprising and innovative.

- There is a feeling of optimism in the business world.

Cost of Increasing Population:

If the population is increasing in size then other things being equal, there is less land and other resources available per capita. If the present population is above its optimum then any further increase will erode living standards as the rate of population growth will exceed the rate of economic growth.

- Building land may become scarce and more expensive.

- More schools, houses, hospitals, libraries and other facilities are required and this means increased staffing in the public sector.

- Services provided by the semi-state bodies will need to be increased. These include transport, telecommunications and energy.

- An increase in population due to a rising birth rate and falling death rate or one or other will increase the dependency ratio and increase the burden of taxation.

Implication of a Falling Population:

- A declining population means more resources available per capita, but there is less incentive to improve technology without the stimulus of a rising population.

- The home market grows smaller and is able to support only a small number of firms in each industry. This results in a lack of competition between the remaining firms and the chance that profits are inflated by charging high prices in monopoly or near monopoly situations.

- A falling population limits the possibilities for business expansion and makes the establishment of new industry extremely difficult.

- Public services are under-utilised resulting in high costs.

- When population is falling the average age increases and people become less mobile and are unwilling to move within the country when opportunities arise.

- If the population is declining due to emigration then the problems caused by, or effects of emigration will exist. Again there is greater dependency, depression, scarcity of skilled workers, failure of the population to reproduce itself and sparsely populated rural areas.

Determinants of Labour Supply:

The main determinants of labour supply are:

- **Demographic Factors:**

The supply of labour is influenced by the level and age structure of the population. As shown in Table 17.3, the dependent or inactive group make up 35.1 of the total population, while the numbers under 15 years fell, those over 65 years have increased. Ireland has an unbalanced population age structure and with the movement from the under 15 age group to working age groups up to 65, there is potential for relatively rapid growth in the labour supply.

- **Emigration:**

Emigration has tended to reduce the number entering the labour force and this was true in the 1950's and 1960's when there was large-scale emigration. This reduced the number that should now be in the older cohorts. During the 1970's many immigrants returned but in the 1980's emigration increased again while in the early 1990's it decreased again.

- **Labour Force Participation:**

The participation rate is the number of persons in the labour force as a percentage of the total population over 15 years of age. The greater the participation rate the greater is the labour force.

Employment in Ireland:

Statistics for measuring the level of employment in Ireland are obtained from the Labour Force Survey that was carried out annually until 1997, when approximately 45,000 households were interviewed each year. Since 1997 a Quarterly National Household Survey (QNHS) compiled under the International Labour Organisation (ILO) standard for measuring the size of the labour force and employment is the official measure now used. The QNHS is required under an EU Council Regulation.

The first QNHS was published on the 26th of April 1997. In it 15 households in 2,600 "blocks" across the country (39,000 households in total) take part in the Survey for five consecutive quarters. Three thousand households are surveyed each week. The same procedure is followed each quarter.

In the ILO method the labour force is classified as:

In employment: Persons who worked for one hour or more in the week before the Survey or were absent from work due to illness.

Unemployed: Persons who, in the week before the Survey were without work and available for work.

Labour Force: Is the sum of those in employment plus the unemployed.

Advantages and Disadvantages of the ILO Method:

The advantages are as follows:
- Internationally standardised;
- Other labour market characteristics can be analysed; and
- Inter -country comparisons can be made.

The disadvantages are as follows:
- Sampling and response errors can occur;
- Expensive to compute; and
- Unsuitable for small areas.

Full Employment:

When we speak of "full employment" in economics, we do not mean that no one is unemployed. There is always a certain amount of unavoidable unemployment and this is known as the " natural rate of unemployment" and it is between 1% and 3%. Monetarists believe in the "natural rate" and contend that any changes in unemployment will only be temporary variations from that rate. There is however no agreement as to what the natural rate is. Keynes believed that full employment could be achieved if appropriate action could be taken.

Labour Force Participation:

Table 17.8 gives participation rates by sex and age for September –November 1997 and the same quarter of 1998. Participation by males in the labour force was much greater in all age categories than for females. This was particularly true for the categories 35-44 and above. Male participation in 1971 was 80.7 when it was 27.9 for females. By 1994 it was down to 69.7 for males and up to 35.7 for females. From the September/ November QNHS 1997 it was 69.4 for males and 44.0 for females while it was 69.8 and 44.5 respectively in the same quarter in 1998. In the case of males participation by over 55 year olds declined due to early retirement, falling numbers in agriculture, earlier age of old age pension and increase in real terms in the labour force pensions. There was increased participation by females, reflecting increased participation by married women.

Table 17.8
Labour Force Participation Rates (ILO) Classified by Sex and Age
September/ November 1997 and 1998

Sex	Age Group Percentage								
	15-19	20-24	25-34	35-44	45-54	55-59	60-64	65+	Total
Male Sept/ Nov1997	31.1	76.8	93.3	93.4	87.1	71.9	52.7	14.9	69.4
MaleSept/Nov 1998	31.2	80.1	93.7	93.1	86.8	72.8	52.8	14.6	69.8
Female Sept/Nov1997	22.9	69.0	73.7	59.4	46.4	30.7	17.7	3.0	44.0
FemaleSept/Nov 1998	23.5	71.3	74.0	60.1	46.6	29.4	17.1	2.8	44.5
All Persons Sept/Nov1997	27.1	73.0	83.4	76.2	67.0	51.5	35.1	8.1	56.5
All Persons Sept/Nov 1998	27.5	75.8	83.8	76.4	66.9	51.3	34.8	7.9	57.0

Source: CSO, QNHS Fourth Quarter 1997 and 1998. May 1999

September/November 1997 while for the same period in 1998 it was 1.650.7mn. The total population over 15 years was 2,839.9 million for September/November 1997 and for the same period in 1998 it was 2,897.8. The overall participation rates were 57.9 and 57.0 per cent respectively. The Table also shows male and female participation rates were 70.3 for males and 45.4 per cent for female for 1997 and 69.8 and 44.5 per cent respectively for 1998. The total number at work in 1997 was 1,472,300 and 1,544,700 in 1998, therefore there was an increase of 72,400 over the period. The total number unemployed according to the QNHS September/November 1997 was 171,600 while it fell to 106,000 in September/November 1998, a From Table 17.9 the labour force was 1.643 million according to the QNHS, drop of 65,600.

Agriculture:

Between 1961 and 1992 the number employed in agriculture fell from 360,000 to 150,000 a drop of 58 per cent. The biggest decline occurred in the 1960's. Th e decline in the 1970's was due in large measure to joining the EU. Further reductions took place between 1981 and 1986 and 1986 to 1991 as seen in Table 17.10. Due to changes in the CAP and GATT it has declined further and will continue to decline over the coming years. The rate of decline has accelerated since 1996 and it is forecast to continue this trend in 1999 and 2000 (Table 17.10). In 1998 agriculture accounted for only 8.9 per cent of total employment down from 34.5 per cent in 1996.(Diagram 17.1).

SERVICES:

Employment in the services sector grew continuously over the period 1961 to 1992 and the growth rate was greater during the 1970's than in the 1980's. This sector includes public as well as private sector services. In the latter part of the 1980's an effort was made to cut back on the numbers engaged in the public sector. Between 1987 and 1992 there was a cut of approximately 10 per cent. The private sector services however grew continuously over the period 1961 to 1992. Service employment has grown every year since 1991 and this trend is set to continue in 1999 and 2000 (Table 17.10). Of the three sectors it is the fastest growing one. Employment in services grew by 2.7% per annum between 1987 and 1997. In 1998 services accounted for 61.2% of total employment (Diagram 17.1)

Table 17.9
Irish Labour Force (ILO Basis) '000 QNHS for September/November 1997 and September/November 1998

	Sept/ Nov 1997 Males	Males		Sept/Nov 1998 Labour Force	Females Total	Females Total
In Employment: Of Which:	881.4	590.9	1,472.3	928.4	616.3	1,544.7
Full Time	810.7	408.0	1,218.8	863.1	432.4	1,295.5
Part Time	70.6	182.8	253.5	65.3	183.8	249.1
Unemployed Seeking:	99.8	71.7	171.6	66.0	40.0	106.0
Full Time	93.6	38.7	132.3	64.2	25.2	89.4
Part Time	6.2	33.1	39.3	1.8	14.8	16.6
Labour Force	981.2	662.6	**1,643.9**	994.4	656.3	**1,650.7**
Not in Labour Force	413.7	782.3	1,196.0	429.3	817.7	1,247.1
Population 15+	1,394.9	1,444.9	2,839.8	1,423.8	1,474.0	2,897.8
Unemployed as % Of Labour Force	10.2	10.8	10.4	6.6	6.1	6.4
Participation Rate %	70.3	45.9	57.9	69.8	44.5	57.0

Source: CSO, QNHS Statistical Release 30 November 1998 and May 1999

Table 17.10
Irish Employment and Unemployment
A: Mid April Estimates 1996 - 2000

Annual Average	1981	1986	1991	1996	1997	1998	1999	2000
				000's				
Industry	363	307	321	355	386	425	452	476
Services	587	606	650	804	818	873	900	922
Agriculture	196	168	154	138	134	127	126	123
Total Employment	1,146	1,081	1,125	1,297	1,338	1,427	1,478	1,521
Unemployed				191	179	155	143	133
Labour Force				1,488	1,517	1,581	1,621	1,654
Unemployment rate %				11.9	10.3	7.8	6.8	6.0
(Live Register)				281	257	231	213	204
Unemployment rate %				18.8	16.9	14.6	13.1	12.3

B Annual Average 000s 1996 - 1999

	1996	1997	1998	1999f
Industry	374	408	442	468
Services	806	845	889	914
Agriculture	136	132	128	124
Total at Work	1,316	1,385	1,459	1,506
Unemployed	185	165	148	137
Labour Force	1,501	1,550	1,607	1,643
Unemployed Rate%	11.5	10.2	7.6	6.4
Live Register	279	254	228	210

•Based on Official Standarised Unemployment Rate ILO definitions.
f = Forecast

Source: ESRI, November 1998 and Labour Force Surveys, various years.

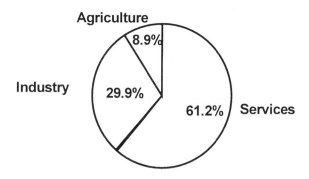

Diagram 17.1 Employment by Sector 1998

Source: Derived from Table 17.10

Growth in Employment 1960-1996:

Table 17.11 gives details of growth in employment between 1961 and 1996. There was a substantial average increase of 4% per annum over the period 1993 to 1996.

Table 17.11
Average Annual Percentage Growth Rate of Employment 1960-1996

	Growth %			Growth%
1961-1965	0.4		1986-1990	1.2
1965-1970	-0.3		1990 1993	0.5
1970-1976	0.2		1993-1996	4.0
1976-1980	2.1		1986-1996	1.8
1980-1986	-1.1		1997-1998	5.3

Source: Irish Banking Review, Summer 1998 and Central Bank Quarterly Bulletin Spring 1999

The composition of this employment growth was as follows:

F.T. male 41%; P.T. male 5%; F.T. female 37% and P.T. female 17%. There are more women returning to work especially on a part-time basis. Over the long term, female employment has grown much more rapidly than male.

Unemployment:

This occurs when individuals are willing to work for the prevailing market wage but are unable to find work at that wage unemployment exists. The unemployment rate can be defined as the percentage of the total labour force without jobs.

Philosophy of Unemployment:

- **Classical Unemployment**

With Classical unemployment demand for goods and services is adequate but producers are unwilling to produce to meet demand as it is not profitable to do so. In this situation unemployment will be high.

- **Keynesian Unemployment**

Keynesian unemployment is due to lack of demand in the economy. Producers are willing to produce more goods and services and to employ more people but there is insufficient demand. Keynes concentrated on the role of aggregate demand as a means of achieving full employment. His advice was that any strategy that increased total expenditure should be used. If consumption or investment could be expanded it would stimulate demand. This was unlikely to be the case in periods of recession in which case the government had to manage the economy and increase its spending or reduce taxes.

- **Monetarists and Unemployment**

Monetarists held that unemployment could be reduced by increasing aggregate demand but only in the short term. In the long term increasing labour mobility, by retraining or by reducing social welfare payments, could reduce it.

Supply Siders and Unemployment:

Supply siders' policies concentrate on labour supply. These include better training and retraining, and more flexible industrial relations. When wage rates are above the equilibrium level, their policy then is to curb the power of trade unions engaging in restrictive practices and to introduce an incomes policy.

Types and Causes of Unemployment:

- **Cyclical Unemployment**

This type of unemployment is associated with economic recession. Firms cannot sell current production for a while so they build up stocks but eventually unemployment occurs. When the recession is over, employment will build up again.

The term cyclical unemployment refers to the alternate booms and slumps in the level of economy activity over the past hundred years. It was the main type of unemployment in the 1930's and Keynes held that it was brought about by inadequate or deficient demand i.e. by downward swings in the pendulum of business activity. Cyclical unemployment is also referred to as demand deficient unemployment.

It is now recognised that demand management alone will not bring about a low level of unemployment. This is due to the high rates of inflation experienced in many countries during the 1970's and 1980's. The emphasis has to be on job creation by encouraging expansion in existing employment and the setting up of new enterprises. Efficiency of the supply side of the economy is now very important.

Changes in world demand and particularly, in Ireland's major trading partners affects the level of employment here. In times of depression the number unemployed increases as it did for example in the early 1990's due to a drop in aggregate demand. Interest rate levels have a bearing on employment and when rates are high there is less investment therefore less employment. With a growing labour force such as Ireland has this means that new entrants or returning emigrants cannot be readily accommodated with jobs.

What is happening in the UK economy is very important since the Irish have been and still are dependent on it to provide employment for a part of the labour force. In the early 1990's the UK was hit by the recession and was not a great source of employment. Consequently some people particularly the young, uneducated or unskilled, who would have emigrated stayed at home and became part of the number unemployed here.

Increasing the level of aggregate demand can reduce cyclical unemployment. The government has incomplete information to work with when trying to estimate what change in aggregate demand is required. It must also decide what measure will give the desired result. Two types of control are available to it i.e. monetary and fiscal and the answer is usually found by a combination of the two. Policies that increase aggregate demand may also increase inflation and the balance of payment's deficit.

We do not have a great deal of control over external economic conditions. Strong growth is necessary particularly in the economies of our main trading partners. Even though the government cannot influence, this it can have the Irish economy in a state of readiness so as to capitalise on any opportunities that arise. With our very open economy we must maintain and improve our competitiveness in international markets. The greater our share, the greater the number employed at home. Government can ensure that it keeps its own house in order and that charges for public services are kept down so as to keep costs competitive. If the cost of running the country can be kept down, less tax will be required, so that the tax element in the cost of production and cost of living is kept down. The government must seek to achieve a high rate of growth in the face of international conditions, some of which it has very little control over, such as the oil crisis in 1974.The Government can encourage investment, exports and consumption. It can, through the development agencies, encourage the setting up of industries particularly indigenous industry.

- **Frictional Unemployment:**

Workers may be "between jobs" having left one job to take up another or having lost a job but unable to immediately secure a new job. They may not get the first job they apply for, or may not accept the first offer received There is friction in the labour market as workers spend some time out of work and this is described as frictional unemployment. It can arise when there is a reduction in the demand for labour in a particular occupation, though jobs are available in other occupations.

It may be the result of lack of knowledge of vacancies by those seeking employment, geographical immobility or mismatching between employment training programmes and the needs of industry.

The Government can try to reduce the period of unemployment and encourage workers to move to where suitable employment is available, by having a good job notification system and by providing the necessary retraining. With technological advance, workers need a high standard of education and a better educational system will enable people to obtain employment.

- **Seasonal Unemployment**

This arises because some industries are kept busy for only part of the year. Employment in some industries is seasonal in nature e.g. tourist industry, sugar beet industry, dairy products area and cereals within the agricultural industry. This type of unemployment is difficult to avoid but in the tourism area, it may be possible to vary attractions so that there is something available all year round. An example of this is the provision of leisure facilities by many hotels as well as the provision of conference centres.

School leavers and third level students must be included in this category. When they come on the labour market, there is a big increase in the number unemployed as it takes time to absorb them into the labour force.

Employers know that the demand for seasonal work is great, therefore they take workers willing to work at relatively low rates for long hours. This is particularly true of students. This prevents the creation of well-paid jobs of a seasonal nature. Employers in preference to ordinary applicants take people on work experience schemes because their wages are subsidised by FAS for example.

- **Structural Unemployment**

Structural unemployment results from the structural decline of industries unable to compete or adapt to changing technology, demand and new products. Growth in international competition has been particularly important as a cause of this type of unemployment.

It is also due to immobility of labour and this may be due to ignorance of opportunities elsewhere within the country or obstacles to movement. The less willing workers are to move the greater the level of structural unemployment.

Occupational immobility may be due to changes in supply and demand in some industries. On the demand side, the price of substitutes may fall or foreign buyers switch to competitors' goods. On the supply side, exhaustion of mineral deposits may cause redundancy.

A regional policy is necessary in order to tackle this type of unemployment. Mobility of labour from an occupational point of view can be improved by providing a high level of education initially, so those workers can adapt to change, if it becomes necessary. Retraining is very important; especially when particular skills are no longer required. The government can try to match jobs to unemployed people and/or give grants to industries to set up in areas of high unemployment.

- **Residual Unemployment**

This is a "catch all" category and includes people who are unemployable because of physical or mental disability. It also includes the "workshy".

If a worker is unemployed for a long period, it may mean that the worker is now unemployable. This can be caused by erosion of job skills and work habits so those workers with recent work experience get preference for the jobs. In the welfare state, which exists in many countries, workers may be better off when unemployed.

There is little a government can do to reduce this type of unemployment. If new jobs are available quickly to replace jobs lost, it may reduce the number going into the unemployable category due to long periods of unemployment.

- **Institutional Unemployment**

This type of unemployment arises because of obstacles to the mobility of labour. For workers living in local authority housing in an area where they have become unemployed, it may be difficult to move to a job in another area because of lack of similar housing. High social welfare payments may be a contributory factor to institutional unemployment. Government can influence the situation here by providing local authority housing when required. It could also make social welfare payments less attractive.

Irish Unemployment:

Causes:

Efficiency Wages: If the labour market was similar to the products market we would expect wages to be flexible so that they fall when there was unemployment (excess supply of labour), making the market clear. It does not however do so and we need to explain why wages are at levels that do not eradicate involuntary unemployment. Since wages do not fall, there is real wage rigidity.

A number of models called efficiency wage theories have been developed to explain this. The argument is that high wages make workers more productive and if wages are cut, workers become less productive and profits fall. Employers use the threat of dismissal to maintain worker discipline. If wages are no higher than in other firms, this is not a real threat unless firms pay higher wages. Higher wages reduce demand for labour and increase unemployment. Workers work harder to the benefit of the firm. Another argument for paying higher wages is to reduce labour turnover. This again benefits the firms, as the costs of recruitment and training can be substantial. Higher wages attract better workers.

Bargaining Models: The activity of trade unions can be the cause of unemployment due to their interference in the labour market. They seek higher wages for their members and firms reduce demand for workers. Supply of labour will increase so that wages should go down. This will not happen if the social welfare system makes it worthwhile for people not to work i.e. the replacement ratio (explained later) is high. As a result wages will not fall sufficiently to clear the market and unemployment will occur. T o over come this difficulty, the power of unions must be reduced and social welfare benefits changed. Unions will say that workers can improve productivity. It is not politically feasible to reduce social welfare benefits.

Programme for National Recovery (PNR), Programme for Economic and Social Progress (PESP), Programme for Competitiveness and Work (PCW) and the current Partnership 2000.

In Ireland we have had wage agreements, national understandings and national programmes in that order since the 1960's with a brief interlude of centralised wage bargaining in the mid 1980's. Their purpose was and is to maintain wage moderation so as to reduce unemployment and improve competitiveness.

Programmes since 1987 have put ceilings on wage increases. These agreements are binding on workers in the public sector but those in the private sector generally adhere to them as well.

It was not until Partnership 2000 that unemployed people were represented in the negotiations and even then only on the fringe. The unions have endeavoured to protect their members real wages with little reference to the unemployed.

Insiders and Outsiders: Insiders consist of people in secure employment so that it is costly to sack them and hire someone in their place. Outsiders are either unemployed or working in the 'informal sector' with little or no job security. Insiders can negotiate higher wages while outsiders cannot. The higher wage then makes it more expensive to hire all the outsiders. It is difficult for the firm to fire the insiders and hire the cheaper outsiders, because the insiders will disrupt production and they know that the outsiders will have to be trained and that it will be some time before the outsiders are as experienced as the insiders. This perpetuates the unemployment of outsiders and to some extent explains long-term unemployment.

Labour Market Policy: The main features are as follows:

- Reduce unions' power to obtain real wage increases for their members which reduces the demand for labour by firms;
- Make social welfare benefits less attractive;

- Reduce the power of unions to preserve restrictive employment practices;
- Tighten social welfare by restricting initial eligibility for benefit, and applying more stringent rules for continued receipt of benefit;
- Reduce employers' costs such as P.R.S.I. (effectively a tax on income);
- Resist the introduction of a minimum wage; and
- Encourage part-time, temporary and self-employment.

The Replacement Ratio: This is a measure of social welfare benefit generosity. It is the proportion of in-work income, lost when one becomes unemployed that the welfare system replaces. It is therefore the ratio of total benefits when out of work compared to average net income when in work.

Tax Wedge: The tax wedge is the difference between the net pay on employee receives and the cost the employer must bear in employing him/her. It arises due to taxes on income and expenditure. Demand for labour depends on the gross amount an employer must pay. This is inclusive of employer levies such as PRSI. The supply of labour depends on the workers' take-home Income tax, PRSI, VAT, and excise duties go towards reducing the disposable wage.

Hysteresis: Hysteresis is a term derived from physics and refers to a situation where the effects lag behind the causes. It has been used to explain unemployment. The explanation makes use of NAIRU – the non-accelerating inflation rate of unemployment. It holds that the level of unemployment is determined by the characteristics of the labour market, for example the number of people who leave schools and colleges. Any attempt to reduce the level of unemployment below the natural rate will only result in higher inflation.

Skills mis-match: This situation arises when the unemployed and in particular the long-term unemployed do not possess skills in demand by the employers. This is true in Ireland at present and contributes substantially to the number unemployed.

Minimum Wage: Theoretically, minimum wages reduce employment on the presumption that the minimum wage is set above the market clearing level that would arise in a competitive labour market.

Measuring Unemployment:
Statistics for measuring the level of unemployment in Ireland are often obtained from the Live Register of unemployment which includes, people entitled to unemployment benefits and assistance or "dole". The Live Register measures the number of Social Welfare recipients claiming unemployment benefit. It does not measure unemployment since it includes part - time workers up to three days a week, seasonal and causal workers entitled to Unemployment Benefit (excluding systematic short- time workers). It also includes applicants for Unemployment Assistance excluding small farmers and self employed plus other applicants for social welfare (excluding those on strike). It excludes persons seeking work that has never worked before and is not entitled to benefits.

Labour Force: Is the sum of those in employment plus the unemployed. It does not include those who have given up hope of getting employment as unemployed, including them instead as inactive or "discouraged workers".

Characteristics of the Unemployed:

Unemployed people can be divided into three broad groupings as follows:

- **Young people:** In Ireland over 25% of those unemployed are under 25 years of age, making it the largest group of jobless people.
- **Older people:** These are in the over 55 group, who tend to be the first to go when workers are made redundant.
- **Unskilled people:** People in this group usually have a low level of education and little or no usable skills.

Table 17.12 gives the figures for unemployment 1982 to 1998 as compiled by the National Office of the Labour Exchanges. On an overall basis unemployment has fallen since 1995. The number on assistance has fallen over the past four years indicating that less people are long term unemployed. These figures do not include people over 55 years who have voluntarily left the labour force and do not have to sign on.

If the population in 1998 is taken as 3.704 million and labour force actually employed as 1.4945 million then only one in two and half of the total population was employed in mid April 1998. Appendix17.2 shows unemployment in the EU15 plus Japan and US over the period 1974-2000. Ireland had the second highest rate of unemployment in the periods 1986-90 and 1991-95 behind Spain. Since 1996 the percentage of the Irish population unemployed has fallen from 11.6 per cent to 8.7 in 1998. It is forecast at 6.2% in 2000 while the EU15 is expected to be 9.0 per cent.

Costs Associated with Unemployment:

The costs of unemployment are felt most directly by those who are without jobs.

For the unemployed person there is the loss of earnings not recovered by unemployment benefits. There is a loss of self- esteem and of spirit which can cause psychological problems.

There are costs to the family of the unemployed person. Their standard of living goes down and they do not have money for luxuries and leisure activities they enjoyed before becoming unemployed.

There is the cost to the Exchequer of paying unemployment assistance. The government also loses tax revenue since the unemployed does not pay tax and they haven't the same purchasing power now that they are on social welfare. Government revenue from VAT and other indirect taxes is also less.

Government has to have officers and administrative staff to administer the social welfare system and pay the recipients.

Crime and vandalism may increase due to lack of something to do, carrying with it the extra cost for law enforcement.

Table 17.12
Unemployed Ireland 1982-1998

Year	Benefit	Assistance	Credit	Total
1982	91,377	82,084	6,406	179,867
1983	97,285	102,837	7,919	208,041
1984	95,771	119,626	10,048	225,445
1985	97,877	129,450	12,540	239867
1986	96,589	140,785	12,840	250,178
1987	90345	145,647	14,091	250,083
1988	78,291	148,899	15,756	242,946
1989	64,433	148,305	17,390	231,128
1990	65,754	152,042	15,011	232,807
1991	78,360	175,123	15,731	269,214
1992	78,872	196,467	17,380	293,719
1993	73,803	207,084	16,202	297,089
1994	65,480	200,198	14,505	280,183
1995	65,180	203,214	17,029	285,423
1996	65,041	186,916	18,199	270,156
1997	70,001	159,825	17,904	247,730
1998	70,432	128,986	16,334	215,752

Source: Direct Communication with CSO

Output is below potential due to unemployed resources being available and as a result income for all is lower.

Reducing Unemployment -Policy Issues:

Many policies have been suggested over the years and the following is an outline of recent policy issues:

- **Reform of Social Welfare System**

Unemployment benefit can be claimed for 15 months in Ireland and then the unemployed person goes on means -tested unemployment assistance that can be drawn indefinitely. It is often suggested that the availability of long-term unemployment assistance gives no incentive to people to look for work. Employers are reluctant to employ people who are unemployed for a long period so they find it difficult to get work and some could be classed as unemployable or "workshy".

It is very important that the net incomes of those at work are greater than those of the unemployed. The market wage cannot go below the social wage. The social wage has been improved at each budget by way of increases in basic payments. Unemployed people are also entitled to free health and education as well as having better access to public housing. At the same time, the market wage has been reduced due to taxation and as a result employers have to pay something over what can be obtained on social welfare if they are to recruit employees. When calculating the gross wage the employer must take into account what is available on social welfare and must offer more. It is also maintained that some social welfare recipients are also working in the" Black Economy" so that what they earn is added to social welfare benefits and they are better off unemployed. There is no income tax on social welfare payments.

A number of proposals have been made on how to reform the social welfare system. A single negative income tax or social dividend approach has been suggested. This would encourage part-time workers or those in poorly paid employment to withdraw from the labour force thus reducing it while at the same time providing others with increased incentives to take up full-time employment. Incremental employment subsidies could be used. An example here would be the forgoing of the employers' part of PRSI on additional workers. The main drawback is that these schemes encourage employers to bring forward jobs they would have created anyway at a later stage. Employer PRSI was reduced in the 1995 Budget as a method of increasing employment.

- **Reform of the Tax System**

The tax wedge is the difference between what the employer pays the employee and what the employee takes home. This is the difference between gross and net pay plus PRSI contributions. The larger the tax wedge the more expensive labour is and the more reluctant are employers to take on workers. This causes employers to employ capital instead of labour. Employees may also substitute leisure for work as the reward for overtime is reduced. If the tax wedge is reduced employment will increase. The Culliton Report (1992) advised on tax incentives as a means of increasing employment and that the tax base must be widened. Even though the tax wedge reduction would reduce revenue from tax in this area, the deficiency could be made up from spreading the tax net to other areas.

Corporation Profits Tax was reduced from 40% to 38% for the service sector. This sector is the employment growth sector and this should encourage employers to create even more jobs. Tax on low paid workers was reduced by an increase in allowances and by a widening of the lower tax band.

- **Education and Training**

People with higher educational attainments are known to have better prospects of obtaining employment. FAS provides training for unskilled and low skilled people with the objective of assisting them in finding employment. It also provides retraining for workers whose skills have become redundant due to ever-changing technology.

Over the years, schemes have been and still are being introduced in an effort to reduce unemployment. These schemes include alternate programme teamwork, social employment scheme, CEDP and now the Community Employment Scheme. These schemes have done much good, with unemployment now falling rapidly.

- **Competitiveness**

As already stated, the Irish economy is very open and is dependent on exports to provide employment. Competition in world export markets is keen and costs must be kept down to remain competitive. This is very true in the Irish case as was demonstrated during the currency crisis of 1992/93. The Irish Punt appreciated against sterling which then left the ERM. As a result, imports from the UK cost more and to sell the same goods at the pre crisis price meant that margins had to be cut. In some cases margins were not sufficient to cover the increased costs and many jobs were in danger. The Government's response at the time was to propose financial assistance for indigenous firms exporting to the UK. Devaluation came before this payment was made. This is not the long-term answer and the policy should be one of ensuring that firms are competitive. Interest rates must be kept at moderate levels and to do so requires fiscal restraint. The wage bargaining system must be such that competitiveness is not only maintained but also improved. Businesses must ensure that for their part, costs are kept down so that combined with other cost maintaining measures they can hold their markets and increase them thus increasing employment.

- **Economic Environment**

The government can promote employment expansion by providing the infrastructure conducive to the expansion of business. EU Structural Funds have helped with this.

Government taxation policy can also be such that it acts as an incentive to enterprise and therefore employment creation. It is possible that if the government wishes to give a tax incentive to one sector, say services, it can do so by putting additional taxes on other sectors. In this way there is no extra cost but rather extra revenue.

Reducing or removing restrictive practices can increase competitiveness. Costs are increased where these practices exist, since firms providing these services are not as efficient as they should be. The cost of their inefficiency is borne by the firms paying for their services, so that their costs in turn are greater than they need be. Restrictions on employment opportunities should be lifted.

- **Regional Policy for Depressed Areas**

There are a number of areas in Ireland where the unemployment rate is above the national average and these can be considered to be depressed areas. There is an outflow of people and the EU and the Irish government must help to stem the flow.

- **Import Substitution**

Firms must try to produce at home what is now imported.

- **Private Promotion of Industrial Development**

There is scope for private promotion of development through community based organisations in particular. This should increase the numbers employed in rural areas where there is little chance of attracting outside firms to set up.

Questions

1. Outline the changes in the Irish population and in the pattern of emigration as revealed by the 1996 Census.

2. Discuss the main characteristics and trends in the Irish labour force. What are the economic implications of these trends?

3. The Irish unemployment problem cannot be looked at separately from the Irish demographic experience. Discuss this statement commenting with the current unemployment problem.

4. Examine the effects of a decline in the birth rate in the short-term and in the longer term.

5. Discuss the possible remedies for Ireland's unemployment problem. To what extent do you attribute high unemployment to government policy failure as opposed to external factors?

6. Analyse selective employment policies directed at increasing the demand for labour with particular reference to Ireland.

7. Outline the costs and benefits of migration to:
   (a) the emigrants;
   (b) the host countries and
   (c) those who remain at home.

8. Ireland's demographic profile has changed towards the EU norm over the past decade. Describe the principal features of this change and the policy implications involved.

9. " The problem of regional unemployment in Ireland could be solved by moving the workers to the work, rather than by taking work to the workers." Critically evaluate this statement.

Appendix 17.1
(Table 17.4)
Projections of Elderly Dependency Ratios EU15 1990-2030

Country	1990	2000	2010	2020	2030
France	20.8	23.6	24.6	32.3	39.1
Belgium	22.4	25.1	25.6	31.9	41.1
Denmark	22.7	21.6	24.9	31.7	37.7
Germany	21.7	23.8	30.3	35.4	49.2
Greece	21.2	25.5	28.8	33.3	40.9
Spain	19.8	23.5	25.9	30.7	41.0
France	20.8	23.6	24.6	32.3	39.1
Ireland	18.4	16.7	18.0	21.7	25.3
Italy	21.6	26.5	31.2	37.5	48.3
Luxembourg	19.9	21.9	25.9	33.2	44.2
Netherlands	19.1	20.8	24.2	33.9	45.1
Austria	22.4	23.2	27.7	32.6	44.0
Portugal	19.5	20.9	22.0	25.3	33.5
Finland	19.7	21.5	24.3	34.7	41.1
Sweden	27.6	26.9	29.1	35.6	39.4
UK	24.0	24.4	25.8	31.2	38.7

Source: EMI Convergence Report 1998

Appendix 17.2
(Table 17.13)

Number of Unemployed in Selected Countries 1974-2000

Country	Percentages								
	1974-85	1986-90	1991-95	1996-2000	1996	1997	1998	1999	2000
Germany	4.2	5.9	7.3	9.4	8.9	10.0	9.8	9.3	8.9
France	6.4	9.7	11.1	11.7	12.4	12.4	11.7	11.1	10.8
Italy	7.0	9.6	10.3	11.9	12.0	12.1	12.0	11.9	11.6
UK	6.9	9.0	9.5	6.8	8.2	7.0	6.3	6.2	6.2
Belgium	7.7	8.7	8.5	8.4	9.7	9.2	8.3	7.7	7.1
Denmark	6.4	6.4	8.6	4.8	6.8	5.5	4.2	4.0	3.7
Netherlands	7.1	7.4	6.4	4.2	6.3	5.2	3.7	3.1	2.6
Sweden	2.4	2.0	7.2	8.5	9.6	9.9	8.3	7.7	7.0
Greece	3.8	6.6	8.3	9.3	9.6	9.6	9.4	9.1	8.9
Portugal	6.9	6.1	5.6	5.9	7.3	6.8	5.7	5.1	4.7
Ireland	10.6	15.5	14.5	8.8	11.6	10.1	8.7	7.4	6.2
Spain	11.3	18.9	20.9	19.0	22.2	20.8	18.9	17.2	15.7
Luxembourg	1.7	2.1	2.5	2.5	3.0	2.6	2.4	2.3	2.2
Finland	4.8	4.3	14.0	12.0	15.3	13.1	11.6	10.4	9.5
EU-15	6.4	8.9	10.0	10.0	10.9	10.7	10.0	9.5	9.0
USA	7.5	5.9	6.6	4.9	5.4	4.9	4.5	4.7	5.0
Japan	2.2	2.5	2.6	3.9	3.4	3.4	4.2	4.4	4.1

Source: Supplement A, Economic Trends No. 10 October 1998

CHAPTER 18

INFLATION

Introduction:

Inflation is defined as a continuing or persistent tendency for the price level to rise. It can also be described as a continuous fall in the purchasing power of money. The most usual measure is that of consumer prices and the CSO publishes the consumer price index on a monthly basis. The annual rate of inflation is the rate of change in the price index between two adjacent years. Deflation is the opposite of inflation. In this Chapter we examine the causes and effects of inflation and assess the policies put forward in the Quantity Theory of Money, and by the Keynesians, monetarists and new classicals for reducing it. We examine the inverse relationship between inflation and employment put forward by A W Phillips i.e. the Phillips curve. Finally the trend in Irish inflation is detailed.

Consumer Price Index (CPI.):

The Irish CPI is calculated on the basis of the average patterns of household expenditure behaviour as obtained from the Household Budget Survey of 1987. This Survey covered a sample of 7,185 households. From this, weights were established for 722 items according to their importance in household expenditure. It is calculated on a monthly basis and attempts to measure changes in the general level of prices for consumer goods and services purchased by private households. Calculation is as outlined in Table 18.1, which shows the weightings, items included and number of times surveyed for each item. Food has a weighting of 24.96% of the total. This means that on average households devote 24.96% of their total expenditure to food.

Problems with the CPI:

The CPI is not an accurate measure of changes in the cost of living and there are a number of problems that can reduce its reliability.

- Different families do not buy similar goods and services. A family with very young children will not purchase the same type of goods as a family with teenage or grown up children.

- The pattern of consumption may change as a result of large price changes. During the currency crises in 1993, mortgage interest rates increased and as a result mortgage holders had to reduce their expenditure on other goods and services. Again reliability of the index may be reduced. When the 1993 devaluation took place, interest rates went back down to a level lower than they were prior to the currency crisis.

- If price changes alone are noted in the index, changes in quality will be ignored. Price changes may reflect improvement in the good or service. An increase in price may be due to better quality so that the real cost of the good or service is the same as it was before the price change.

- It is difficult to consider changes in prices which consumers actually pay. Goods and services can be purchased from different outlets e.g. corner shops, supermarkets and prices do not always change simultaneously or even by the same amount in these outlets.

- Index numbers are of limited value for comparison over long periods of time due to the fact that new products come on the market, and changes in fashion and tastes increase demand for some goods and services and reduce it for others. It is also due to the fact that the composition of communities change as does the distribution of the population.

Table 18.1
Irish Consumer Price Index weighting used in measuring Consumer Price Index

Category	Number of Prices Surveyed in Category	Weight in overall Consumer Price Index %
Food	126	24.96
Alcohol	13	12.28
Tobacco	4	3.41
Clothing & Footwear	68	8.07
Fuel & Light	10	6.12
Housing	24	5.71
Household Durable Goods	70	5.13
Other Goods	116	5.69
Transport	92	16.70
Services	199	11.93
	722	100.00

Source: CSO

Uses of Consumer Price Index:

- Since a rise in the CPI means a fall in living standards i.e. a rise in the cost of living, trade unions use the CPI when they seek wage increases for their members.

- It is used to calculate the rate of inflation, and this in turn is used to calculate among other things, the real GNP.

- Some savings institutions like the Post Office have index-linked savings accounts and the interest on deposits is related to changes in the CPI.

- It is used to indicate what increase is required in social welfare payments in order to maintain the real value of these payments. The Government uses it when indexing social welfare payments and calculating tax free allowances.

- Other countries have similar indices, for example the UK has a Retail Price Index that is an index of the prices of goods bought by a typical household and comparison can be made.

The Consumer Price index for 1996 was 135.4 and for 1997 it was 137.4.

To calculate the rate of inflation from the C.P.I. for 1997

$$\frac{\text{CPI 1997 - CPI 1996}}{\text{CPI 1996}} \times \frac{100}{1} = \frac{137.4 - 135.4}{135.4} \times \frac{100}{1} = \frac{2}{135.4} \times \frac{100}{1} = 1.5\%$$

Theories and Types of Inflation:

The Quantity Theory of Money is the oldest theory of inflation. Classical School economists based their analysis of inflation on it. In its simplest form it states that the general level of prices depends on the supply of money.

The Quantity of Money and the Price Level:

Price is the relationship between a quantity of money and a quantity of goods. Thus the higher the price of a good, the lower the value of a unit of money in terms of that good. Here we are concerned with movements in the general price level - the average level of prices. Changes in aggregate demand affect prices as well as income and output.

The Quantity Theory of the Demand for Money:

The original and most elementary theory of the demand for money was Irving Fisher's Quantity Theory given as MV = PT. M is the stock of money in existence; V is the velocity of circulation; P is the average price at which a transaction takes place; and T is the number of transactions in the period. It forms the basis of the monetarist theory of inflation and the role of monetary policy in the economy. The theory may be related as MV = PY. M is the money supply when in equilibrium between the demand for and supply of money. V is the income velocity of circulation, which is the number of times per year that the money stock is used to purchase the annual production of goods and services. P is the general price level as given by the (Consumer Price Index). Y is the real level of National Income.

The demand for money (M) can be written:

MV=PY where PV= Nominal GNP $M = \frac{PY}{V} = M = 1/V.PY$

If the velocity of circulation (V) remains constant as Fisher stated it did, the demand for money would rise in direct proportion to increases in prices (P) and real income (Y).
M is the equilibrium position between money demanded and money supplied. Thus if the Central Bank increased the amount of money in circulation, M would increase. Assuming V is constant, this would result in an increase in P and Y according to the last equation. Whether the increase is in Y or P depends on whether the economy is in a full employment

situation or not. If there is unemployment in the economy, an increase in M will result in an increase in Y (real income). If, however, the economy is at full employment, an increase in M will result in an increase in the price level (P).

Quantity Theory Equation, MV = PY $P = \dfrac{MV}{Y}$

Assuming that V remains constant, for P to remain stable, M must change at the same rate as Y. Growth in M in excess of Y will result in an increase in P i.e. inflation.

The Cambridge Version:

Economists in Cambridge developed a version of the quantity theory that relates the quantity of money to the level of income. Whereas in the Fisher version, V and P refer to all transactions, the Cambridge version is concerned with transactions affecting final goods. Instead of PY, we now have $P_1 O$, where O is the physical output of final goods and services and P_1 is the average of prices. The substitution of O for Y means that the velocity of circulation is the income velocity of circulation (V_1). V_1 is the rate of turnover of money in the purchase of final goods and services. It is

$$V_1 \quad = \dfrac{\text{National Income}}{M}$$

The equation now is $MV_1 = P_1O$ and since $P_1 O$ = National Income MV_1 = Y or M = kY where k is the average fraction of income which people hold in money. It can be shown as k = $1/V_1$.

If money turns over 5 times a year, then each unit is held on average for a fifth of that time. If V^1 is 5, then people wish to hold, on average, 1/5 of their real income as money. M = kY shows that when the supply of money (M) and demand to hold money (kY) are equal, there is equilibrium. This means that on average a pound was used 5 times during the year or £1 bought £5 worth of final goods and services during the year.

Under monetarist theory, monetary policy plays an essential role in the economy. Where there is unemployment, an increase in the money supply leads to an increase in the growth of the economy towards full employment. When there is full employment, increases in the money supply greater than the growth in the economy, causes inflation.

Monetarists base their theories on historical evidence that all inflation of moderate duration were caused by increases in the size of the money stock. They quote the examples of the inflow of gold and silver into Europe as a result of the Spanish Conquest of the Americas and German hyperinflation of the 1930's. This does not prove that changes in price are caused by changes in money supply.

The Quantity Theory assumes that V remains constant. If an effort is made to curb the growth of M so as to curb the rate of inflation, V would increase as the limited stock of money is just worked harder.

Critics of the monetarist theory argue that it is very simplistic to ignore the rate of interest, in the demand for money. They also hold that it is not reasonable to expect that the quantity of money demanded will increase on a linear (straight line) basis irrespective of the level of income. This means that the quantity of money demanded may decrease relative to the growth of the money supply as income increases.

Keynesians and the Quantity Theory:

The equation of exchange is just an identity and indicates that the amount spent in an economy always equals the amount bought. To make a Quantity Theory out of this identity the following assumptions have to be made:

- the price level is determined by the money supply and not vice versa; and

- V the velocity of circulation and Q real output or income are relatively constant.

Keynesians used these two assumptions to attack the Quantity Theory. One such attack was by Lord Kaldor who argued that the functional relationship between the money supply and the price level is specified the wrong way round. It is changes in the price level that cause the money supply to change, not the opposite. Inflation is caused by cost push factors. The money supply changes to suit the level of transactions required at the newer higher price level.

They do agree that the money supply must increase in order to finance an inflation and to keep it going. They do not concede that the increase in the money supply is the cause of inflation. If control of the money supply is too tight in an effort to halt inflation, it is possible that the result will be that activity will fall because transactions cannot be financed.

Keynesians also question whether V and Q are constant. Evidence from the 1970's and the 1980's suggests that V has not remained constant, but has slowed down in response to increases in the money supply. The monetarists as a result have changed from insisting that V is constant to it being relatively stable and predictable. V is a function of the interest rate. However it would appear from data that there is no systematic relationship between interest and V in the short run. An increase in the money supply may increase real output (Q) rather than the price level (P), especially if there is spare capacity and unemployment in the economy. They accuse monetarists of faulty statistical techniques and manipulation of evidence to support the Quantity Theory.

Revival of the Quantity Theory:

Revival is due to the work of Milton Friedman and economists known as the Chicago School. They hold that the determinants of the demand for money are fairly stable and change only slowly over time, whereas money stock may rise or fall fairly rapidly. Changes in nominal national income are due mainly to changes in the supply of money. This indicates to monetary authorities the necessity of paying more attention to the quantity of money and less to the rate of interest.

Current Position:

The debate centres on what is an effective substitute for money balances. Keynesians held that the only one was securities. If the money supply is increased excessively, the public will try to shed its excess liquidity by purchasing securities. Price of securities will rise and interest rates will fall. The latter means that the cost of holding money falls and it is a more attractive option. The rate of interest will continue to fall until the increased volume of money is willingly held at the current price or rate of interest. The effect on levels of consumption and spending may be very small. Investment demand, which depends on expectations rather than rate of interest and effects of changes in value of financial assets, would not be great as far as the propensity to consume is concerned.

The present day quantity theory looks on money as a substitute for all assets whether real or financial. Anyone short of money will forego some planned expenditure rather than sell securities.

The monetary school holds that an increase in the money supply will lead to spending on a wide range of income yielding assets. Some of these assets will be securities yielding an explicit rate of interest.

The modern theory holds that the impact of changes in the quantity of money will be widely dispersed rather than working through changes in interest rates. Money supply is the important determinant of the level of economic activity. Changes in money supply are the best indicators of future changes in aggregate expenditure.

Money Supply and Inflation Policies:

Monetarists hold that money supply should only grow at the same rate as growth of output in the economy. This usually requires a cut in the budget deficit and cutting public expenditure can do this. There is also the possibility of holding present spending and taxation levels but to finance the budget without borrowing from banks. Interest rates would need to be maintained at a high level. Taxation could be increased thus reducing the budget deficit. This may put people off work and would certainly be a disincentive to effort. It would be very unpopular. Monetarists link inflation with money supply and there is no satisfactory proof of this. There may be other causes in which case inflation cannot be controlled by concentration on one factor. High interest rates reduce investment and reduction in government expenditure reduces aggregate demand and causes unemployment.

Demand Pull Inflation:

At the outbreak of World War II Keynes adapted his theory of how deficient demand in a deflated economy can cause unemployment to explain how excess demand can cause inflation in a fully employed economy. Demand pull inflation may be defined as a situation where aggregate demand persistently exceeds aggregate supply at current prices so that prices are being 'pulled' upwards. This type of inflation is usually associated with conditions of full employment. If unemployed resources exist, bringing them into use can cover an increase in demand. Supply will rise and the increase in demand will have little or no effect on the price level. When resources are fully employed, there is an increase in prices.

Excess demand can arise under full employment conditions as follows:

- Government may increase spending without a corresponding rise in taxation. If the deficit is made up of bank borrowing the additional spending is financed by an increase in the money supply.

- It may arise if a country tries to achieve an export surplus, in order maybe, to pay off external debt. Exports generate inflation because they generate income in the domestic economy but reduce supplies in the domestic market. Imports could make up the difference but if exports exceed imports, there will be excess demand unless savings and taxes are increased to absorb the additional purchasing power.

- Demand inflation can occur when a country tries to increase its rate of economic growth while at full employment. Resources need to be transferred from production of consumer goods to capital goods so as to increase the rate of capital accumulation.

- Incomes do not fall but the supply of goods demanded will decrease. Without an increase in taxation and/or savings, there will be excess demand and rising prices.

In the situation of excess demand, suppliers try to employ more workers to increase output to meet demand. In conditions of full employment, workers are scarce and as a result, demand exceeds supply and wages are bid up and the increase in wages causes an increase in costs and so prices go up.

Policies to Reduce Demand- Pull Inflation:

Deflationary policies such as higher taxation lower government expenditure or higher interest rates can be introduced to control demand-pull inflation. A reduction in the level of aggregate demand is necessary when inflation is caused by excess demand. Even though this leads to more people being unemployed, it was still done in the 1950's and 1960's to achieve price stability. There is, however, evidence that inflation is not now associated with a high level of demand as it once was. Ireland does not, at present, have full employment or excess demand but if it had, at a later stage then demand-pull inflation would reappear.

Cost- Push Inflation:

Creeping inflation continued in the Keynesian era even when excess demand was not apparent. In the 1960's Keynesians switched from the demand-pull to the cost-push theory of inflation. Prices rise because of some factor independent of the level of aggregate demand. Cost inflation is due to autonomous increases in firms' costs and is primarily a wage inflation process.
Cost- push inflation can be divided into two categories internal and external.

Internal Cost-Push:

Internal cost-push can be described as 'wage-push'. If increased wages are not accompanied by a similar increase in productivity, costs of production will rise. Wages can increase when there is no excess demand in the economy. There must be an independent factor pushing up wages and there are a number of factors that could account for this:

- Higher indirect taxation will directly raise price levels and result in demands for higher wages. Greater direct taxation that reduces disposable income also leads to demands for higher pay.

- If the prices of imports go up, the cost of living goes up and the value of real income goes down, resulting in demands for higher pay.

Restriction on permitted wage increases can be used but if relaxed, they lead to large-scale effort to catch up and make up ground considered lost.

- If economic growth is slow, workers will not achieve the standard of living they expect, and will try to obtain this level through wage increases. This happens even though it works against the workers in that prices go up and growth goes down because profits are reduced.

- An effort to close the gap between high paid and low paid workers by granting a substantial wage increase brings about cost-push inflation. Once the process starts, it continues and there is a wage-price spiral. In periods of continuous inflation, workers expect that it will continue to increase and they seek even higher wages and the vicious circle continues.

External Cost-Push or Imported Inflation:

External cost or imported inflation can start with an increase in import prices, as it did in 1973/74 following the rise in oil prices. It occurs when the cost of essential imports rise regardless of whether or not they are in short supply. A country can try to reduce the quantities or the price of imports. However an individual country can do little about a rise in world prices.

Polices to Reduce Cost Push Inflation:

These can be divided into internal and external:

- **Internal**

Here inflation is due to wage increases being in excess of productivity increases and Government must endeavour to reduce the rate of wage increase. This can be done by moderating the increases in incomes and prices or by preventing such increases. This has been attempted through prices and incomes policies, the Programme for Economic and Social Progress (PESP) Programme for Competitiveness and Work (PCW) and Partnership

2000. Government can try to show people that one person's pay increase is another person's price rise. Generally, this type of moral suasion achieves little or nothing. Government can also hold down price rises in nationalised or semi-state industries and can put a ceiling on public sector pay. An all out effort to increase productivity to offset wage increases will reduce or eliminate inflation.

- **External**

Little can be done in a situation where world prices are rising as was the case during the oil crisis of 1973/74 when the price of oil quadrupled. A country must seek to prevent external factors from starting a wage-price spiral. Compensatory wage claims to offset increased prices of imports must not be conceded. The country must work to prevent depreciation of its exchange rate, as it would cause import prices to rise.

Prices and Incomes Policies to Reduce Inflation:

- **Incomes Policy**

An incomes policy is an effort to influence wages and other incomes directly while, at the same time, curbing the growth of prices. If the policy is statutory, it will cause industrial unrest and if voluntary, it is unlikely to be effective. A norm for wage increases must be set and the question arises as to level. If the norm is too high, inflation will not be greatly reduced and if too low, workers will resist it. There will need to be exceptions to the norm otherwise the agreement will not last as it will be too rigid. Once exceptions are made, others will seek to become exceptions as well. There is also the possibility that the limits set will be avoided by some e.g. the self- employed, and people working in the black economy.

- **Prices Policy**

If all the increase in price requested is not allowed, productivity is expected to make up for the difference in costs. This can lead to great difficulty for firms unable to increase productivity as their profit margins are reduced. There must be exceptions made as otherwise, certain products will cease to be produced or will be exported at a higher price. It is, of course, impossible to check adherence to the policy.

All previous attempts at prices and incomes policies in Ireland have failed since it is impossible to control and supervise such policies.

Devaluation Inflation:

If there is a fall in the country's exchange rate, import prices go up and trigger inflation since they increase the cost of living and workers seek higher wages to make up for this. The wage-price spiral follows.

Suppressed Inflation:

As noted already inflation involves a rise in prices but it is possible for a government to prevent this while the inflationary process is still ongoing. This was done in the former USSR when instead of prices rising there were shortages, queues and black markets.

Creeping Inflation:

This occurs when the inflation rate is fairly stable for a period but gradually creeps up. This happened in Ireland in the 1960's and mid 1970's. It also happened in other advanced countries and contributed to the crisis in Keynesian economics and the monetarist counter-revolution.

Strato-Inflation:

Here the inflation rate is between 10% and hundreds per cent without ever reaching hyper-inflation. Between 1973 and 1983 - with the exception of 1978 - Ireland had this type of inflation.

Hyper-Inflation:

Hyper-inflation occurs, when inflation rates are very high. The most famous example is the German experience of 1922-23, when the Government had a big deficit that it financed mainly by printing money. So great was the increase in the money supply that the Government had to buy faster printing presses. This was not enough so they took in old notes and added zeros to them and reissued them as larger denominations. A more up to date example is that of Bolivia which had 11,000 per cent inflation in 1985 also Yugoslavia in the early 1980's. It is usually the result of a political crisis. The functions of money break down and normal economic activity ceases.

Stagflation:

This is a period of both high inflation and high unemployment. It combines price inflation with stagnation in economic activity. This went against the Keynesian demand management policies and politically is inadvisable as a method of controlling inflation and unemployment. Inflation is no longer exclusively associated with excess aggregate demand due to the arrival of stagflation in the 1960's.

Mark-up Inflation:

This is due to the impact of indirect taxes. It occurs when suppliers strive to maintain a steady percentage profit level when prices are rising. If for example VAT goes up the supplier will calculate his mark-up on a higher base resulting in higher prices. This increase is passed on to the consumer and mark-up inflation is generated.

The Phillips Curve:

Keynesians divided between the demand-pull and cost-push theories of inflation continued the debate aided by a statistical relationship discovered by A.W. Philips. He had found a fairly stable relationship between the increase in money wage rates and the level of unemployment over a long period. When there was low unemployment and high increase in wage rates, aggregate demand was high. With high unemployment and a low increase in wage rates, there was low aggregate demand.

This relationship is shown in Diagram 18.1

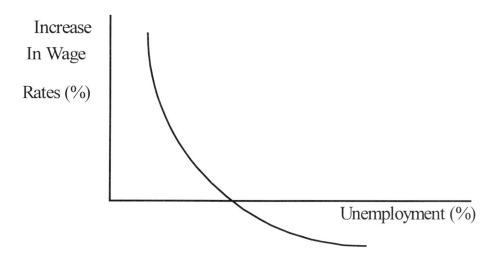

Diagram 18.1 Phillips Curve

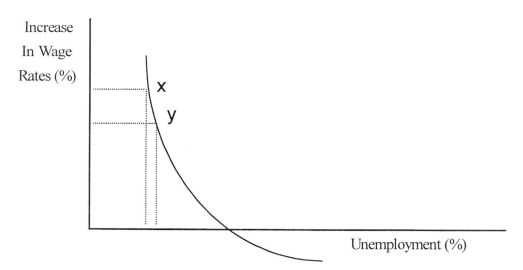

Diagram 18.2 Trade off Between Unemployment and Inflation

Diagram 18.2 shows that a choice can be made between full employment and wage increase. If, at point x with full employment, growth of money wages is causing too much inflation then the economy could go to point y. Full employment is sacrificed but the increase in wages is brought down. This relationship broke down in the mid 1960s when wages increased by more than would have been predicted given the level of unemployment. This simple trade-off between inflation and unemployment no longer exists. Many considered after the mid -1960s that some factors 'push up' wages and other costs. The 1970's and 1980's saw higher unemployment and higher inflation than the 1950's and the 1960's.

Expectations Augmented Phillips Curve:

This was introduced by Milton Friedman in 1968. He explained that the Keynesian theories on the Phillips curve were based on a misunderstanding of the relationship between inflation and unemployment. He said they wrongly took into account only the current rate of inflation as it affects workers and firms but ignored the influence of the expected rate of inflation. He also believed that a stable relationship between inflation and unemployment, allowing a long -term trade off, never existed.

For him the only "true" long term relationship between unemployment and inflation lies along a vertical line on which trade offs are not possible, running through the natural rate of unemployment or the non accelerating inflation rate of unemployment. (N.A.I.R.U).
Diagram 18.3 shows the short run and long run expectations augmented Phillips curves. In Diagram 10.3 P_1, P_2 and P_3 are short run Phillips curves, and U is the "natural" rate of unemployment i.e. frictional and structural. We assume that labour productivity does not grow so that price inflation equals the increase in wages or wage inflation. Now suppose the economy is initially at A in Diagram 10.3, unemployment is at U and the rate of increase of money and wages are zero. Workers expect inflation in the future to be zero since the current rate is zero.

If the government expands demand in order to reduce unemployment from U, it trades off along P_1 to say B. The cost of achieving U_1 appears to be an inflation rate of 3%. Friedman considers point B to be unstable and holds that it cannot be maintained in the long run. Workers will only supply labour beyond the "natural" rate if real wages go up which if it happens, makes employers demand less labour. Workers may suffer from money illusion thinking that a 3% rise in wages is also a real wage increase. He believed that workers and employers see through their money illusion. He argues that employment can only be sustained above it's "natural" level if inflation continuously accelerates to keep workers expectations of inflation from the previous period below the actual rate to which it has risen. As expectations change, P_1 moves to P_2 and then to P_3 and so on. These curves would move to the left if the expected rate of inflation falls.

According to Friedman unemployment can be kept below the "natural" rate in the long run if the government allows the inflation rate to accelerate through a continuing monetary expansion. This will in the end lead to hyper-inflation. Unemployment will go over the "natural" rate.

If the government now decides not to allow the money supply to grow by more than 3% per annum, thus not allowing accelerating inflation, it may succeed in keeping the rate of inflation at 3%. Money illusion will be recognised and employment will return to the "natural" rate. The economy can only return to zero inflation and unemployment at the "natural" rate, when the expected rate of inflation has fallen to zero.

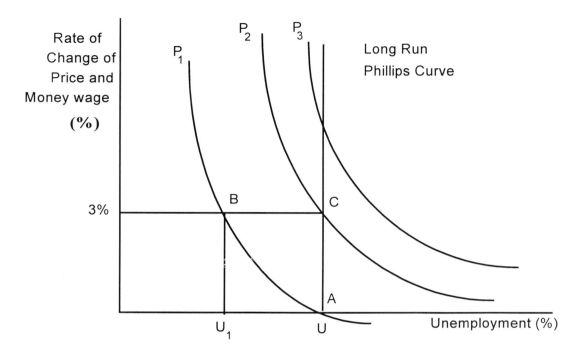

Diagram 18.3 Expectations Augmented Phillips Curves

The New Classical Position:

These economists have rejected the theory that expectations are based on past experience and argue that they are based on up to date information. They accept the concept of the "natural" rate of unemployment but do not accept the idea of money illusion, even in the short run. If the government seeks to reflate the economy, what it does, is anticipated by workers and firms and they modify their behaviour to offset the effects intended by it.

Friedman considered that a lengthy period is required to "bleed" the system of inflationary expectations. The New Classical School believe that if the government's stated intention is to reduce the rate of inflation, workers and firms will lower their expectations regarding wages and prices if they regard the governments intentions as credible. Inflation can be reduced without a great deal of suffering.

Effects of Inflation:

- **Effects on Income Distribution**

Inflation redistributes income among people in an arbitrary way so that there are winners and losers. Among the losers are those whose incomes are fixed or relatively fixed in money terms. This group includes incomes from fixed interest securities and some private pension schemes. All income recipients in this group will suffer a fall in their real incomes. Debtors and borrowers will gain by going into debt and repaying in money whose value has declined.

The lender loses out if the actual rate of inflation turns out to be higher than the expected rate built into contracts. Inflation can redistribute income way from the private sector and towards the government. If income tax allowances are fixed in money terms, inflation can raise tax revenue by pulling more people into higher tax brackets - a process of fiscal drag. Prices rise so that revenue from VAT increases, provided sales do not fall to offset the price increases.

- **Efficiency**

Demand-pull inflation is associated with buoyant business conditions and sellers markets. Pressure to improve the product and performance is less and can lead to inefficiency. The opposite is true in the case of cost-push inflation. Productivity must increase to absorb extra costs otherwise the firm may fail. The firm can reduce its labour force and thus contribute to unemployment. Demand inflation leads to increased investment and expansion. Since the value of money is falling, savings fall as people will spend more leaving less for investment.

- **International Trade and Competitiveness**

Economies dependent on international trade can encounter severe problems due to inflation. If domestic prices rise faster than those of overseas competitors, imports rise and exports fall, resulting in a balance of payments deficit and a rise in unemployment. Domestic industry becomes less competitive resulting in a fall in exports, employment and growth.

- **Repayment Tilt**

With inflation, repayments on nominal debt contracts, such as mortgages are highest at the start of the loan. This repayment tilt distorts the markets in which it works. A current example is the housing market where the perceived cost of houses increases with inflation.

- **Peoples Behaviour**

People and firms expect inflation and build it into their behaviour. They bring forward purchases and hoard if they expect inflation to accelerate. It can lead to a loss of confidence in money. Firms when unsure about long -term trends in inflation, find it difficult to carry out long-term planning. They may divert funds from productive investment in fixed capital into land, property, commodity hoarding and speculation.

- **Anticipated and Unanticipated Inflation**

The size and seriousness of the effects of inflation depend on whether it is anticipated or unanticipated. If it can be anticipated, we would expect people to be able to allow for it in the economic decisions they make. There would be few problems if inflation could be anticipated with certainty, but this is not so. Unanticipated inflation can cause serious and severe problems.

- **'Shoe Leather Costs'**
When inflation is greater than expected, people are forced to modify their behaviour and there will be little incentive to hold money. This results in more trips to the bank to withdraw

cash. The additional trips are known as 'shoe leather costs'. This loss of liquidity means that people are less able to take advantage of unexpected bargains.

- **'Menu' Costs**

During periods of inflation prices are rising and price lists and labels must be changed. The 'menu' costs of inflation refer to the resources required to change price lists when prices are rising or falling. The introduction of bar codes has reduced this cost.

- **Fiscal Drag**

This occurs when tax bands are not fully inflation adjusted. Workers who anticipate inflation seek higher wages and this moves them to higher tax brackets. Net income does not rise in line with gross income. Tax revenues received by the government increase even if the government does not change the rates of taxation.

Benefits of Inflation:

In times of rapid inflation real rates of interest are often negative. For example, if the nominal rate of interest is 10% and inflation is 15% then there is a negative real rate of interest of 5%, as inflation exceeds the nominal interest rate. Inflation thus acts as a hidden tax, redistributing wealth and income from lenders to borrowers, which for example benefits house buyers. The real value of the mortgage is gone down while the value of the property keeps rising.

Inflation tends to reduce the real burden of the national debt. However the cost of servicing the debt held by domestic lenders goes up as the Government may have to increase the rate of interest if it is to obtain new funds.

Inflation in Ireland:

The first Consumer Price Index was compiled in 1914 with a base of 100. After the 1914/18 war the index was 188. During the war period goods and services were scarce so that consumers had large cash balances. After the war when goods became available the surplus cash was spent and this brought about inflation, caused by excess demand.

By about 1921 production or output increased so that excess demand no longer existed and prices fell. They did not fall to the pre -1914 level. At this time wages were cut therefore demand was reduced. The downward trend continued up to 1935. After 1935 there was inflation and this grew over the period of World War II but in the period 1945/1950 the rate of inflation slowed down.

Between 1950/1955 inflation accelerated due to the Korean War, but it fell in the late 1950's when there was a period of depression and large-scale emigration.
In the 1960's increases in inflation were moderate (Table18.2), while the early 1970's saw rising inflation which was aggravated by the rise in oil prices in 1973/74. As shown in Table 18.2 inflation hit a high of 20.9% in 1975. This was due not only to the quadrupling of oil prices in 1973/74 but also to the fall of almost 25% in the exchange rate of the pound due to

the fall in the value of sterling at that time. This and the rise in the price of oil were classified as imported inflation.

Inflation fell in 1976, 1977 and by 1978 it was down to 7.6%. However, we were hit by a second oil crisis in 1979 and to counteract this crisis, the government financed the public sector deficit by monetary expansion. This drove the inflation rate back up over 20% in 1981. In the early 1980s inflation in the UK was lower than in Ireland. This was disappointing for us as we had blamed the UK for our high rate of inflation. The government found it easier to print money to spend than to raise taxes sufficiently to balance the budget.

Since 1984 the rate of inflation has been a single figure and even though it has varied, has been at relatively low levels in Ireland. This is due to a number of factors including reduction of monetary financing of the Exchequer deficit after 1987, agreed negotiated moderate pay increases and a slow down in domestic demand. Another factor in the late 1980's was the fall in the price of oil due to substitution of other forms of energy and the economical use of oil. Imported inflation due to Irelands link with sterling ceased in 1979 when we broke the link on joining the European Monetary System.

For 1993 the inflation rate was 1.5%, the second lowest in the EU and the lowest in Ireland since 1960. The reasons for this drop in the rate are the devaluation of the IR£ in January 1993 and the substantial decrease in mortgage interest rates. It was 1.7%, 1.5% and 2.4% in 1996, 1997 and 1998 respectively. The forecast shown in Table 18.2 for 1999 is 1.9%.

Table18.2
Irish Inflation 1968 to 1999

YEAR	RATE %	YEAR	RATE %	YEAR	RATE %
1968	4.8	1981	20.4	1994	2.4
1969	7.4	1982	17.1	1995	2.3
1970	8.2	1983	10.5	1996	1.7
1971	9.0	1984	8.6	1997	1.5
1972	8.6	1985	5.4	1998	2.4
1973	11.4	1986	3.8	1999*	1.9
1974	17.0	1987	3.2		
1975	20.9	1988	2.1		
1976	18.0	1989	4.1		
1977	13.6	1990	2.7		
1978	7.6	1991	3.5		
1979	13.2	1992	2.25		
1980	18.2	1993	1.5		

*Forecast

Source: CSO Statistical Bulletins Budgets

EMU and Inflation:

The ECB has set itself the medium term goal of a maximum annual increase of 2% in consumer prices. It must take action if the rate differs from the target. From Table 18.3 it can be seen that euro zone states did not have uniform rates of inflation even in the year of convergence. It is very unlikely that they be the same into the future as shown in Table 18.3.

In the case of Ireland if interest rates fall, it will further fuel house price inflation. If we have, inflation induced loss of competitiveness we will have to increase taxes and/or cut spending as we no longer have the option of depreciating our exchange rate to off set any loss in competitiveness.

Table 18.3
Inflation Rates in Selected Countries, 1997 to 2000

Country	Rate of Inflation (%)			
	1997	1998	1999e	2000f
Austria	2.0	1.1	1.3	1.5
Greece	2.5	2.3	2.1	2.1
Finland	1.5	1.5	1.6	1.9
Germany	1.8	1.0	1.1	1.5
Sweden	2.2	2.3	1.8	2.2
France	1.1	0.6	1.2	1.4
UK	2.6	2.0	2.2	2.0
Italy	2.5	2.2	2.0	1.9
Ireland	0.9	2.7	3.3	3.3
Belgium	1.6	1.1	1.4	1.5
Netherlands	2.0	2.2	2.3	2.3
Denmark	2.2	1.9	2.4	2.2
Spain	2.5	2.3	2.1	2.1
Portugal	2.5	2.6	2.4	2.1
E.U 15	2.1	1.6	1.7	1.8
EU 11	1.9	1.5	1.6	1.7
US	1.9	0.9	2.2	2.6
Japan	1.6	0.7	-0.2	0.4

e Estimate   f Forecast.
Central Bank Various Quarterly Reports

Questions

1. Explain what is meant by the quantity theory of money based on the identity MV=PT. Is there a relationship between the quantity of money and the price level?

2. Explain how the Consumer Price Index is constructed and assess its accuracy in measuring changes in the cost of living. What are the uses of the CPI?

3. " The Phillips curve is no longer a useful guide to economic policy". Discuss.

4. Distinguish between Demand-Pull and Cost-Push inflation.

5. Assess the effectiveness of prices and incomes policies.

6. Examine the monetarist view that "inflation is always and everywhere a monetary phenomenon".

7. What are the sources and effects of inflation in an open economy? What policy measures might be suggested to lower the rate of inflation in Ireland?

CHAPTER 19

GOVERNMENT AND THE ECONOMY

Introduction:

Governments everywhere adopted a policy of laissez-faire during the 19th century. Intervention took place only when absolutely necessary. Employment of women and young children was regulated and legislation to control monopolies and to provide essential services such as water and sewerage was introduced. The outbreak of World War I in 1914 forced governments to become involved in the management of their economies. Further pressure was added by the depression of the 1930's, and by the Second World War (1939 – 1945). After 1945, Great Britain's government was committed to a policy of full employment and in the same year, introduced a comprehensive social welfare scheme. Other governments followed along similar lines.

In this Chapter the objectives of macroeconomic policy are discussed, together with the instruments to achieve them. Direct intervention by the Irish government is examined and the arguments for and against state enterprise are assessed. Planning and social partnership are described. The Chapter concludes with an assessment as to what may be included in The National Development Plan 2000-2006.

Policies Requiring Government Intervention:

♦ **Social Policy;**

Social policy covers transfers of income and services to those who cannot provide them themselves. In advanced economies, this policy also covers education, health and housing. Expenditure in this area is usually very substantial and as such is an important influence on the economy.

♦ **Development of Infrastructure:**

Development of infrastructure covers transport, roads, railways, energy requirements, postal and telecommunication services, sewerage facilities, refuse collection and internal security. By providing the above, the state encourages economic activity and everyone is better off.

♦ **Macro-economic Objectives:**

The main aims of government economic policy are to achieve:

1. Full employment;
2. Economic growth;
3. Price stability;

4. Equilibrium in the Balance of Payments; and
5. Other objectives.

1. Full Employment:

Employment was discussed in Chapter 17. Full employment in term of GDP is a measure of the output that the economy is capable of producing when all its resources are employed. For labour it means that work is available for all those willing to work at existing wage rates. All, however, will not find work for reasons already outlined.

Unemployment is both a social and an economic problem and it represents a waste of resources and a permanent loss of output. It creates hardship for the dependants of the unemployed and damages the morale of those out of work. It can also lead to crime and general public disorder. There are, therefore, sound economic, social and political reasons for having full employment as a major objective of government policy.

As an economy approaches full employment, people previously under-employed in family businesses, including farms, seek employment since the family members are unable to increase productivity with the existing number employed. Married women currently not working may seek employment as well as older people who now see a chance of work, as the economy approaches full employment.

2. Economic Growth:

This has been defined as the long run tendency for GNP per capita to grow. A growing economy means that the standard of living is also growing with more goods and services for people to consume. There has been much criticism of the growth objective in many advanced countries. The argument is that growth creates social costs that outweigh the benefits to be gained. It continues, however, to be a major objective of economic policy since governments see it as the key to bringing material benefits to the millions who still experience poverty.

It is doubtful whether enough is yet known about the causes of growth so that governments are handicapped in their efforts to determine the conditions required so as to achieve a given growth rate.

The government attempts to achieve this objective by:

- Adopting fiscal policies that encourage private enterprise e.g. low -rate of tax on company profits.

- Providing the economic infrastructure suited to the establishment and expansion of private and public enterprise.

- Promoting industry by way of grants for fixed assets, training and export promotion; provision of industrial estates; and technology transfer.

- The provision of semi-state companies e.g. IDA Ireland, Agricultural Credit Corporation (ACC) and many others.

3. Price Stability:

The maintenance of a stable price level has been and still is a major objective of government policy in all countries. Price stability refers to the general price level as measured by some price index such as the Harmonised Index of Consumer Prices (HICP) introduced by all EU member states in January 1997. It does not mean that prices remain absolutely stable. Prices are, however, generally inflexible in a downward direction so that changes in supply and demand usually mean a gradual increase in the price level. The objective is to keep the annual level of price increase to some moderate level or average percentage. The ECB has set a level of 0 to 2% increase in consumer prices per annum.

Governments seek to control inflation for the following reasons:

- There is a loss of competitiveness in international trade if a country's rate of inflation is greater than that of its competitors. As a result, it is difficult for it to sell its exports, while at the same time, imports outsell domestic products on its home market.

- If, as a result of inflation, production costs are high, foreign industrialists will be discouraged from investing in the country.

- Persistent inflation may result in the toleration of inefficiency. In periods of high demand, prices obtainable are high and they cover the costs of inefficient firms thereby keeping them in business. When there is a shortage of skilled workers, inefficient and less productive operatives may be employed. This will affect all workers as inefficient work practices become established and these have a tendency to remain even when the particular shortage has passed.

- People will expect inflation to keep on increasing and they will spend rather than save.

4. Equilibrium in the Balance of Payments:

This does not mean that the target is an exact balance of receipts and expenditure on foreign account. Governments must aim at a current balance or small surplus in the long run. A persistent deficit will lead to the exhaustion of a country's reserves as will its ability to obtain short-term loans and it would require crisis economic measures which would disrupt the smooth running of the economy. A persistent surplus means sending abroad resources greater in value than is being imported which is not a good idea either.

The Irish economy is an open economy as for example, in 1997 imports were 81.6% and exports 83.5 % of GNP. It is important, therefore, to have equilibrium in the Balance of Payments. The necessity to remain competitive imposes a discipline on the management of the economy. This is referred to as "The Balance of Payments Constraint".

5. **Other Objectives**:

• **Improvement of Conditions in Particular Regions:**

This is a major objective of most governments, as development tends to be uneven internally. Areas that are not well endowed economically receive more assistance. There are, of course, strong social grounds for such a policy.
The aims of regional policy, if achieved, assist in the achievement of overall aims of:

• Economic growth - when economic activity is more evenly spread around the country, it leads to greater efficiency.

• Full employment- a large proportion of total unemployment is due to regional unemployment.

• **Reducing Inequalities in the Distribution of Wealth and Income:**

The use of the taxation system is one way of achieving this aim. Provision of a wide range of social services is also a means to this end. Many regard this as a social rather than an economic objective.

• **Improving the Allocation of Resources:**

 - The government can set up a number of institutions to promote competition and industrial re-organisation as a means of getting a more efficient utilisation of resources.

 - How much of the National Income should be at the disposal of private citizens? This is a question of optimum allocation of resources.

 - To influence resource allocation, the state uses public funds and instruments of fiscal policy such as taxes, grants and subsidies to influence the structure, performance and location of privately owned industry. It can also go into business for itself.

 - Government must assist in the socially desirable allocation of resources. This includes agricultural and industrial policies.

Interaction between Objectives of National Economic Policy:

Most would agree on the necessity of achieving the objectives already discussed. There may, however, be some disagreement as to priorities. Some of the objectives may be compatible with each other in which case they can be achieved at the same time and the achievement of one will help to achieve the other (and vice versa). Some of the objectives may be incompatible with others in that they are difficult to achieve at the same time. Achieving one will mean the sacrifice of the other (and vice versa).

Some examples of compatibility and incompatibility are now discussed:

Compatibility:

- Compatibility between the objective of 'full employment' and 'economic growth'.

The economy operates at full capacity in a situation of full employment. Demand for firms' products exceed supply and they increase productive capacity through increased investment in order to meet the demand. As a result, output increases and there is economic growth.

Due to this growth, there is optimism among business people and it is a sign that the economy is healthy. New jobs will be created and even though some are lost due to declining sectors, there will be a net increase. The circular flow of income will be increased by injections of investment spending. This will assist in maintaining a high level of total expenditure in the economy and full employment will be maintained.

- Compatibility between the objectives of 'balance of payments equilibrium' and 'price stability'.

When prices are stable, a country's exports become more competitive and this improves the balance of payments. This is particularly so if other countries or trading partners are experiencing inflation or at least a higher rate than the home country. Export earnings increase and there is greater ability to purchase capital goods that will further increase exports and these will have a cumulative effect.

Incompatibility:

- **Incompatibility between the objective of 'full employment' and 'balance of payments equilibrium'.**

Policies that are designed to achieve an increase in employment will increase demand and part of this increased demand will be for imported consumer goods. If the price of domestic goods increases, demand for imported consumer goods will result in a balance of payments deficit. An increase in industrial activity will bring about an increase in demand for imported raw materials and machinery and this will, at least in the short run, put stress on the balance of payments. There is a possibility that, in the long run, it may lead to an increase in exports and/or a reduction in imports.

- **Incompatibility between the objectives of 'full employment' and 'price stability'.**

Policies pursued to stimulate the economy may result in buoyancy in demand that will result in an increase in the general price level. As total spending is increased to achieve full employment, prices are 'pulled up' i.e. there is demand-pull inflation. When the full employment level is reached, labour in general and some skills in particular become scarce and wages are bid up resulting in higher prices. Other factors that may contribute to rising costs of production are increases in the price of materials and capital goods. The choice is between high employment and high prices or low employment and low prices.

- **Incompatibility between the objectives of 'economic growth' and 'balance of payments equilibrium'.**

When an economy is growing rapidly, imports of raw materials, intermediate goods and consumer goods also grow rapidly. This leads, in the short run, to deterioration in the balance of payments, as exports do not keep pace with imports, even though they may increase in the long run.

- **Incompatibility of 'economic growth' and 'redistribution of national income'.**

The redistribution of national income in favour of the economically disadvantaged requires a transfer from those who are economically most productive. To obtain the resources required to give effect to the transfer, businesses and individuals must be taxed. This is a disincentive to effort and, as such, will tend to reduce the pace of economic development.

- **Incompatibility of 'balanced regional development' and 'economic growth'.**

Firms will be reluctant to locate in areas of a country that will put them at a cost disadvantage as these areas are economically sub- optimal for them. A firm locating in such an area will suffer from increased cost of production and as a result, it will be unable to compete. Governments must compensate for this by way of additional grants.

Having sorted out the matter of objectives and their mutual consistency or otherwise, policy makers can choose specific policy instruments.

Instruments of Macro-Economic Policy:

The means by which a government attempts to achieve its objectives are referred to as tools or instruments of macroeconomic policy. These instruments are as follows:

- **Monetary Policy** Generally this refers to action that influences the quantity of money in circulation, the availability of credit or the level of interest rates. This was discussed in Chapter 12. The European Central Bank now decides on monetary policy for Ireland.

- **Fiscal Policy** is defined as the deliberate use of government income and expenditure as an active instrument of economic policy. The major instrument is the budget. Fiscal systems may have built-in stabilisers. Fiscal measures were discussed in Chapter 14. It is now a very important instrument of economic policy as it is under the control of the Irish government.

- **Exchange Rate Policy** refers to government action that influences the external value of a country's currency. The movement from fixed to floating rates has meant that the management (or non-management) of the exchange rate has become an important feature of government policy. This topic was discussed in Chapter16.

- **Direct Controls** The difference between this instrument and others is that it seeks to reach the objective by controlling the economic variables directly whereas other instruments seek to influence the way the variables behave. Examples are statutory control of prices and incomes; control over the level of imports by means of quotas or rationing of foreign exchange; grants used to influence the location of industry; rationing of foodstuffs and petrol in wartime.

- **Institutional Changes** - economic policy can be achieved by the establishment of specialised institutions so as to achieve particular objectives.

Nationalisation is an example of institutional change although it may be used for non-economic as well as economic reasons.

How All Objectives can be Simultaneously Achieved:

Achieving one objective helps to achieve the others as follows:

- Full employment promotes economic growth by stimulating investment.

- Economic growth i.e. increased productivity absorbs wage increases so that costs do not rise and inflation is kept down.

- Price stability helps the balance of payments.

- Economic growth improves the quality of exports and in the long run, this improves the balance of payments position.

- A stable balance of payments brings about good economic growth; and

- Together good economic growth and healthy balance of payments maintain full employment.

West Germany achieved all objectives simultaneously. However, many governments are unable to do so and this is difficult to explain. It may be due in part to inadequacy of the analysis of the working of the economic system.

Policy Problems:

One of the most debated issues is the apparent conflict between the objectives of price stability and full employment. The possibility of a trade-off between inflation and unemployment has arisen. If there is an inverse relationship between movements in the rate of unemployment and movements in the general price level, what level of inflation is acceptable while, at the same time, maintaining full employment? Five per cent inflation may be an acceptable rate if unemployment is kept below say 4 per cent. The problem is that this rate of inflation may cause imports to exceed exports and therefore, result in balance of payments difficulties.

Policies with regard to balance of payments encounter many difficulties. When demand in the domestic market is reduced, in order to reduce imports, the result may be an increase in unemployment and a check on economic growth. Protective measures such as tariffs and quotas will bring about a reduction in exports due to retaliatory measures by trading partners.

An effort to speed up the rate of economic growth may result in an accumulation of stocks. Growth depends on increased productivity and efficiency. These require incentives to bring them about but by providing them, inequality in the distribution of income may be increased.

Choice between Conflicting Objectives:

A choice must be made and the concept of opportunity cost can be applied. This means that the cost of pursuing one goal is failure to achieve the other. Here we examine the conflict that exists between achieving full employment and reducing inflation. When a policy of monetary restraint is in force, unemployment tends to increase.

If inflation is given priority business people will have more confidence; interest rates will be lower; people on fixed incomes will suffer less and overall, the economy will be expanding.

The costs of giving priority to reducing inflation are higher unemployment; economic recession resulting in business failures; high interest rates which damage business confidence and reduce investment and loss of markets to foreign competitors.

As shown by this example, it is difficult to decide which policy should be given priority. The same concept of opportunity cost can be used for any scheme of government expenditure.

Reasons for the Economic Role of Government:

Intervention has in the past taken place on the basis that there are deficiencies in the operation of a free enterprise laissez-faire economy and that the government must itself remedy these deficiencies.

Some of the reasons for intervention are as follows-

- Certain goods and services, required by the community as a whole, must be provided by the state since they cannot be charged to any one individual. These include defence, street lighting and many other services and they are financed out of taxation.

- There are certain goods and services which constitute an important element in the production process of all firms so that any deficiency in the quality, availability or cost competitiveness of these goods and services e.g. transport communication and electricity would put an unacceptable burden on many firms. The government is expected to provide them as part of the country's infrastructure.

- Competition may be reduced by the emergence of large firms with a degree of monopoly power and it is the obligation of the government to promote competition and to look after the interests of the consumer.

- There are certain costs and benefits which are external to the firm in the sense that they do not appear in the costs incurred or revenues received by the firm. Private enterprise will usually ignore such costs (e.g. pollution) and they will be unable to charge for the benefits (e.g. the amenity provided when an attractive building replaces a derelict property). Semi-state bodies will be under strong social and political pressures to take account of these externalities. Railways operate unremunerative lines because if they did not do so, certain communities would be isolated.

- Organisations within the public sector may have access to funds from international sources such as the EU and the World Bank which private enterprise does not since it hasn't got government financial backing. Moreover the public sector may secure finance at more competitive rates.
- Government helps to manage the economy. Nationalised industries can be used to subsidise employment during a recession or depression. Their investment programmes might be increased to produce multiplier effects during a depression and slowed down during a boom in order to reduce aggregate demand. Government may require semi-state bodies to hold prices down in order to slow down the rate of inflation. This may mean difficulties for government in its efforts to carry out long-term planning.

- It is argued that workers will enjoy better working conditions due to the fact that the state is the employer and not a company out for its own profits and this will have a psychological benefit resulting in increased worker productivity.

Direct Intervention in the Economy:

In a mixed economy like Ireland, direct intervention is an important government control. Direct intervention can be carried out in any of the following ways:

- **Legislation**

Laws are there to prohibit certain activities and are sometimes used to ban or limit the importation of particular goods with the aim of protecting home industry. Legislation is there to control companies, competition and to protect the consumer and the environment. The government will, from time to time, introduce such legislation as it sees fit to control economic activity in the public interest.

- **Tariffs and Subsidies**

By imposing tariffs, imported goods become more expensive and less attractive to consumers. Tariffs can be used to protect home produced goods until they become established on the market.

A subsidy exists when the government makes a contribution to the costs of production. It may be related to the number of units produced or can be a lump sum. Its main aim is to encourage production of goods where such production is considered to be socially desirable though it may not be economically viable.

- **Nationalised or Semi -State Bodies**

In a few cases such as the Post Office, the state is directly involved through a Government Department. Most state involvement is by way of statutory corporations set up by acts of the Oireachtas. The relevant minister holds practically all the shares. State ownership is often advocated on political grounds but this wasn't the case in Ireland where nationalisation was done in the belief that to do so would promote economic development. State involvement has been at the expense of the private sector and the latter would find it difficult to enter the relevant markets now. This is due to the dominance of the state- sponsored company in the market place. In areas like broadcasting with the exception now of local radio, the state has protected its position by means of legislation. In other areas like transport the state has crowded out other firms by providing a service at below cost.

Semi -state bodies are to be found in almost every sector- transport, industry, energy, banking, tourism, communications and others. They account for almost 10 per cent of GNP. Irish Governments over the years have set up a substantial number of bodies to provide service for the public. Direct intervention is substantial and occurs when:

- The government engages directly in trading for example through Bord na Mona to exploit the bogs and The Electricity Supply Board (ESB);

- When through its agencies it offers incentives to the private sector by way of grants, advice and encouragement. Examples here are the IDA, Forbairt, Irish Tourist Board, Agricultural Credit Corporation and many more;

- The main objective is to bring about a self reliant and self sustaining economy in the long run.

Arguments for State Enterprise:

- Overall control of the economy is possible with state control e.g. in the past the ESB could be told to postpone or reduce price increases to help in the control of inflation.

- To ensure the supply of goods and services which could not be provided by private enterprise. Again electricity is a good example.

- Some industries are not as efficient when structured as competitive markets as they would be when monopolised under state ownership e.g. the supply of electricity and public transport. Waste is eliminated which occurs when there is more than one supplier and fixed investment is high e.g. ESB network of poles

- State corporations may have an advantage over private enterprise in risk taking because the risk is spread over the whole economy rather than it being concentrated in the hands of a few. It may have an advantage in risk taking, decision making and innovation because of better access to information that makes its calculations more accurate.

- Nationalisation allows the state to control monopoly power. In areas like electricity and water supply, monopoly is inevitable because any other market form would be impractical and duplication would result in waste.

- Industries such as railways require large amounts of capital to set them up. Private industry will be unwilling to become involved even if the required finance could be raised. If Iarnrod Eireann was in private hands it would probably close some of the lines and this would be against the national interest.

- Politically socialist parties prefer the nationalised approach in the belief that the people have control.

- Waste will occur when there is high fixed investment unless there is a monopoly. Even if there is competition in say electricity, the second company would have to be limited to new consumers and there are few of these in any particular year. Due to very large economies of scale in electricity generation the optimum number of stations is unlikely to be sufficient for competition. This is very true in the case of Ireland and when electricity was introduced in the 1920's the government alone was able to take advantage of these economies of scale.

Arguments against State Enterprise:

- A public monopoly is as bad as a private monopoly, since it may incur losses through increasing prices rather than through cost reducing efficiencies.

- Profit constitutes a target for firms and a measurement of their efficiency. For state sponsored bodies, the profit motive is absent and there is less incentive to improve product, quality and service. There is little incentive to operate in the most efficient manner possible.

- Semi -state bodies are accountable to the public and their directors may adopt a very conservative approach to risk taking.

- People appointed as directors and chief executives may not have the required ability or knowledge to run an organisation of this nature.

- The Boards of the semi state bodies may be subject to pressure groups who wish them to undertake non-economic activities.

- The operations of these bodies may be made more difficult due to government intervention in their day-to-day business.

Control of State -Sponsored Bodies:

The following are ways in which the relevant minister exercises control:

- the minister sets policy;

- directors are appointed by the government;

- annual accounts must be presented to the Minister and these and other matters can be debated in the Dail;

- any state body can be investigated by the Oireachtas Joint Committee and findings can be published.

Privatisation:

Privatisation means the sale of shares in previously nationalised enterprises to the public. Irish Life, Irish Sugar Company, B and I and Irish Steel were privatised. Shares were eagerly sought and these are now public limited companies quoted on the Stock Exchange. These sales yielded just over £640mn for the exchequer. It means a reduction of the role of the state and an expansion in the private sector.

Arguments for Privatisation:

- When a company is privatised it is exposed to market forces and this should lead to greater efficiency, growth and service to consumers. If for example the ESB or Telecom Eireann were privatised but only after they are split into competing parts, supernormal profits will be competed down. Separate parts will have to keep costs at a minimum to stay in business.

- Another benefit may arise from a reduction in the ability of trade unions to obtain wage increases unrelated to productivity improvements.

- Some companies like Aer Lingus are already competing with RyanAir but are still helped by government subsidies. If there is deregulation i.e. when the government removes barriers to competition such as licences, the consumer will gain from competition.

- When privatised, the company must obtain capital for investment purposes and must issue shares or borrow from the banks or other financial institutions. Criteria are stringent and it must show that it will make profitable use of the funds if obtains. It promotes a positive attitude to business, risk taking and the enterprise culture.

- Shareholders will insist on an adequate return and if this is not obtained they will sell their shares. As a result the share price will drop and the company may be taken over or go out of business.

- Borrowing by semi-state bodies is part of the Public Sector Borrowing Requirement (PSBR). Privatisation brings in funds so that government can reduce P.S.B.R. This allows the government to reduce taxation and also to keep inflation down.

- When a company is in state control the minister is the shareholder. Even though the public owns these companies, people generally do not think of it in this way and show little interest in them. When privatised the owners show a great deal of interest.

- Management can be paid at a level comparable to other private companies whereas in semi state companies they are paid considerably less. They can therefore attract high calibre people and retain them.

- Privatisation means that there is no chance of political influence determining policies.

- Capital markets can be built up and developed so that there is scope for further growth, lack of which is causing domestic capital to go abroad.

Arguments against privatisation:

- The argument for market forces breaks down if a private monopoly replaces a public one. When nationalised the company doesn't seek to maximize profits. Since a monopoly can maximise profits being private does not necessarily mean it is more efficient. The argument then is will the private company be afraid of going out of business and the answer is no because it can raise prices. Some of these monopolies may close down unprofitable sections of the business if privatised, while if they are semi-state bodies the relevant minister is reluctant to do so for political reasons. While this was the case in Ireland, the position has now changed and as shown in the case of the former Sugar Company, the Tuam and Thurles factories were closed down as was Irish Shipping. There are of course social reasons for providing some services such as bus and rail as some areas would not have a service if private enterprise alone was involved.

- Even though regulations are made they can be insufficient to prevent the abuse of monopoly power. These include:

- Regulations built into legislation such as constraints on pricing policy. Government can retain a "golden share", as is the case in Ireland.
- A regulatory agency can be established to monitor the business of the company and to regulate policy if required.

- The existing methods and agency to control monopolies can be used.

Even though PSBR and Debt/GNP ratio are reduced due to privatisation there are a number of problems:

- Profits from semi state bodies go towards reducing PSBR and many of them earn profits contrary to common belief that they do not. Once these are privatised there is no further profit therefore there is no contribution to the exchequer.

- Semi-state bodies can be used to promote economic development. If the industries use local raw materials the following benefits occur:

- Goods can be produced at lower cost due to lower transport costs and can compete with imports.

- Imports can be reduced thereby improving the balance of payments.

- The use of local materials increases the effect of the domestic multiplier on expenditure on the products of the industry.

- The price of the shares may be too low or shares may not be taken up. In the former case future sales will only command this price and in the latter it will be very difficult to sell the next nationalised industry.

- People already own shares in nationalised industries therefore they buy their own shares. However the number of shareholders after privatisation is very small considering that all the people of the country were shareholders when the industry was nationalised.

Economic Planning:

Economic planning is the defining of future objectives and showing how they are to be achieved. The following are a number of conditions of economic planning:

- It must be active in the sense that it is broken down to individual or product level so that people trying to achieve targets have a hand in setting them;

- When different groups are involved in the planning process, their representatives must ensure that they communicate the details to their colleagues;

- All areas of the public sector must be involved and play their part;

- Government grants and other incentive schemes must be continuously monitored to ensure that they are serving their purpose in implementing the plan;

- There must be good communications between the public and private sector;

- Trade unions have a part to play at individual firm level as they can exert pressure on management to strive for more growth in the interest of employers and employees;

- Consultations must take place at individual firm level.

Indicative Planning:

Indicative planning is a voluntary system of planning practised in many western countries. It involves meetings of a wide range of interests in the economy. It was first introduced in Ireland in the late 1950's with the First Programme for Economic Expansion. It is a form of national economic planning in which a target is set for the growth of national output over a number of years, usually five.

Quantitative estimates are made as to what might happen to particular industries and sectors of the economy if global expansion is achieved. The figures are accompanied by a list of policy measures intended to help achieve what is planned. The figures are an "indication" of how the economy might develop. The policy measures can include incentives or disincentives to push the economy in the desired or required direction. Policies are not however tied to the targets of the plan and there is no method of enforcement of sanctions against firms or industries failing to achieve the targeted output.

Planning in Ireland:

First Programme for Economic Expansion (1958 - 1963):

This was published in 1958 and outlined the objectives of economic policy in agriculture, industry and other main sectors of activity. It dealt with the role of the state in promoting economic development by investment and indirectly by way of grants, loans and other incentives to the private sector. Additional resources were directed towards agriculture and industry and away from hospitals, public housing and other social type services. A target of an 11 % growth in the volume of GNP was set over the period 1959-1963 but 23% was achieved.

A number of guidelines were given:

- Agriculture was to provide the impetus to growth;

- Income tax was reduced because of the adverse effect of high income tax on savings and enterprise. The overall burden of tax was not eased;

- Salaries and wages were to stay behind those in the U.K; and

- To stimulate public and private enterprise.

Overall dependency on agriculture was emphasised as was the need to increase productivity.

Few of the recommendations were implemented but it did involve a greater number of people in talking about economics and the economic performance of the country. Agriculture did not prosper. Industry led in the area of growth and there were large inflows of capital due partly to the dismantling of trade barriers.

Second Programme for Economic Expansion (1964 - 1970):

Complete methodological structures were used. It forecast a 4% increase per annum in real GNP and it had the following characteristics: -

- To raise the real income of the community by 50% in the 1960's to bring it up to the OECD target level;

- To reduce involuntary emigration so that by 1970, net yearly emigration would be 10,000 at most;

- Special attention was to be given to education and other types of 'human investment'; and

- To give increased aid to developing countries.

It was based on the assumption that Ireland would be a member of the EU by 1970. Targets set for the Second Programme proved to be unrealistically high but at the same time it helped achieve the growth obtained over the period. This was perhaps a period when economic growth in Europe was high and Ireland gained due to the fact that she had become more outward looking, particularly with regard to foreign trade and investment.

Third Programme for Economic Expansion:(1969-1972):

This programme also forecast a growth rate of 4% per annum. The main aims of the Programme were:

- To bring about a sustainable increase in employment;

- To seek the highest growth possible having regard to its effect on future prospects. The rate of growth taken was four per cent; and

- Arrangements were made to adjust the programme if necessary.

This plan was very detailed and input - output models used were not appropriate at the time. Targets were not achievable from an early date in the Programme and this was especially true of targets for employment.

Like the Second Programme, the Third was carried along by the developments taking place in other economies. It perhaps helped but was not essentially the cause of any growth that took place. Confidence in Irish planning was dented due to the unrealistic and unrealisable targets set.

National Development Plan 1977 -1980:

A Department of Economic Planning and Development was established in 1977 and the National Development Plan 1977 –1980 was introduced. It set targets for growth in employment and output.

The national aims were outlined as follows:

- to increase employment;
- to curb the rate of inflation;
- resume growth in living standards while maintaining competitiveness;
- to extend the productive base of the economy;
- to promote efficiency in the economic system; and
- to give priority to areas of social concern.

For a number of years prior to 1977 the Irish economy had lost momentum, employment had fallen; living standards had either fallen or remained as they were; private sector investment had been reduced; and inflation was higher than in any post war period. Wage rates had risen sharply as people sought to maintain their real incomes. Recession was hitting hard as a result of the oil crisis of 1973.

In its pre-election manifesto the government had set out its strategy that included immediate action to increase employment and output and to curb inflation. It also indicated the policy measures it would use to bring about faster growth. The public sector was to give the initial boost to the economy.

This necessitated increased public expenditure and employment in the public sector, which subsequently proved to be a very heavy burden on the economy. Targets again were unrealistic especially when the second oil crisis occurred in 1979.

The Way Forward (1982):

This was a Manifesto from Fianna Fail covering the years 1983 to 1987 and its main objectives were as follows:

- to halt and reverse the rising trend in unemployment;

- to lower inflation and interest rates to improve competitiveness;

- to improve social equity in society by reducing unemployment;

- to protect the living standards of those on social welfare;

- by promoting equity in taxation to reduce the burden on the PAYE group;

- to reduce Exchequer borrowing progressively to ensure ability to repay;

- elimination of current budget deficit by 1986;

- create an economic environment conducive to private investment; and

- to bring the balance of payments under control by increasing exports.

It was never implemented as Fianna Fail didn't form the government as a coalition of Fine Gael and Labour did so.

Building On Reality (1985 - 1987):

This Plan came in three stages:

1. Report of the Committee on Costs and Competitiveness that pointed to the severe decline in international competitiveness;

2. White Paper on Industrial Policy (1984);

3. Proposals for Plan (1984 -1987) which was to form the basis for Building on Reality and gave 241 recommendations covering economic and social policy was published.

One of the main recommendations was the need to cut public sector borrowing by cutting expenditure.

The Plan itself addressed such problems as unemployment, public sector deficits and the balance of payments. Compared to previous plans this one made no extravagant promises. Projections however were too optimistic and public finances continued to deteriorate up to 1987.

Overall it was seen as a political document and it did little to tackle inherited problems such as the large -scale state involvement in the economy and the level of state indebtedness by that time had reached crisis proportions.

Programme for National Recovery (1987 -1990):

This was a Programme put forward by the minority Fianna Fail government formed in 1987. It included a detailed pay agreement for the public and private sectors. By 1987 the magnitude of the debt/GNP ratio and the fiscal imbalance was so large that immediate action was needed to reduce them. It was successful in adhering to the 2.5 per cent annual wage increase for the three- year period, helped by low inflation rates over the period.

Programme for Economic and Social Progress (PESP) 1991 to 1994:

The main objectives were:

- sustained economic growth to narrow the gap in living standards between Ireland and the rest of Europe;

- a substantial increase in employment; and

- a major assault on long term unemployment.

Policy Aims:

- The aim of fiscal policy was to reduce the debt/GNP ratio to 100% by 1993. This would have been achieved except for the currency crisis and devaluation in January 1993;

- Monetary policy was to keep interest rates low. Towards the end of the period they were low but they were high at other times;

- Exchange rates were to be kept stable but again, the currency crisis and the collapse of the ERM 1993 complicated things; and
- Structural policies were aimed at increasing competition in both sheltered and exposed markets.

Fianna Fail and Labour Programme for Government (1993):

The parties agreed to a Programme in January 1993 and some of the main points are as follows: -

- Three new Government departments- Enterprise and Employment; Tourism and Trade; and Equality- were established;

- Exchequer Borrowing Requirement to be held at 3% of GNP;

- Creation of a State bank through the merger of ACC, ICC and Trustee Savings Bank and also involving An Post;

- A national economic and social forum to tackle unemployment;

- tourism plan for 35,000 extra jobs over five years;

- Development of the Food Industry;

- Modernisation and expansion of the Irish fishing fleet;

- New laws on employment equality;
- A £270 million jobs fund increased to £750 million in 3 years to help create 30,000 new jobs each year;

- The commercial future of Air Lingus secured or guaranteed; and

- Four light rail lines and 10 quality bus corridors in Dublin.

Programme for Competitiveness and Work (1994-1996):

Employers, trade unions and government agreed to adhere to a 8.24% change in nominal wages over a three year period.

National Development Plan (1994 -1999):

This Plan was launched on August 11th 1993 after very extensive consultation with all interested parties. It was the most ambitious Plan ever proposed and its main thrust was one of creating 200,000 gross jobs over the period of the Plan and to put 1.2 million people into education and training programmes. Employment was the cornerstone and if the Plan was to work, pay and related conditions could only improve in a way that facilitated a progressive and sustained improvement in Ireland's competitiveness. This was achieved under the Programme for Competitiveness and Work and Partnership 2000. A real growth rate of 3.5% per annum was forecast but it turned out to be much higher.

Core Elements in the Plan:

Basically there were four core elements in the Plan:

1. Investment in the growth potential of the economy i.e. in industry, agriculture, natural resources and tourism;

2. Investment in transport, transport infrastruture and the environment;

3. Local development initiatives; and

4. Education and training to help Irish business to be more competitive and to attract industry.

Finance for the Plan came from the EU under the Community Support Programme. These funds have helped Ireland to strengthen its infrastructure and to increase employment.

Partnership 2000 (1997-1999):

The primary aim of this programme is to secure and to strengthen the economy's capacity for sustainable employment and economic growth. It is based on acceptance by all its' participants of the following:

- A commitment to a reduction in the tax burden;
- Moderate wage increases in the context of low inflation with a strong focus on competitiveness;
- A commitment to improved social measures to tackle long- term unemployment and social exclusion.
- Agreement on the management of the public finances including a slow down in the rate of increase in current public spending.

The National Development Plan 2000 – 2006:

Ireland is now in the process of compiling this Plan with the intention of submitting it to the EU in the summer of 1999 for its consideration. Separate Community Support Frameworks are expected to be agreed for the BMW(13) counties as well as the Southern and Eastern regions.

ESRI Report "National Investment Priorities 1999"

The Government commissioned the ESRI to study investment requirements and to identify priorities. The latter include areas such as roads, public housing, education and training, public transport and research and development. Its Report entitled 'National Investment Priorities' was submitted to the Government. This incorporated and evaluated inputs from many sources including state agencies, government departments and the social partners. What follows is a summary of the main recommendations contained in it.

A Plan to concentrate investment in certain key centres is suggested as the long-term strategy for promoting balanced regional development. For the economy to reach its potential of 5% growth per annum to 2006, the poor state of infrastructure must be addressed. The boom will continue with average economic growth of 5 per cent per annum provided the government puts £47bn into what the ESRI describes as our crumbling infrastructure.

It suggests Cork, Limerick (including Ennis/Shannon), Galway, and Waterford with a Derry/Letterkenny hub as target areas. They also suggest a second-tier of local development hubs. It calls this a "nodal" strategy that it says is better than letting development radiate out from the major centres like Dublin or a "scatter gun" approach trying to invest everywhere.

- **Industry**

Industry including tourism, it states, no longer need government grants or tax breaks. Cost per job in tourism is £30,000 and the Report recommends the phasing out of tax relief and other financial assistance to the sector. A tourism-marketing fund is recommended and it should be funded from EU and domestic sources. To obtain EU funding in this area, it will be necessary to place an emphasis on the need to help the long- term unemployed, early school leavers and women returning to the labour force. Supports for indigenous industry capacity and expansion programmes that are oversubscribed are too generous. It backs a major cut back of grants except for less developed areas. The programme for inward investment measures aimed at helping fixed asset development and employment grants are heavily oversubscribed. There should however be a general phasing out of industrial grants in the case of the less developed areas.

Support for the tradeable sector should be limited to measures that overcome identifiable market failures. It recommends that an equity fund be established by the development agencies. The fund should invest in ordinary equity solely in 'seed' and early stage projects. A special programme for regional development for the three least developed regions should be included in the next Plan. Job creation should not be the explicit criterion. The telecommunications and energy industries, it suggests, can be left to the private sector. It recommends more spending on small farms and on those on lower incomes. It feels that the government will get little more return from investment in the fishing industry but should further develop angling.

- **Research and Development**

The ESRI holds that spending on research and development is the key to economic growth but Ireland has lagged behind other counties in this respect. There is a case for significantly increasing the level of public funding for research and development. It recommends that there should be one programme with separate budgets for applied and basic research.

- **Education**

The Report suggests that education should get £6.5bn of spending over the period. £770mn of this should be spent on helping the long-term unemployed.

Western Development Commission (WDC):

The WDC a statutory body published its Plan to develop the west – the seven western counties from Clare to Donegal -on the 26th April 1999. Funding should come from the EU and the Exchequer and amount to £3.7 billion up to 2006. It highlights the failure of the IDA to attract industry into this region and states that if its Plan is implemented it will bring about sustainable economic development of the region.

In the 1997/1998 period, according to the Plan, only 12 out of a total of 102 IDA backed projects were located in the region. Of the 24,000 jobs created nationally, only 6.6% were in the region. It suggests that industrial development incentives should be used to attract small foreign and indigenous industries to locate in small urban centres. " This should be achieved by a significant restriction on incentives offered to such firms in the major centres of population," it states.

The Report gives detailed economic data on a county- by –county basis and deals with all the major sectors of the economy. While it does not put forward any radical proposals for the marine sector it does emphasise the potential of fish processing and fish farming.

Bord Iascaigh Mhara (BIM) Plan:

BIM carried out a study of the marine sector published in March 1999 and it argues that a doubling of EU and state expenditure on the marine sector would yield a 20 per cent increase in jobs over the next seven years. The marine sector receives only 1% of EU structural funds.

The BIM plan puts forward nine development programmes that depend on £154 million in EU investment support.

The Irish Business and Employers Confederation (IBEC):

In 1998 IBEC made a submission to the Government in which it identified a £14 billion "infrastructural deficit" and gave its removal as the national priority. It states that all of the Cohesion Funds and 60% of the European Regional Development Funds should be spent on improving infrastructure. In April 1999 IBEC together with the Construction Industry Federation (CIF) presented a report to the Government in which it called on it to speed up spending on infrastructure in order to bring the State up to international standards by 2006. They want the Government to join with private enterprise for carrying out vital projects e.g. the Eastern link bridge in Dublin.

Questions

1. Identify the main objectives of government economic policy and discuss the interaction between them.

2. Is it possible to reconcile the objectives of economic policy? To what extent has this been achieved in Ireland?

3. Discuss the objectives of national economic policy. To which objective would you give priority at present and how would you attempt to achieve it?

4. "State involvement in our affairs is necessary for the overall public good, but privatisation can provide the state with significant benefits." Examine the relevance of privatisation in to-day's economic climate.

5. Discuss indicative planning outlining the advantages claimed by supporters and disadvantages claimed by opponents.

6. Describe the advantages and disadvantages of privatisation.

CHAPTER 20

ECONOMIC GROWTH AND DEVELOPMENT

Introduction:

In Chapter 20 we explore the theory of economic growth and examine government policies to promote it. Irelands growth performance since the 1950s is assessed as is the outlook for the future. Irish and EU regional policies are outlined and the impact of Agenda 2000 on Ireland is discussed. The main characteristics of developing countries are examined. Various theories of development are then discussed.

Economic Growth:

Economic Growth can be defined as a steady increase in gross domestic product of a country as a result of an increase in the economy's productive capacity. It is concerned with improving living standards and this is a result of growth in physical output of physical goods and services.

Actual Growth:

This is the annual percentage increase in national output i.e. the growth in what is actually produced. Statistics give actual growth rates. Whether actual growth increases or not is dependent on how increases in potential are utilised.

Potential Growth:

This is the speed at which the economy could grow, if all productive resources were fully employed. Some of the factors that contribute to potential growth are:

- an increase in resources such as capital, labour or natural resources; and

- increased efficiency in the use of these resources such as improved management, technology or labour skills.

If potential growth is slow; the government will adopt supply side policies.

Production Possibility Curve and Growth:

The distinction between actual and potential growth can be shown on a production possibility curve. In Diagram 20.1 suppose that manufactured goods and services aggregated together are Good X and that agricultural goods are Good Y. The curve shows potential output in the form of a movement from Curve 1 to Curve 2. Actual growth is shown as a movement out from A to B to C to D. If an increase in GDP occurs in the short run it is likely that it is not due to an increase in productive efficiency but rather to an increase in aggregate demand which brought into use resources up to then under-utilised.

In Diagram 20.1 this is a movement from A to B. An example would involve the greater use of available machinery. To obtain growth over a period of time Curve 1 must move out to Curve 2, i.e. there must be an increase in output, which enables the economy to move beyond B to C and on to D.

A movement from a situation where resources are unemployed and demand is deficient does not mean that economic growth has occurred if there is a movement to full employment. There is no growth in productive potential. When combining one year with another it is necessary that the level of resource utilisation is similar. The effect of population growth must also be considered. Take a country where GDP is growing at four per cent per annum but the rate of growth in the population is six per cent, average per capita GDP is falling.

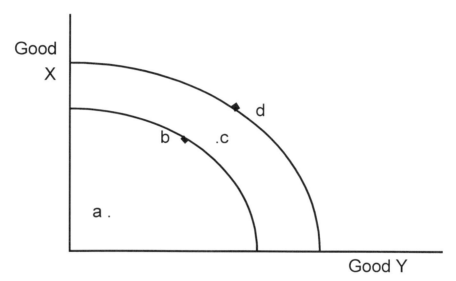

Diagram 20.1 Production Possibilities Curve

Causes of Actual Growth:

The rate of actual growth is influenced by the changes in Aggregate Demand (AD = C+I+G+X-M). A high level of AD will encourage firms to invest in more capacity, when the slack if any is taken up. If AD falls, firms will cut back and will have increased stocks. AD and actual output fluctuate together in the short run.

In the long run growth in AD determines whether potential output will be achieved. Another important determinant of actual growth is growth in potential output.

Causes of Potential Growth:

Now attention is turned to the supply side of the economy in an effort to determine the capacity of the economy to produce. Economic growth refers to an increase in the output of an economy following an increase in the amount of available resources. Increased output can be attributed to an increased input of the factors of production and increased efficiency.

Increased Output Due to Increased Input of the Factors of Production:

This comes about due to increases in the supply of labour, capital, land and raw materials.

- **Labour**

If the working population increases then there will be an increase in potential output. This increase could be the result of a previous rise in the birth rate or fall in the infant mortality rate. An increase is possible from net immigration as happened in Australia and other countries and now Ireland. Another way to increase the supply of labour is through an increase in the number of women at work.

- **Capital**

An increase in the stock of capital will increase output. The larger the proportion of GNP which a nation diverts to investment the greater will be the stock of capital. A greater capital stock results from total (gross) investment being in excess of capital depreciation, i.e. net investment. Economists however record gross investment as beneficial. Investment or gross capital formation is a major determinant of growth. Increasing the amount of capital to labour is known as capital deepening while increasing the capital stock in order to keep up with a growing labour force is known as capital widening.

The quality of the capital is very important, as is its composition from the point of view of modern technology and developments. The modern day development of Japan and Germany is attributed to their replacement of capital stock destroyed during the war with up to date productive capacity. Advantages in productivity due to better quality rather than quantity of capital are known as embodied technical change.

Incremental capital output ratio (ICOR) refers to the increase in output relative to the increase in net investment (capital) over a period of time. It therefore reflects the productivity of capital. If ICOR is low relative to other countries it may mean that the quality of investment decisions isn't good.

- **Land and Raw Materials**

There is not much scope for increasing the amount of land available as it is essentially fixed. Raw materials can be discovered. Discovery is regarded as a once-off benefit, as was the finding of natural gas off Cork for Ireland. Output of the raw material as a result of this will reach its maximum and as it runs out, output will fall. Of course as an increasing amount of one factor is added to fixed factors diminishing returns set in. This problem can only be solved if there is an increase in the productivity of resources.

Classical Growth Theory:

In general the classical economists had a very pessimistic outlook with regard to economic growth. History would dismiss this theory of growth. They held that the end result of capitalist development is stagnation. Classical theory assumed a stationary state with growth but at a very slow steady rate. Growth as we understand it, takes place by fits and starts. They held that in the long run growth would cease and economies would settle at a stationary state with only basic subsistence wages.

Government Policies to Promote Growth:

There is general agreement that the government can influence economic growth but there is disagreement as to what policies should be adopted. The following are some ways the government can influence economic growth:

- **Labour**

The quality of labour can be improved by providing basic education so that school leavers are numerate and literate. Training schemes can be provided so that workers are either trained or retrained in up to date technology and work practices.

- **Public Sector Investment**

Public sector investment can be used as a source of growth and capital spending in the form of infrastructural development can be especially beneficial.

- **Maintenance of law and order**

This is a primary function of government and over the years many other services have been added. Maintenance of law and order provides the climate for enterprise and is an attraction for outside business to establish in Ireland.

- **Tax System**

Government must be careful when taxing profits because if the taxation levied is considered to be excessive, it will take away the incentive to invest. Differential rates of Corporation Tax on retained profits and dividends can be used in an effort to get increased retention of profits and through this increased investment. This policy is considered to be controversial at the present time. Countries such as Germany and France have lower marginal rates of tax than Ireland and they place greater reliance on indirect taxation as a source of government revenue. Overall they have a lower rate of direct taxation so that there are greater incentives for businesses.

- **Aggregate Demand**

A high and stable level of aggregate demand is conducive to economic growth but if it is up and down it reduces confidence and investment. A high level of domestic demand can be achieved by way of fiscal and monetary policy. The latter may have costs in terms of inflation and balance of payments which may damage long run growth prospects.

- **Competitiveness**

Competitiveness in an economy is very important as when it is at a high level it encourages innovation. This in turn leads to new production techniques and methods.

- **People's Attitudes:**

People need to have attitudes that are favourable to growth and enterprise since these attitudes determine the degree of risk taking and the level of saving. Attitude to profit taking will determine the level of enterprise.

- **Interest Rates**

Every effort should be made to keep interest rates low especially long-term interest rates. If the cost of borrowing is high, investment will be low. By giving tax relief on interest paid and thereby reducing the cost of borrowing, projects will be undertaken that would not have been without this relief.

- **Research and Development**

A country needs to encourage research and development. Establishing the framework for research and development and making finance available will encourage it. When the state sponsors research, it must disseminate the findings in order to assist business and encourage further research.

- **Level of State Intervention**

It is difficult to establish the optimum level as too much intervention is viewed as central planning and too little as neglect.

Supply- Side Economics:

Supply side economics is defined as a study of how changes in aggregate supply affect variables such as national income. Supply side economists advise against government intervention in the economy at both micro- and macroeconomic levels. It is an approach that focuses directly on aggregate supply and how to shift the aggregate supply curve outwards. "Supply Siders" hold that this can be done by applying total freedom of operation to those aspects of the economy that affect the factors of production, goods and services. They are advocates of legislation banning monopolies, cuts in income tax, retraining grants for labour, and curbing the power of trade unions. This approach was used by the Reagan administration in the US (1981 - 1989) to decide on fiscal policies. It was also used in the UK when Mrs. Thatcher was Prime Minister (1979 - 1990). In both cases the core of their policy was to rely on the market, reward enterprise and keep the government on the sidelines.

Until the late 1970's the aim of policy was to counter unemployment and inflation. This was introduced after World War II and was based on Keynesian demand management principles. If unemployment increased, tax cuts were made and/or expenditure was increased. When inflation increased, tight fiscal and monetary policies were used to control it.

Change from Demand Management:

Towards the end of the 1970's the Keynesian approach was abandoned by many and the emphasis was changed to policies which focussed on factors that would increase the growth in potential output. These factors include increased saving and investment as well as reduced taxation on capital income and in this way enterprise is encouraged as is competition. There has been a shift from Keynesian policy of stabilisation in the short run to one of increasing long run economic growth.

Role of Incentives:

Supply side economics holds that incentives play a key role by ensuring an adequate return to saving, working and enterprise. They emphasise the loss of incentive due to high levels of taxation under demand management.

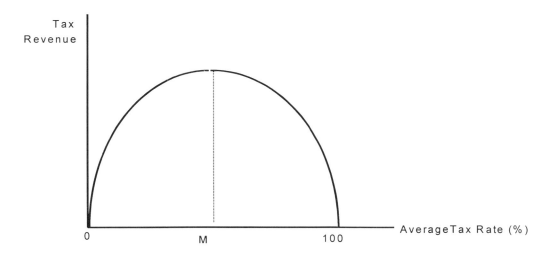

Diagram 20.2 The Laffer Curve

Relationship between Tax Policy and Economic Activity:

One policy with which supply-siders have been associated is that of cuts in income tax. They suggest that high taxation induces people to reduce their labour and capital supply. Some suggest, like Arthur Laffer, that high tax rates may lower tax revenues. He made the point by drawing what is now known as the Laffer Curve shown in Diagram 20.2.

Tax revenue is zero when the average tax rate is zero. It would also be zero where the average tax rate was 100 per cent, as nobody would have the incentive to work (except in the Black Economy). There is some tax rate at which revenue is maximised and in the Diagram it is M per cent. If the rate is above M then a cut will increase revenue. If the tax rate was 100 per cent, national income would be zero, so that as the rate falls national income increases. During the Reagan administration in the US, taxes were cut and they did result in economic expansion but they also led to a very large US budget deficit during the 1980's.

Supply Side Policies and Inflation:

Cost-push pressures may cause inflation but it can be reduced by supply side policies:

- By reducing the power of the trade unions and/or firms, thus improving competition in the labour and/or goods markets; and

- By introducing a prices and incomes policy to prevent people from exercising this power.

Inflation was reduced in the early 1990's but it was costly in terms of high unemployment.

Unemployment and Supply Side Policies:

Supply side policies concentrate on the supply of labour. The aim here is to make workers more responsive to changes in job opportunities. They argue that the labour market is in equilibrium most of the time in the sense that the wage rate just balances the demand for labour with the supply of workers ready to accept jobs. Unless incentives are changed, no more workers can be hired at this rate. Supply siders in the US stressed tax cuts, as already stated, as an incentive to work. In the UK it was suggested that social welfare benefits were too high relative to after tax pay of low paid workers and were a disincentive to work. It was also suggested that the trade unions could restrict entry to a job thus keeping wages artificially high.

Policies to Encourage Competition:

In the UK the Thatcher government concentrated on the private sector, i.e. privatisation and deregulation. Increased competition would, it was felt, improve efficiency and consequently at the macro level output would increase and inflation decrease.

Market-oriented supply side policies in the 1980's:

The aim of these policies was to increase the rate of growth in aggregate supply by encouraging private enterprise. The policies are as follows:

- Reducing taxes so as to increase incentives;
- Reducing government expenditure in order to release more resources for the private sector;

- Reducing the monopoly power of trade unions;

- Abolishing exchange controls;

- Reducing entitlement to certain welfare benefits;

- Encouraging competition through privatisation and deregulation e.g. The Irish government deregulated air transport in the 1980s by allowing Ryanair to compete with Aer Lingus; and

- Reducing obstacles to investment and risk taking.

Costs of Growth:

- Greater consumption may not make people happier while it may reduce the overall quality of life.

- Growth can increase income inequality as the go ahead obtain more while the others remain as they are. Certainly if taxes are cut to promote growth, the better off will benefit more than the less well off.

- To finance growth, consumption must be cut either by increased taxation or savings. This is true of the short-run so that either way, higher growth results in lower consumption.

- It is possible that growth will just generate greater additional demand as people want more and more. There is no increase in their utility but they become more materialistic.

- If people relentlessly pursue economic growth then they may become greedy and selfish, as a society. These social costs are borne by society, not the producer. People can become lonely, stressed, lacking in motivation and in many cases turn to violence and crime. The incidence of heart disease is also likely to increase.

- There are environmental costs associated with growth. Most people desire an environment that is clean and free from pollution. Growth may cause pollution that can be in the form of noise, acid rain and depletion of the ozone layer.

- Growth involves a greater use of resources and finite or non-renewable resources such as oil and other fuels are going to run out.

- With innovation and technological advance, skills will become redundant and workers will be involuntarily unemployed.

Regional Development:

Regional policy is designed to influence the geographical distribution of economic activity. There are inequalities and imbalances and various measures are taken to reduce these and they constitute regional policy. These measures are a means to encourage the growth of some areas as well as overall growth resulting from a further use of resources, mainly labour and capital.

Regions:

Since regional policy is concerned with bringing about a more even geographic distribution of economic development, the country must be divided into regions. This is a process of classification and depends on policy objectives. When classification is done it must be remembered that there are different types of regional problem areas and these can be put into groups as follows:

- Regions that are traditionally less developed: These are areas dependent on agriculture and are characterised by low incomes, outward migration and poor infrastructural facilities. There are such areas in Ireland.

- The once rich areas or regions based on industries now in decline, e.g. coal and textiles. Ireland does not really fit into this group even though there are declining traditional industries the effect is not as severe as in other parts of the world.

- Congested inner city areas, examples of which are found in Ireland.

Market Approach to Regional Problems:

The market can in theory correct regional disparities. The free market approach suggests that any interference in the locational decisions of firms will lead to decisions that are inefficient and sub-optimal.

Regional unemployment means disequilibrium in the labour market and if wages are reduced equilibrium will be restored. Workers will go where wages are higher and employers will be attracted to the low wage areas and this, at a later stage, will bring wages back up. Opponents say that this process is very, very slow.

Advocates of the market approach suggest that when the government becomes involved it brings with it other burdens for firms in the form of bureaucratic controls and taxation.

Social costs are ignored with this approach and as labour leaves an area, there are more social costs and existing ones are added to. Facilities will not be fully used e.g. hospitals and schools. Areas attracting people will not have adequate facilities. Property such as housing will be expensive in the growth area and prices will fall substantially in the declining area.

Labour leaves the declining area and population falls so that markets are reduced and unemployment increases. Labour will not easily move due to economic and social ties to the area.

Labour markets are not without friction as there is collective bargaining and Partnership 2000 in Ireland. This reduces wage differences between regions if such differences exist.

Approaches to Regional Policy:

When an area is depressed the government can take some short term measures to assist it such as works programmes. However in the long term workers must be persuaded to move from the depressed area or work must be found for them in the area. There are two policy options i.e. bring workers to work and work to workers.

- **Workers to Work**

- Unemployed people are reluctant to move from their own area particularly when there is unemployment in an area that is more prosperous.

- Firms can expand in their own area therefore location decisions do not enter into the matter. It may be that they could not expand due to a shortage of suitable labour.

- Community life in the area from which workers move will be seriously affected.

- Housing will cost more in the new location and this may prevent mobility.

- Unemployment benefit may remove the incentive to move.

- If incentives are given to move, people who are employed in the depressed area may go and these are usually skilled people.

- **Work to Workers**

- In this case firms are encouraged to set up in depressed areas. This means that mobility of capital is the aim of policy. Community life is maintained and perhaps strengthened.

- External diseconomies of scale are avoided, as there isn't excessive localisation of industry that would lead to higher costs.

- External diseconomies of scale are avoided, as there isn't excessive localisation of industry that would lead to higher costs.

- Since bringing workers to work is not very feasible this would appear to be the only policy left.

- By helping the more immobile workers such as older people and married women it stimulates the labour force participation rate.

- Moving workers into an area produces a positive multiplier effect.
- Firms locating in depressed areas may not operate at greatest efficiency and thus incur higher costs. This will happen even when they obtain assistance from the government.

- If grants to firms are weighted on the side of investment, firms are encouraged to substitute capital for labour and the number of jobs provided may be very small.

- It is an expensive policy and the benefits arising from it may be small.

European Union Regional Policy:

EU regional policy seeks to:

- Co-ordinate national regional policy of member states to ensure their conformity with the Treaties;

- Help members develop their underdeveloped areas to achieve balanced development in all areas;

- Support declining industrial regions; and

- Make community policies and financing instruments more sensitive to regional needs.

To introduce these policies financial resources are required. There are three structural funds: the European Regional Development Fund (ERDF) set up in 1975 with the objective of assisting in the development of Community problem areas; the European Social Fund (ESF) 1958; and the Guidance Section of the Agricultural Fund (FEOGA). In 1993 a Cohesion Fund was set up in recognition that the Single Market would cause poor areas of the EU to lose out. The funds were given to help the countries of Ireland, Spain, Portugal and Greece to catch up. These funds were used to improve roads, airports, and telecommunications and third level educational institutions.

ERDF:

The main objective of this is to fund physical infrastructure in less developed areas of the EU including roads, railways, ports, telecommunications and other areas. Receipts are on a 'national quota' basis and areas receiving support are identified by national regional policies. This ensures that every member state gets some support from ERDF regardless of its level of development or prosperity. From 1979 quota ranges rather than fixed quotas are used and funds cover educational institutions. In 1989 significant new arrangements for the ERDF came into force as part of reform of the Structural Funds. Funds were to double by 1993 and there is now greater complimentary between the three Funds mentioned above.

The Single European Act 1987 recognised that parallel action to promote economic and social cohesion to go with the Single Market was needed. As the EU has increased its membership the differences between the rich and poor regions have increased and was expected to increase as a result of greater competition after January 1993 when the Single European Act came into force.

Elements of Reform of Structural Funds:

The following are the key elements in the reform of the Structural Funds:
- Concentration on five main objectives thus preventing the wastage of funds when spread over too many aims;

- Annual programme basis instead of on individual projects;

- A partnership effort with EU national, regional and local bodies with the involvement of people at every level;

- greater examination and monitoring of supported projects so as to evaluate the contribution made to economic and social cohesion; and

- Better co-ordination between the funds.

A review took place in the course of the five- year period 1989 to 1993. It basically found that the reforms were working but that there was still a great deal to be done before the gap in living standards and opportunities was closed between people in the rich and poor areas of the EU.

Objectives of Structural Funds:

There were seven objectives:

1. Promoting the development and adjustment of the regions lagging behind with expenditure concentrated on particular member states or regions identified, on the basis of socio-economic criteria. The whole of Ireland is included. 80 per cent of ERDF is devoted to Objective 1 regions. Funds involved are ERDF, ESF and EAGGF.

2. Converting the regions badly affected by industrial decline with assistance from, the ERDF and ESF.

3. Combating long -term employment is Objective 3 and it comes under the ESF.

4. Objective 4 is to facilitate the occupational integration of young people, through the ESF.

5. Objective 5 deals with CAP:

6. Speeding up the adjustment of agricultural structures, using EAGGF.

7. Development of rural areas, using EAGGF guidance section, ESF and ERDF.

ERDF is concerned mainly with Objectives 1 and 2. Over the five–years (1989 – 1993) Ireland got 5.4% of the ERDF.

Agenda 2000:

The Commission of the EU proposed a series of measures to prepare for enlargement of the EU and policy reforms and these were contained in Agenda 2000. In 1997 the EU Commission set out draft proposals.

The Structural and Cohesion Funds Package:

The aim of this package is at concentrating, simplifying and clarifying responsibilities so reducing objectives from seven to three. The measure used for allocating structural funds is GDP and for cohesion funds it is GNP. Both measures are used simultaneously when aid per person is calculated.

Objective 1:

This promotes the development of regions lagging behind. To be eligible a region must have a per capita income that is less than 75% of EU per capita GDP. When this rule is applied, ten regions that qualified previously will lose their Objective 1 status.

Objective 2:

A new Objective 2 covers regions experiencing industrial change, fragile rural areas and urban areas highly dependent on fisheries.

Objective 3:

Regions becoming ineligible for Objective 1 and 2 status are awarded a transitional status. A new Objective 3 cares for the modernisation of policies with regard to education, training and employment. Innovative financial instruments, such as loan guarantees and risk capital funds to increase the leverage of the Structural Funds are introduced. A new regulation to govern the Structural and Cohesion Funds and the Instruments for Structural Policies for Pre-Accession (ISPA) between 2000 and 2006 are also proposed.

The proposals for a new financial perspective for 2000-2006 are presented on an EU 15 basis. Ceilings are set for expenditure on agriculture; structural funds; internal and external policies; administration and research. The Commission estimates that by 2006 it will need only 1.13% of the EU GNP to cover its traditional tasks.

Irish Regional Policy:

The establishment of the Congested Districts Board in 1892 was the first attempt at regional development in Ireland. It only lasted until 1923. There is very little indication that there was any attempt again until the 1950's and 1960's. In 1949 the Industrial Development Authority was set up in an effort to attract foreign manufacturing industry to Ireland so that Ireland had an outward looking policy. In 1952 the Underdeveloped Areas Act introduced regionally differentiated grants in an effort to correct regional imbalance and An Foras Tionscail was set up to administer the grants. This was recognition of the difference between the west and east and south -west where the west was underdeveloped relative to the other areas.

Gaeltarra Eireann was set up in 1956 to promote development in the Gaeltacht. Shannon Free Airport Development Company (SFAD Co) was set up to promote the Shannon area and the world's first airport duty free industrial estate was set up.

The Local Government (Planning and Development) Act of 1963 set up nine regions for physical planning purposes. In 1965 the government noted its intention to promote urban centres that would cater for a region. Wright (1967) and Lichfield and Associates (1967) were commissioned to prepare plans for Dublin and Limerick respectively, and Buchanan & Partners for the country (remaining regions) in 1969.

Buchanan reported in 1968 and suggested the development of two major centres of industrial growth at Cork and Limerick/Shannon. Dublin growth was to be limited to its natural increase.

Six other regional centres were suggested, as were four local centres. The debate at the time was on the advisability of concentrated growth as against dispersed growth. The Buchanan report was never implemented and the government issued its "Review of Regional Policy" in 1972, supporting dispersed growth.

The IDA brought out Regional Industrial Plans for 1973/77 and the government accepted these as a basis for dispersed growth. Its objective was to achieve a greater dispersal of industry outside the selected large growth centres. These plans were fairly successful and further plans for 1978/82 were issued when a certain amount of progress was made.

The Telesis Report 1982 was very critical of policy, in particular stating that incentives given were too generous, favouring capital formation rather than the provision of employment. The four regions were largely ignored and use of natural resources was very inadequate.

Dependency on foreign firms does not generate self- sustained growth and a country needs a strong indigenous exporting sector.

Changes were made in regional policy objectives after the publication of a White Paper on Industrial Policy in 1984. Up to this the grant system was biased towards designated areas which were mainly in the west of Ireland. After 1984, grants were given to industrial sectors and areas badly affected by the recession taking place at that time. Commitment was short term rather than long term. Priority was given to target sectors that included pig meat, beef, indigenous mechanical engineering, DIY products and others.

Regional Changes in the 1980's and 1990's:

By 1987 the government had realised that borrowing would have to be curtailed and that fiscal rectitude would have to commence. As a result policy switched from spatial development to national development. The whole of Ireland at this stage was designated as a single area eligible for aid under the ERDF set up in 1975. The movement towards sectoral development (or by industry) had begun with the 1984 White Paper.

National Plan and Community Support Framework:

Under the 1988 reforms of the Structural Funds there were three phases involved when seeking assistance:

- A multinational plan for three to five years listing requirements;

- Community support framework (CSF) giving agreed priorities; and

- Implementation of CSF through use of different forms of assistance while monitoring, assessing and adjusting if required.

Irish Regionalisation, 1999:

The Government decided to divide the State into separate regions. Fifteen counties Donegal, Leitrim, Sligo, Cavan, Monaghan, Louth, Mayo, Roscommon, Galway, Longford, Westmeath, Offaly, Laois, Clare and Kerry considered to be disadvantaged were selected. It was hoped that these would secure special Objective 1 status for EU Structural and Cohesion Funds for 2000 – 2006, since they are considered to have incomes of less than 75% of average EU GDP per capita. However Eurostat decided on thirteen counties leaving out Clare and Kerry, two counties added on by the Government at a late stage. EU officials wanted to ensure that the regional structures agreed in 1994 remained in tact. Ireland is thus divided into rich and poor regions. The Commission accepted regionalisation on condition that Ireland devolved power to the regional bodies.

The thirteen counties (Objective) will receive maximum direct funding from EU structural and cohesion funds. The 1.1mn people in the thirteen Border, Midland and Western (BMW) counties will receive £900mn or £750 per resident. The thirteen counties in the east and south will receive £1.5bn or £600 per resident. In 1992 Ireland received £2,293 per person while the other member states received £826 per person. Regionalisation brought in an additional £430mn. Exchequer saving due to Objective 1 status for the BMW counties will be used to tackle urban unemployment black spots.

The state is allowed to give up to 40% in grants to industry setting up in the Objective1 region but only 20% in the remainder of the country. This will make the BMW counties attractive locations for foreign industry. After 2006 they may benefit from Objective 2 status through a transitional arrangement.

Ireland received £400mn from the special Cohesion Fund and this will be spread across the entire country.

This division of the country skews structural funding and industrial development away from Dublin, Limerick and Cork. The thirteen countries have not benefited from the 'Celtic Tiger' to the same extent that the remaining 13 counties have. The southern and eastern counties will receive a special "transition" arrangement with current top levels of aid being cut back slowly over the earlier years of the budget period. The IDA has been moving away from giving maximum direct grants to industry. It now offers logistical assistance to new firms setting up in Ireland and loss of Objective 1 status will not affect this assistance. It may be possible for the Objective1 areas to get approval from the EU for bigger tax incentives for commercial operations. A new National Plan is being prepared and it is based on this form of regionalism.

Economic Growth and Ireland:

Ireland is a Small Open Economy (SOE) in the sense that it is very dependent on foreign trade and in competition with a very large number of sellers. Since Ireland is part of the larger economic system it is affected by what happens in it and has very little influence over what happens. It is dependent on investment from outside Ireland to create growth. For this reason incentives which are as good if not better than those of other countries must be offered. Growth policy consists mainly of making Ireland attractive as a location for foreign firms.

Measuring Irish Growth:

There are some problems when measuring Irish growth. Over a period of years GDP has been exaggerated. Transfer pricing and profit outflows of foreign firms can distort the GDP growth rate while both are unrelated to economic activity in Ireland. Taxation policies can affect the flow of goods between the various subsidiaries making up a multinational enterprise and also the price at which these goods are transferred. Ireland is a low tax country with a 10% tax on manufacturing industry and internationally traded services. Transfer pricing is used to minimise the company's tax liabilities, internal prices being set so that the greatest profit is earned in those countries with the lowest rate of company taxation. In Ireland this practice is followed in the pharmaceutical, electronic and manufacturing sectors thus creating the illusion of high exports, output and productivity growth. To these companies Ireland is a tax haven and they move their profits here from their enterprises around the world.

In Ireland GDP is greater than GNP as Net Factor Income from Abroad is negative. Over 90 per cent of GNP is represented by exports and prices of some of these goods are falling all the time e.g. electronics. The terms of trade are hit and this results in Irish disposable income falling. This fall is estimated at 1% thus reducing Gross National Disposable Income (GNDI) by 1% per annum below GNP. Other problems in measuring national income are discussed in Chapter10.

Growth 1950s to 1999:

Growth in the Irish economy can be broken down into six periods as follows:

The 1950's:

When the economy is broken down into sectors Ireland had a high dependency on agriculture. The industrial sector was made up a few foreign and many indigenous firms, with the latter catering mainly for the relatively small Irish market. Ireland had a very serious unemployment problem alleviated by emigration as a safety valve at the time.

In the late 1950s the Irish economy was opened to the modern world. 'Economic Development' by T. K. Whittaker was published in 1958 and its main recommendation was to develop agriculture. It also suggested that Ireland should seek to attract foreign industry by giving them tax and other concessions. Due to protectionism, Ireland missed out on the post-war boom and the period of general economic growth that lasted until about 1973 in the developed world.

1960 - 1973:

Ireland applied to join the then EEC in 1961 but was turned down. By the end of the 1960's Ireland had changed from being an agricultural country to an industrial one. Agriculture grew due to the large subsidies given in the course of the First and Second Programmes. In 1965 the Committee on Industrial Organisation was established and it found that Irish industry was badly managed and equipped. To remedy this situation grants were given to firms to help them modernise. An Chomhairle Oiliuna (ANCO) was set up to provide industrial training. As seen in Table 20.1 the average annual growth rate for Ireland in the period of growth 1960-1973 was 4.4 per cent compared to the EU 4.7%. The increase in growth started with the First Programme for Economic Expansion (1959-1963). Even though the change in the Irish growth rate was substantial, it was not enough to bring it up to the EU average. Spain and Greece had much higher rates of growth than Ireland. Japan had more than double the Irish rate at a high of 9.6 per cent. During the 1960's and 1970's the net increase in manufacturing employment came from foreign firms in the export sector.

1973 - 1979:

Starting with the oil crisis of 1973 there was a global slow down in economic growth and the average rate fell to 3.4 per cent of GNP for Ireland (Table 20.1). This was relatively high by international standards as the E U average was down to 2.5%, and in Japan to 3.6%. Ireland joined the EEC in 1973 and this benefited agriculture. The Irish economy showed recovery towards the end of the 1970's but this was mainly due to large-scale government borrowing. In 1977 the government, troubled by high unemployment, increased spending and this set the economy back until 1987 when fiscal rectitude was introduced.

1979 - 1987:

Annual average growth rate for Ireland in this period was extremely poor at 0.3% compared to 1.6% for the EU (Table20.1). This slow growth is explained in various ways by different commentators. Over this period there were huge swings in Irish fiscal policy and these contributed to this low growth. Adverse conditions in economies generally made the situation worse. During the 1970's borrowing was large and debt was built up and this affected the rate of growth in the early 1980's. Not alone was debt large at this time but interest on it was high so that Irish Debt/GNP ratio rose substantially. Action had to be taken in 1987 at a time when there was a downturn in the world economy. Inward direct foreign investment slowed down and consequently so did the rate of growth in output. With fiscal rectitude introduced in 1987 has come a vast improvement in public finances, one of the key features of economic performances during the suceeding period.

1988 - 1993:

From Table 20.1 it is seen that the Irish economy grew by 5.5% per annum on average over the period 1988 to 1993. The EU average for the same period was 2.0%. These were very high growth rates for Ireland relatively. In this period there was a large volume of foreign direct investment into Ireland. With the Single Market coming into being in January 1993, foreign firms sought to locate here before a "Fortress Europe" was established. Pharmaceuticals and data processing sectors made up the greater part of this investment. Perhaps the relatively low Irish labour costs formed part of the attraction as a location.

1994 - 1999:

There was a strong recovery in the Irish economy over this period as there was in the world economy generally. Irish recovery was generally assisted by the recovery in other economies. In 1987 Ireland was one of the poorest countries in the EU with a GDP per capita of less than 63% of the UK's. In 1998 the Irish economy has surpassed the UK's and is now very close to the EU average.

From Table 20.1 it can be seen that the economies listed plus the EU on average all showed increases in the rate of output over this period. Ireland's rate of growth for 1994 to 1998 and forecast for 1999 as shown in Table 20.1, has greatly exceeded all of the countries listed in the table. Real GNP grew by 7.4%, 8.8%, 6.0%, 7.7%, 1994, 1995, 1996, 1997 respectively giving an average of 7.5% per annum over the period. It is estimated to have grown by 10.0% in 1998 and the forecast for 1999 is 8.5%. The Government has forecast an average growth rate of 6% per annum for the three- year period 1999, 2000 and 2001.

This spectacular growth led to Ireland's economy being called the "Celtic Tiger". This is a punning reference to the longer-established term "tiger economy" that was used to describe the more successful Asian economies e.g. South Korea in the 1980s.

Table 20.1
Annual Average % Growth Rates of Output in Selected OECD Countries GDP

Country	Period									
	1960/73	1973/79	1979/86	1988/93	1994	1995	1996	1997	1998	1999f
United States	4.0	2.4	2.5	1.9	3.9	2.0	2.8	3.9	3.5	1.5
Japan	9.6	3.6	3.6	3.0	1.0	0.9	3.5	0.8	-2.6	0.2
EU	4.7	2.5	1.6	2.0	2.5	2.5	1.7	2.7	2.8	2.2
Ireland	4.3	3.4	0.3	5.5	7.4	8.8	6.0	7.7	10.0	8.5e
Spain	7.2	2.2	1.6	2.0	1.7	2.0	3.0	3.4	3.8	3.4
Portugal	6.9	2.9	1.9	2.7	1.0	2.3	3.3	4.0	4.0	3.3
Greece	7.6	3.7	1.5	1.3	1.0	2.0	2.6	3.5	3.0	3.2
France	na	na	na	na	2.2	2.2	1.5	2.3	3.1	2.4
Denmark	na	na	na	na	4.7	2.7	3.5	3.2	2.4	2.0
Belgium	na	na	na	na	2.3	1.9	1.5	2.9	2.7	2.3
UK	na	na	na	na	3.5	2.5	2.3	3.4	2.7	0.8
Germany	na	na	na	na	2.8	1.9	1.4	2.2	2.7	2.2
Italy	na	na	na	na	2.2	6.7	3.0	1.5	1.5	2.1

f = forecast e= estimate

Source: OECD Economic Outlook 1998. No 51 CSO and Eurostat

Government growth forecasts are 5.7 and 5.2% for 2000 and 2001 respectively indicate a significant slow down on previous performance. The reduction for 1999 is made in the expectation that the external balance will be reduced as export growth slows. This is based on weaker demand growth in a number of our trading partners. The ESRI in its Quarterly

Economic Commentary February 1999 revised downwards its estimate of growth in GNP for 1998 from 8.25% to 7.25%. These are still very high growth rates.

In 1998 tax revenue increased by 13%, the current budget surplus was over £2 billion and the Exchequer financing surplus £747mn even though the capital deficit increased substantially. This trend continued in the first quarter of 1999. Tax revenues were up 13.3% on the same quarter in 1998 well ahead of the Budget forecast of 7.5%.

Inflation has not increased despite the high growth rates and has averaged 2% per annum in the period 1994 -1997. It was 2.4% in 1998 and the Central Bank forecast for 1999 is 1.5%. Another key feature is the increase of 26% in the number employed over the period 1991 to 1998. The ESRI forecast is for this growth in employment to continue to 2000.

Outlook for Irish Economic Growth to 2006:

Concern has been expressed about the sustainability of the current rates of Irish economic growth. There are a number of factors that may check or reduce growth and some of these are examined here.

- **Labour Shortages**

Over the last decade the flexibility of the Irish labour market has increased and there has been a rapid growth in the supply of skilled labour. During 1999 the rate of increase in the labour supply began to slow down and this will continue over the next decade. There is an emerging labour shortage in certain sectors e.g. the technology, building construction and financial services sectors. This is confirmed by substantial increases in pay as employers seek to attract skilled workers. If this trend continues and there is a downturn in the economy, workers will either have to take a cut in nominal pay or be unemployed. The latter is the more likely outcome and would result in a fall in economic growth.

The shortage of skilled labour is a structural one and requires a long-term policy to overcome it. Investment in education is essential to the growth process. Growth cannot continue unchecked if the input of skilled labour is constrained.

- **Infrastructure**

Failure to develop adequate infrastructure means logistical problems now and this threatens further economic expansion. The inadequacy of infrastructure is evident in areas such as housing, roads and railways. In its Report outlined above, the ESRI states that "A key to the growth potential of the economy over the next decade will be the country's ability to absorb the increasing numbers of households." There is a serious shortage of serviced land and this has led and will continue to lead to substantial increases in house prices.

- **Overdependency on a few Products**

Many economists are of the opinion that Ireland is over-reliant on a small number of Multinational Corporations (MNCs) operating in the chemicals, pharmaceuticals and electronics. Ireland has been successful in attracting MNCs mainly because of the 10% tax on companies engaged in manufacturing, Financial Services Centre and other export services. Our trading partners, especially the US and Germany, are unhappy with this arrangement. The 10% tax was to go in 2010 but now we are introducing a 12.5% tax across the board for all companies manufacturing and non-manufacturing alike.

- **Growth in Credit**

Credit growth can be a spur to economic growth and it has acted as a spur in Ireland's case. However as credit becomes excessive in relation to income available, it slows down economic growth. This could become a problem in Ireland in the years ahead.

- **World Recession**

A general world recession now seems likely. This will affect foreign direct investment in Ireland as well exports. We must ensure that Ireland remains a good location for foreign direct investment. The attitude of outsiders is changing towards us. In recent years we have alienated our EU partners by pursuing policies inappropriate to a country with income close to the EU average.

Ireland and the EU Budget 2000 – 2006:

Ireland has an infrastructure deficit and the EU summit in Berlin concluded "the Commission will maximise the leverage effect of EU funds by encouraging greater use of private sources of financing." This means that the EU will require the government to identify projects that will be developed using a private- public approach. A guiding principle is that if a project is worth undertaking with EU funding, it is equally worth undertaking using tax payers' funds.
In the period 1994 to 1999 Ireland received just under £7bn in EU funding but this is to be reduced to £3bn in the seven -years from 2000 to 2006. The total EU budget is frozen at a ceiling of 1.27% of Community GNP for the period to 2003.

Each member's EU contribution is 1.27% of GNP plus a proportion of VAT receipts. Ireland's annual contribution to the EU Budget is expected to rise to £788mn in 2000 and to £1075mn in 2006 from its 1998 level of £630 mn. CAP receipts to Ireland of £1.5 billion annually and £400mn per annum in structural funds will make her a net beneficiary over the period 2000 –2006. Receipts from social and regional funds will fall sharply towards the end of the Budget period and there will be a loss of Cohesion Funds in 2003. In 1998 receipts are estimated at 3.5% of GDP whereas they were 6.5% in 1991. From 2002 contributions will be based less on VAT and more on GNP. This will favour Ireland and as much as £132mn could be saved.

In 2006 EU will allocate funds again and by then the EU will have additional members from Eastern European countries. These new member states will have GNPs much lower than even the poorest parts of Ireland. Agricultural incomes will be lower than those of Irish and other EU states. Ireland with its outstanding economic growth will by 2006 be among the richest states in the EU. At this stage Ireland will be on a different side of the bargaining table trying to keep the lid on contributions and arguing against generous grants to poorer regions, a very different scenario than has pertained since we joined the then EEC in 1973.

Economic Development:

The term development can be used to describe the process of economic and social transformation within a country. It therefore implies change.

Developed and Developing Economies:

Economies, such as the United States, Germany and Japan, are generally referred to as developed economies. These contain large manufacturing sectors and even larger service sectors. Remaining countries comprise the developing world. This is not a very satisfactory label since it includes the very poor as well as the newly industrialised countries of East and North East Asia (NICs). Collectively, all the countries of the developing world are called the less developed countries (LDCs). Other labels used are 'North' and 'South' and the "first", "second" (old communist countries) and "third" worlds. Most of the developed economies are located in the northern part of the Northern Hemisphere. Countries of the 'South' are the tropical and sub-tropical LDCs lying to the south of the developed world.

Defining Developing Economies:

A developing country is one with real per capita income that is low relative to that pertaining in advanced countries. This definition conceals the human side of development. Developing countries have populations living at a subsistence level in poor health, having low levels of literacy and in very inadequate accommodation. They vary greatly one from another in terms of size, infrastructure, climate, political structure, resources, and degree of urbanisation and industrialisation.

Distinction between Economic Growth and Economic Development:

A distinction is sometimes drawn between the related concepts of economic development and economic growth. Both terms are concerned with changes in the level of Gross National Product and productive capacity. The term economic development is often used to define the situation in which an increase in the level of income in the economy involves a change in the structure of society. Economic growth is however used to describe a situation in which an increase in the level of GNP is attained without an alteration in the structure of society.

Main Characteristics of Developing Countries:

- **Per Capita Income**

The World Bank categorises countries into three income groups as follows:

- Low-income economies, with per capita income of $725 or less in 1994;

- Middle-income economies with per capita incomes of between $726 and $8,955;

- High-income economies, with per capita incomes of $8,956 or more.

From Table 20.2 it can be seen that 57 per cent of the world's population are in the low income group and their per capita GNP in 1994 was $380. The middle income group or 28% of the world's population had per capita GNP of $ 2,520 per annum while the remaining 15% had incomes over $23,420 in 1994. Care must however be taken when using the standard method of comparison as the use of official exchange rates causes distortions. Also as the per capita figure is an average it says nothing about the distribution of that income. Market valuations ignore non- market items such as own consumption by peasants. A new method of looking at what money buys i.e. 'purchasing power parity' shows that incomes in this category are greater than thought. The poorest country in 1996 was Ethiopia with a per capita income of $120 per annum! The richest country on the same date was Switzerland with a per capita income of $37,930. Since all or most of incomes earned in LDCs go on consumption there is little or no saving and as a result no investment either.

- **Population**

People in low -income countries tend to have large families to provide security against old age since there are no pensions or other benefits. The 40 poorest countries have 55 per cent of the world's population but have to share 5 per cent of world income. During the 1980's population in the poorer countries grew by 2.5 per cent per annum, compared to 1 per cent in the developed countries. Malthus predicted a return to a subsistence culture and it would seem that this is true for over 80 per cent of the world's people. Any surplus produced is consumed away, leaving very little for capital formation. High population growth rates put pressure on the available land to support the increased number of people. More people may be working on the land but add little to output. Nature can interfere with the productivity of land and it is disastrous when there is too little or too much rain for example. At times of famine, over-population is cited as the root cause and often the only cause. It is a major contributor but this is not the complete case. In Japan for example the population density is 310 persons per square kilometre while in Nigeria it is 90 persons per square kilometre. Japan has few natural resources whereas Nigeria has many including oil.

- **Weak Agriculture**

This weakness is demonstrated in LDCs by productivity trailing far behind population growth. This means that most people must work on the land to feed themselves so that only a small number is available for other work necessary to improve productivity e.g. drainage, irrigation or better equipment. Improved productivity can be brought about by institutional change such as land reform. Often attempts at land reform are negated by large landowners

- **Insufficient Capital and Traditional Techniques**

Capital is a produced means of production and consumption must be foregone to do it and this as already mentioned is practically impossible for the poorer countries. Lack of capital together with traditional techniques of production keeps productivity low.

- **Illiteracy**

Only the privileged have access to education and much of the population is illiterate (Table 20.2). This reduces the productivity of labour and there is a shortage of skilled workers which impedes progress even further.

Table 20.2

Important Economic Indicators for Different Country Groups

Country Group	Population 1994 Millions	Adult Literacy (%)	Life Expectancy at Birth	GNP per capita $	GNP per capita Average Annual Growth % 1985-1994
Low Income	3,182.2	34	63	380	3.4
Middle Income	1,569.9	n.a	67	2,520	-0.1
High Income	849.9	<5	77	23,420	1.9

Source: World Bank, World Development Report 1996

- **Dualistic Economies**

Most of the LDCs have a small modern sector and a large traditional sector. In the traditional sector old and primitive techniques are used but in the modern sector mainly established by foreigners, modern techniques are used. Profits are repatriated and various minerals and primary products are exploited on behalf of the foreign country.

- **Political Situation**

Even though this is non -economic in form it has very serious economic implications. The politics of these countries are often a hangover from the past and dominate economics to the detriment of economic development. Different ethnic groups can cause division as can different religious beliefs. Countries colonialised often have prolonged civil wars based on tribal differences. Where political control changes hands frequently there is a grave lack of continuity in any development policies being pursued.

- **Employment/Unemployment**

In LDCs there is a high rate of unemployment and disguised unemployment. Disguised unemployment occurs when people are at work but have not enough to do. If, for example, three people work a bit of land but all three are not fully employed and one leaves to work elsewhere, then the two remaining are fully employed and agricultural output doesn't drop.

- **Economic Backwardness**

Low labour efficiency, factor immobility and lack of incentive for economic change are some of the signs of economic backwardness. Generally traditional values discourage the full utilisation of human resources, as in the case of class distinction.

- **Foreign Trade Orientation**

LDCs as a rule are foreign trade oriented. They export primary products and import machinery and consumer goods. They are over dependent on primary products and this can have serious effects on their economies. It can lead to concentration on one sector to the detriment of all others. The economy can become susceptible to fluctuations in the international prices of the exported commodities. There is also a dependence on imports for fuel, machinery and manufactured goods.

Elements of Development

- **Human Resources**

This deals with labour supply, education, discipline and motivation. In order to attain economic development, a country needs to:

a) Control disease and improve health and nutrition in order to improve productivity and the quality of life of the population.

b) Education must be improved as it makes workers more productive. People must first have a basic primary education after which, they must be trained in new techniques applicable to industry and agriculture. Those with ability should be sent abroad and after a period, should bring back knowledge of business and engineering.

c) Improvement is required in the utilisation of labour as in developing countries there is usually widespread disguised unemployment. Rural output need not fall much when people transfer to industrial jobs. Food production is then increased so that those leaving the land can move to cities and towns where industrial job opportunities should be growing.

- **Natural Resources**

Many of the poorest countries in the world have little or no natural resources. The land and resources they have must be divided between large numbers of people. Even when there is a major natural resource, such as copper or oil, there is no guarantee of development. In fact, it could be that possession of natural resources and the development of these can lead to the neglect of others. Possession of a mineral does not mean that a country can become a modern industrial power.

Agricultural land is perhaps the greatest natural resource of developing countries and usually engages much of the labour force. Output of food can be increased thereby increasing national output. If farmers become more productive, workers can be released for work in other industries. Security of tenure, access to credit and advice encourages farmers to increase productivity.

- **Capital Formation**

In order to accumulate capital, it is necessary to forego current consumption over a period of time. Poor countries are living at subsistence level with no surplus over and above their current consumption needs. Even when they can save, it amounts to approximately 5 per cent of national income as against 15 to 25 per cent for advanced countries.

The savings of low- income people go towards providing themselves with housing and other basic equipment leaving little or nothing for development. Too little saving is perhaps the greatest problem developing countries have. It takes many years for a country to develop its infrastructure i.e. roads, railways, airports and factories, all very necessary for a productive economic structure. There is also the problem of maintaining the infrastructure after it has been successfully put in place. Countries with wasting assets, such as mining or oil must be careful that they do not live beyond their means during the productive life of these resources only to find that when they have run out, they are unable to sustain growth and the standard of living.

- **Social Overhead Capital**

Social overhead capital is an essential ingredient for the development of a private economy. This consists of roads, railways, public health, etc. Investment here is on such a scale that only the state can provide it.

Technological Change and Innovations:

Technological changes are related to changes in the methods of production which are the result of some new technique of research or innovation. They lead to an increase in the productivity of labour, capital and other factors of production.

Developing countries are benefiting from the very large pool of knowledge available from advanced or developed countries. It is, however, necessary to adapt and modify the techniques to suit the developing countries' needs in accordance with their economic, social and technical capacity and requirements.

To avail of this technology transfer, the recipient country must encourage entrepreneurs to take the ideas and employ them. It must be remembered that conditions differ greatly from those in advanced countries. In the latter, there is a plentiful supply of capital relative to labour, high wages and skilled workforce, conditions that do not exist to the same degree or at all in poorer countries.

It is the government's responsibility to foster the entrepreneurial spirit, achieved through training, education and respect for private enterprise.

- **Social Environment**

A social environment receptive to change must be established. Persuasion and not coercion should be the method used. Education and demonstration can do a great deal in this direction. If people can see the benefits of development, they will make a greater effort to provide themselves with the means to achieve something similar for themselves.

The Debt Crisis:

The origin of the debt problem of LDCs can be traced back to 1973/74 when OPEC forced up the price of oil by approximately four times in the space of a few months. This caused a big increase in import bills and deterioration in balance of payments of countries with no domestic oil production. There was also a decline in demand for LDCs' primary commodities. Foreign exchange earnings dropped due to a reduction in exports and deterioration of terms of trade. As a result there was a massive widening of current account deficits.

Up to 1973/74 LDCs obtained external finance by way of aid from governments of developed countries and private direct investment. Aid consisted of cheap loans and servicing was not a problem. By heavily borrowing abroad, developing countries continued to grow at a relatively rapid rate during the second half of the 1970's. In the early 1980's however their large and growing debts caught up with them. Only for intervention by the IM.F large scale defaults would have occurred.

LDCs had to renegotiate on their debt repayment schedules and interest repayments with their banks with the help of IMF. Conditions were placed on them as a result and they had to adopt austerity measures to reduce imports and cut inflation and wage increases. By the mid 1980's the Latin American countries were rejecting the IMF austerity plans.

In 1985 the then US Treasury Secretary James Baker argued for a shift of emphasis from austerity to growth in the debtor countries, which should be allowed to increase their debt further to finance investment and export expansion. It was based on the assumption that growth would resume in the advanced countries, something that didn't materialise.

In 1989 there was the Brady Plan which saw debt forgiveness as the solution. Banks would write off the debts and receive compensation from their governments. Costs would be borne by taxpayers and this wouldn't endear the government to them especially since the latter would be bailing out the banks. Banks, however, are writing off debts out of their profits on an annual basis. It would seem that greater direct investment in LDCs is required and less reliance should be placed on short -term borrowing.

Vicious Circle:

Developing countries face great difficulties in combining capital, labour resources and entrepreneurship. They find that these difficulties reinforce each other in a vicious circle of poverty.

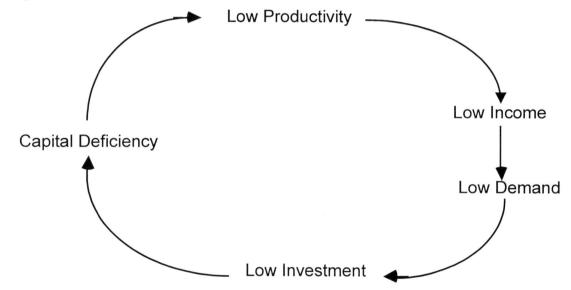

Diagram 20.3 Demand Side of Vicious Circle

The basic vicious circle stems from the fact that any less developed country's total productivity is low due to deficiency of capital, market imperfections and general underdevelopment. The demand side of the vicious circle is that the low level of real income leads to a low level of demand, which in turn leads to a low rate of investment and hence back to deficiency of capital and low productivity. This is shown in Diagram 20.3. Low productivity is reflected in low real income that means a low level of saving. The latter leads to a low level of investment and to deficiency of capital. The deficiency of capital in turn leads to a low level of productivity. The vicious circle on the supply side is thus complete and is shown in Diagram 20.4. The common feature of both is the low level of real income, reflecting low investments and capital deficiency.

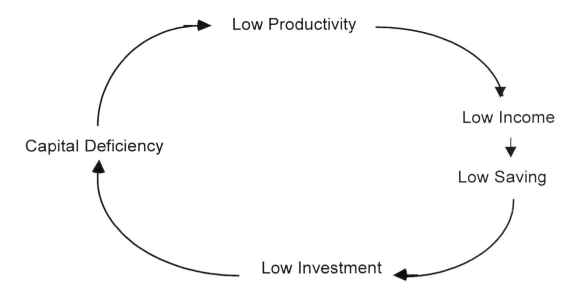

Diagram 20.4 Supply Side of Vicious Circle

Some Theories of Economic Development:

• **Adam Smith (1728-1790)**

Smith wrote 'An Inquiry Into The Nature And Causes Of The Wealth Of Nations', which was published in 1776. His theory points out how economic growth came about and what factors and policies impede it. He thought that capital accumulation, saving, improved technology and division of labour were important.

Society was made up of capitalists and labourers. Capitalists, landlords and moneylenders save according to Smith. He omitted income-receivers, the major source of savings in an advanced economy. He neglects the role of the entrepreneur in development whereas it is the entrepreneur who innovates and thus brings about capital formation.

His theory has only limited validity for LDCs. Market size is small and as a result, the capacity to save and the inducement to invest are low. It also means that productivity is low and this implies a low level of income. Low level of income results in small capacity to save and inducement to invest and they keep the size of the market small.

In LDCs competition has been replaced by monopoly and this has tended to perpetuate poverty. Development is possible through government intervention rather than through a policy of laissez-faire as suggested by Smith.

His theory of economic development is helpful to LDCs as it points towards factors that assist the process of development. Farmers, traders and producers, the three agents of growth mentioned by him, can help by increasing productivity in their areas. Their interdependence points towards the importance of balanced growth for these economies.

- **David Ricardo (1772-1823)**

Modern economists have adopted Ricardo's ideas on economic growth. He emphasised the importance of agriculture and held that industry depended on it. Ricardo felt that the profit rate should be increased because capital accumulation depends on it as it does on saving. International trade is important as it gets the maximum out of resources and thereby increases income.

There are weaknesses in his theory. He neglected the impact of technology and held that improved technology in the industrial area displaced labour. The most serious defect in his theory is his neglect of the role of the interest rate in economic growth.
He does not regard the interest rate as an independent reward of capital but includes it in profits. His theory is based on the impractical notion of laissez-faire and neglects the role of institutional factors.

On an overall basis, his theory is applicable to LDCs in that it emphasises capital accumulation, agricultural development and an increase in savings and profits.

- **Marxist Theory of Economic Development**

Karl Marx (1818-1883) contributed to the theory of economic development by his economic interpretation of history, outlining what brings about capitalist development and putting forward an alternative path of planned economic development.

His theory, however, is not directly applicable to LDCs and he did not think much about them. He failed to see that population pressures exist in them and for this reason, his theory is inapplicable. His departmental scheme is applicable to LDCs where dualism exists, namely a capitalist sector and a subsistence agriculture sector making two departments. The former sector yields a large economic surplus and the latter a small one. Rapid economic development is possible by reorganising and expanding the capitalist sector (Department 1) and transforming the subsistence sector (Department 2) into the former so as to increase the economic surplus. This necessitates planning for industrialisation and an increase in the supply of agricultural commodities to meet the expanding demand of the capitalist sector.

A number of countries such as India, Ghana and Burma have followed the Marxian Departmental Schema. The basic strategy has been to increase investment in capital goods industries and to increase the supply of consumer goods. The main thrust has been to increase employment and purchasing power, build a strong capital base and increase and improve the ability to produce.

- **Schumpeterian Theory**

Joseph Schumpeter outlined his theory in the 'Theory Of Economic Development' published in 1911. Its applicability to LDCs is limited. It is based on a socio-economic order existing in Western Europe and USA in the 19th century and today socio-economic conditions are very different in LDCs. He held that there must be an entrepreneurial class, but that in developing economies adequate entrepreneurship is lacking due to lack of profit incentive and sufficient infrastructure.

The innovator envisaged by Schumpeter does not fit well into a mixed economy where the government is the largest entrepreneur and the public and semi-public sector provides the main impetus for development. LDCs need to assimilate existing innovations rather than to innovate themselves. He held that change comes from within but in the case of LDCs change comes about due to ideas imported from outside and to technology and capital also obtained from outside.

Schumpeter does not consider population growth and its effect on development. He did not consider that high growth of population retards the growth rate of a developing country.
He held that inflationary impulses form an integral part of the development process. There is no secular inflation involved and the long-term price level remains stable. In developing countries, inflationary forces are very powerful and LDCs are demand-oriented economies.

Keynesian Theory:

John Maynard Keynes (1883 - 1946) changed the nature of economic science by creating modern macroeconomics. His book "The General Theory of Employment, Interest and Money", published in 1936, is a great and influential book.

Keynesian theory does not analyse the problems of developing economies as such and it is relevant mainly to advanced capitalist countries. It is based on assumptions that limit its applicability to underdeveloped countries.

Cyclical unemployment Keynes held occurs during a depression and is caused by deficiency in effective demand and can be removed by an increase in the level of effective demand. Unemployment in LDCs is, however, chronic rather than cyclical. The problem is one of shortage of capital resources not demand. LDCs have a problem with disguised unemployment rather than involuntary unemployment on which Keynes concentrated. What is needed is a solution to chronic and disguised unemployment yet he gave no solution for these.

Keynes based his theory on a closed economy yet all LDCs are open economies as they are dependent on foreign trade. He assumed that there was a surplus of labour and other resources in the economy. This is not so in LDCs where skills, capital and infrastructure are all lacking or inadequate.

The main ideas put forward by Keynes and their validity or applicability to LDCs is now examined.

- **Effective Demand**

Unemployment is caused by deficiency of effective demand and his solution is to increase consumption. In an underdeveloped country, there is disguised unemployment but no involuntary unemployment. In developed economies, unemployment is due to excess savings and can be reduced by increasing consumption and investment through different monetary and fiscal measures. In developing economies, income levels are extremely low, propensity to consume is high and savings are very small. If monetary and fiscal measures are used, the result will be price inflation. The problem is one of trying to increase employment and per capita incomes.

- **Propensity to Consume**

This suggests that as income increases, consumption increases but by less than the increase in income. As income rises, so do savings. This is not so in developing economies. Marginal propensity to consume in underdeveloped countries is very high and consequently the marginal propensity to save is very low. In an underdeveloped country, it is not possible for production to match an increase in the marginal propensity to consume due to lack of productive resources. Prices, therefore, increase and employment does not.

- **Propensity To Save**

Saving in excess was a vice to Keynes since it caused a reduction in aggregate demand. To LDCs, saving is a virtue as it is by saving they can form capital and it is through capital formation that they can develop. They must reduce consumption even below subsistence and increase saving.

- **Marginal Efficiency of Capital (MEC)**

The MEC to Keynes was an important determinant of investment. When investment increases, the MEC falls and when investment falls, the MEC rises. This relationship does not hold for underdeveloped economies since in them, investment is at a low level as is MEC. Many factors such as lack of capital, small markets, low income, low profit etc. tend to keep MEC and investment at a low level.

- **Rate Of Interest**

This is the second determinant of investment in Keynes theory. Liquidity preferences and the supply of money determine it. It is only demand for money for speculative motives that affects the rate of interest. In underdeveloped economies, the liquidity preference for speculative motives is low and does not influence the rate of interest. Keynes held that an increase in the supply of money lowers the rate of interest and encourages investment, income growth and the level of employment. In LDCs, an increase in the money supply leads to a rise in prices rather than to a fall in interest rates.

- **Multiplier**

Keynes never looked at underdeveloped countries from the point of view of their problems or the relevance of his theory to them.

The concept of the multiplier is based on four assumptions:

1. Involuntary unemployment: In developing countries, there is no involuntary unemployment and there is disguised unemployment so that the operation of the multiplier towards increasing output or employment is retarded.

2. An industrialised country has an upward sloping supply curve to the right but it does not become vertical until a substantial interval has elapsed. The supply curve of output in an underdeveloped country is inelastic and this makes the working of the multiplier more difficult. Consumption goods industries are unable to expand output and to offer employment. Agriculture, the chief consumption goods industry, has a backward sloping supply curve that means that an increase in the value of output does not always mean an increase in the volume of output. This is because, in the short run, farmers do not have the facilities to increase output. The primary increase in income is spent on food so that the multiplier effect is lost.

3. A comparatively elastic supply of working capital is needed to raise output. Underdeveloped countries have an inelastic supply of working capital for increasing output of consumption goods.

4. Absence of excess capacity in consumption goods industries prevents the required increase in output of consumption goods industries and the resultant employment therein.

Overall, the applicability of Keynes General Theory to underdeveloped countries is very limited. There is the danger of unintelligent application by people versed in the economics of advanced economies but lacking in understanding of underdeveloped or developing economies.

Rostow's- Stages of Economic Growth:

W.W. Rostow believes that economies go through five stages of economic development as follows: -

1. The Traditional Society

Traditional societies are primitive and usually poor, with very little change from generation to generation. They have a low ceiling to their total production that is largely agricultural.

Social structure is hierarchical in which family and tribe connections play a dominant role. More than 75 per cent of the people are engaged in agriculture. It is not necessary that a country pass through this stage, as was the case with the United States, Canada, New Zealand, Australia and Ireland.

2. Traditional Society Preparing for Take-Off:

During this period the preconditions for sustained growth are created. People begin to accept that change is possible. Some of the preconditions are the establishment of a nation state and build up of the spirit of enterprise.

Banks appear together with other financial institutions and they mobilise saving into productive investment. In the case of 'preconditions', it is not necessary that they must precede the take-off.

3. The 'Take-Off':

Rostow describes this as the great watershed in the life of modern societies when the old blocks to steady economic growth are overcome. The analogy is with an aeroplane that can fly only after attaining a critical speed. It is normally associated with the Industrial Revolution or with the change from a largely agricultural to an industrialised economy.

The conditions necessary for the 'take-off' are:

- A rise in the rate of productive investment from 5 per cent to over 10 per cent of national income;

- The development of one or more manufacturing sector with a high rate of growth; and

- The existence or quick emergence of a political, social and institutional framework which exploits impulses to expansion.

The concept of the 'take-off' is a spur to development in the case of underdeveloped countries. Capital formation of over 10 per cent and the creation of a leading sector are helpful in the effort to industrialise. The first condition of 10 per cent saving/investment ratio needs to be modified in the context of worldwide inflationary pressures during the past three decades or so. A more realistic figure may be 20 to 25 per cent. Regarding the development of a leading sector, agriculture could be the one. Developing countries have an advantage in that they can draw on the capital, technology and skills of the advanced countries.

4. The Drive To Maturity:

Rostow believes that the Drive To Maturity is a period lasting approximately 60 years immediately following the 'take-off' in which modern technology and methods of production are extended across a much wider area of economic activity.

5. Age Of High Mass Consumption:

As societies attain economic maturity, there is an increase in real income per head of population and the community enjoys a standard of living which transcends the basic needs of food, clothing and shelter. The pattern of demand shifts towards durable consumer goods and services.

Lewis' Theory of Unlimited Supplies Of Labour:

W. Arthur Lewis developed a two -sector model of economic development in his article *'Economic Development with Unlimited Supplies of Labour'* in 1954. He examines the expansion of the capitalist or industrial sector as supplies of cheap labour feed it from the agricultural sector. Surplus labour is directed to industry and it is in this manner that development takes place. He views the typical underdeveloped economy as divided into two compartments i.e. a capitalistic sector and a traditional subsistence sector. In his dualistic system, the capitalist sector is the source of dynamic stimuli and the rate of growth in the economy as a whole is held to be regulated primarily by reinvestment from capitalist profits. Expansion of the capitalist sector requires it to be in contact with the subsistence sector. The latter, in his view, is characterised by backward techniques, low output per capita and a large amount of underemployment. Capitalists can draw off labour by offering wages slightly better than subsistence earnings and about 30 per cent less than industrial workers, receive.

He sets out to show how a capitalist economy expands through profits earned in industry being returned as investment in it. Capital is also created out of bank credit and this leads to an inflationary rise in prices for some time. When the surplus labour is engaged in the capitalist sector and paid out of created money, prices rise because income increases, while consumer goods output remains constant. This is only temporary, since as soon as capital goods such as machinery start producing, consumption goods prices start falling.

Every underdeveloped country does not have unlimited supplies of labour as many of them are sparsely populated. The wage rate is not constant in the capitalist sector, as it continues to rise over time in the industrial sector of underdeveloped countries. He suggests that the capitalist surplus is reinvested in productive capital. If, however, productive capital is labour saving, it would not absorb the labour and the theory breaks down. Skilled labour is not a temporary bottleneck in underdeveloped economies but is rather long term.

Balanced Growth Theory:

This has been advocated by a number of economists including Rosenstein-Rodan and Ragnor Nurkse in "Problems of Capital Formation in Undeveloped Countries," in 1953.

The term 'balanced growth' is used in many different senses, but the original exponents of the doctrine of balanced growth had in mind the scale of investment necessary to overcome indivisibilities on both the supply and demand side of the development process. Indivisibilities on the supply side refer to the 'lumpiness' of capital particularly social overhead capital and the fact that only investment in a large number of activities at the one time can take advantage of external economies of scale. On the demand side, they refer to small size of market and profitability as they affect economic activity. The doctrine was later extended to refer to the path of economic development and the pattern of investment needed to keep the different sectors of the economy in balance so that lack of development in one does not impede development in another.

Unbalanced Growth:

The foremost proponent of unbalanced growth is A. Hirschman. He outlined his development strategy in his book, '*Strategy of Economic Development*', published in 1958. It is his contention that the best way to achieve economic growth in an underdeveloped economy is to deliberately unbalance the economy. Investment in strategically selected industries or sectors in the economy will bring about new investment opportunities and so pave the way for further development. If the economy is to be kept moving ahead, the job of development policy is to maintain disequilibrium and tensions.

Balanced Versus Unbalanced Growth:

Vicious circles of poverty are at work in underdeveloped countries and the result is small markets. A balanced pattern of investment is needed in order to build up a number of mutually supporting industries so that the size of the market is enlarged. The argument against this is that these countries do not have the resources required for simultaneous investment in a few industries.

The 'unbalanced' doctrine puts forward sectoral development on a selective basis rather than all together. It also seeks to remove scarcities in underdeveloped countries by induced investment decision making. It is, however, possible that in these countries decision making itself is scarce. Creating imbalance within the economy by making investments in strategic sectors when there is a shortage of resources leads to balance of payments difficulties and inflationary pressures in underdeveloped countries.

The two doctrines have two common problems: one concerns the role of the state in development and the other is the role of supply limitations and inelasticities.

Nurkse believes that balanced growth is relevant primarily for a private enterprise system. However, state help is required in taking investment decisions in underdeveloped countries and planning is required. In the unbalanced growth case, the state plays a major role in encouraging social overhead capital investment thereby creating disequilibrium. Unbalanced growth also needs state planning.

Nurkse's theory of balanced growth is mainly related to lack of demand and neglects the role of supply limitations. This is not correct since underdeveloped countries are seriously lacking in the supply of many resources including capital, skills and infrastructure generally. Unbalanced doctrine neglects the role of supply limitations and inelasticities. It emphasises scarcity of decision making but not scarcity of other resources in an underdeveloped economy

Dualistic Theories:

Dualism refers to economic and social divisions in an economy such as geographical differences in the level of development, differences in the level of technology between sectors and differences in attitudes and customs between the native population and foreigners settled in the country. The basic origin of dualism is the introduction of money into a subsistence barter economy and development depends on the extension of the money economy. Development must, therefore. contend with the existence of dualism in all aspects. Here we look at social and technological dualism.

- ## Social Dualism:

The problem is one of a traditional society with no modern exchange sector and a modern society. Incentives must be given to those in the subsistence sector so as to get them into the money economy. Social dualism can be regarded as the inevitable consequence of development rather than as a basic cause of underdevelopment. It can cause problems of its own in that different development strategies are required to cope with dissimilar conditions in the two sectors.

- ## Technological Dualism

Technological dualism implies the use of different production functions in the advanced sector and the traditional sector of an underdeveloped economy. Its existence has added to the problem of disguised unemployment in the rural sector and technological unemployment in the industrial sector.

As with social dualism, technological dualism can be regarded as an inevitable feature of development. Two disadvantages are commonly associated with it. One is that when technological dualism is the result of a foreign enclave, a proportion of the profits is repatriated thus reducing the level of saving and investment in the home country. The second is that when production processes are labour intensive in the non- monetised sector and capital intensive in the industrial sector, it is possible that the technology of the industrial sector may impede progress in the agricultural sector.

Questions

1. Describe the main factors on which the rate of growth in an advanced industrial economy depends.

2. Set out and explain the conditions that are necessary to enable a country to embark on a programme of economic development.

3. What are the barriers to growth in less developed countries?

4. Define the term " economic growth" and with regard to Ireland identify and analyse features that you consider to have contributed to economic growth.

5. Outline Rostow's analysis of the stages of economic growth.

6. Discuss the main characteristics of developing countries.

7. What are the main instruments of Irish regional policy?

8. Critically evaluate Irelands National Development Plan 2000-2006.

9. Assess the Western Development Commissions Plan 2000-2006 and evaluate its progress to date.

10. The Irish economy has grown at an outstanding rate over the past decade. Give reasons for this and assess the prospects for continuing high rates over the period 2000 to 2006.

11. Critically evaluate the regionalisation of Ireland in 1999 into two regions.

12. Ireland has been given the title "Celtic tiger" economy. Explain the reasons for this and compare it with the Asian tiger economies.

GLOSSARY
- A -

Absolute advantage: A country has an absolute advantage if its output per unit of inputs of all goods is larger than that of another country.

Accelerator theory: This theory states that an increase in demand for final goods will produce a proportionally greater increase in the demand for capital goods.

Aggregate Demand: Total value of all planned expenditures on the output of a particular economy over a given time usually a year.

Aggregate demand curve: This shows what the total planned spending would be at various average price levels.

Aggregate monetary demand: The total spending on goods and services for a particular economy in a given period.

Aggregate supply: The total supply of goods and services available from domestic production plus imports to meet aggregate demand.

Aggregate supply curve: This shows what the total planned supply would be at various average price levels.

Allocative efficiency: The situation that occurs when no resources are wasted.

Automatic stabilisers: Tax revenues that rise and government expenditure that falls as nominal GNP rises and falls.

Average fixed cost: Total cost divided by total output.

Average product: Total product or output divided by number of variable inputs.

Average propensity to consume: The proportion of national or individual income that is used for consumption purposes.

Average propensity to save: The proportion or percentage of income of an individual or the whole economy, which is not spent on consumption goods and services.

Average revenue product: Total revenue divided by the quantity of the factor of production hired.

Average revenue: Total revenue divided by the quantity sold.

Average total cost: Total cost divided by output, which also equals the sum of average variable cost and average fixed cost.

Average variable cost: Total variable cost divided by output.

- B -

Balance of payments: This is a record of all the financial transactions between one country and other countries in a given period.

Balance of trade: The value of exports minus the value of imports.

Balanced or neutral budget: A situation where government revenue is exactly equal to government expenditure.

Barriers to entry: Legal or natural impediments protecting a firm from competition from firms wishing to enter that market.

Barter: An economy where people exchange goods and services directly with one another without any payment of money.

Birth rate: The crude birth rate is the average number of live births occurring in a year for every thousand population.

Black economy: That part of a country's economic activity that is not officially recorded as part of the National Income.

Budget deficit: This occurs when government expenditure exceeds its revenue from taxation.

Budget surplus: This occurs where government revenue exceeds government expenditure.

- C -

Capital: All inputs into production that have themselves been produced.

Cartel: A group of producers that enter into a collusive agreement to restrict output in order to increase prices and profits.

Central bank: Banker to the banks and the government.

Ceteris paribus: Other things remaining constant or other things being equal.

Closed economy: An economy that has no transactions with any other economy.

Cobweb theorem: A model in which the quantity currently supplied depends upon the price that prevailed in the previous market period. It is usually applied to agricultural products.

Collusion: Agreements between firms, whereby they accept limitations on their freedom of action. It may take many forms ranging from cartels to price leadership.

Command economy: An economy in which the basic functions of resource allocation are carried out by a central administrative process as opposed to a price system.

Common Agricultural Policy (CAP): The system of intervention in agricultural markets operated by the European Union to maintain farm incomes and encourage structural improvements in farming.

Comparative advantage: A country has a comparative advantage with respect to another country in the production of a given commodity if the opportunity cost of the commodity in question is lower in that country than in the other country.

Complement: A good that is used jointly or in conjunction with another good.

Constant returns to scale: Technological conditions under which the proportionate increase in a firm's output is equal to the proportionate increase in the input in all factors of production.

Consumer price index: A measure of the overall cost of the goods and services bought by a typical consumer.

Consumer surplus: Excess of total consumer benefit that a good provides over what a consumer has to pay.

Cost push inflation: Arise in the general level of prices caused by persistent rises in the costs of production.

Cross price elasticity of demand: Is a measure of the responsiveness of demand for one product to a change in the price of another product.

Crowding-out effect: This occurs when increased public expenditure leaves total expenditure or activity unchanged because it causes a compensating fall in private sector expenditure or activity.

Current account: A record of all transactions involving the purchase or sale of goods and services abroad.

Customs union: This is established within two or more countries when all obstacles to free trade between members are removed and a common external tariff against all non members is put in place.

Cyclical unemployment: Unemployment, which results from a decline in the country's total production in the trade cycle.

- D -

Decreasing returns to scale: Technological conditions under which the proportion of change in a firm's output is less than the proportion of change in the input in all factors of production.

Deflation: A reduction in the general level of prices.

Deflationary gap: The excess of National Income over expenditure at the full employment level of National Income.

Demand: Demand for a good or service is the total quantity that will be purchased at any given price over a given time period.

Demand curve: A graph showing how much a consumer is willing to buy at each price.

Demand-pull inflation: Inflation that is created and sustained by an excess of aggregate demand over the full employment level of output of goods and services.

Derived demand: Demand for a factor of production or input not for its own sake but in order to use it in the production of goods and services.

Devaluation: The reduction in the official rate at which the domestic currency is exchanged for foreign currencies.

Diminishing marginal returns: If one factor of production is fixed in supply and successive units of a variable factor are added to it, a point will be reached when output rises at a slower rate, i.e. marginal product will decline.

Diminishing marginal utility: As a consumer consumes more of a good in a given period of time the total utility increases, but it does so at a decreasing or diminishing rate.

Diminishing marginal rate of substitution: Is the rate at which a consumer needs to substitute one product for another in order for the utility derived from the two products to remain constant.

Discounting: Calculating the present value of a future payment by using a rate of return.

Disinflation: Is a fall in the rate of inflation.

Disposable income: Personal income including transfer payments after all direct taxation has been deducted. It gives an estimate of the amount available for consumption and saving.

Dissaving: Dissaving occurs when consumption exceeds disposable income.

Division of labour: The breaking up of a production process into different tasks in order to facilitate specialisation of labour and/or mechanisation.

Dumping: The sale of a good on a foreign market at a lower price than on the domestic market or for a price less than its cost of production.

- E -

Economic good: Any physical commodity or service that gives utility and that commands a price if bought or sold on a market.

Economic growth: Increase from one period to the next in real GNP.

Economic profit: Revenue less cost when the opportunity costs of production are included in cost.

Economic rent: The return to a factor in fixed supply that is considered to be a surplus over and above the amount required to induce the owner to offer the factor for use.

Economies of scale: These are present when an increase in output causes average costs to fall.

Elasticity of demand: The responsiveness of quantity demanded to changes in price.

Elasticity of supply (price): The responsiveness of quantity supplied to changes in price.

Entrepreneurs: Individuals or groups of individuals who engage in risk taking and innovation.

Equilibrium: A position from which there is no inherent tendency to move away. It is the solution of an economic model.

Euro: The currency of the EMU.

Euro currencies: Currencies deposited with a European bank outside their country of origin.

Exchange controls: Limitations on citizens' ability to conduct transactions requiring the use of foreign currencies or gold.

Exchange rate: The price of a currency expressed in terms of another currency. It is the rate at which the currencies can be exchanged.

Expansionary fiscal policy: An increase in government expenditure and/or a reduction in tax aimed at increasing the level of aggregate demand.

Externality: A cost or a benefit arising from an economic transaction that falls on a third party and not taken into account by those who undertake the transaction.

- F -

Factors of production: The inputs or resources used in production.

Fiat money: Money, which is not backed by some commodity such as gold that, has some intrinsic value.

Fiduciary issue: Paper money not backed by gold.

First-degree price discrimination: This type of discrimination occurs when each unit is sold for the maximum obtainable price.

Fiscal policy: Government policy concerned with raising revenue through taxation and deciding on the level and pattern of expenditure for the achievement of macro economic goals.

Fixed cost: The cost that is independent of the level of output.

Fixed exchange rate: A system whereby a group of countries agree to maintain a par value for their own currency relative to the others by means of intervention on the foreign exchange markets.

Floating exchange rate: A rate freely determined by the interaction of demand and supply.

Foreign Exchange Swaps: This occurs when banks have the ability to swap some of their holdings of foreign currency for Irish currency.

Free rider: Anyone who enjoys the benefit of a good or service without paying for it.

Free trade: The free exchange of goods between countries without artificial barriers such as quotas or tariffs.

Frictional unemployment: Unemployment that results from the time lag between labour becoming unemployed and locating a job.

Full employment: In terms of gross domestic product it is a measure of the output that the economy can achieve when all its resources are employed.

- G -

Giffen good: A good for which demand increases after price rises due to the positive income effect outweighing the negative substitution effect.

Gross Domestic Product: The market value of all final goods and services produced within a country in a given period of time.

Gross National Disposable Income (GNDI): Gross National Product adjusted to take account of changes in the terms of trade.

Gross National Product (GNP) The market value of all final goods and services produced in an economy over a given period.

- H -

Hard currency: A currency traded in a foreign exchange market for which demand is persistently high relative to supply.

Human resources: All forms of labour used to produce goods and services.

Hyper inflation: Very rapid and constantly growing rate of inflation causing money to lose its value to the point where barter becomes the preferred means of exchange.

- I -

Imperfect competition: A market model in which there is more than one firm but the necessary conditions for perfect competition do not exist.

Imports: The goods and services that we buy from other countries.

Income effect: Effect on the consumption of a commodity of a change in real income resulting from a change in its price.

Income elasticity of demand: The percentage change in the quantity demanded divided by the percentage change in income.

Indifference curve: A curve that shows all the possible combinations of two goods that yield the same total utility for a consumer.

Infant industry: Developing domestic industry whose average costs of production are higher than those of established industries in other countries.

Inferior good: Goods for which demand falls as consumers income increase.

Inflation: A sustained rise in the average price of goods and services.

Inflationary gap: The excess of aggregate monetary demand over aggregate supply at the full employment level of output.

Injection: Spending in the economy other than consumption spending.

Inter-bank market: The market in which banks lend to each other on a wholesale basis.

Interest: The payment made by a borrower in payment for the use of capital.

Intermediate goods: Goods that are inputs in the production of final goods.

Invisibles: The export or import of a service such as banking or tourism.

- J -

J-curve: A curve, which depicts the changes in the Balance of Payments current account after a devaluation of the currency.

- k -

Kinked demand curve: A curve that has a discontinuous slope, the result of two distinct price reactions of competitors to changes in price.

- l -

Labour force: The number of people employed plus the number of people available for work.

Laffer curve: A curve showing the relationship between tax revenue and average tax rate.

Laissez-faire economy: A market economy that is allowed to operate according to competitive forces with little or no government intervention.

Leakages: These are withdrawals from the Circular Flow of Income, i.e. saving, imports and taxes.

Lender of last resort: An essential function of a Central Bank is the willingness to lend to the Banking system at all times although it does so on its own terms.

Less developed countries (LDC's): Low income countries with rapid population growth, low saving rates and dependence on subsistence agriculture.

Liquidity preference theory: The extent to which individuals wish to hold their wealth in the form of money rather than other assets such as bonds.

Liquidity: The ease with which any asset or commodity can be converted into money.

Long-run: The period of time in which the firm can adjust all its factors of production, both variable and fixed.

- M -

Macroeconomics: Macroeconomics is concerned with the economy as a whole and it studies the determinance of total output inflation employment and unemployment and National Income.

Marginal cost: The additional cost resulting from a small increase in the output of a good.

Marginal physical product: Addition to total output as a result of employing one extra unit of a factor of production.

Marginal Propensity to Consume (MPC): Is the proportion of a rise in National Income that goes on consumption or that fraction of a person's additional income which is spent on consumer goods.

Marginal Propensity to Import (MPM): The change in imports that occurs as a result of a change in income divided by that change in income.

Marginal Propensity to Save (MPS): Is that part of any small increment of income, which is saved.

Marginal Propensity to Tax (MPT): This is the change in tax paid that occurs as a result of a change in income, divided by that change in income.

Marginal revenue product: The change in total revenue that results from employing one more unit of a variable input.

Marginal revenue: The change in total revenue that results from selling one additional unit of output.

Marginal utility: The change in total utility resulting from a one unit increase in the quantity of a good consumed.

Market economy: A system where economic decisions are decentralised and made by owners of factors of production, consumers and producers.

Market failure: A situation that occurs when the price system fails to produce a socially optimal quantity of the good.

Markets: Arrangements that bring sellers and buyers together for the purpose of determining conditions of exchange.

Medium of exchange: Anything that is generally acceptable in exchange for goods and services.

Microeconomics: That branch of economics, which deals with small parts of the economic system and is a model which explains the behaviour of individuals and firms in the economy.

Mixed economy: An economy based partly on markets and partly on a command mechanism to co-ordinate economic activity.

Monetarists: Economists who believe that changes in the money supply bring about changes in nominal GNP which in the long run is reflected in a higher rate of inflation.

Monetary policy: This is the term applied to actions which influence the money supply interest rates or the availability of credit.

Money illusion: This occurs when people confuse nominal and real changes.

Money: Anything that is generally accepted as a means of payment for goods and services or in the settlement of debts.

Monopolistic competition: A market characterised by a large number of firms competing with each other by producing similar but differentiated products.

Monopoly: The sole supplier of a good, service or resource that has no close substitutes.

Monopsony: A single buyer of a resource or product in a market.

Multiplier (The): A measure of the effect on National Income of a change in one of the components of aggregate demand.

- N -

Narrow money supply: Referred to as M_1 it is equal to notes and coins in circulation plus current accounts in banks.

National debt: The cumulative total of outstanding debts owed by successive governments.

National income: The sum of incomes received by residents of a country in a given period usually a year.

Natural resources: The non-produced factors of production, i.e. gifts of nature including water, air and land.

Nominal GNP: Value of final goods and services for a given year expressed in that year's prevailing prices.

Non price competition: Any method used to attract customers other than price cuts.

Normal good: A good the demand for which increases when income increases.

Normal profit: Earned when total revenues equal total opportunity cost.

Normative statement: A statement about what ought to be, based on an opinion that cannot be verified by observation.

- O -

Oligopoly: An industry characterised by a few firms that produce either a homogeneous product or differentiated products that take into account their mutual interdependence.

Open economy: An economy of a country that engages in international trade.

Open market operations: The purchase and sale of securities by the Central Bank on the open market.

Opportunity cost: The cost of doing one thing in terms of the alternative foregone.

- P -

Participation rate: This is the proportion of the population of working age who are employed or seeking employment.

Per capita income: The income per individual found by dividing total income by the total number of people.

Perfect competition : A market structure that is characterised by a large number of buyers and sellers of a homogeneous product.

Permanent income hypothesis: A hypothesis that consumption depends on some estimate of expected long run income rather than current income.

Phillips curve: A curve that shows the relation between the rate of inflation and the rate of unemployment.

Positive statement: A statement about what is and that can be verified by careful observation.

Precautionary motive: Money held for the purpose of meeting unforeseen expenditures.

Price ceiling: This the legal maximum price that can be charged for a good.

Price discrimination: This is the selling of a good or service on two markets at varying ratios between price and marginal cost.

Price elasticity of demand: This measures the responsiveness of quantity demanded to a change in price.

Price elasticity of supply: This measures the responsiveness of quantity supplied to a change in price.

Price index: A device used to estimate the average percentage change in the prices of a particular bundle of goods.

Price leadership: A characteristic of some oligopolistic markets where the firms explicitly or implicitly follow the price changes of one firm, the price leader.

Price taker: A firm that cannot influence the price of its product.

Primary liquidity ratio: This is the ratio of a bank's holding of cash and balances in the Central Bank to its deposit liabilities.

Private good: A good or service each unit of which is consumed by only one individual.

Privatisation: The sale of government holdings in nationalised industries to the private sector.

Product differentiation: Making a product slightly different from that of competitors.

Production possibility curve: A curve showing the maximum output that an economy can produce given its existing resources and a given level of technology.

Productivity: The relationship between output and the input used to produce that output.

Progressive tax: A tax that takes a greater proportion of income from the better off and a smaller proportion of income from the less well off.

Protectionism: This is restrictions on international trade.

Public good: A good which provides benefits which are not confined to any one individual or household once it has been provided to another.

Public Sector Borrowing Requirement (PSBR) : Borrowing by the central government for current and capital purposes, plus borrowing by the semi state bodies, plus borrowing by local authorities.

Purchasing power parity: Holds when the exchange rate between two currencies reflects the relative purchasing power of those two currencies in their respective countries.

- Q -

Quantity theory of money: The quantity theory of money states that a change in the nominal money supply leads to an equivalent change in the price level but does not affect output or employment.

Quasi rent: Payment over and above the opportunity cost necessary to induce the owners of factors to offer them to the market in the short run.

Quota: A restriction on the quantity of an imported good.

- R -

Real GNP: Measures the volume of real goods and services produced by the economy by removing the effects of rising prices on nominal GNP.

Real income: The quantity of goods and services that an individual, or a country can consume with the money received from all sources of income.

Real rate of interest: These are interest rates which take into account the current rate of inflation.

Recession: A reduction in business activity or a decline in real GNP.

Rediscount rate: The rate of interest charged by the Central Bank to the Irish commercial banks when it acts as lender of last resort.

Reflation: Government measures to increase aggregate demand closer to the full employment level of National Income.

Regressive tax: A tax which takes a decreasing proportion of income as income rises.

Rent: A payment to a factor of production in excess of its opportunity cost.

Resources: Land and natural resources, labour and capital that can be combined to produce goods and services.

Revaluation: An increase in the official rate at which a country's currency is exchanged for other currencies.

- S -

Saving: Saving is income minus consumption and is measured in the National Income accounts as disposable income minus consumption expenditure.

Scarcity: Exists when the amount of the good or resource offered to users is less than the amount they would wish to have if it were given free of charge.

Secondary liquidity ratio: This is the ratio of a bank's holding of liquid assets to its deposit liabilities.

Short run: An amount of time that is not sufficient to allow all inputs to vary as the level of output varies.

Short term credit facility: This is the rate of interest charged by the Central Bank when acting as lender of last resort.

Special Drawing Rights (SDRs): Assets created by the IMF which give holders unconditional drawing rights.

Speculative motive or demand: The amount of money individuals and businesses wish to hold in the expectation that bond prices will shortly fall.

Stagflation: A combination of high inflation and high unemployment in a stagnant economy.

Standard of deferred payment: The unit in which loans and future contracts are fixed provided its value is stable.

Structural unemployment: Unemployment that results from the long run decline of certain industries.

Subsidy: A payment made by the government to producers that depends on the level of output.

Substitutes: Goods that may be used in place of other goods.

Substitution effect: That part of an increase in the quantity of a good demanded whose price has fallen which is attributed to consumers substituting cheaper goods for relatively more expensive goods.

Supply: This is the relationship between the quantity of a good supplied and it's price.

Supply side economics: The effort to increase real production by providing incentives to businesses and workers.

Surplus: The amount by which quantity supplied exceeds quantity demanded when the price in a market is too high to equate the quantity demanded with the quantity supplied.

- T -

Tariff: A tax on imported goods designed to encourage domestic production.

Tax incidence: Shows who pays a tax after prices adjust to the tax.

Tax wedge: This is the difference between the net pay an employee receives and the cost the employer must bear in employing him/her.

Terms of trade: The terms of trade express the relationship between the average prices of exports and of imports.

Total cost: The sum of fixed costs (FC) and variable costs (VC).

Total revenue: The total amount of money received by a firm from selling its output in a given time period.

Total utility: The total benefit or satisfaction a person gets from the consumption of goods and services.

Traditional society: An economic system where economic questions are determined by customs and habits handed down from generation to generation.

Transfer payments: Payments by the government to individuals without requiring any service in return.

- U -

Unemployment: A situation that exists when members of the labour force wish to work but cannot obtain a job.

Unemployment trap: The availability of social welfare benefits reduces the incentive to work.

Unit of account: A common measure such as pounds and pence that expresses the relative values of goods and services.

Utility: The benefit or satisfaction that a person gets from the consumption of a good or service.

- V -

Value added: Total revenue minus the sum of purchases of raw materials components and services.

Value added tax: A percentage tax on consumer expenditure.

Variable costs: Those costs which vary directly with output.

Velocity of circulation: Measures the average number of times money changes hands in the course of a year.

Vicious circle of poverty: Countries are poor because they do not save and invest in capital goods and they cannot save and invest because they are poor.

Visible trade: Exports and imports of physical goods.

- W -

Wants: Quantities of goods and services people would like to have if the price were zero.

Wealth: Total assets of an individual, firm or government minus its total liabilities.

- X -

X-inefficiency: The failure of management to ensure that production occurs at as low a cost as possible.